Magnificent Decay

Under the Sign of Nature: Explorations in Ecocriticism
Serenella Iovino, Anthony Lioi, and Kate Rigby, Editors
Michael P. Branch, SueEllen Campbell, and John Tallmadge, Senior Advisory Editors

Magnificent Decay

MELVILLE AND ECOLOGY

Tom Nurmi

UNIVERSITY OF VIRGINIA PRESS
CHARLOTTESVILLE AND LONDON

University of Virginia Press
© 2020 by the Rector and Visitors of the University of Virginia
All rights reserved
Printed in the United States of America on acid-free paper

First published 2020

9 8 7 6 5 4 3 2 1

Library of Congress Cataloging-in-Publication Data
Names: Nurmi, Tom, author.
Title: Magnificent decay : Melville and ecology / Tom Nurmi.
Description: Charlottesville : University of Virginia Press, 2020. | Series: Under the sign of nature : explorations in ecocriticism | Includes bibliographical references and index.
Identifiers: LCCN 2020010301 (print) | LCCN 2020010302 (ebook) | ISBN 9780813945019 (hardcover ; acid-free paper) | ISBN 9780813945026 (paperback ; acid-free paper) | ISBN 9780813945033 (epub)
Subjects: LCSH: Melville, Herman, 1819–1891—Criticism and interpretation. | Nature in literature. | Human ecology in literature. | Ecocriticism.
Classification: LCC PS2388.N3 N87 2020 (print) | LCC PS2388.N3 (ebook) | DDC 813/.3—dc23
LC record available at https://lccn.loc.gov/2020010301
LC ebook record available at https://lccn.loc.gov/2020010302

Cover art: Storm in the Mountains, Frederic Edwin Church, 1847. Oil on canvas. (Cleveland Museum of Art)

For Carm

. . . how thrive the ferns
About the ruined house of prayer.
—Herman Melville, *Clarel: A Poem and Pilgrimage in the Holy Land* (1866)

Contents

Preface xi

Introduction 1

1. Pearl: *Mardi* 47
2. Tendril: *Pierre* 84
3. Honeycomb: *The Piazza Tales* 145
4. Pebble: *John Marr* 199

Conclusion 225

Acknowledgments 231

Notes 233

Index 269

Preface

The first decades of the twenty-first century have dramatically altered how we understand the boundaries between humans, animals, plants, and rocks. In the summer of 2018, for example, Seattle residents were captivated by a mother orca carrying her dead calf through the San Juan Islands in what ethologists believe was an extended ritual of mourning. A few years earlier, plant researchers reported new advances in phytosemiotics, or the ability of vegetal life to communicate with other plants and fungi, sometimes across great distances. And in 2016, mineralogists suggested that the hundreds of exclusively human-generated minerals found in the debris of nuclear testing, amid ore dumps, or clinging to mine-shaft timbers and shipwrecks represented marker "lithologies" of the Anthropocene: definitive signatures of the human species in the geologic record.[1] Animals grieve. Plants signal. Humans have geologic force. These anecdotes—alongside other developments in microbiome science, virology, molecular phylogenetics, and, of course, anthropogenic climate change—prompt us to tell a different story of the human species through the prism of the nonhuman, a prism that refracts our constituent animal, vegetal, and mineral selves.

This is the story that Herman Melville, one of the most celebrated but misunderstood authors in American literature, sought to tell. Although he may be best remembered for his sea tales, Melville's lesser-read fiction and poetry reveal him to be a truly *planetary* writer. He was a writer of relations, networks, and systems that we now term "ecological." In his own vocabulary and distinctive style, Melville understood that our planet is defined by ensembles of emergent complexity crisscrossing borders of life and nonlife, human and nonhuman. Neither a self-regulating Gaia nor a harmonious whole, Earth is an asymmetrical, mutative territory interweaving kingdoms of life against unimaginable magnitudes of time. Such an integrated vision of the planet characterizes the science of ecology and provides the context for *Magnificent Decay: Melville and Ecology*, a small book with a strange title premised on the potential of literature to motivate human communities to see themselves in new, planetary ways. *Magnificent Decay* argues that ecological thought develops and flourishes in the imaginative scenes of literary texts with more power and endurance than any other form of expression. This is why returning to Melville, and to nineteenth-century literary cultures more generally, is a lively intellectual task for anyone concerned with understanding our current moment of environmental precarity. Because, perhaps surprisingly, nineteenth-century conditions are eerily familiar to us: increasing energy use and reliance on large-scale mining and drilling, growing awareness of climate changes with little political action, enduring legacies of imperialism and racism, and evolving technologies in transportation, medicine, and communication that transform the frontiers of the human body and its proximity to—or distance from—other beings.

The key word is distance. If 8 percent of the human genome comes from viral DNA inserted by retroviruses, if our health is inextricably linked to the trillions of microbes in our digestive tracts, and if we share genetic material with plants and marine ooze in hydrothermal ocean vents, then one of the central achievements of the twenty-first century must be the recognition that we are, all of us, more nonhuman than human.[2] Yet this recognition does not necessitate veering into anti-humanism, nihilism, determinism, or utopic technological fantasy. The following chapters demonstrate how a heightened awareness of our intimacy with nonhuman worlds, our very lack of distance, discloses the qualities that exemplify our humanness. Our creativity, for example. Our capacities for story, responsibility, grief, and communal life. Our potential to adapt to and endure in changing conditions of planetary existence. These conceptions of the human hinge, sometimes unnervingly, on being knotted within other forms of being.

But to guide us through this tangle of relations, we need a narrative through line, a "monkey-rope" like the one Ishmael uses to support Queequeg dangling over ravenous sharks. We need a way to articulate, as Ishmael puts it, our "connexion with a plurality of other mortals" and, crucially, *nonmortals*.[3] So, by closely reading his stories and lyrics, *Magnificent Decay* demonstrates how Melville anticipated the two principal insights of contemporary environmental humanities: (1) the illusory division between natural and human histories and (2) the difficulty of representing multiple scales of planetary change far beyond the relatively limited vantage points of our species. Unfolding the implications of these two insights in Melville's writings allows us to see how ecological aesthetics—the elegant symmetries that persist between biotic and abiotic spheres of being—might offer a conduit between science and art that clarifies our reliance on, and obligation to, unfamiliar nonhuman worlds.

The challenges of the Anthropocene also come at a time when American public education is under threat, when STEM and humanities study appear distant and disconnected, and when the rich heritage of human storytelling seems drained of ambiguity and nuance, buried under Twitter feeds or anesthetized by Instagram scrolls. Yet the most recent, exciting, and incisive work in the humanities has been directed toward the intersection of science and society, particularly the role of narrative in shaping both domains of human endeavor. Scholars and artists have called our attention to the historical and philosophical origins of the paradigms that govern our reactions to the Anthropocene, drawing on neuroscience and evolutionary genetics as much as literary, assemblage, or systems theories. Their histories probe the "basic structures of thought, values, feeling, expression, and persuasion" that ecocritic Lawrence Buell argues "may indeed be more influential in the remediation of environmental problems than the instruments of technology or politics."[4] Perhaps the chief feature of Anthropocene debates—especially those around climate change—is the almost incalculable power of story to influence our senses of place and community in both digital and material worlds, as well as our prophecies for the next centuries of life on Earth. Narrative and ecology, in other words, uncover the assumptions that guide our responses to strangers and environments alike. *Magnificent Decay* is dedicated to Melville but is equally a reply to, and rallying call for, all artists whose work gives us a sharper view of ourselves from outside the boundaries of our species as we hurdle toward a shared, perilous planetary future.

Magnificent Decay

Introduction

Alas, for America as I must so often say, the ungirt, the diffuse, the profuse, procumbent, one wide ground-juniper, out of which no cedar, no oak will rear up a mast to the clouds! it all runs to leaves, to suckers, to tendrils, to miscellany.
—Ralph Waldo Emerson, *Journals* (1847)

What is Melville beyond the whale? For most twenty-first-century readers, he has become synonymous with the mysteries of the white leviathan, yet Melville's contemporaries knew him as something else entirely: a Pacific sailor among the cannibals, an adventurer at the ragged edges of the map, even a sex symbol returned from years of isolation with Tahitian beauties. Still, Melville's best-known sea novels—*Typee: A Peep at Polynesian Life* (1846) and *Omoo: A Narrative of Adventures in the South Seas* (1847) in his day, *Moby-Dick; or, the Whale* (1851) in ours—only make up a portion of his writings. The rest of his work experiments with an astonishing array of forms and genres that take readers far from the "wilderness of waters."[1] Seedy New York City alleys to Palestinian deserts, Himalayan ridges to Andean lightning clouds, Melville's more obscure romances, gothic tales, sketches, and poems shift our attention away from the ocean and its charismatic megafauna. Instead, we are confronted with stranger tableaus of intertwined phenomena. We face grotesque amalgams of minerals, plants, humans, animals, fungi, rivers, and storms. In these neglected fictions and lyrics, Melville meditates on what he called the "havoc" of the natural world, a havoc that nonetheless produces "grace of form" in the processes of creation and destruction, mutation and death, upheaval and decay.[2]

This is Melville beyond the whale. A writer attuned to the intricate entanglement of human and nonhuman realms, not in pantheistic or transcendental terms but in terms we now recognize as hallmarks of ecology. I elaborate on my use of the term "ecology" below, a decision that raises questions of method and the purview of historical context in the study of literature and science. But, at the outset, I want to note how the "semantic slipperiness" of the word causes some degree of confusion, misunderstanding, and even disciplinary entrenchment that has undermined productive discussions across forms of knowledge in recent decades.[3] Ecology has three interrelated but distinct meanings. First, it designates a certain professional scientific practice (e.g., marine ecology) that developed in the twentieth century; second, it stands for a philosophical or ideological concern for "nature" and its many environments, broadly construed; and third, in its most technical sense, it signals an orientation toward planetary life that emphasizes the relations between discrete organisms and their immediate surroundings and/or wider habitats. Ecology tracks the living and nonliving elements, structures, pressures, and flows that make existence on Earth possible, all characterized by the interactive properties of complexity and emergence at various magnitudes.

Magnificent Decay argues that Melville is best understood through the third definition, as part of a network of trained scientists and curious nonscientists in early America whose thinking and writing about organism-environment relations make them "protoecologists" before the professionalization of ecology proper.[4] As we will see, these protoecological thinkers have a very specific history in the nineteenth century, and they teach us something important. Not just about the history of ecological thought, where it came from and what it might be, but about the construction of knowledge itself. In this sense, a more precise term might be *peri*ecological, from the Greek meaning "surrounding," which conveys an intuitive awareness of interconnectivity without the technical discourses of twentieth-century ecological science. For example, any sensitive reader of Melville is struck by his elaborate layering of multiple narratives within a single story. A story that, on first glance, seems so human centered unexpectedly swerves away from the human to explore the surrounding verdure, measure a stony outcropping, or creep inside an animal den. All of a sudden—in the eye of a whale peering from the depths or in the flash of lightning that illuminates a newly split tree—we glimpse the world from unfamiliar vantage points, sometimes from what Emerson called "the poise of the planet."[5] Seen from "a broader view," as Melville put it in "The Encantadas" (1854, 1856), the human species becomes a trace in a wider smear of organic viscosities and inorganic drifts.⁶ In Melville's writing, we can appreciate the human as an emergent property in the history of life, a species that shares common origin with pearls and bones, mosses and ferns, tortoises and bees, pebbles and sea-dew.

Although Melville was indeed a tree hugger—on a walk with Hawthorne in 1850 he spent time "patting" his favorites "upon the back"—his environmental vision departed from both Enlightenment deism and Romantic metaphysical sublimity.⁷ Melville emphasized the discontinuities, ruptures, and chaos that were quickly becoming unavoidable features of nineteenth-century science, features that could not be fully accommodated by long-held philosophies of nature. By the time Charles Darwin insisted in *The Origin of Species* (1859) that the "economy of nature" depended on "constantly destroying life" to support adaptation and evolutionary persistence, Melville had already declared that "the natural advance of all creatures" means that they "bury themselves over and over again in the endless resurrection."⁸

Melville's literary ecologies were motivated by the realization that humans cannot easily *think their species*—let alone grasp their relation to the planet—beyond narrow narratives of competition and dominion: patriarchy, monoculture, resource extraction, slavery, colonialism, capitalism. Ishmael, for instance, is overwhelmed by the project of writing even a single whale. The "outreaching comprehensiveness of sweep" needed to properly represent the whale is simply too much for poor Ishmael. Such a project demands grappling with "the whole circle of the sciences . . . [and even] the universe."⁹ Ishmael's struggle mirrors the famously digressive structure of *Moby-Dick* that has long frustrated readers expecting more familiar contours of narrative fiction, with emphasis on individual character and discrete events in sequential arc. Readers of Melville in search of life disentangled or resolved are left longing because works like *Moby-Dick* subvert the individualist, singularly organismic thinking that has directed Western thought for centuries. Separating human from animal, animal from plant, and plant from mineral has installed taxonomy and compartmentalization as the paradigms for reason. This logic extends not only to the sciences but also to identity, gender, politics, religion, and most Western ethical systems. With the rise of the Lockean individual as the center of economic and social life in the modern West, our sense of collective obligation to other beings, human and nonhuman, has eroded. The corresponding inability to visualize where the human fits in the scale of our planet's spatial and temporal histories provides the starting point for Melville's ecological imagination.

This book shows how Melville's fascination with the emergent complexities and magnitudes of our planet's systems informs his fiction and poetry, especially under-appreciated texts like *Mardi: and A Voyage Thither* (1849) or *John Marr and Other Sailors* (1888). The project began with a simple list of the accumulating materials, bodies, and forces in Melville's writing. Over time, unusual phenomena began to crowd out the once-dominant images of cetaceans and captains. Suddenly, a perceptive reading of Melville meant thinking about boulders, mushrooms, and bird's nests. Ecology is vital for reading Melville in the Anthropocene because we have finally begun to see the planet as Melville did: a terrain of unevenly distributed agencies that upend recognizable thresholds of species and scale. It is important to remember that the term "Anthropocene" is itself contested, and I take up these debates in chapter 3, but whatever we call it, Melville helps us see that the history of human intervention in local and planetary ecosystems is more precisely the history of "how modernity became 'disinhibited' in its relation to nature," to quote historian of science Jean-Baptiste Fressoz.[10] In Melville we discover the history of how we forgot the extent of our relations to bodies of all kinds.

Today, global ecological degradation happens before our eyes: from biodiversity loss, ocean acidification, bio-accumulative chemical pollution, and ozone depletion to fertilizers interfering in phosphorus-nitrogen cycles and the aggregate, transformative effects of climate change. But not because we don't understand the science. It is because, as critic Yves Cochet put it, "the social psychology of human life does not allow the right decisions to be made at the right time."[11] We humans are always late, belated, deferring and deferred, out of time. We are a delayed species, forever lagging behind that which we have created and that which may, in the end, make us extinct. Contentedly, we defer. An undercurrent of this book is about how the rapidity of modern life—carefully, obsessively synced to Apple watches, Amazon orders, and hourly time sheets—actually produces the existential difficulty of *keeping time*, a difficulty that obscures the fact that "humanity is growing / Toward the fullness of her fate," as Melville phrased it in his Civil War retrospective *Battle-Pieces and Aspects of the War*.[12] We know what is happening to the planet. We knew the data in 1980 and intuited it much earlier. But it seems that human "nature" prevents us from telling the story of "nature" in a way that generates action.

The human species is not prepared to see itself from the perspective of the nonhuman Other or from a vantage point beyond the organism, beyond the whale. But Melville was. Instead of new data or models, confronting the human footprint on the planet requires new stories, more sharply and richly articulated ones, about our bonds with other forms of existence. To truly communicate, human beings need a shared context. We need a collective set of metaphors that ground the narratives through which we make sense of our species. For, as nineteen-year-old Melville wrote to the editors of the *Albany Microscope* in 1838, "what doth it avail a man" to possess "all the knowledge of a Locke or a Newton, if he know not how to communicate that knowledge"?[13] *Magnificent Decay* contends that Melville provides us that set of stories by making the complexity of human-planetary relations accessible to a broad spectrum of readers, in ways that climate science, environmental policy, law, or formal philosophy simply cannot.

TRIBE OF FUNGI

In the past fifty years, literary critics have recognized that Melville's interest in animals, plants, oceans, and islands is rooted in nineteenth-century philosophies of nature that bear influences of Spinoza, Goethe, and, eventually, Schopenhauer. But I'm less interested in pantheism, for instance, as a way of indexing attitudes toward "nature" or "identity"—what Richard Hardack terms the "deep structure" of the American Renaissance—because Melville was suspicious of such metaphysical claims even as he trafficked in them and because they ignore Melville's nuanced understanding of science as an orientation to materiality without transcendental purchase.[14] I turn instead to Melville's education in, and reading of, a range of Earth sciences.[15] Recent work in Melville studies has unfolded fresh, material dimensions in the Melville canon, and this book traces the many intersections between Melville's ecological imagination and his sustained reading in the history of religion and philosophy that scholars have explored for more than a century. *Magnificent Decay* is thus a twenty-first-century elaboration of very early Melville criticism that, from the start, saw the natural world as a guiding force in his prose and poetry.

The latest scientifically leaning scholarship follows Melville's explorations of "material humanity," as he called it in *Typee*, because through sciences like biology and geology Melville found answers to age-old philosophical problems, including the nature of free will and the meaning of creativity.[16] Our knowledge of Melville's reading demonstrates that his metaphysical and spiritual musings are bound up with his study of materialist and protoecological perspectives on life and nonlife, difference and sameness.[17] Via ecology, Melville approached questions of determinism and ethical responsibility within elegant and experimental literary forms that blurred the distinctions between "natural" and "artistic," the patterning of a beehive and the syntax of a sentence. Moreover, although advances in astronomy, zoology, and chemistry taught Melville many things, a thorough reading of his work uncovers several sophisticated philosophies of ecology that, ultimately, *teach ecology about itself.* Melville's searching literary examinations of the natural world disclose the very conditions that produce ecological knowledge as we understand it today. These conditions characterize the transdisciplinary field of *human ecology* and provide a horizon of interpretation that connects twenty-first-century empirical science to nineteenth-century literary fiction.

This is a bold claim. But there are historical, biographical, textual, and theoretical foundations that, when overlaid, structure my reading of Melville's environmental-literary epistemology. First of all, in the nineteenth century, budding physical and life sciences captivated artists, writers, and thinkers of all stripes. In antebellum America, art and science were allies in the quest to understand the natural world. Melville read deeply in the major scientists of his day, and his writing refers often to the work of, for instance, Carl Linnaeus, Georges Cuvier, James Hutton, Charles Lyell, Louis Agassiz, John Dalton, Michael Faraday, and Charles Darwin.[18] And Melville was not alone in his polymath reading habits. His mutual interests in science, art, and literature reflect the capacious quality of nineteenth-century education on both sides of the Atlantic. Highly educated Europeans and Americans pored over paleontology and botany alongside fiction and poetry and in between visits to art galleries and public exhibitions.[19] For example, William Cullen Bryant, one of the most popular early American poets and for decades the editor of the *New-York Evening Post,* wrote extensively on geology, mineralogy, and botany. And when famed London publisher John Murray III reprinted Melville's first two novels, *Typee* and *Omoo,* in his *Home and Colonial Library* series (1843–49), he featured them alongside the 1845 second edition of Darwin's *Journal of Researches,* now known as *The Voyage of the Beagle.*

Throughout the nineteenth century, writers like American technologist Jacob Bigelow recognized the "intimate connexion and dependence [that] exists between sciences and arts." Bigelow concluded that the "discovery" of science corresponds to the "invention" of art.[20] Emerson concurred:

"Science does not know its debt to imagination."[21] For Melville, the imagination was the great gift of the human species, the mechanism needed to access the "all comprehending abstracted essence of the infinite remoteness of things. Without it, we were grass-hoppers."[22] Imagination—and particularly the literary imagination—was a precondition for the human practices of empathy, storytelling, and mourning that generate periecological awareness and might, just maybe, deliver a planetary framework for dwelling ethically with other species. Melville was one of many American writers who, before and after the Civil War, pinpointed the convergences between science and imagination, material and concept, landscape and nation. But, as I noted earlier, Melville's ambivalent stance toward science is rooted in larger concerns about the human species' capacity to tell truthful stories about itself, concerns inevitably linked to questions of free will. Long-dominant mechanistic and deterministic views of natural history—the unstoppable drive of "nature's automatonism," as Melville described it in *The Confidence-Man: His Masquerade* (1857)—were suddenly pushed to the forefront of social discourse by revolutionary developments in nineteenth-century geology and biology.[23] Each of these fields reshaped debates over human will and the nature of sociality in Melville's lifetime, and they appear in a variety of forms and avatars over the course of his career as a fiction writer and poet.

So Melville's most productive writing years, between 1846 and 1876, offer a window onto the thicket of connections that brought science, technology, philosophy, and literature together in nineteenth-century America. In these decades, science became professionalized in trade journals, universities took on new public roles as centers of knowledge, and the exchange between scientists, governments, and private industry drove innovations that would foster an age of cooperation between corporate interest, scientific research, and public works. The story of American science 1846 to 1876 is thus the story of America undergoing radical transformations. Between the Mexican War—which opened half a million acres for westward expansion and settler colonialism—and the election of Rutherford B. Hayes—which effectively ended Reconstruction and reinstated a brutal regime of racial violence in the Jim Crow South—the bloody spectacle of the Civil War was amplified by technological supplements that would forever change our conceptions of what counted as "natural" and "artificial." This is the story of how we got from the Hoe printing press and the Howe sewing machine to Alexander Graham Bell's telephone and the first U.S. World's Fair: the Centennial

Exposition in Philadelphia that drew thirty-seven countries and ten million visitors. I consider Melville's attitudes toward technology in more detail in chapter 3, but, up front, it is important to recall how tightly Melville's novels and Darwin's finches were entwined with the technological history of mass communication and globalization in nineteenth-century planetary history. Because Melville's life (1819–1891) is coterminous with the dawn of the industrial West, his unprecedented attention to the scales of modern technological intervention in environmental systems offers a unique opportunity to theorize "the natural" at the exact moment when it began to be redefined and redeployed for the techno-modern world we came to know in the twentieth and twenty-first centuries.

During the tumultuous nineteenth century, Melville saw science, technology, and art wrestling with essentially the same problem: originality. Whether framed in national, literary, or evolutionary terms, the question of originality remained at the heart of Melville's writing life, absorbing discourses across science and art so that creativity and reproduction became the dominant tropes of his cognitive universe. For Melville, originality was a philosophical knot that bound national identity, ecological knowledge, and literary form together in interrogations of iteration and plagiarism, difference and sameness. Originality, in other words, had consequences for conceptualizing America's extraordinary democratic experiment as well as the very story of our species. "No writer," Melville declared, "has produced such inconsistent characters as nature herself has."[24] And by 1866, the fractured, postwar American nation seemed to bear out this insight in the social realm as the country struggled to accommodate the acceptance of difference on which it was ostensibly premised.

Magnificent Decay is organized around these principles of sameness and difference, principles that operate in the domains of communication and politics *and* in the biogeochemical origins of life itself. Chapter 1, for example, deals with the atomic consistency of all matter when seen from mineralogical and geological perspectives, while chapter 2 transitions to Melville's vivid descriptions of plant life that thrives so differently from humans and animals. This emphasis on difference culminates in Melville's animal fables (the subject of chapter 3), stories in which definitions of animality and humanity meet under the architecture of shelter, dwelling, and nesting. Chapter 4 concludes with a return to geomorphological force, a look at the cycles of weathering and erosion that reduce life, eventually, to worn pebbles on a shingle beach. In the context of ecological difference,

Darwinian evolutionary theory was for Melville a single example of how widening perspectives in science only confirmed his intuition about the impossibility of truly original creation, in nature as in literature. Again in *The Confidence-Man*, Melville writes that "the sense of originality exists at its highest in an infant, and probably at its lowest in him who has completed the circle of the sciences."[25] There is, Melville's narrator continues, "but one point in common" between originality in fiction and "all other sorts: it cannot be born in the author's imagination—it being as true in literature as in zoology, that all life is from the egg."[26] While Melville's fictions undermine and complicate this specifically zoological assertion, the sentiment shows how matted together ecological and literary claims to creation and originality were in Melville's mind, as they were in many early Americans' perceptions of the purpose and even spiritual mission of the New Republic.

Indeed, the rhetoric of American democracy has always been suffused with botanical and animal metaphors that highlight protoecological thinking folded into discourses of American identity. In *Common Sense* (1776), for instance, Thomas Paine called America "the tender rind of a young oak" in need of protection, and Emerson would later write that while government has in other places "been a fossil," in America "it should be a plant."[27] More elaborately, in his enormously popular collection of essays and short stories *The Sketch Book* (1819)—which Melville owned and referenced throughout his life—Washington Irving suggested that the processes of creation are analogous across national, literary, and ecological domains. He marvels how "the conveyance of seeds from clime to clime" by birds resembles the process of writing. For Irving, to write was to transplant the "fine thoughts of ancient and obsolete authors" and let them "flourish and bear fruit in a remote and distant tract of time." "Thus it is in the clearing of our American woodlands," Irving tells us, "where we burn down a forest of stately pines, a progeny of dwarf oaks start up in their place; and we never see the prostrate trunk of a tree mouldering into soil, but it gives birth to a whole tribe of fungi."[28]

An inheritor of Irving's protoecological theory of writing, Melville was obsessed with the implications of difference raised by eco-literary problems like originality and iteration. And Melville's fellow Americans were likewise dealing with questions of diversity, both before and after the war. Though he was devastating in his explication of the philosophical grounds that underlie the racial, gendered, classist, and colonialist violence that defines American history, Melville was famously oblique on many of the hot-button political issues of his day. But *Magnificent Decay* maintains that Melville most powerfully approaches the question of difference, the "slumbering volcano" beneath the veneer of sociality, through the ecological.[29] This premise propels Melville from his century into ours, an age of extraordinary interest in our species' collective, historical impact on the planet and an age of ongoing (some would say renewed) hatred and racism. "We live," Cornel West has proclaimed, "in the age of Melville . . . an age of spiritual blackout and moral meltdown against the backdrop of an American empire in cultural collapse and political breakdown. No one in America, past or present, understood more deeply and depicted more vividly than Melville, the lived experiences of Americans of all colors and classes . . . Neglected in his own day, American realities have caught up with Melville's art."[30] To "cultural collapse and political breakdown" I want to add the planetary crisis initiated by Anglo-American empires. This book cannot rehearse all of Melville's important engagements with race, class, or gender that West forcefully outlines and that Melville scholars continue to explore. Those concerns remain vital to our own moment, but *Magnificent Decay* offers a more literal and material reading of what West identifies as Melville's "vivid" depictions of the "lived" American experience. These two words—one about literary style and one about embodiment—join together questions of language with questions of health, corporeality, and a host of life sciences that are themselves enmeshed within discourses of race, gender, and class. The merging strands of science, philosophy, and literature in nineteenth-century culture therefore provide the interface for Melville's ecologies, for the lived to become vivid.

And although I begin the book by situating Melville in the industrial-scientific context of nineteenth-century America, the influence of science on Melville transcends the *thematic* motifs of his fiction and poetry. The striking depictions of geological and hydrological processes in *Mardi*, for example, or the detailed sketches of food chain networks in *Pierre, or the Ambiguities* (1852) produce not just awareness of ecological complexity but literary expressions whose forms *are themselves* emblems of complexity. As we will see in much more detail, Melville's perplexing, blotchy writing—his "purpleness," as he puts it in *Pierre*—does not simply analogize ecological wonders, translating phenomena to text. Melville's opaque art maps the internal logic of ecology itself. Melville provides fleeting glimpses of the delicate, relational geometries created by networks of life and nonlife through the equally complex, relational structures of syntax. In this way, I argue that

Melville's purple prose generates in his readers the kind of species thinking that has the potential to rewrite the story of human planetary dwelling, a story that encompasses built environments and architectural edifices as much as hives and burrows.

I use the word "dwell" here, and throughout this book, to mean "inhabit" and "cohabit." But the term also retains its original philologies from the old English *dwęllan,* meaning to be "delayed" and to "linger on" with full attention. To dwell is to be made conscious of habit, habitat, and the multiplex forms of cohabitation that surround us. Probing the capacity of literary forms to represent ecological complexity by slowing time and forcing readers to linger on purple passages, Melville carves a place for fiction in an America, then as now, increasingly yielding to the authority of absolutist politics, commoditized distraction, and the unblinking speed of techno-modernity. Melville's literary experiments deserve careful study to see how literature and science can, together and at the same time, tell new stories about dwelling within the turbulence of the Anthropocene.

AMERICAN MAGNITUDES

One of the most remarkable characters in Melville's writing appears early in *The Confidence-Man:* a huckster simply named "the herb-doctor." A peddler of tinctures and homeopathic remedies on the decks of the Mississippi steamship *Fidèle,* the herb-doctor markets his brews as "natural," full of "health," and without "error" or disease.[31] He relies on this romantic vision of the natural world to sell his snake-oil potions, and he is successful because he affiliates himself with a passive and unpolluted image of "Nature." Herb-doctors, he tells one passenger after the next, "claim nothing, invent nothing; but staff in hand, in glades, and upon hillsides, go about in nature, humbly seeking her cures" like the "Omni-Balsamic Reinvigorator" or the "Samaritan Pain Dissuader."[32] But the ship's resident skeptic Pitch doesn't buy it. How, he asks, do you account for diseases like cholera or toxic plants like nightshade, both of which are just as "nat'ral" as flowers or herbal tonics? What can the herb-doctor say about Pitch's flooded farm, "swept clean away" by excess "alluvion" left by the very waters that now sparkle picturesquely off the *Fidèle*'s decks? Pitch loudly laments the "dangerous" side of nature, nature with less "wonder than terror" for humans and animals alike. Clover and dandelions may be pretty, but what of the "hailstones [that] smashed my windows?" he asks. The whole of human history is, for

Pitch, the story of how our species has tried to "bar" Mother Nature from our homes: to "bolt her out" and, by stuffing the cracks in our walls, "lint her out" of our lives.[33]

The herb-doctor's debate with Pitch, like all of the conversations between the con man and his marks in the novel, is Melville's way of posing a binary of opposites about the "natural" world, neither of which is tenable or satisfying. Both rely on a reductionist understanding of the human's relation to environments, disease, and security. Both suggest the limits of human imagination under forms of sociality whose expressions of value are rooted so completely in money. Yet this moment enables Melville to interject an honest realism into his protoecological thinking, an ironic acknowledgment of the practical limits of environmental idealism. In fact, Pitch's response nicely captures the average nineteenth-century American's attitude toward environmental risk. By staging opposing visions of "Nature"—which he had been deconstructing since his time sailing the Pacific—Melville shows how environmental discourses are always bound up with economic ones, how ecology poses a challenge to notions of individuality and freedom in precisely the same ways that the confidence man does, with his masquerades of compassion and self-reliance. If "Nature" is neither intrinsically healing nor always baleful, and if we can never "lint out" external environments because they constitute our very bodies, then we are lost in a zone of environmental ambiguity without sturdy binaries to stand on. Without firm ground, we retreat to familiar categories of economy, security, and individualism, not despite our alluvial "natures" but because of them.

This scene also points out how limited scientific knowledge really was for most Americans in the antebellum period. On the whole, average nineteenth-century Americans were just not that interested in science.[34] As the abundance of new data from western exploration made its way back east and eventually to Europe, American science was hamstrung by the reluctance to think slowly, think big, or induce any "general law," as Harvard scientist Louis Agassiz put it, from environmental phenomena.[35] The American haste in all things scientific was motivated by the economic pressures of scientific exploration and conditioned by the threat of herb-doctor charlatanism. But, more commonly, it was habituated by poor communication of science to the general public. As the epigraph to this introduction makes clear, Emerson saw American science as "diffuse," without the stability of a "cedar" or "oak" tree to support it: "It all runs to leaves, to suckers, to tendrils, to miscellany." He may have been right, at least until after the

Civil War, but his botanical metaphors about the state of American science are nonetheless revealing. Emerson's emphasis on tendrils and miscellany conjures a field of parts without wholes, elements and processes without discrete organismic entities. Emerson depicts ecologies unbounded by "Nature" or other forms of metaphysical "inclosure," to quote the narrator of Melville's story "The Piazza."[36]

Still, American science did put the young nation on the international intellectual map. Many nineteenth-century European scientists relied on data from the wildernesses of North America to support their theories and sometimes to generate new ones. Historian of science Robert Bruce explains: "Europeans thought little of American ideas, but they needed American facts."[37] European scientists needed the lived American experience of the continent's geological and ecological diversity. Darwin's 1857 correspondence with American botanist Asa Gray, for instance, helped the Englishman formulate his theory of evolution. And earlier in the century, Yale professor Benjamin Silliman had pioneered American mineralogy while Albany Academy scientist Joseph Henry made advances in electromagnetic resistance independent of Ohm's theory. (Henry also developed the commercial telegraph and, independent of Faraday, worked out the principle of mutual induction.) By the 1890s, the early professionalization of ecology had become a symbol of American science's work to gain independence from, and equal stature with, its European counterparts. Darwin gets the bulk of the fame in the history of nineteenth-century science, and deservedly so, but advances in physiology, microscopy, and biochemistry were hugely formative for American scientific research as it formalized and expanded at the turn of the twentieth century.

But in early America, it was geology that brought together citizens, scientists, and the federal government to survey the continent's mineral wealth. With money on the line, amateur and professional rock hunters were suddenly concerned with the physics and chemistry of geological features, which, in turn, promoted interest in tracking down and classifying long-extinct forms of life. Historian Nathan Reingold reminds us that nineteenth-century geology had "an ambiguous role, being at the same time part of natural history and of natural philosophy."[38] Put differently, geology intruded into the domains of history and philosophy, forcing both disciplines to grapple with new conceptions of time. Not only were middle-class consumers increasingly able to afford clocks and pocket watches—a subtle index of changes in the administration of labor during nineteenth-century industrialization, particularly around the working day—but national history itself, especially in America, had to be recalibrated to accommodate new scales of time beyond the limited duration of historical memory. This recalibration turned out to be enormously productive for American national identity in the antebellum period. In his excellent history of American time telling, Thomas Allen notes that "the expansion of the temporal scale from thousands to millions of years by the science of geology" anchored American time within geological chronologies. "Geology gave the American land a history," writes Allen, "and, through both scientific study and artistic representation, gave the people a felt connection to that history."[39] David Spanangel goes so far as to say that the early American Republic should be understood as a "social experiment whose cultivation and deployment of natural knowledge depended essentially upon the practice of geology."[40] Or, to quote the atheist geologist Margoth in Melville's epic poem *Clarel* (1876), for nineteenth-century Americans "All, all's geology."[41]

As science and philosophy converged in the study of geological features, writers of the day began to experiment with the "vividness" of literary forms to think through the unsettling implications of scientific discoveries. For example, as we will see in chapter 1, Melville turns to the mineral in the fantastical worlds of *Mardi* because minerals are metonyms for the human species' relationship to a planet running on geological time, a relationship that a single person cannot easily grasp without conceptual help. In *The Origin of Species* Darwin observed that the human mind "cannot possibly grasp the full meaning of the term of even a million years; it cannot add up and perceive the full effects of many slight variations, accumulated during an almost infinite number of generations."[42] This is because, as Stephen Jay Gould has argued, "Deep time is so alien that we can really only comprehend it as metaphor."[43] Since geology offered material residues of deep time and metaphors for thinking in million-year scales, it aligned science and language in the contemplation of cause and effect across alien magnitudes. Scientific breakthroughs in geology and biology thus reshaped nineteenth-century narratives of embodiment and selfhood, contouring the initial outlines of "complexity" as a pivotal term in the philosophy of science. Darwin's challenge, still with us today, was how to represent this new sense of geo-evolutionary time within language systems that were structured by past, deeply anthropocentric ordering schemes. How could words ever express the Darwinian trauma, as Freud called it, which wounded our species-ego by exposing us to the mysteries of time beyond human comprehension? Built on a bedrock of human agency and theological exceptionalism, what good was language for understanding a profoundly nonhuman planetary history? Might literature, with its linguistic play and fictional freedom, provide a way forward? Many writers thought so, and looking back at them today, we can see that their attempts to represent degrees of planetary complexity (unfolding through vast scales of time) partially explain why nineteenth-century writing, and especially Melville's, is often so difficult, so weird, so speculative, and so explicitly philosophical during this period of conceptual upheaval.

To read Melville alongside the history and philosophy of nineteenth-century science is to discover a hidden trajectory in his work, one that enables us in the twenty-first century to think simultaneously about the vivid and the lived, about the literary and the ecological. In this way, Melville tests the insights and limits of materialist philosophies by making ecological complexity visible, paradoxically, in the most "unscientific" narrative forms of fiction and poetry. Melville intervenes in scientific discourses to sketch complexity from the multiple vantage points afforded by the flexibility of literary fiction. For Melville, the openness of literary forms—their ability to multiply streams of thought—lets readers "collectively behold the marvels which one pair of eyes sees not," to quote *Mardi*'s self-appointed philosopher Babbalanja.[44]

Before Melville, scientifically attuned American fiction had blended eighteenth-century discourses on scientific methods (especially observation) with narrative theory (especially the sympathy elicited by another's story) to heighten the authority of fiction in understanding "natural" wonders. At the turn of the nineteenth century, for example, gothic novelist Charles Brockden Brown distinguished history from romance by suggesting that romancers establish "cause and effect," while historians are limited to observation and mere notation of fact. Historians archive "catalogues of stars, and mark their positions at given times," Brown writes, but a romancer "will arrange them in *clusters* and dispose them in *strata,* and inform you by what influences the orbs have been drawn into sociable knots and circles." Novelists give literary form to scientific fact, Brown claimed, by arranging clusters and strata to better see the designs of nature. The very best scientists—Brown cites Isaac Newton and William Herschel as examples—are historians *and* romancers because they assign "motives to actions" and trace the "connections" between adjacent actions to unfurl the "magnificent fabrics" of planetary causal relations. In this paradigm, literary narrative's emphases on plot, action, and consequence become perfect tools to investigate the "series of motives and incidents subordinate and successive to one another." The complexity of a single action radiates outward in an "empire of romance," Brown's term for his literary philosophy of causality.[45]

Melville's entire oeuvre might be summarized as "an enlarged study of mankind" across this empire of romance, supplemented by a post-Darwinian awareness that "whatever man might be, man is not the universe."[46] As I wrote in the preface, Melville takes the planetary view, one that requires moving between massive scales of time and space within the seemingly narrow confines of an alphabet, a word, a sentence, a line, a paragraph, a book. At the beginning of *John Marr,* Melville observed that "the microscope, telescope, and other inventions for sharpening and extending our natural sight" enable us merely "to enlarge the field of our original and essential ignorance."[47] Plus, that enlargement is incredibly disorienting. Looking retrospectively over Melville's career, an early reviewer of *The Confidence-Man* articulated this sense of disorientation, one that only increased as Melville matured as a writer. The early Pacific stories, the reviewer declares, "were all stars, twinkles, flashes, vistas of green and crimson, diamond and crystal," but by *The Confidence-Man,* ten years later, Melville had "now tempered himself, and studied the effect of neutral tints . . . His fault is a disposition to discourse upon too large a scale."[48] From a planetary perspective, everything becomes "insignificant in the curve of the sphere," as Emerson phrased it, leaving plot-hungry readers confused and abandoned to the vagaries of details.[49] For Emerson, the human sciences often neglect scale by focusing on "microscopic criticism," and therefore one of the hallmarks of American Renaissance writers was their attention to large, metaphysical, even universal scopes of imagination.[50]

From the Puritans to Emerson and onward, Americans have been keenly attuned to "bigness," which Max Weber would later describe as a uniquely American "romanticism of numbers."[51] Whitman, the most famous celebrant of celestial multitudes, jubilantly concluded near the end of his life that America had finally become "poetry" with "cosmic and dynamic features of magnitude and limitlessness . . . never possible before."[52] For Whitman, American landscapes reflected the scale-bending symmetries of the cosmos, its "magnitude and limitlessness." A more capacious term than "scale" or "scope," "magnitude" empowered writers as different as Anne Bradstreet, Jonathan Edwards, and Emily Dickinson to theorize the spatio-temporal and spiritual implications of the U.S. democratic experiment.[53]

In an era of railroad timetables and daily newspapers set against the deep time of recently discovered geologic epochs, "magnitude" had diverse resonances across nineteenth-century disciplines, including mathematics (order of magnitude), astronomy (brilliance of stars), and eventually seismology (earthquake intensity). But in antebellum America, "magnitude" became shorthand for *formal correspondences,* like the spherical similarities that aligned atoms with the newly observed moons of Saturn. Ishmael's transcription of a whale skull, for example, had to be "scaled down to the human magnitude" and thus serves as an emblem of the kind of scalar thinking required of nineteenth-century readers as they took up the fluid temporal ranges of Melville, Whitman, and Darwin.[54]

Properly understood as experiments in magnitude, this strain of nineteenth-century American fiction and poetry anticipates a critical approach in contemporary environmental humanities, what Derek Woods and Timothy Clark have called "scale critique."[55] Facing the scalar disjunctures of contemporary environmentalism that tend to split responses into local responsibility—recycle!—or global activism—capitalism!—without addressing the feedback between both scales, Woods and Clark ask that we accept the "anachronistic" nature of modern life to create new time scales for environmental ethics, scales that early American writers were already poised to offer.[56] Further, although antebellum definitions of magnitude tended toward bigness, toward immensity, the concept also worked (despite Emerson's warnings) in the opposite direction: toward a renewed appreciation of the very small, the microscopic, and the elemental. Melville's contemporary Karl Marx, for example, invokes the inorganic grounds of existence in his famous description of how capitalism alienates a worker from his universal "species being": "The life of the species, both in man and in animals, consists physically in the fact that man (like the animal) lives on inorganic nature; and the more universal man is compared with an animal, the more universal is the sphere of inorganic nature on which he lives. . . . The universality of man is in practice manifested precisely in the universality which makes all nature his *inorganic* body."[57] Marx concludes that *"inorganic* nature" is always within the human body because, after all, "man is a part of nature." Both Melville and Marx were responding, in their own domains, to the magnitudes of inorganic materiality that influence how we delineate "natural" from "human" history. Marx and Melville share a vision of the inorganic that stresses the fact that nonlife dwells within life, structures it, and makes it possible. And all of this before talk of identity, society, or politics.

As far back as *Omoo,* Melville had emphasized the flows of energy and inorganic matter that formed the wild landscapes readers so appreciated in nineteenth-century travel fiction. For instance, describing the estuaries on the island of Loohooloo, *Omoo*'s narrator Paul theorizes the role of salt concentrates in the formation of coral: "It is said that the fresh water of the land, mixing with the salts held in solution by the sea, so acts upon the latter as to resist the formation of the coral; and hence the breaks." He then explains the spread of vegetation on coral barrier islands: "Here and there, these openings are sentineled, as it were, by little fairy islets, green as emerald, and waving with palms. Strangely and beautifully diversifying the long line of breakers, no objects can strike the fancy more vividly."[58] Paul's natural history of coral islands begins with salinity of tidal waters—its admixtures and marine chemistry—to demonstrate how the drifts and pressures of inorganic substances generate the territory of organic life. In Paul's telling, the aesthetic beauty of emerald islets and waving palms depends on the humblest of salt molecules and the unique tidal ranges of a given coastal area. Paul's observations move readers past a conception of life housed in distinct, organismic bodies and toward an ecology of "transcorporeality," to borrow a useful term from Stacy Alaimo.[59]

Melville's most creative twentieth-century reader, Charles Olson, was the first critic to recognize these dynamics in Melville's fiction. Writing in the 1950s, Olson argued that nineteenth-century thinkers like Melville, amazed by discoveries of "energy and motion," were suddenly possessed by the sensation of being merely "a thing among things."[60] For writers of the period, "discrete" details no longer corresponded to "the real" in the same way: "classification was exposed as mere taxonomy; and logic (and the sentence as poised on it, a completed thought, instead of what it has become, an exchange of force) was as loose and inaccurate a system as the body and soul had been, divided from each other and rattling, sticks in a stiff box. Something like this are the terms of the real and of action Melville was an early inheritor of, and he is either held this way or he is missed entirely."[61] Olson's point is that "matter offers perils wider than man if he doesn't do what still today seems the hardest thing for him to do, outside of some art and science: to believe that things, and present ones, are the absolute conditions." Yet the structures of these "absolute conditions" are, simultaneously, "flexible" because, as Olson poetically describes it, "quanta do dissolve into vibrations, all does flow, and yet is there, to be made permanent, if the means are equal."[62] I don't take Melville to be an unqualified materialist, but Olson exposes the crucial tension between Melville's philosophical realism—his anti-transcendentalism, his emphasis on the absolute conditions of material existence—and the spiraling, fluid poetics that typify the strangeness of his literary style and its constant metamorphoses. Olson is thus a major figure in our understanding of Melville's relationship to science, for he alone in the twentieth century noticed a central paradox in Melville: the intractable, contradictory, but necessary fact that absolute materiality—which, for humans, is most clearly understood in death—is at the same time a feature of the mutable conditions that produce life through complex dynamics of emergence. Building on Olson's insights, *Magnificent Decay* claims that any reading of Melville must take into account his sensitivity to the complexity of life's dependence on nonlife, a sensitivity that came to define ecological thought from the twentieth century onward.

RETROSPECTIVE ECOLOGY

I want to pause here to address the use of "ecology" in the context of Melville and nineteenth-century America more broadly. Is this an anachronistic error, that fatal blunder feared by historians and critics? In one sense, yes, because Melville never used the term himself.[63] And yet, how are we to understand Melville's ties to science when his thinking and writing are so concerned with the network of relations between humans, animals, plants, and minerals that we now recognize as ecological? We are faced with two horizons of interpretation that nonetheless converge in the retrospective story of ecology, a field that, even before it had a name, had a point of view and a history.[64] The criticisms of ecology as a science—namely, that sequence and antecedent do not necessarily equal causality—apply to the history of ecology as well. Tracking the "phylogeny of ecology," to use historian Robert McIntosh's phrase, means tracking a *"retrospective* ecology" necessarily colored by the historical messiness of defining ecology as scientific practice, as environmental concern, and as relational philosophy.[65] In other words, in the history of ecology we find a welter of conflicting methodological approaches to the past that circumscribe historiography, literary criticism, and the philosophy of science. The history of ecology teaches us that knowledge is never quite on time. It is always out of joint. And if our experience of the Anthropocene is similarly anachronistic—when a morning commute requires the burning of Mesozoic fossil fuels, and carbon footprints from two centuries ago still linger in the atmosphere—might our methods of diagnosis and inquiry *need* to be anachronistic? Might we abandon the fantasy of historical purity and decontamination to properly grasp the nature of our anachronistic species? Perhaps the answer lies in the history of ecology, a history of a conceptual framework as much as a word or a formal discipline.

In a story recognizable to many of us, the word *oecologie*—from the Greek *oikos* meaning "household," or, more precisely, "dwelling"—first appeared in German biologist Ernst Haeckel's *Generelle Morophologie der Organismen* (1866) and was later elaborated by Haeckel to mean "the science of the relations of living organisms to the external world, their habitat, customs, energies, parasites, etc."[66] I fully address the implications of *oikos* in chapter 3, but for Haeckel, the term "ecology" simply enlarged the scope of biological inquiry to include, for example, botany and zoology. Ecology allowed biological science to be concerned with related disciplines like physiology and morphology. As a set of scientific practices, ecology is a definitively modern science that could not have existed until the development of evolutionary biology, which itself required the discovery of modern chemistry and geology. And it took another century after Haeckel's coining of the term for ecology to become fully recognized as a field by mainstream science. But the most important methodological aspect of early ecological thinking was the stress on inductive reasoning, rooted in field observations, which attended to Earth processes in their spatial and temporal dimensions. Ecology is premised on the notion that we can conceptualize life without relying solely on the species as a foundational unit of analysis, enabling us to accommodate disorder and slip past clumsy dualisms (e.g., mechanistic vs. holistic perspectives). From its early roots, ecology has also tended to be a more theoretical than applied science, one concerned not just with observation but with the vexed status of interdisciplinary knowledge and the problem of coherence between fields, systems, and methods. The "major difficulty of ecology," McIntosh admits, "has been developing a body of theory to accommodate the vagaries of the phenomena it purports to explain."[67]

This book argues that Melville's supple literary forms provide that body to ecological theory, intervening between "reader" and "nature" to map the complexity of relations that generate the ecological configurations we see in forests, oceans, and deserts. As Melville knew well, the origins of ecological thinking are entrenched in eighteenth-century European theories about the interrelations between life forms, often glossed as "the economy of nature."[68] This is a familiar narrative, wherein philosophers from

Rousseau to Gilbert White seized on the Arcadianism of rustic coexistence with nature while scientists like Carolus Linnaeus flexed their taxonomic muscles to create rubrics of knowledge that shaped the field of biology for two centuries. But the imaginary of "nature's economy" was also attractive to early nineteenth-century Romantic writers and artists because it recast the authority of science, challenged the burgeoning capitalist ethos, and resisted the vision of a dominated nature articulated by some Christian theology. For the Romantics, the economy of nature became a counter-vision to industrialization's estrangement of human beings from dirt, streams, and stones.[69] But Romantic writers often used nature's economy as evidence for their own philosophical musings, inducing grand transcendental and metaphysical truths that Melville cautioned against.

Even more significant for our purposes, in its initial phases protoecological thought was especially concerned with *spatiality*. Early nineteenth-century geographers, for instance, tried to represent the topological dimensions of species relations by studying how animals and plants were dispersed across regions, what they called "biogeography" or "phytogeography." In an 1856 letter, Thoreau described his own motivation to understand the environment in conspicuously spatial rhetoric; he wanted a "sense of the breadth of the field on whose verge I dwell."[70] George Perkins Marsh's popular *Man and Nature* (1864), later reprinted in 1874 as *The Earth as Modified by Human Action*, took a similar spatio-theological perspective on the ways that human endeavors transformed the landscape. Marsh argued, in terms striking to readers today, that we had a responsibility to recognize how human modifications "must rank among geological influences," and therefore it was our moral duty to dedicate resources and innovations to remediating our ecological imprint.[71]

It is critical to underline, however, that ecology as a science did not develop from the transcendentalism of Thoreau or the visionary urgings of Marsh, but from the professionalization of life sciences in the late nineteenth century. It is equally critical to recognize that writers like Marsh, along with other figures in the history of ecology like geologist Nathaniel Southgate Shaler and sociologist Lester Frank Ward, situated organism-environment relations (to varying degrees) against the wider backdrop of American territorial expansion that often saturated scientific insight with the optimistic, sometimes racialized, rhetoric of social progress.[72] Along these lines, one can trace a history of protoecological progressive thought as far back as Hippocrates, Theophrastus, and Pliny the Elder up through the European exploration of North America. Then there is the rich protoecological history of eighteenth- and nineteenth-century European science, including, for example, the biological materialism of Erasmus Darwin (Charles's grandfather), Jean-Baptiste Lamarck's farsighted work on environmental conditioning, and the spiraling plant morphologies of Johann Wolfgang von Goethe, which we will take up in chapter 2.

Another prominent figure lurking in the background here is the German polymath Alexander von Humboldt, sometimes identified as the "first ecologist."[73] Humboldt's goal, as he laid it out in his masterwork *Cosmos: A Sketch of a Physical Description of the Universe* (1845, 1850), was to follow "the chain of connection, by which all natural forces are linked together, and made mutually dependent upon each other."[74] Humboldt was beloved by Emerson, Whitman, and especially Thoreau, who used Humboldt's model of plant ecology to theorize New England's ecological and social climates, including forest succession and seasonal changes.[75] Humboldt saw the cosmos as a "harmoniously ordered whole" and understood "Nature's forms" as hidden patterns waiting to be discovered.[76] However, when scientists like Humboldt tried to understand "the rich luxuriance of living nature, and the mingled web of free and restricted natural forces," things seemed "as if shrouded in a vapory vail."[77] Humboldt's rational science aimed to "lift the vail that shrouds [Nature's] phenomena."[78] Whereas Humboldt declared his science "rational empiricism" and not "speculative philosophy," Melville's fiction is *precisely* speculative philosophy: an investigation into the primary relations between thought, language, and environment.[79]

Although some scholars have criticized Humboldtian science for its relationship to nineteenth-century colonialism, Humboldt frequently denounced imperial power and its consequences in the Americas.[80] Laura Dassow Walls has argued that while Humboldt may have been seduced by the intellectual potential of a scientific archive, it was not because the archive supported empire but because the archive produced various forms of excess. Humboldt, like Melville, saw this surplus of uncategorized botanical and biological knowledge overwriting and destabilizing the internal structure of empire, a vision evident in Humboldt's most archival work, *Political Essay on the Kingdom of New Spain* (1811).[81] Still, we should contrast Humboldt's archival fascination with Melville's life-long practice of destroying his work and letters. In chapter 1, I examine this anti-archival instinct, one that radicalizes Melville's vision of ecology by performing in his own "artificial" archive the same decay and extinction he sees in the "natural" one.

But the point here is that, reading Humboldt and other transatlantic scientists, antebellum Americans were primed to think ecologically. Uniting spatial and linguistic modes of representation, protoecology was a conceptual matrix that produced philosophical and literary experiments as well as practical methods for dealing with life and death issues in early America. In the 1830s, for instance, medical pioneer and New Jersey physician Daniel Drake was studying what today we would call disease ecology, and in the early years of the nineteenth century Canadian naturalist Titus Smith founded the field of "geobotany" (now plant ecology) by searching out the relations of plants to local and regional environments. In fact, professional ecological science truly started with plant geography, usually for agricultural and weed control problems, and the first book in English with "ecology" in the title was L. H. Pammel's 1893 *Flower Ecology*. Nevertheless, it was the earlier intersection of geology and biology—for example, Lyell's influence on Darwin—that produced tectonic shifts in how scientists theorized the history and evolution of life by considering the relics of very ancient, paleoecological systems. In this sense, Melville's vision of "Nature" was always closer to Darwin's than Humboldt's, with its hallmark emphases on randomness, mutation, and decay. Melville's disenchanted vision of the Galapagos Islands in "The Encantadas," for example, uses geological time to read planetary history through biology, extending Darwin's insights on evolutionary creation to human ecologies and the (creative) destruction wrought by our species.

In October 1835, when Darwin surveyed the Galapagos Islands for the first time, he recalled being "astonished at the amount of creative force" displayed on the islands.[82] Darwin saw in the Galapagos the geological origin of all islands: a geo-biological insight that would eventually coalesce into the germ of the idea of evolution. "Hence, both in space and time," he wrote, "we seem to be brought somewhat near to that great fact—that mystery of mysteries—the first appearance of new beings on this earth."[83] Melville visited the Galapagos almost exactly six years later, on October 30, 1841, early into his years roving the Pacific. He likely read Darwin's 1839 edition of *Journal of Researches* aboard the frigate *United States* on his journey home from the Marquesas Islands between 1843 and 1844, and he later owned a copy of the Harper Brothers' two volume 1847 edition.[84] As with Darwin, the Galapagos Islands occupy a central place in Melville's imagination and in the development of his environmental philosophies. The opening of *Typee* takes place "some twenty degrees to the westward of the Gallipagos"; *Mardi* begins with a voyage to the "Gallipagos, otherwise called the Enchanted Isles"; and even the Pequod's carpenter appreciates the equatorial uniqueness of "Gallipagos."[85] Additionally, in the "Extracts" that open *Moby-Dick*, Melville quotes a passage on whales from Darwin's *Voyage*, and as Jennifer Baker has suggested, we might read Darwin's observational method—representing scientifically known objects to "evoke emotional, intellectual, and bodily responses"—as a model for Ishmael's literary method and musings on extinction.[86] Recent work on Melville and evolutionary thought has further identified Darwin's influence on Melville's writings after 1871: what was known as "Darwin's year" and in which the publication of *Descent of Man* (1871) was followed by new editions of *Origin of Species* (1871), Lyell's *Antiquity of Man* (1872), and Thomas Huxley's *Man's Place in Nature* (1872).[87]

Despite reading widely in Romantic and later Victorian poetry—including Wordsworth, Tennyson, Browning, Arnold, Swinburne, Meredith, and Hardy—Darwin hesitated to unknot the ties that bind literature and science. But twentieth-century scholars have carefully analyzed Darwin's own literary style, pointing to the influence of his distinctive syntax on the articulation of his ideas in works like *Researches, Origin,* and *Descent*. Gillian Beer argues that, at the level of grammar, Darwin's writing performs the fundamental tenets of his thinking about how life changes over time. In particular, Darwin's syntax in *Origin of Species,* especially in chapter 4, often branches off into successive clauses so that his "prose succession imitates the order it describes, branching out into further and further similitudes."[88] George Levine, perhaps Darwin's most astute literary critic, writes that "in submitting all things to time" Darwin challenged the notion that there were any universal forms of nature and, further, any "permanent categories of thought."[89] For Levine, Darwin's work on evolution should be read alongside other cultural forms of the era—the overpopulated, multiplot Victorian novel, for instance, and even early European experiments with modernism—that similarly challenged static models of scientific and social experience. Darwin's "tangled bank" of nonteleological, continuing change has therefore become a recognizable tableau for the convergence of evolutionary science and literary style in the fin-de-siècle Atlantic world.

By the end of the nineteenth-century, literary-philosophical questions over the nature of representation—the molding power of language in the expression of thought—suddenly became applied problems within newly defined scientific disciplines like evolutionary biology and geology. As ecologists diverged from evolutionary biology in the 1890s to develop their own distinct field of study, the equilibrium model of nature's economy had been finally shot through with the accepted realities of disorder, accident, and chaos. But it was far less clear how these realities might be represented. Scientific method and linguistic mode seemed to collapse into one another as they each approached the limits of human-centered models for explaining planetary phenomena. By the mid-twentieth century, ecology had become a refuge from overspecialization in the sciences. Ecologists were increasingly interested in what complexity theorist Melanie Mitchell calls "the demise of the reductionist dream," instead seeing individual scientific disciplines as local approximations of much more global, complex systems.[90] Mitchell notes that ecology allowed twentieth-century scientists to contemplate "how large numbers of relatively simple entities organize themselves, without the benefit of any central controller, into a collective whole that creates patterns, uses information, and in some cases, evolves and learns."[91] These anti-reductionist dreams, which emphasize self-organization and disorder, saturate Melville's weird fiction of the 1840s and 1850s. The man who lived among the cannibals had begun to apply Darwinian insights to literary composition a century before ecology became established as a field of inquiry.

In short, the protoecological antecedents we've been tracking provide a way to think through the arrival of ecological thought within literary form. So, although it is ostensibly about fiction and poetry, *Magnificent Decay* conjoins two ways of thinking ecologically. It juxtaposes mereological ecology, or autoecology (emphasizing discrete parts of an environment, as in population ecology), and holological ecology, or syncology (which emphasizes the material and energy flows that characterize ecosystem ecology).[92] If ecology is an "architectonic science" where methods of analysis and synthesis are always in tension, then Melville's transitory fictional spaces—islands in *Mardi*, meadows in *Pierre*, nests in "The Encantadas"—can be read as expressions of this tension without resolution: fictional abeyances that heighten the reader's capacity for ecological thought.[93] For, as the narrator of *Pierre* tells us, any single "event" is actually a "product of an infinite series of infinitely involved and untraceable foregoing occurrences" and thus represents "only one link in the chain; but to a long line of dependencies whose further part is lost in the mid-regions of the impalpable air."[94] *Pierre*'s philosophy of causality captures Melville's awareness of where he found himself in imperial modernity: caught between scales and turning to methods of expression that blurred long-settled definitions of form, rhetoric, genre, and translation. Julian Yates has argued persuasively that formerly distinct scientific and literary methods are increasingly understood today simply as "ways of moving, ferrying, or shifting things (persons, concepts, plants, animals) between and among different spheres of reference."[95] Ecological questions have become literary ones, all hovering under a common "sign of nature," the apt title of the series in which this book appears. Without valorizing science as a privileged epistemology, Melville's writing investigates how "Nature" is made legible and at what scales.

Take ferns, for example. Ferns are mentioned in many of Melville's writings—in *Omoo,* the verdant banks of Tahiti are "carpeted with a minute species of fern" called "nahee"—and Melville makes it is clear that these sporophytic plants thrive in habitats where flowering plants may not.[96] We now know that ferns support a massive diversity of invertebrate life. Ecologically considered, they are vital nodes for a wide range of organic systems. A single tropical epiphytic fern, like the bird's-nest fern that takes root in the limbs of other trees, has been estimated to contain half of the entire invertebrate biomass within a hectare of rainforest canopy.[97] Such compressions of ecological magnitude in a single organism challenge our understanding of *complexity* as a meaningful concept in Earth system science. I use the term "complexity" here to mean contemporary interdisciplinary attempts to represent the scale-warping patterns emergent from the interactions between environments and organisms. Especially from *Pierre* onward, Melville's motifs and poetics hinge on the meaning of complexity, and the word deserves some explanation given its central role in this book.

BOWERS OF COMPLEXITY

"Complexity" derives from the Latin root *plectere* (to weave, entwine) in the term *complexus:* surrounding, encompassing, and encircling. When John Locke used the word in 1690—"Ideas thus made up of several simple ones put together, I call Complex; such as are Beauty, Gratitude, a Man, an Army, the Universe"—it still retained a sense of building-block, Enlightenment order in which great chains of being were "put together" from simpler forms.[98] But by 1847, when Emerson used it in an essay on Goethe, complexity had come to mean structural and organizational elegance. The "highest simplicity of structure is produced," Emerson wrote, "not by few elements, but by the highest complexity."[99] Taking "complexity" into the realm of biology, Darwin concluded his famous 1859 letter to Lyell by declaring that life has "a tendency to advance in complexity of organization."[100]

Both Emerson and Darwin use complexity to refer to systems that exhibit what we today call *non-additive properties*. In other words, the aggregate expresses properties not reducible to a summation of its parts.

Complexity theory in the late twentieth and early twenty-first centuries has moved far beyond Emerson and Darwin's notions to adduce more strictly mathematical properties of complex phenomena (nonlinearity, for example). Complexity is extraordinarily difficult to measure, just as "wetness"—an emergent property of aggregate drops of water—is extraordinarily difficult to approximate, and so modeling complexity requires a nuanced understanding of the fundamentally nonlinear nature of emergence that characterizes it. After Darwin, analysis of complexity demanded that scientists find "recurring patterns in the system's ever-changing configurations," like "motifs" in molecular genetics or "lemmas" in Euclidean geometry.[101] Complexity prompts us to think about a world that is "perpetually novel," a world unceasingly active and full of accident. But because a property like emergence cannot be captured in itself—any example is unique and temporally bound—and because emergence is most often not visible from a human vantage point so limited in space and time, complexity resists our most familiar representational modes, modes that have historically produced the fiercest imperial gazes.

But before I continue my discussion of complexity and its relation to Melville's literary forms, I need to directly address the problem of anachronism raised in the previous section: the incongruity of using present knowledge (like complexity theory) to read the past, consciously or unconsciously. Although I'm drawing on the vocabulary of complexity theory here—vocabulary that would have been foreign to Melville—the *concepts* of complexity and emergence were not foreign to him or to his audiences at all. In fact, Melville's literary terminology, styles, and forms invite present-day readers to linger at the limits of representation in fresh and unexpectedly relevant ways, in ways that capture the correspondences between human thought, writing, and ecological networks. Rendering the intricacy of geological, botanical, and zoological phenomena within the intricacy of literary texts, Melville's fictions and lyrics are roadmaps for how nature becomes "natural," how it gets constellated into patterns, words, metaphors, syntaxes, and stories. Yet seeing these constellations from the vantage point of the twenty-first century means embracing German philosopher Hans-Georg Gadamer's concept of *wirkungsgeschichtliches Bewußstein* ("effective-historical consciousness"), the fusing together of two horizons of interpretation: then and now.[102] This form of reading concedes the impossibility of pure and absolute objectivity in historical understanding and accepts the realities of contamination and pollution, partiality and obscurity, which are, of course, the very foundations of ecological thought.

The intermixture of past and present, influence and iteration, is classic Melville. His prose swims with allusions, his narrators tinker with source material, and his descriptions overlay disparate landscapes in which the human appears and then fades just as quickly. Following Giorgio Agamben's contention (in a very Melvillean turn of phrase) that "the investigation of the past is nothing but the shadow cast by an interrogation directed at the present," my approach in this book reframes anachronism as a literary-historical problem embedded within Melville's wider concerns over originality in nature and in writing.[103] Folding a discussion of anachronism into the arguments over "nature" at the heart of this book enriches Melville's contribution to the philosophy of history as much as the philosophy of ecology, entwining the two discourses around literary problems of interpretational authority, originality, and context.

In this way, anachronism "need not be thought of as the enemy of historicism—a license to overwrite the past with the present"—but rather, echoing critic Marjorie Levinson, as "using the knowledges and imaginaries of our own time to summon up particular pasts and make them flash upon us in ways that neither they nor we could have anticipated."[104] Similarly, in her groundbreaking work on natural history and sexuality in the eighteenth-century Atlantic world, Greta LaFleur juxtaposes scholarly methods that emphasize historical objectivity with those that emphasize present-day concerns: "archival fidelity" against a presentist "erasure" that threatens to efface the "relentless specificity" of historical pasts. LaFleur rightly points out that dedication to archival objectivity "runs the risk of reading objects as metaphors for subjects, of assuming the unremitting knowability of the past and thus failing to account for the drive toward problematic mastery that underlies this scene of interpretation." On the other hand, by clothing past centuries "in the vestments of the twenty-first," critics risk "the colossal, devastating erasure" of "the everyday realities of people very different from us, people who were grappling, in their own time and in their own terms, with the both philosophical and ethical question of making sense of human difference."[105] Elaborating LaFleur's nuanced take on anachronism, *Magnificent Decay* is organized in large part by the specific terminology of Melville's own lexicon as it is filtered through the strangeness of his environmental imagination. The resulting terms—for example: "contour," "cluster," "verdure," "honeycomb"—are at once resonant and dissonant to our twenty-first-century ears, and this book retunes our frequencies through anachronistic discourses to better hear the diction of environmental thought, then and now.

So while Melville would not have understood words like "fractals" or "nonlinearity," his vocabulary and literary style impress on the reader the patterns and phenomena that would later become codified into scientific definitions. This explains why Melville dwells for extended passages on seemingly excessive descriptions of lush verdure or living seabeds, like the "marine gardens" of Papeetee harbor in *Omoo*. The harbor is populated by "coral plants of every hue and shape imaginable:—antlers, tufts of azure, waving reeds like stalks of grain, and pale green buds and mosses . . . crawling among these are strange shapes:—some bristling with spikes, others clad in shining coats of mail, and here and there, round forms all spangled with eyes."[106] Here, seabed habitats are transmuted into various hues, shapes, and contours to emphasize the activity *between* organisms: sprouting, crawling, bristling, spangling. Attending to passages like this one, to the strangeness of Melville's own language and style, enables us contemporary readers to defuse the dilemma of anachronism without discounting the specific historical worlds Melville is writing in and about, and without discounting how the powerful insights of Melville's ecological visions remain relevant for our current moment. The marine gardens of Papeetee harbor suddenly become striking scenes of ecological diversity characterized by the perpetual movement, modification, and chance that drive evolutionary change over thousands of years. And all of this change is captured by the interpenetrating hues and hazy syntax of Melville's sentences.

Throughout the book, I rely on Melville's unique diction, idiosyncratic grammar, and repeated phrasings to articulate his ecological foresight. Chapter 1, for example, focuses on Melville's use of the term "cluster," as in clusters of minerals and the clusters of meaning contained within the term "mineral" itself. Minerals are geophysical objects composed of elements in certain formations, but they also make their way into the bodies of corals and crabs. From points of bio-interface, amorphous minerals become biominerals and sometimes get fully mineralized into tissues like mussel shells, fish tendons, and human teeth. In chapter 2, I emphasize the word "verdure," which Melville often uses in descriptions of landscapes so dense with life that it is difficult to discern where individual species end and others begin: masses of foliage "spread with such rich profusion, that it was impossible to determine of what description of trees it consisted."[107] The impossibility of description, of expressing that which lies at the outer reaches of representational capacity, signals Melville's awareness that the "universal verdure" of planetary ecosystems is a constant reminder of our impoverished categories of ecological thought. In chapter 3, I focus on Melville's use of "honeycomb" to refer to the nested layers of human-animal inhabitations. Human houses and animal nests are artifacts of interrelations between species and materials at different scales, in ways similar to Melville's descriptions of Pacific islands: "On one hand was a range of steep green bluffs hundreds of feet high, the white huts of the natives here and there nestling like birds' nests in deep clefts gushing with verdure."[108]

If the exchange of ideas, microbes, plants, and animals between the colonies and Britain in the eighteenth century collectively constituted the transatlantic cultures of natural history, then clearly Melville is invested in the nineteenth-century cultures of natural history on a planetary scale. Take, for instance, the political ecologies of human-animal relations onboard the whaleship *Julia* in *Omoo*. The crew's biscuits have been "honey-combed" by worms while cockroaches and "regiments of rats disputed the place" with the sailors. The narrator notes that the "vermin" seemed to take "actual possession" of the ship, "the sailors being mere tenants by sufferance."[109] On the *Julia*, "every chink and cranny swarmed" with cockroaches. They "did not live among you, but you among them . . . clustering and humming among the swarms lining the beams overhead, and the inside of the sleeping-places . . . buzzing in heaps almost in a state of fusion."[110] Hair-raising descriptions of swarming insects brought readers into the sensory world of the far-flung whaleship, but they also indicated Melville's appreciation for human-animal networks of cohabitation and mutual influence, from Columbian exchanges of the fifteenth and sixteenth centuries to Pacific transfer ecologies in the nineteenth.

Melville goes on in *Omoo* to detail the introduction of South American horses, cattle, and sheep to Tahiti, along with fruits like figs, pineapples, lemons, and limes (the latter "highly valued as an anti-scorbutic").[111] Observing that smallpox and other forms of "virulent disease" were completely unknown to Tahitians before European contact, Melville's narrator Paul is a sort of early disease ecologist, recognizing that the life is uninterrupted exposure to outside influence, to contagion.[112] Paul represents this exposure in a brief meditation on his own threadbare sandals, whose worn soles took

"The Round-Robin," from Herman Melville, *Omoo: A Narrative of Adventures in the South Seas* (New York: Harper Brothers, 1847), 104. (University of California Libraries)

"a sort of fossil impression of every thing trod upon."[113] Paul's fossil-sandals provide a metaphor not only for the bidirectional impacts of human-environmental contact but also for writing itself. Here, the famous "Round-Robin" image that Melville included in *Omoo* takes on wider significance.

The "Round-Robin" was a grievance made by sailors against the captain of the *Julia*, written out on two blank sheets torn from a book ("A History of the most Atrocious and Bloody Piracies") and fastened together with pitch. The sailors imagine that, because they all sign the document in a circle without hierarchy of leadership, they stand together, and no one can be singled out as the ringleader. "For ink," Paul tells us, "some of the soot over the lamp was then mixed with water, by a fellow of a literary turn; and an immense quill, plucked from a distended albatross' wing, which, nailed against the bowsprit bitts, had long formed an ornament of the forecastle, supplied a pen."[114] This image is an icon for Melville's ecologies of writing. Individual signatures radiate outward from "All Hands," mutually bound together in a non-additive complex without readily discernable causal patterns. But the material composition of the "Round Robin" doubles its meaning; written in soot-ink (water and burned organic matter, likely whale oil) with an albatross feather, the emblem melds minerals, plants, and animals in the collective signature of a human community. Meaning, style, and material converge in a single inscription.

I've lingered on the "Round-Robin" in *Omoo* because it helps clarify my use of the term "ecology" throughout this book. As I noted earlier, "ecology" has three specific definitions: scientific discipline, environmental concern, and interactions between organisms and environments. Though the word and its derivatives have come to refer variously to "nature," "sustainable living," or anything "green," in the following pages I use "ecology" to mean only interrelations and influences between individuals and larger systems, whether cockroaches, smallpox, or sailors-turned-writers. Ecology is the consideration of relations over entities, form over content, and style over meaning. Ecology is collapse and absorption, exchange and resistance. To more closely explicate this approach, we need a few more detailed examples from Melville's work that disclose the power of style and form in his ecological thinking. Let's turn then to a passage deep in *Moby-Dick*. In the short but famous "Bower of Arsacides" chapter, Ishmael describes how a beached sperm whale skeleton is slowly absorbed into the mossy "sea-side glen" of Pupella, somewhere in the endless expanses of the South Pacific.

At Pupella, Ishmael observes that the trees "stood high and haughty, feeling their living sap; the industrious earth beneath was as a weaver's loom, with a gorgeous carpet on it, whereof the ground-vine tendrils formed the warp and woof, and the living flowers the figures." He continues:

> All the trees, with all their laden branches; all the shrubs, and ferns, and grasses; the message-carrying air; all these unceasingly were active. Through the lacings of the leaves, the great sun seemed a flying shuttle weaving the unwearied verdure. Oh, busy weaver! unseen weaver!—pause!—one word!—whither flows the fabric? what palace may it deck? wherefore all these ceaseless toilings? Speak, weaver!—stay thy hand!—but one single word with thee! Nay—the shuttle flies—the figures float from forth the loom; the fresher-rushing carpet for ever slides away. The weaver-god,

he weaves; and by that weaving is he deafened, that he hears no mortal voice; and by that humming, we, too, who look on the loom are deafened; and only when we escape it shall we hear the thousand voices that speak through it.[115]

One of the definitions of complexity is "a system that exhibits nontrivial emergent and self-organizing behaviors," and the key question for ecologists and systems scientists is how this "self-organizing" comes about, how the "green, life-restless loom of that Arsacidean wood" creates the "ever-woven verdant warp and woof" that "intermixed and hummed" around the whale skeleton.[116] All "woven over with the vines," Ishmael exclaims, the whale is "every month assuming greener, fresher verdure." In the bower of Arsacides, "Life folded Death; Death trellised Life; the grim god wived with youthful Life, and begat him curly-headed glories." Like the innumerable ecologies Melville would describe at the base of Mount Greylock in *Pierre* or in the fish-filled, "honey-combed" grottoes beneath the islands of "The Encantadas," the bower of the Arsacides discloses ranges of hidden life that trellis, and are trellised by, nonlife in ceaseless thickets of unwearied verdure.

Thematically, Melville's attention to the endless cycles of life is not groundbreaking. But the power of the "Bower of Arsacides" passage comes not from its imagery of the humming glen but from its poetics: the formal linguistic conventions that shape our reading experience and reproduce emergent complexity in the very event of reading. Melville's interlinked, semicolon-dense syntax performs on the page the "ever-woven" intermixture of organisms and environments that he wants to highlight for the reader. Like his sailors' slang, Melville's writing has a self-confessed "flowery style," and the act of reading the chapter draws attention to a lattice poetics of network thinking wherein vegetal motif is mirrored in literary style.[117] Here and in other places, Melville's poetics correspond to contemporary network theory that, as Melanie Mitchell puts it, tries to find "a novel language for expressing commonalities across complex systems in nature . . . thus allowing insights from one area to influence other, disparate areas."[118] Just as network theory plays the role of a hub to twenty-first-century scientific discourses, Melville's writing plays hub, trellis, and lattice to protoecological nineteenth-century discourses.

Melville makes readers aware that all thought assumes a certain style, a certain form of expression, which provides a shorthand for the thinker's relationship to his or her historical context. Though style has become a neglected term in current studies of nineteenth-century American literature, contemporary critics like Sam Otter and Dorri Beam argue that highly wrought styles—especially Melville's—provide a "space from which dominant assumptions can be brought into view and reformulated."[119] For Otter, Melville's style is rooted in the "articulation of discontinuity," which begins with the limitations of human vision: the "ridges, gaps and transits" that appear in Melville's Marquesan landscapes.[120] This attention to perspective (and voyeurism) is inaugurated in *Typee*, where Nukuheva bay is first described as a "vast natural amphitheater of decay, and overgrown with vines, the deep glens that furrowed its sides appearing like enormous fissures caused by the ravages of time."[121]

To cite one final example of Melville's literary-style-as-ecological-thought, recall the third section of "The Encantadas," titled "Rock Rodondo." According to the narrator, the islands that make up the Galapagos chain were designated "Enchanted" by sailors because the "strong and irregular" currents that swirled around them were "unaccountable" and resisted navigators' best efforts to map the "fleetingness and unreality of the locality of the isles."[122] Amid the hydrodynamic disorder of an open system like the Pacific Ocean, pilots were challenged to locate pockets of order, islands of momentary stability that constitute "dissipative structures," to quote the famous twentieth-century chemist Ilya Prigogine.[123] Melville intuits the ecological complexity of these dissipative structures in his description of Rock Rodondo. A two-hundred-fifty-foot rock island in the Galapagos "rising straight from the sea," Rock Rodondo ascends "in entablatures of strata to a shaven summit."[124] Rodondo seems to the narrator "a high stone tower" of "some perished castle" which, at its peak, like "any old barn or abbey," comes "alive with swallows" and other birds that crowd the "rocky ledges with unnumbered sea-fowl." On Rock Rodondo, "the tower is the resort of aquatic birds for hundreds of leagues around. . . . It is the aviary of the Ocean," full of penguins, pelicans, albatrosses, "gannets, black and speckled haglets, jays, sea-hens, sperm-whale-birds, gulls of all varieties."[125] "Eaves upon eaves," the narrator marvels, "nests upon nests."

The precarious nests atop Rodondo are spaces of evanescent order at the margins of chaos. A century after Melville, Gaston Bachelard would argue that the nest is the "very impetus of the imagination" because the animal life is usually "concealed by the immense volume of vegetal life." But "when we examine a nest, we place ourselves at the origin of confidence in the world."[126] "The world," Bachelard concludes, "is a nest."[127]

Swallows make nests of mud and saliva. Hermit crabs take up residence in abandoned mollusk shells. Humans check in and out of hotel rooms. On Rock Rodondo, Melville sketches the nested intersection of three scales of ecological diversity: alpha diversity (α: the "local" pool of birds), beta diversity (β: local-meets-regional birds, or the "landscape" pool) and gamma diversity (γ: total diversity, or "regional" pool), where $γ = α \times β$.[128] This formula is a handy index to understand bird ecology as well as the wider gamma diversity of the Galapagos, in which the diversity of birds finds its "full counterpart in the finny hosts which peopled the waters" at the base of Rodondo.[129] Underwater, the narrator sees "one honey-comb of grottoes affording labyrinthine lurking places for swarms of fairy fish . . . Here hues were seen as yet unpainted, and figures which are unengraved." Cataloguing bird's nests and fish grottoes, vegetal novels and stony lyrics, *Magnificent Decay* surveys the gamma diversity of Melville's ecologies, from 1848 to 1888.

Furthermore, although the remarkable examples above emphasize animal ecologies, gamma diversity extends to human ecologies as well. Thus the following chapters track Melville's network thinking beyond Pacific glens and Galapagos rocks into New York City law offices and the industrial factories that dotted rural New England landscapes. In this way, writing *about* ecological practice and writing *as* ecological practice dovetail when we consider our species' unique modes of dwelling, sociality, and inhabitation. For example, a number of Melville's short stories published in the 1850s, notably "Bartleby, the Scrivener" (1853) and "The Tartarus of Maids" (1855), were overtly concerned with how material networks of paper production and distribution might bear literal and metaphoric implications for human ecologies. Melville's knowledge of paper production in western Massachusetts—exemplified by his 1851 visit to Dalton, a paper mill on the Housatonic Falls where quartz in the surrounding hills produced a purified water supply ideal for paper making—directly informed the material poetics of his short fiction. Such works obsessively conjure images of paper, both as a physical product of modern industrialization and as the primary medium for writing about modernity: a medium "marked by ephemerality," as Melville scholar Graham Thompson phrases it, because modern chemical additives accelerated the decomposition of paper.[130] In Melville's hands, paper became an emblem of industrial ecologies that scrambled the borders between man and nature, literature and chemistry.

As the bower of Arsacides, the birds of Rock Rodondo, and the mill at Dalton suggest, Melville's midcareer writing is structured by a poetics of ecological networking that ignores various boundaries that might usually distinguish inner from outer, dead from living, manmade structures from "natural" ones. By the same token, Melville reminds us that while traversing boundaries more closely approximates ecological networks, it does not mean an absolute flattening of difference and agency—the straw man of new materialism—because there are different intensities of relation, degrees of influence, and strengths of agency. In the chapters that follow, I take seriously, as nineteenth-century thinkers like Melville did, the capacity of literature to *preserve* difference, both by describing the asymmetrical agencies within natural systems and by working within a relational linguistic system of signs and syntaxes that exhibits complexity in its own right.

Contra Thoreau, who in *Walden* sees himself mining the "richest vein" of the Concord hills armed only with his mind (an "intellect" that "discerns and rifts its way into the secret of things"), Melville was suspicious of pantheistic, transcendentalist rhetoric that reinstalled concepts like "Me," "God," and "Nature" at the center of experiences.[131] "Perhaps, after all," Melville famously wrote to Hawthorne in 1851, "there is *no* secret" to the "Problem of the Universe." Rather, he mused, it may be that "it is this *Being* of the matter; there lies the knot with which we choke ourselves. As soon as you say *Me*, a *God*, a *Nature*, so soon you jump off from your stool and hang from the beam."[132] Even though Melville does dabble in mining-as-thinking metaphors, his method resists the transcendental secret truth, the literary masterwork, or the skeleton key to Nature. His method is accumulative, digressive, hybrid, multiple, ecological. Like the sailor in *Omoo* trying to fall asleep by reciting the "multiplication table," Melville multiplies thought, eventually summoning up "a grayish image of chaos in a sort of sliding fluidity."[133] Melville knew that writing could never make an image or concept or word fully present. The whale remains incomplete, "unpainted to the last."[134]

Understood this way, Melville's attention to the aesthetic forms of unstable geodynamic and biochemical processes—the structure of mineral clusters or the chemistry of lightning bolts—becomes a way of thinking about the complementarities between science, philosophy, and art. At its most ambitious, this book demonstrates how the junctions between science and art are visible in the commitment to *anti*-disciplinary thinking, a nomadic course of research that does not presume barriers between the humanities and the sciences, does not "bridge the gap" because there is no gap. Melville's insatiable appetite for vividness and lived experiences of all kinds motivated him to cross disciplinary knowledge silos, and his fiction and poetry teach us many lessons about the narrowness of our conceptual schemas today, inside and outside the academy, during an especially dangerous time for democracy. "Degrees we know, unknown in days before," the narrator of *Clarel* tells us. But our increased knowledge only means that as the "light is greater, hence the shadow more."[135]

THE LIVING CONTOUR

While I hope that *Magnificent Decay* will be of interest to nonspecialist readers familiar with Melville or acquainted with recent work in the environmental humanities, the book primarily intervenes in three academic fields: Melville studies, literature and science studies, and the various theoretical strands of new materialism and new formalism that have shaped the humanities in the past twenty years. However much *Magnificent Decay* contributes to each of these fields, it also participates in contemporary conversations about scale and environmental ethics in the Anthropocene.[136] *Magnificent Decay* will find additional audiences in scholars of animal studies, plant studies, and the geohumanities who have returned again and again to Martin Heidegger's controversial distinction that "the stone is worldless, the animal is poor in the world, and man is world-forming."[137] These post-Deleuzean critics have taken up Agamben's call to move beyond the illusion of "a single world in which all living beings are situated," focusing instead on how the worlds of animals, plants, or stones should be understood as zones of *"inhabitation rather than access,"* as Jeffrey Nealon puts it.[138] Nealon's archaeology of the plant in Western thought, Cary Wolfe's reconstruction of the animal in biopolitics, and Nathan Brown's account of the "inorganic open" at the frontiers of contemporary materials science each provide lively and necessary challenges to Heidegger's influential account of ecological metaphysics.[139] Like these thinkers, I maintain that the birth of the biological sciences at the end of the eighteenth century did more than foster organismic thinking that would create the conceptual grounds for contemporary biopower regimes. The life sciences also created the conditions for countervailing paradigms of ecological thought. Nineteenth-century writers like Melville sidestep the animal-man, plant-man, or stone-man distinctions by highlighting the emergent, nonlinear interrelations between animals, plants, and stones within nonscientific but scientifically rich forms of literary fiction.

To show the inter-animating discourses of literature and science in Melville's work, I reference throughout the book Melville's reading of geologists, botanists, and biologists such as Robert Chambers, Baron Cuvier, Charles Lyell, and, of course, Darwin. But I also read Melville's literary ecologies through popular introductory science textbooks with which antebellum Americans would likely have been familiar, such as William Phillips's *Elementary Treatise on Mineralogy: Comprising an Introduction to the Science* (1844) and Maxwell Masters's *Botany for Beginners: An Introduction to the Study of Plants* (1872). These texts allow us twenty-first century readers to inhabit the scientific imaginations of Melville's nineteenth-century readers, providing a shared context for the protoecological thinking and pattern identification that organize Melville's environmental consciousness. *Botany for Beginners,* for example, notes that the "spiral arrangement" of fir cones obliges observers to take a "geometrical turn of mind" in order to see the "whorled" patterns in the firs and in the wider forest.[140] The dissemination of scientific knowledge in such textbooks created a discursive matrix in which Melville's ecologies could be received and understood, then and now. And the visual material that often accompanied scientific manuals affords yet another mode of engagement with the vast and intricate interactions between species. The zoological compendium *The Pictorial Museum of Animated Nature* (1844), which we will encounter in chapter 3, offers readers amazing sketches of animal life alongside encyclopedic entries on behavioral ecology, as does Oliver Goldsmith's *A History of the Earth, and Animated Nature* (1807, 1825), which Melville owned and references in *Typee, Mardi,* and *Moby-Dick.*[141]

But... so what? Why does a nineteenth-century fiction writer's ecological vision matter for the frenzied, daily crises of the twenty-first century? In a late, unpublished poem from *Weeds and Wildings, Chiefly: With a Rose or Two,* Melville describes a charioteer who lashes a "way-side Weed" as he speeds on his way. The speaker of the poem asks: "But knows he what it is he does?"[142] Rigorous, historical humanities scholarship answers this exact question for the human species by, as Nealon phrases it, paying attention to how "concepts are conformed with certain conceptual territories." It is through literary and scientific histories that we are able to more accurately "diagnose what our 'doing does' within an expanded mesh of life."[143] This may seem obvious, but what seems obvious in the Anthropocene is precisely what needs examination and elaboration. Looking back to the ancestors of ecological thinking in the nineteenth century unearths genealogies of biopower whose origins of subjecthood are built from "scientific" reasoning. I want to recover a Melville whose conception of the world moves past individual, organismic subjectivity and into stranger configurations of bodies, matter, and power.

The main thread of *Magnificent Decay* is how Melville aligned literary and ecological processes in his writing to think more incisively about both modes of knowledge production around the axis of sameness and difference. And, as we've seen, Melville was one of many nineteenth-century transatlantic thinkers who recognized the power of narrative form to convey or distort the disquieting truths of post-Darwinian science. Adelene Buckland has written about how British Victorian writers "elaborated new *literary* forms with which they could explain, interpret, order, describe, argue about, and bring into existence a science whose claims and insights were both complex and new."[144] In geology, "problems in literary form were often used as a conceptual tool for thinking through the problems of geological form," so that the techniques of literary representation became essential in imagining the material history of the planet.[145] Nineteenth-century Anglo-American writers—Melville, Whitman, Eliot, and Hardy among them—tested how literary form might defamiliarize the Earth and its processes, while simultaneously forcing the reader to consider the *craft* of writing. In effect, these writers fissured the fantasy of the canonized product (*Moby-Dick*, the classic doorstop) and returned the reader to "the torqued process of its production," to quote Nathan Brown.[146] Reading with an eye for craft—for the act of creation rather than completion—heightens the sense that our understanding of material "reality" has much to do with the "forms" by which it is made perceptible. "What is real in the cosmos," writes critic Rebekah Sheldon, becomes "forms wrapped inside of forms."[147] This is precisely how Giorgio Agamben sees the origin of modern biopolitics. By separating materiality from form, *zoe* from *bios*, the state suppresses the far more radical and unmanageable potential of what Agamben calls "form-of-life . . . a life that is linked so closely to its form that it proves to be inseparable from it."[148]

However, literary form has always been notoriously difficult to define, and the history of literary criticism is littered with various interpretive schemas that get roped into "isms" and attendant ideological rules. As a way of circumventing this knotted history, I again look to Melville's own vocabulary for a set of coordinates that opens new ways of thinking about form. Ishmael, for example, recognizes that capturing "the true form of the whale," the whale's "absolute body," is impossible. Instead, Ishmael talks about the whale's "contour," its sketchy outer limit and "varying shape." He notes that representing the "difference in contour between a young suckling whale and a full-grown Platonian Leviathan" is not just a constraint on the writer's ability to capture the whale; it is also a liberating fact, a freedom of impermanence that elevates the epistemological authority of fiction. To write in the presence of the whale's "living contour" is to encounter complexity at two levels of experience, one physical and one representational, and neither can come close to a pure "symmetry of form," as the narrator of *Billy Budd, Sailor* (1924) calls it.[149] Truth "uncompromisingly told will always have its ragged edges."[150] Thus Melville's work traffics in varying shapes, ragged edges, and partial forms to generate geometries of representation at the perimeters of human perception: pearls, tendrils, honeycombs, pebbles. His eagle-eyed readers become Pip-like, drowning in visions of the "strange shapes of the unwarped primal world" that await beneath the Pacific.[151]

Melville's "contours" are in this sense formal experiments in nearly every literary genre. Travelogue, encyclopedia entry, romance, science fiction, fantasy, gothic novel, stage play, sketch, short story, anecdote, tale, elegy, epitaph, epic, epigram, and lyric. *Magnificent Decay* focuses on four relatively understudied texts—*Mardi, Pierre, The Piazza Tales,* and *John Marr*—to draw new contours around Melville by looking at the boundaries and margins of his career. Readers of this book will inevitably notice the absence of an entire chapter dedicated to *Moby-Dick,* and this is intentional. Though *Moby-Dick* skulks in each of the chapters, I purposefully make absent Melville's most obviously ecological novel to restructure the story of Melville's writing life. Instead of foregrounding Melville's popular texts—*Typee, Moby-Dick,* or "Bartleby"—this book pushes into the light four of his strangest and least understood works, unwiring the organismic logic of the masterwork and tracing a network of ecological poetics across individual texts.

Each of the four chapters looks at a different ecological process and the form of life it produces: the clustered crystallization of a deep-sea pearl, the spiraling reach of a vine's tendril, the inhabitation and abandonment of a honeycomb, and the erosion of pebbles on a windswept beach. This ecoformalist method allows me to ask four questions with implications for literary studies more broadly: (1) How does the romance accommodate geological time in *Mardi*? (2) What do the gothic, botanical worlds of *Pierre* have to do with the reproductive politics of the sentimental novel? (3) Can the improvisational qualities of the literary sketches in *The Piazza Tales* approximate what it means to dwell among other animals amid the asymmetrical agencies of a damaged planet? (4) How might the lowly pebbles of *John Marr* represent an intersection of the material and the artistic, a condensation of atmospheric pressures and flows that shrink planetary magnitudes to the palm of hand?

Magnificent Decay is structured around the realization that people do not act out of logical reasoning alone. They act on what they find beautiful, moving toward the objects and bodies they desire within the spaces they occupy, day to day. This awareness guides a broader inquiry. How do we witness, fit within, and live on the planet? Melville has answers. He prods us to remember that we witness at different scales of materiality, time, and space; that we fit into the world by acknowledging our mineral, vegetal, and animal selves; and that we live by rules that become the forms of our lives, rules that we must change if the planet is to support our species as we know it in the coming centuries.

PEARL, TENDRIL, HONEYCOMB, PEBBLE

Chapter 1 opens *Magnificent Decay* by arguing that while Melville may be famous for his oceanic exploits, his obscure third novel *Mardi* reminds us that he was also a writer of the Earth, *terra scriptor,* whose insights into our planet's rocky, inanimate worlds are increasingly relevant for contemporary discussions of environmental ethics in the Anthropocene. After the Pacific-roving adventures of *Typee* and *Omoo,* Melville creates in *Mardi* a lithic romance, a sustained engagement with planetary scale and deep time through the nascent sciences of geology, mineralogy, and astronomy. Read against the backdrop of the California gold rush and ongoing territorial expansion across the American West, *Mardi* provides the skeletal frame for Melville's geologic imagination, one that would shape his environmental philosophies for the rest of his career. At first glance, reading the significance of geological compounds like minerals in a novel or a poem seems weird, a kind of absurd materialism that takes seriously physical geography in the imaginative spaces of literary expression. But it is equally weird *not* to notice how often minerals crop up in Melville. They regularly stud his descriptions of processes and transformations of all kinds. Uncovering the peculiar presence of minerals in *Mardi* and other writings—shaping plots, themes, and even styles—I show how the mineral molded Melville's conception of the indefinite boundaries between life and nonlife. Melville's specific emphasis on inorganic materials like gold, pearls, and bones in *Mardi* forces readers to confront the shared minerality of existence, the molecular *sameness* that persists across spatiotemporal magnitudes and levels of evolutionary complexity. Further, *Mardi*'s alluvial form, its constant attention to "earthy matter," and its explicitly geological characters like Yillah and Babbalanja give us pause to consider how minerals mediate human and environment, then as now.

Chapter 2 tracks a significant shift in Melville's writing after *Mardi*: his return from the inorganic to the organic, from the mineral view of planets and pearls to the vegetal worlds of flowers and vines that characterized *Typee* and *Omoo*. This shift would have far-reaching implications for Melville's understanding of the "nature" of writing and its hidden kinships with organic life. For example, when we are first introduced to Isabel—the most important character in Melville's widely panned seventh novel *Pierre*—she poses a series of profound ecological questions: "What was it to be dead? What is it to be living? Wherein is the difference between the words Death and Life? Had I been ever dead? Was I living?"[152] Meditating on the difference between life and nonlife, materially and linguistically, Isabel's questions venture into the eerie places and unsettling phenomena that distort borders between the inanimate and animate. *Pierre* celebrates the subterranean fungi, vaporous clouds, and muculent foams that fall through the cracks of Linnaean taxonomies. It is thus a novel of "mutilated stumps," whose attention to decay and partiality makes perceptible the interstitial spaces where life and nonlife intersect, deform, and inter-merge. Pierre's gloomy ruin offers the contrast necessary to see how "life" became defined in modernity via biological, chemical, botanical, and other protoecological sciences in midcentury America, with help from the literary and scientific crosscurrents of European Romanticism. In *Pierre*, *Mardi*'s geological prophecies about the mineral commonalities between forms of existence are seen in the light of vegetal "greenness" that defines both the novel and the prismatic "fresh-foliaged heart of Pierre."[153] Tracing the figure of the spiral that dominates *Pierre*, this chapter argues that Melville uses the familiar gothic romance as a way to explore the unnervingly unfamiliar, the "cunning purpleness of hidden life" veiled by the apparent chaos of wildernesses. The spiral also helps readers realize the significance of Melville's entangled, helical syntax, which mirrors *Pierre*'s swirling narrative as a whole. The novel circles back and forth in time and space to disfigure the traditional form of the sentimental novel and its tidy norms of heterosexual reproduction, patriarchal order, and genealogical stability.

Written in the wake of *Pierre*'s failure, the stories collected in *The Piazza Tales* (1856) take up the question of the animal. Multiplying the many marine and terrestrial animals in Melville's earlier work—not only whales but elephants, camels, tortoises, dogs, scorpions, and many, many birds—*The Piazza Tales* swerve from *Pierre*'s vegetal spirals to think about the similarities and differences between animal and human life. Superimposing huts, towers, prisons, and ships onto shells, trees, nests, and honeycombs, these stories reveal the layers of inhabitation that have come to typify the science of human ecology: "Nature, house and all."[154] Viewed through the lenses of human ecology, architecture, and animal studies, familiar characters like Bartleby and Benito Cereno—and unfamiliar ones like Bannadonna and Hunilla—start to look very different. Chapter 3 argues that, together, *The Piazza Tales* provide a series of interlocking animal-human fables that stage the four primary, conflicting human responses to dwelling within their environments. These I term "eco-consciousness," "eco-technical optimism," "economic progressivism," and "eco-pessimistic eschatology." Melville's experimentation with the form of the literary sketch in his midcareer magazine writing phase affords him an innovative medium to address the most socially and politically sensitive issues of his day, and ours. With special attention to spaces of religious seclusion—abbeys, hermitages, and monasteries—the chapter concludes with an outline of Melville's neo-monastic, eco-spiritual ethics: a concern for the animal-other rooted in a grief that sees a "monastery of earth" in the residues of planetary cinders, present and future.[155]

The fourth chapter of *Magnificent Decay* looks to Melville's poetry, which he began to write seriously in 1859 after the perceived washout of his career as a fiction writer. Until relatively recently, Melville's poetry has been disregarded as postscript to the major novels and stories of the 1840s and 1850s. But Melville wrote poetry far longer than he wrote fiction and considered it the true "business" of his literary life. Without ignoring his war-weary *Battle Pieces* or the despair of *Clarel*, this chapter focuses on a collection of poems written only three years before Melville's death, *John Marr and Other Sailors*. In this last stage of his ecological philosophy, Melville becomes interested in how the planetary phenomena most resistant to representation—storms, weather, atmospheres—influence biogeochemical pathways through the processes of erosion and weathering. Maintaining that *John Marr* is Melville's poetic representation of erosive force and thermodynamic energy ecologies—a place where stones and poems take a common form—the chapter dwells on the series of poems that concludes the collection: seven epigrammatic verses grouped under the title "Pebbles." In more ways than one, and in ways not dissimilar to Melville's own writing life, *John Marr* becomes pebbles. Melville's lyrics in "Pebbles" are, in other words, the debris of an eco-literary career. Topographic signatures of erosion, pebbles constitute a material-poetic outline for the recursive processes of composition and erasure, sedimentation and erosion. His philosophy of abiotic magnitude may have developed through *Mardi*, *Pierre*, and *The Piazza Tales*, but in the sand, wind, and aerosol sprays of *John Marr*, Melville closes a lifetime of thinking about the ways in which writing corresponds to the fractal patterns of the nonhuman world. As *John Marr* demonstrates, Melville's ecologies are, in the end, present in his readers' very bodies, in the ephemeral dust of page turning, and in the moisture of our breath as we read.

Each of the chapters in *Magnificent Decay* builds on existing work in what has been called the ecological humanities, a field that, as Wendy Wheeler has noted, is greatly informed by evolution but resists the "mechanistic reductionism of neo-Darwinian theory."[156] For Wheeler, the eco-humanities accept a "complicated realism" that follows distributed agencies athwart domains of life and nonlife to reconsider the most basic premises of our environmental visions. Taken as a whole, *Magnificent Decay* recasts the arcs of Melville's career, showing how his enchantment with the ecological dynamics of stability and instability correlate with the crescendos and diminuendos of his writing. Accordingly, the book moves from the relatively stable mineral geometries of *Mardi*'s geologies and the dynamic topologies of plant spirals in *Pierre*'s forests to the transcontinental topographies and planetary energetic systems of *The Piazza Tales* and *John Marr*.

By anticipating in the mid-nineteenth century the most contemporary visions of the cosmos, Melville must be seen as one of the founders of literary ecology, a first practitioner but also a first critic who continually challenged the defining concepts of ecological thought and their relations to literature. Melville's irresolvable doubt, humility, and ironic sensibility encourage ongoing unsettling of the grounds of ecology, particularly around dwelling and its very real political implications. The sense of *oikeiôsis*, meaning affinity or belonging, that develops from Melville's "integral ecologies" must be capacious but provisional, idealistic but pragmatic, hopeful but ironic.[157] More generally, Melville shows us how the provisional nature of the eco-humanities is itself a source of strength. For example, the process of writing this book led me in totally unexpected directions, and its provisional form, its raggedness, allowed my thought to range and retrace itself in ways that began to disclose wider patterns in eco-humanities theory as much as in Melville. Such unforeseen patterns and lines of inquiry constitute the joy of writing. In *Magnificent Decay* I found that my writing taught me what I think and humbled the postures of my arguments. For in writing, as in geology, sedimentation makes certain features visible, but, over time, erosive revision decays all monuments. To quote Rolfe in *Clarel*:

> The flood ebbs out—the ebb
> Floods back; the incessant shuttle shifts
> And flies, and weaves and tears the web.[158]

Melville demonstrates, in other words, that ecologies of writing flood and ebb in the ceaseless attempt to capture the living contours of life on our planet. We are all the "baffled hunter" in *Mardi*, lost and wandering "round and round some purple dell, deep in a boundless prairie's heart." Then, suddenly, we come upon the "open plain. . . . The universe again before us; our quest, as wide."[159]

CHAPTER 1

Pearl
Mardi

Think you there is no sensation in being a rock?
—*Mardi*

When Melville visited the Boston Gallery of Fine Arts in May 1847, along with his sisters Augusta and Sophia, he was confronted by a series of rock-strewn landscapes hanging on the walls. Among them was Thomas Cole's *Course of Empire* (1833–36), the celebrated five-panel allegory of civilization's imprint on the Earth.[1] Eight months later—after newlyweds Herman and Lizzie Shaw had settled into their New York City life—the discovery of gold in the Sierra Nevadas forever altered the topography of northern California, generating a mining boom that triggered one of the largest internal migrations in U.S. history.[2] Also in January 1848, New York City society was enthralled by Scottish scientist John P. Nichol's lectures on astronomy, which incorporated poetry into discussions of the Milky Way.[3] The course of empire, gold fever, and the immensity of the stellar universe. Together, these three moments in Melville's life and times provide a useful way to approach his least-read and first fully ecological novel, *Mardi: and A Voyage Thither*.

Rich with "sedimentary strata" and imagery of terrestrial "treasures"—gold, silver, diamonds, granite—*Mardi* shows Melville thinking on a planetary scale through the nineteenth-century sciences of geology, mineralogy, and astronomy.[4] For Melville, the geologist and the novelist share a common fascination with the pressures of creation, especially the elegant patterns that follow from creative processes, nonhuman and human alike. From *Mardi* on, Melville experimented with different literary forms to articulate the implications of Earth sciences at a moment when, all of a sudden, the human no longer occupied the center of planetary history. But before his more famous meditations on whales and tortoises, Melville turned in *Mardi* to the Earth's surfaces and interiors, to the compressed and propulsive worlds beneath our feet that remain mostly invisible and largely unthought. *Mardi* takes as its central problem the givenness of the Earth in relation to the human.[5]

In *Mardi*, Melville's careful attention to geological materials—as well as the geothermal and weathering processes that shape them—marks his first attempt to make sense of the "inscrutable inhumanities" that exist in magnitudes far beyond our species' capacity to represent them.[6] From our twenty-first-century perspective, thinking inside the Anthropocene has meant taking seriously our debt to and responsibility for the nonhuman, from microbes to oil to rainforests. But we have not fully recognized the extent of our entanglement with inorganic spheres of existence, the often-obscured elements and minerals that support bone chemistry and power iPads. Ironically it might be the third and most abstruse work of a seafaring novelist that provides a vital but unfamiliar vision of our species through the scale-bending perspective of inanimate matter.

This chapter recovers *Mardi* as an essential text in Melville's oeuvre. *Mardi* not only inaugurates Melville's interest in eroding the barriers between literature and science; it also makes an initial case for Melville's relevance to our own moment of environmental crisis. Melville wrote *Mardi* at a transformative time in world history, when mid-nineteenth-century developments in metallurgy and industrial mining led to the appearance of what Christopher Jones terms "mineral energy regimes." These developments lowered technological barriers to expansion, thereby structuring modern economies of scale. Increased energy production and consumption generated new "landscapes of intensification," and America became the proving ground for the economic potential and environmental limit of a modern, mineral democracy.[7] In particular, anthracite coal, or "stone-coal," dramatically reshaped mid-Atlantic landscapes via energy transportation networks that connected the country to the city, creating (uneven) geographic development and contributing to America's first large-scale environmentally degraded areas.

As mined resources fueled industrial capitalism, by the late 1840s economic roadblocks appeared to vanish completely, and the nation's mineral prospects took shape from Pennsylvania to California. Ores like copper and iron provided the matrix for the "blending of organic and mineral energy regimes" that would bring America into the age of empire.[8] At the end of the century, solid coal could be railroaded for heat and fuel, liquid oil could be pipelined for refining and manufacturing, and flows of electricity could be channeled from dams to light the eastern seaboard. And the shift from harvesting wood to extracting oil was a conceptual leap as well as a technological one. Consciously or not, oil companies intervened in geologic timelines in ways that jumbled distinctions between prehistoric past and modern present. Even though consumers tend to repress the organic nature of fossil fuels like oil, the origins of its carbon energy are quintessentially ecological: sea-floor plankton and mineral matter become sedimented into kerogen petroleum, which is then trapped in shale formations that, hundreds of thousands of years later, yield petroleum-field riches and illuminate kitchens. Many of Melville's breakfasts, for instance, were cooked on a box stove, a hotplate for burning million-year-old coal, with windows made from quarried New England mica.

Such scrambled senses of time, energy, material, and environment bear not just on Melville's meals or his literary philosophies but on embryonic nineteenth-century scientific disciplines like biochemistry and modern medicine, where new, post-vitalist categories of organic life reorganized definitions of what counted as an "environment" at all. In chemistry, for example, German scientist Friedrich Wöhler's laboratory in Göttingen drew American students throughout the 1850s, riveted by Wöhler's 1828 synthesis of urea from ammonium carbonate. Wöhler demonstrated that organic matter could be created from inorganic compounds, erasing hard distinctions between "natural" and "artificial" and paving the way for modern pharmacology. Another German, Felix Hoppe-Seyler, opened the field of physiological chemistry by pioneering syntheses of alkaloids and antipyretics (fever-lowering compounds). And by the early twentieth century, the Haber-Bosch synthesis of ammonia from nitrogen in the air would revolutionize agricultural fertilization and increase global crop yields to allow for the massive human population growth in the past hundred years. These materialist sciences, which undergirded fields as diverse as oil production, medicine, and agriculture, disclosed the elemental-mineral ties between apparently unrelated histories, defying familiar organizing principles like scientific field or "natural" conditions.

Moreover, colonial and early national studies of what would come to be known as disease ecology had previously showed that the internal environments of the body were always already penetrated by external ones. Shaped by ancient climate and humoral theories of the body's susceptibility to outside influence, many eighteenth-century physicians—like William Falconer in his *Remarks on the Influence of Climate* (1781)—believed human traits, such as character and even race, were essentially *environmental*. Greta LaFleur has noted that eighteenth- and early nineteenth-century conceptions of the porous body were, in this sense, "deeply ecological."[9] At the same time, scientists like Lamarck argued that human societies were making unalterable modifications to local and global environments. As early as 1803, Lamarck had pondered these mutual networks of influence, posing a question about hydrogeology that stood for environmental arrangements more broadly. "What," Lamarck asked, "are the general effects of living organisms on the mineral substances which form the earth's crust and external surfaces?"[10] And, we could add, vice versa?

Reading *Mardi* today, one hundred and seventy years after it was published, it is remarkable how Melville offers the contours of a Lamarckian-inspired, geo-environmental history with which we are still coming to grips, one that understands all objects as "increasing assemblage[s] of ancient times and dispersed spaces," as Bruno Latour phrased it.[11] In the mid-twentieth century, Charles Olson contended that narrative fiction had the uncanny ability to trace these assemblages across orders of magnitude, dilating Ahab's famous doubloon into an entire planet. "This round gold," Ahab murmurs, "is but the image of the rounder globe."[12] For Olson, part of Melville's enduring appeal is his "unique ability to reveal the very large (such a thing as his whale, or himself on whiteness, or Ahab's monomania) by the small."[13] In other words, the freedom of literary form opens thought to hidden topologies, networks of scale that highlight the continuities between a mollusk's shell and the coil of a galaxy. This is why minerals—the most foundational building blocks of "earthy matter" visible to the human eye—warrant closer inspection in nineteenth-century literary history. These geological clusters and formations offer material clues into the problems of magnitude, time, and modernity with which writers were grappling in Melville's lifetime. To account for the nature of the mineral was to account for the nature of the galaxy. Babbalanja, our guide through *Mardi*'s stony landscapes, agrees: "Other worlds differ not much from this, but in degree. Doubtless, a pebble is a fair specimen of the universe."[14]

ETERNAL GRANITE

Branded a strange, "shapeless rhapsody" by one reviewer, *Mardi* begins as an anonymous sailor's adventure-turned-quest for a mysterious woman named Yillah as he travels through the fictitious but Pacific-inspired isles of

Mardi.[15] But once the narrator assumes the name Taji (the sun god of Mardi) and is joined by five companions—Babbalanja, Media (the king), Mohi (the historian), Yoomy (the poet), and Vee-Vee (the fool)—the novel transforms into something else entirely. From the gold mine to the Milky Way, the bulk of *Mardi* explores the planetary imprint of the human species at different vantage points in space and time. "Mardi is not wholly ours," Babbalanja explains. "We are the least populous part of creation . . . a census of the herring would find us far in the minority. . . . We inhabit but a crust." "We are," he concludes, "but a step in a scale."[16] So Taji and his crew spend time considering the human as a thing among and "in things."[17] They inspect fossils, discuss volcanic eruptions, debate the origin of the Earth, analyze the structure of human bones, argue theories of mineral chemistry, and even examine a butterfly locked in amber. Like Ishmael, self-professed geologist and fossil reader of "antechronical creatures," Babbalanja finds in scientific paradigms the vocabulary to speculate on Mardi's past, referencing a litany of scientists including Linnaeus, Cuvier, Hutton, Lyell, Agassiz, and Darwin.[18]

By the time of *Mardi*'s composition between April 1847 and November 1848, Melville had closely read Cuvier, Lyell, and Darwin, but the many references to geology, paleontology, and cosmology in the novel suggest a much broader scope of Melville's reading than extant records can confirm.[19] However, from the mystified first reviews until now, *Mardi* has remained an illegible obelisk, a flawed precursor to *Moby-Dick*, or, worse, a colossal and inchoate allegory. But such monumental rhetoric is appropriate for a novel full of relics and ruins, a novel that contemplates the literary impulse to achieve the immortality of "ponderous stone."[20] "More enduring monuments are built in the closet with the letters of the alphabet," Melville would write a year later in *Redburn: His First Voyage* (1849), "than even Cheops himself could have founded, with all Egypt and Nubia for his quarry."[21] Moving below the palm tree landscapes of *Typee* and *Omoo*, in *Mardi* Melville carved out a "petrific" romance, as he would put it in *Clarel*, by exhuming the substances usually ignored in narrative representation: the elements and minerals whose composite materiality warps familiar definitions of originality and authenticity.[22]

Frustrated with his British publisher John Murray's insistence on novelistic realism—what Murray referred to as "documentary evidence"—Melville began writing *Mardi* as an experimental dive into the meaning of authenticity, that elusive and grounding credibility we demand of a good story.[23] In his opening preface to the novel, Melville states the problem outright. *Mardi* is about whether "fiction might not, possibly, be received for a verity."[24] He saw Murray's emphasis on authenticity as a philosophical problem and a personal attack, both of which betrayed the "desire to test the corporeality of H—— M——," as he put it in an 1848 letter. Although Melville ultimately found another publisher for *Mardi*, he responded to Murray's corporeal test by hewing the novel out of "different stuff altogether," out of rocks and stones and bones.[25] *Mardi* breaks down the facile concept of biography-as-authenticity that had shadowed Melville's previous two island adventures, addressing instead the material substrata whose iterative, erosive natures spoke to his growing enchantment with the parallels between writing and geology.

Throughout his career, Melville routinely associated "the great Art of Telling the Truth" with excavating, tunneling, and quarrying.[26] *Pierre*'s avowed goal as a writer is to "come to the latent gold in his mine," and in his famous "Quarter-Deck" speech, Ahab demands we look under "the little lower layer" for the bedrock truths masked by our performances.[27] Then there is the narrator of "The Encantadas"—a Galapagos "geologist" observing unique minerals like "malachite," a green mineral found with copper—who was created a dozen years before *Clarel*'s Margoth would rake the Holy Lands for minerals like an obsessed scientist chipping away at "old theologic myth" with "geologic hammers."[28] Even Melville's reviewers drew on metallurgic metaphors to describe his work. *Clarel*, for instance, was "labored over as a blacksmith hammers at his forge."[29] For Melville, to think deeply was to mine ever further into the lower layers, only on occasion finding "wondrous, occult properties—as in some plants and minerals."[30] Knowledge was stratigraphic, "surface stratified on surface," and true insight was revealed "by some happy but very rare accident (as bronze was discovered by the melting of the iron and brass in the burning of Corinth)."[31] These linked metaphors of knowing, mining, writing, and smelting had particular import during *Mardi*'s composition. As Melville got deeper into his novel, newspapers heralded gold bonanzas out west. America's mineral future loomed.

As I note in the introduction, recent scholarship on Melville and the nonhuman has gestured at the importance of animals, plants, and other ecologies in the major works, but critics have rarely scrutinized the material substructures, like *Mardi*'s stones and ores, that frame questions of monumentality and scale in Melville's writing. For example, early in *Mardi* Taji proclaims: "It is not the Pyramids that are ancient, but the eternal granite whereof they are made."[32] Taji's stress on granite—an intrusive igneous rock composed mostly of quartz and feldspar, the two most abundant minerals in the Earth's crust—dissolves anthropocentric pyramid time into the vastness of mineral time. The minerals in granite are forged by cooling magma, by high temperatures and pressures beneath the Earth's surface, by weathering and erosion, or by unfathomable explosions of neutron stars billions of years ago: the absolute markers of what is distant, ancient, and enduring. Yet other minerals, like apatites or zincs, are so intimate that they structure our crania and maintain the neuronal processes that generate our very thoughts.

Whether defined strictly (gold, calcite) or loosely (coal, oil), minerals embody the "folded heterogeneous temporalities" of all objects.[33] They contain the elemental architecture of the planet's antiquity and even prophecies for its future, as the exclusively human-generated minerals from mining, dumping, and nuclear testing have become markers of human "lithologies" that characterize the Anthropocene.[34] (Not to mention all the manufactured "mineraloids" like glasses and microplastics whose thousand-year half-lives haunt landfills, amassing in oceans and in our bodies.) The convergences of minerals and humans raise intriguing questions about creativity and legacy in an epoch of anthropogenic minerals that never before existed in our solar system, and perhaps the universe.[35]

Although Melville lacked the technical mineralogical knowledge that would develop in the twentieth century, he nonetheless appreciated the philosophical implications of minerality at the genesis of the modern age. Today, we recognize more accurately *how* the mineral mediates human and environment. Minerals not only deliver the energy required to generate modern economies of scale; they also make the human species visible in the landscape. From manganese-based pigments that color cave drawings to conflict minerals like tantalite that activate cell phones, minerals contour the human species' relation to itself and to the Earth. Minerals give material form to our creative impulses as well as our destructive ones. They facilitate an ever-evolving technological capacity to alter the planet, in hydroelectric dams and weapons of mass destruction. They also demand that we reimagine planetary ecology to include human-mineral constructions: concrete buildings, asphalt pavements, and, more dramatically, compounds like tungsten carbide or boron nitride, whose creation represents the "single largest change to the Earth's mineral storehouse since the early Proterozoic era," according to geologist Jan Zalasiewicz.[36] If the materials and effects of human technology are fundamentally geological, then the human is not just "tool-being," as Graham Harman would have it, but *mineral-being*.[37]

To be precise with my terminology here, by "mineral" I mean primarily its current, technical definition: "a naturally occurring, inorganic, crystalline compound with a definite, but sometimes variable chemical composition."[38] But, as we will see, in Melville's day "mineral" was also a byword for the rocks that contained minerals (like mica) or, even more confusingly, carbon-rich, once-organic compounds (like coal). Similarly, today's terms like "conflict minerals" or "rare earth minerals" that are applied to ores such as coltan (columbite–tantalites) really refer to the valuable, technology-critical elements niobium (Nb) and tantalum (Ta) derived from the ores to manufacture capacitors and other electronic components.[39] Linguistically, minerals are metonyms of elements; materially, they are human access points to those elements. This is why, starting in the eighteenth century, an "earth" referred to an acid-soluble element that could be processed for wide-ranging domestic and industrial applications. Throughout this chapter, I use "mineral" as an abbreviation for the interface between elements and organisms, the porous boundary between "earths" and ecosystems that reminds us how, as Emerson phrased it, "the world is all outside: it has no inside."[40]

But my primary claim in this chapter is that, more than a century and a half ago, Melville was already rethinking the territory of geology by contemplating how the liquidity of scale presented by the mineral might correspond to literary form in the alluring but bewildering complexity of *Mardi*. Although the novel is ostensibly a Polynesian travel-quest in the tradition of *Typee* and *Omoo*, its concern with the diagenetic (rock-making) processes that sculpt the islands of Mardi interrupts the romance, giving readers a chance to reflect on the role of inorganic materials and processes in human and planetary histories. Minerals are thus useful in literary fiction and in theorizing the Anthropocene because they concretize multiple scales of time in easily apprehensible ways (unlike, for example, tectonic plates). In our current "epoch of diachronicity"—Andreas Malm's pithy phrase—minerals provide a tactile index of the Anthropocene's conceptual challenges.[41] We can hold granite in our hands, recognizing that this relic of force precedes us and will persist far after the living tissues of our palms decompose. Aggregating into rocks, minerals constitute the medial zone between the very large ranges of mountains and planets and the very small orbits of the atomic and subatomic. Minerals may not be *for* us, but they are *in* us and, to a certain degree, legible *to* us: a paradox of anthropocentrism that melts the literary into the geological. In fact, for antebellum mineralogists like William Phillips, minerals were "the very *alphabet to the older rocks*," a geological grammar that aligned literary and scientific imaginations in reading the mysteries of cosmic time.[42] Geologically considered, Emerson's famous dictum—"Language is fossil poetry"—could be inverted, and American fossils began to speak a poetry all their own.[43]

As Melville contemplated the literary repercussions of geology in *Mardi*, he revised his understanding of the indefinite borders that demarked life from nonlife, human from stone. He began to explore the creative homologies between literary form and "earthy matter."[44] Working in the tradition of what Noah Heringman has termed "aesthetic geology," Melville advances an ontology of earthy matter in *Mardi* developed both thematically—in his focus on geological phenomena—and formally—in the novel's diffuse structure and alluvial poetics.[45] The sprawling organization of *Mardi* allowed Melville to probe the capacity of literary form to represent the emergence of complex systems in geology *and* in human society. At the same time, Melville incorporated scientific insights of his day into the novel and, through the malleability of his fictional worlds, even anticipated others to come. In this context, *Mardi* can be read as an example of "abstract geology," Jussi Parikka's mode of inquiry that follows the geological across life/nonlife divisions to challenge the disciplinary knowledge silos that delineate one environment from another, delineations naturalized by the conveniences that mineral energy regimes afford us.[46] Melville's method in *Mardi* is intentionally nonlinear, but his itinerant course of writing, while rhapsodic at times, nonetheless has discernable patterns. The novel is far from shapeless. Seen as a whole, *Mardi* constellates for the reader a tableau of minerals, rocks, and ores at different magnitudes, uncovering the symmetries between ocean bivalves and the formation of distant planets. The following sections trace *Mardi*'s abstract, aesthetic geologies by highlighting the three primary expressions of minerality in the novel—gold, pearls, and bones.

My approach here transgresses traditional precincts of literary criticism just as the minerals themselves transgress traditional boundaries of values, bodies, and systems. They function as commodities (gold), biogeochemical mechanisms (pearls), and structural matrices for complex forms of life (bones). They are objects, dwellings, and foundations. They compose the ink used to print these words and the capacitors required to read the digital version.[47] Furthermore, minerals organize our relation to memory itself by structuring creative technologies like books, photographs, and computers.

Mineral chemistry, for example, played a key role in the development of daguerreotypy and photography between 1840 and 1900 (silver ores and chloride of lime especially), laying the foundation for media that, today, shape how we remember the past and articulate the present. As the toxic history of photography makes clear, the technological practices that permitted humans to see the world more clearly beyond the naked eye—through telescopes, microscopes, and cameras—now threaten to pollute that world. Also ironically, the very technologies whose production generated the Anthropocene now enable us to measure its effects, as in the remote sensing needed for climate research which itself requires the products of industrial mining.

Understanding how Melville deals with minerality in *Mardi* requires layering materialist, historicist, and formalist readings together to show the power of the inanimate made visible by the spatiotemporal freedoms of fiction. I begin with a brief history of American geology, detouring through the 1848 California gold rush, to set up *Mardi*'s emphasis on telling time or, more precisely, the difficulty of reconciling human time with mineral time. This framework enables us to appreciate why Yillah's mystical pearl and Babbalanja's skeleton play such significant roles in the novel, functioning simultaneously as narrative devices, thematic figures, and emblems of the novel's geomorphological design. Ultimately, following *Mardi*'s shifts in magnitude—gold nuggets to solar nebulae—becomes a way of tracking the appeal of planetary sciences for nineteenth-century Americans: the desire, as Ishmael explains it, "to have one's hands among the unspeakable foundations, ribs, and very pelvis of the world."[48]

GENERATION DECAY

A democratic science of the everyman, antebellum geology lent objectivity and historical depth to growing national pride in the grandeur of American landscapes. Long walks in the woods taught amateur rock hunters to read the histories of ordinary American stones, and the physical encounter between rock and would-be geologist created a momentary sensorium, a kinesthetic connection to prehistory amid the boisterous early years of the young Republic. Hands-on, "personal instruction"—as recommended by Phillips's *Treatise on Mineralogy* (1844) and other field manuals—disciplined budding mineralogists in the art of identifying and collecting samples. These manuals urged readers to move beyond mere "possession" of minerals in order to apprehend the deeper "principles" in the rocks.[49] Readers

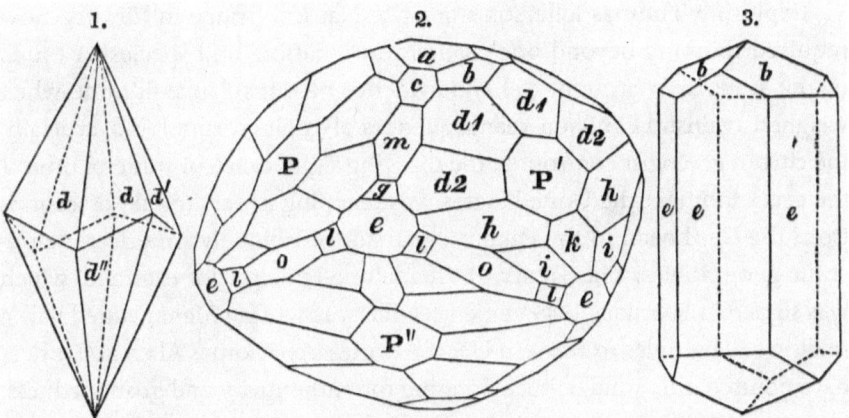

Carbonates of lime, from William Phillips, *An Elementary Treatise on Mineralogy: Comprising an Introduction to the Science*, 5th ed. (Boston: William B. Ticknor, 1844), 265. (Harvard University Library)

saw the crystal geometries found in iron meteorites (called Widmanstätten patterns after 1808) and traced the patterns that differentiated one mineral cluster from another. By midcentury, geology texts sometimes rivaled novels in popularity, mineral cabinets began to appear in upper-middle-class American homes, and treatises like Edward Hitchcock's *The Religion of Geology* (1851) tried to reconcile geological knowledge with Christian faith.[50]

An 1853 article in *Putnam's Monthly Magazine of American Literature, Science and Art*—published in the same issue as "Bartleby, the Scrivener"—even claimed that the mineral was "the basis of all specific forms. . . . [I]t gives body, so to speak, to all individual organizations." Imagining the "distance of the mineral from man in the scale of existence," the article ponders man's "mineral experience" of *becoming-stone*: the sensation of "falling from a building," for instance, powerless in the grip of forces like inertia and gravity.[51] The *Putnam's* article is one example of how nineteenth-century physical sciences reoriented philosophy around magnitudes of materiality. Human beings had abruptly moved from the center of planetary consciousness to merely a thing among things. The reimagining of our material existences—our relative distance from stone—features prominently in Emerson, Thoreau, Poe, Melville, and Whitman, as well as in such painters as Cole and Frederic Edwin Church. These writers and artists confronted the dissolving frontiers of the human in relation to nonhuman bodies that, for millennia, had signaled its absolute limit.

Exploring Thomas Jefferson's favorite Natural Bridge in Virginia now required thinking beyond one's generation, nation, and species. A touch of the stone arch brought to hand evidence of our relative finitude when weighed against the million-year sequences of geologic time. And, crucially, the citizen geologist confronted the dizzying significance of mineral time at the exact moment the United States was mapping its territorial possessions from the Caribbean to the Pacific in pursuit of uniquely American democratic geographies. The Treaty of Guadalupe-Hidalgo, for example, which was signed in February 1848 while Melville was writing *Mardi*, added half a million square miles to western U.S. territories. As Thomas Allen and others have pointed out, amid cultural longing for authenticity and groundedness, nineteenth-century natural science supplied the physical excavation of North American history, anchoring national destiny in the continental crust.[52]

And landscape painting—like Church's rendering of *The Natural Bridge, Virginia* (1852)—offered the visual schemes for American geo-authenticity, quickly becoming both an important representative medium for geological insights and a mode of socio-moral interpretation. Rebecca Bedell reminds us that nineteenth-century American landscape painters including Church, Cole, Asher B. Durand, John Frederick Kensett, William Stanley Haseltine, and Thomas Moran maintained a "conservative geology" in their work, "a geology that could draw moral and spiritual lessons from stones."[53] In this context, much has been written about Cole's *The Course of Empire*, which Melville saw in Boston while in the early stages of *Mardi*. Most notably, critics have theorized the presence of erratic boulders or glacial erratics—known in Cole's day as a "perched boulders"—in the background of each panel of *Course*. Cole owned and read J. L. Comstock's popular *Outlines of Geology* (1834), and the perched boulders in *The Course of Empire* conveyed to viewers the power of geologic force to shape the landscape in scale and power far beyond human history and its relatively puny monuments.

These images would have appealed immensely to Melville, whose own lifelong habit of burning correspondence seems to have something to do with the impermanence of writing and perhaps the impermanence of civilization itself. Melville's "immolations"—"sacrifices to the gods of fire" as he called them—turned letters to ash and literary meaning to mere matter.[54] Unsurprisingly, similar scenes of fiery sacrifice make their way into nearly all of his fiction and poetry. Early in *Moby-Dick*, for instance, Queequeg lights a "sacrificial blaze" for Yojo, and, late in the novel, Ahab addresses the flames directly: "Oh, thou foundling fire . . . I worship thee!"[55] Throughout human history, fire has been linked to power, visibility, and territorial sovereignty through a web of relations Michael Marder has termed "pyropolitics."[56] In *Pierre*, fire signifies the essence of creation. Torching the letters and memorials that tie him to the Glendinning line, our hero Pierre sees that fire "is neither a respecter of persons, nor a finical critic of what manner of writings it burns; but like ultimate Truth itself, of which it is the eloquent symbol, consumes all, and only consumes."[57] This brief passage, one of the most significant and undertheorized in Melville's work, aligns the truth of writing with all-consuming fire, "that most honest and summary of all elements."[58] Melville's peculiar practice of burning letters and destroying manuscript plates suggest that, in Melville's mind, the fleeting span of a human life somehow corresponded with the fleeting temporality of (burning) writing. And, in fact, Melville's whole career was marked by both accidental fires and the self-destruction of his own writing archive.

On December 10, 1853, for example, a fire at Harper Brothers in New York City burned all of Melville's unsold books and printing plates, including the original set for *Typee*. In March of 1879, *Putnam's* asked Melville if they could send the remaining unsold copies of *Clarel* to the paper mill to be recycled. He agreed. Eight years later, in 1887, *Harper's* melted the plates of *Mardi* and *Pierre*, again with Melville's permission.[59] Against the backdrop of the cutthroat world of midcentury American print capitalism, Melville's constant need to be published (for family, fortune, and fame) clashed with his urge to burn and destroy his creations. This tension organizes a number of his most famous fictions, usually figured as the reduction of a writing self to a "charred landscape within," to quote the narrator of *Pierre*.[60] Ishmael describes America itself as a "scraggy scoria of a country," and the opening sentence of "The Encantadas" commands the reader to imagine "five-and-twenty heaps of cinders . . . magnified into mountains."[61] This process of magnification is one of Melville's tools for ecological representation, moving from local fires that devastate individual families to cataclysmic fires that erupt in "flame" from a mountain peak on Ahab's doubloon: fires that perhaps foreshadow mass extinctions to come.[62]

For Melville, fire, like writing, was a "fugitive" process, an agent of creative transformation and a reminder of the material frailty that writing strives to overcome. Pierre's compositions at Saddle Meadows—he had "written many a fugitive thing"—are carelessly discarded, swept away out the window, and used as kindling for the fire.[63] Bartleby's previous career, we are told, was spent burning undeliverable correspondence in the "Dead Letter

Office." The destructive, elemental power of fire, in Melville's biography and in his writing, thus denatures how we read his archive and understand the letters and manuscripts that do survive. As detailed in chapter 3, one of the differentials between human and animal cultures is the very survival, from elemental forces, of an archive: the formal and always partial project of human memory that chains us to, and distracts us with, the past. But the archive can also free us to more clearly see the present. Through the imagery of fire, Melville realized that, because the future must always be a fiction, so the present must be fictional insofar as we give it archival context, provide it historical unity, and stabilize it by creating structures—material and conceptual—to guide the sociality of present-day arrangements. Instead of feeding the imperial fantasy of a permanent, monolithic archeology of knowledge, Melville's "archive-destroying" drive, as Derrida would later phrase it, resists the nostalgia of individual authorship and of national literature itself.[64] This Promethean paradox, in which creativity and destruction are united in the heat of *techne* and enshrined in the archive, will come to define a certain strain of Melville's writing in the 1850s, especially in *Moby-Dick* and *The Piazza Tales*, where Melville tracks the implications of fire for technology, architecture, and visions of future ecological life on the planet. But in the 1830s and 1840s, Americans' fascination with the geologic past in the landscapes of Cole and his Hudson Valley cohort betrayed a competing desire. Americans also wanted to imagine a *ruined future* similarly marked by geo-apocalyptic decay.

Take the scene late in *Mardi* when Media, Babbalanja, and Yoomy encounter a mob in North Vivenza, Melville's allegory for the northern United States in the 1840s. The angry crowd finds an anonymous scroll on a palm tree, which poses provocative questions for the "democratic" mob. "Time is made up of various ages; and each thinks its own a novelty," the scroll proclaims, "But imbedded in the walls of the pyramids, which outrun all chronologies, sculptured stones are found, belonging to yet older fabrics." It continues: "And as in the mound-building period of yore, so every age thinks its erections will forever endure. But as your forests grow apace, sovereign-kings! overrunning the tumuli in your western vales; so, while deriving their substance from the past, succeeding generations overgrow it; but in time, themselves decay . . . republics are as vast reservoirs, draining down all streams to one level; and so, breeding a fullness which can not remain full, without overflowing."[65] Melville's aqueduct metaphors—"republics are as vast reservoirs" that must eventually overflow—remind

Vivenzans of the enduring eco-hydrological systems that persist after the downfall of human empires. In the Vivenza scroll, Melville's accumulating clauses oscillate between a proleptic unraveling of Vivenza's future and a meditation on its deep past, those "sculptured stones" that predate even the ancient pyramids. So while the Vivenza chapters have clear satirical weight for Europe and America at the end of the 1840s—specifically revolutionary activity in France and England as well as the 1848 Free Soil Convention at Buffalo—Melville's incorporation of desolate, post-imperial imagery in *Mardi* binds the novel's rhetoric to larger cultural projects like Cole's *Course of Empire*, which refract a turbulent post-Jacksonian democracy marked by increasing pressures of an expanding market economy, a context we will return to in the next chapter.

Vivenza's stones represent the arrogance of man's quest for immortality, for edifices that "will forever endure." As they overrun Western tumuli, remapping the landscape in their pursuit of permanent, legible territories, new generations of Vivenzans only *seem* to grow or to make progress. In reality, over time, they too decay into the desolate ruins of once-immortal kingdoms. New forests and old waters overrun forgotten burial mounds and skeleton cities alike. Even the fifteen-year-old Wellington Redburn recognizes this truth: "I am filled with a comical sadness at the vanity of all human exaltation," he muses. "For the cope-stone of to-day is the corner-stone of to-morrow; and as St. Peter's church was built in great part of the ruins of old Rome, so in all our erections, however imposing, we but form quarries and supply ignoble materials for the grander domes of posterity."[66] In *Mardi*, *Redburn*, and eventually *Moby-Dick*, Melville prophesizes the consequences of Babbalanja's dis-anthropocentric maxim—"if not against us, nature is not for us"—before developing the theme even further in *Pierre*, *The Piazza Tales*, and *Clarel* to emphasize the relics of vanished humanity that that litter Ozymandian deserts with the remnants of empire. But in 1848 America, the empire-builders were hunting for gold in California, an image Melville takes up directly when his band of travelers encounter Mardi's own gold rush on the island of Kolumbo, the "land of mints and mines."[67]

THE POVERTY OF GOLD

The strike at Sutter's Mill in January 1848, the epicenter of the American gold rush, was officially reported in the *New York Tribune* on August 19, 1848, and then again on September 16, where Melville likely read of it while finishing *Mardi*.[68] "Farmers have thrown aside their plows, the lawyers their briefs, the doctors their pills, the priests their prayer books," one reporter wrote, "and all are now digging gold."[69] Four months later, in his State of the Union address detailing the impact of gold on the nation's future, James K. Polk described the "peace, plenty, and contentment" that "reign throughout our borders." He announced that American geological riches presented "a sublime moral spectacle to the world." "We are," Polk boasted, "the most favored people on the face of the earth."[70] Between 1848 and 1850, more than one hundred thousand people migrated west with mineral dreams, literally paving the way for an American empire. The mineral capital extracted from California accelerated western growth and drew the international investment needed to support America's rise to global power in the late nineteenth and early twentieth centuries. Territorial expansion suddenly became subterranean as well as westward, and America's underground mineral archives—meticulously accounted for in geological survey histories like Josiah Whitney's *The Metallic Wealth of the United States* (1854)—seemed confirmations of American continental destiny. Plus, minerals were more than just energy stores or sources of capital. They were integral to the structural integrity of the mining technologies themselves (rock drills, for example), which in turn laid the foundation for transportation infrastructure that would bring America into the industrial period.

It is no surprise, then, that gold features prominently in *Mardi*. But Melville's interest in metallic wealth moves past the fever of 1848. In some places, Melville does level straightforward criticism of extractive mining, but in others, gold becomes a figure of creativity and transformation. When King Media describes the isles of Mardi as "the retributive future of some forgotten past," he outlines a messianic account of gold in American history that equally describes *Mardi*'s diffuse geological scope: a massively distributed history of future rewards materialized in the rocks beneath its characters' feet.[71] Still, for Melville a gold rush was a symptom of capitalism's infectious but numbing spirit. Gold fever? An extension of the theological colonialism he saw in the Pacific. Indifferent to wealth disparities or the consequences of ever-expanding empire over all forms of life, the mineral capitalist's law of labor was diametrically opposed to the energy of free-ranging inquiry that characterizes much of *Mardi*.

This is why the novel is dotted with critiques of commerce and labor, from the corrupting effects of silver mining to the exchange of teeth as commodities and, eventually, a full-on populist revolt.[72] Most directly,

Babbalanja preaches against the allure of Mardi's gold on Kolumbo. "Gold is the only poverty," Babbalanja cautions, "of all glittering ills the direst." He warns his companions that the Mardian god-force Oro had purposefully hidden Mardi's gold "with all other banes," like saltpeter and explosives, "deep in mountain bowels, and riverbeds. But man still will mine for it; and mining, dig his doom."[73] "Oh curse of commerce!" fumes Babbalanja, "that it barters souls for gold."[74] Mineral wealth is obviously significant for the novel's arc, demonstrated by the abrupt changes in Media and Babbalanja when the group reaches Serenia, a theo-economic utopia where property is communal. Along these lines, the most compelling criticism of *Mardi* has examined the relation between the novel's emphasis on property and Melville's investigation of freedom and authorial control at a formative moment in the nation's history and his own career.[75]

Yet key moments in *Mardi* hint that, for Melville, possession—of gold, of territory, of the planet—is ultimately the ur-mirage of the human species. As we've seen, in the North Vivenza scroll Melville reframes the rhetoric of U.S. democratic expansionism in far greater magnitudes: "imbedded in the walls of the pyramids, which outrun all chronologies, sculptured stones are found, belonging to yet older fabrics."[76] Following the logic of the Vivenza scroll, we might measure the weight of the 1848 gold rush on *Mardi* quite differently. *Mardi* juxtaposes gold time to geologic time, Kolumbo to Vivenza, to reassess the "moral spectacle" of Polk's California. Read this way, Sutter's strike becomes an expression of the violence that exposes the "natural" chronologies of the mineral to alternate, human temporalities. The explosive creation of a mineshaft shatters "sculptured stones" into economic time, into nuggets in a miner's hand that soon become a groom's wedding band. *Mardi*'s treatment of gold reminds us that while for billions of years geophysical forces alone shaped mineral temporalities, human endeavors like large-scale mining have produced unprecedented geological agency for our species. As mineral mining and oil drilling intervene in millennial timelines, they disinter "older fabrics" of time and stitch geological epochs together so that the most mundane economic activity becomes akin to time-traveling science fiction.

Here the novel's concerns clearly coincide with a rich vein of twenty-first century literature and criticism that charts the intersections between the humanities and physical sciences like geology. But it is not quite accurate to suggest that Melville was ahead of his time in his geological focus. More specifically, the conditions of *Mardi*'s composition eerily parallel our own, and Melville's insights into geo-environmental processes resonate with recent essays by scholars like Dipesh Chakrabarty and Tobias Menely. These critics address three distinct threads of Anthropocene humanities scholarship deeply woven into *Mardi:* (1) the collapsing distinction between natural and human history, (2) the difficulty of representing scales of time and space that can capture our species' relation to the planet, and (3) the potential of literature to motivate reading communities to see human-nonhuman relations in new ways.[77]

For example, in "The Climate of History" (2009) Chakrabarty observes that technologies and population growth have given humans new planetary power, forcing us to "scale up our imagination of the human."[78] This is *Mardi*'s chief task for the reader, a task that implies a complex lesson. Shifts in scale necessitate shifts not just in vision or language but in *narrative form.* The literary thus becomes a critical category for species-being. Conceptualizing the human at the planetary level produces what Chakrabarty terms "rifts" in thinking as we negotiate "different scales simultaneously."[79] Melville's readers faced analogous rifts in antebellum America. Hungry for natural history to provide secular answers to questions of origins, amateur geologists were met with unnerving descriptions of infinitude, as in the concluding sentence of Hutton's *Theory of the Earth* (1788): "We find no vestige of a beginning,—no prospect of an end."[80] In *Mardi*, Melville goes further: "There is no place but the universe; no limit but the limitless; no bottom but the bottomless."[81]

These intimidating galactic perspectives challenged the ability of nineteenth-century readers to coordinate magnitudes of time, to reconcile a granite boulder with an infinite universe. We remain equally challenged today. Humanists have responded by grounding their work in material histories, but as Mark McGurl writes, when we take sciences like geology seriously, we realize that "what we call the 'ground' is no ground at all but the result of a process whose own ground is another, antecedent process extending backward in time."[82] Confronting the materiality of gold only unfolds other, more elemental histories (of supernovae nucleosyntheses or colliding neutron stars, for example).[83] *Mardi*'s gold suggests the poverty of our knowledge systems, the inadequacy of our temporal imaginations, and the dearth of narrative mechanisms that might tie together different "grounds" of existence. Similarly, Rob Nixon and others have argued that the long-term effects of industrial pollution and global climate change elude traditional narrative modes because they operate across "nonsynchronous temporal orders" and deploy "slow violence" invisible to individuals and even generations.[84] We are caught in the "obscurity of the present," to quote Menely, which chains us to self-serving organizing principles—genre, period, discipline—and thwarts our ability to interrogate time's magnitudes: its recursive spirals of past, present, and future masked by the comfort and distractions of mineral energy regimes.[85]

Obscurity is an appropriate word for *Mardi* given the novel's largely bewildered reviews, but it is more precise to say that the novel pierces the obscurity of the past by playfully compressing and dilating time, both within the narrative world of Mardi and in the reader's experience of reading *Mardi*. Threatened by a geological scale that "burdened the nineteenth century with a sense of time that exceeded the limits of plot," as Virginia Zimmerman puts it, Melville plots an excess of time in *Mardi*.[86] Each of *Mardi*'s chapters is but a cluster of hours for the characters, taken up by *Mardi*'s readers in minutes. There are long sections where the plot dissolves into Mardian prehistory or where Taji is so mesmerized by fleeting memories that "all the Past smote all the Present."[87] We readers are left to think about our own time spent reading the novel, a fourth dimension that binds *Mardi*'s temporalities to the immediate, embodied moment of page turning. The experience of reading *Mardi* generates what Wai Chee Dimock calls a "relativity effect" that bridges distant times and spaces through a network of literary relations that are materially structured by mineral ones.[88] In other words, we labor through a travelogue-turned-romance about time and minerals that is itself an exemplary product of the extractive economies it wants to critique.[89]

Mardi's focus on telling time remains a crucial (meta)interpretive problem while also buoying its relevance almost two centuries later, amid another era of increasing temporal complexity. Lyell's and Darwin's introduction of indeterminacy into natural and human history—the irruptions of accident and chance in the clean, linear logic of Enlightenment taxonomies—was perhaps most disturbing to nineteenth-century thinkers because it put limits on the human's ability to tell time at all. We have not yet recovered. This is one of the reasons why Melville's fiction continues to awe and frustrate contemporary readers. Melville captures the beauty and terror of temporal indeterminacy by slipping across magnitudes, especially moving from large to small. Against Chakrabarty's advice to "scale up," Ishmael asks, "Why then do you try to 'enlarge' your mind? Subtilize it."[90] By "subtilize," Ishmael means to "sharpen" or "refine" but also to "introduce subtleties or fine distinctions into . . . make thinner" or "more fluid or volatile."[91]

If thinking the color of whiteness, for instance, seems to elude analytical logic, then maybe Melville teaches us to scale *down* our imagination of the human to its constituent, subtle, mineral parts: to the "essence of things," as Babbalanja phrases it, "the elements of the tear which much laughter provoketh . . . the precious pearl within the shaggy oyster."[92]

PEARLS AND PLANETS

At its most ambitious, *Mardi* transforms sculptured stones and gold deposits from objects of contemplation into the structural principles of literary expression. The novel as a whole is patterned on the uncanny similarities between inorganic forms and organic ones, ruined monuments and human bodies, the decay of rocks and the creation of books. Like Lombardo, the author of the Mardian epic "Koztanza" hidden within *Mardi*, Melville "did not build himself in with plans" for writing an extended narrative. Rather, he "got deeper and deeper into himself" as he went deeper into Mardi's geological past.[93] As a result, "Koztanza," like the isles of Mardi, "lacks cohesion; it is wild, unconnected . . . nothing but episodes; valleys and hills . . . boulders and diamonds."[94] The scattered geologies of Mardi, its boulders and diamonds, parallel the expansive and digressive 195 chapters of *Mardi*.

But *Mardi* only appears to be a sedimentary assemblage of characters and conversations with little plot to connect the dots. The many mineral compounds strewn throughout the narrative, most notably Yillah's rose-colored pearl, actually help the reader track the nonlinear arcs of character and theme. The search for Yillah and her "Golconda locks" frames the majority of the novel, beginning and ending with repeated imagery of the pearl she wears around her neck.[95] When Yillah suddenly disappears in chapter 64, Taji describes his memories of her as "tearful pearls beneath life's sea," foreshadowing one of the novel's final scenes in which Taji is forced to dive for pearls in Hautia's mystical cavern of "many Golcondas."[96] Shadowy antagonist and Yillah's dark twin, Hautia harasses Taji throughout *Mardi*, but in the end Taji finds himself trapped in his enemy's mineral cavern, feeling "crystalized in the flashing heart of a diamond."[97] Taji ultimately refuses Hautia's seductions, and Yillah's rose-pearl is rewarded to him once more. The pearl becomes an enigmatic symbol of Yillah's endurance, her hovering between life and death. It sets Taji in pursuit again, alone, "over an endless sea."[98]

Yillah's pearl clearly motivates the plot of the novel, but the pearl's complex mineral composition deepens its significance. Wild pearls are made of calcium carbonate (aragonite and calcite minerals) and conchiolin (a protein matrix for minerals) sedimented over years into nacreous layers. Nacre, a composite of organic and inorganic material whose formation is still not fully understood, represents the ambiguity of the pearl's status within an organism. It is a cluster of life-within-nonlife-within-life. Housed inside mollusks, pearls appear to be generated over time by the mollusk's immune system.[99] *The Penny Cyclopaedia of the Society for the Diffusion of Useful Knowledge* (1833–43), a key source for Melville while writing *Mardi*, describes the "carbonate of lime and albumen" composition of the pearl, but today we recognize that the pearl is likely an evolutionary relic of biomineralization, the inorganic material produced by a living organism for structural integrity and protection from predation.[100] An immuno-mineral amalgam, the pearl discloses an essential mineralogical presence within life. It makes visible the animate's dependence on the inanimate at micro scales, but with implications far beyond seafloor ecology.

Melville likely did not know that the pearl oyster (*Pinctada imbricate*) was the first animal to be depleted by colonial Europeans in the Americas in the sixteenth century, but he certainly understood the rapacity of the

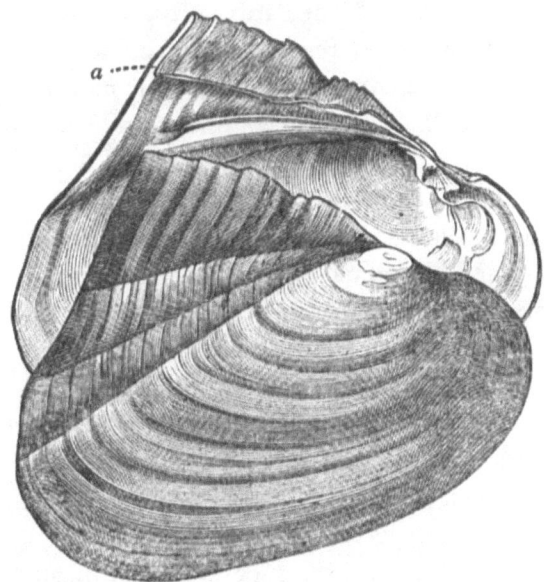

Unio alatus, from *The Penny Cyclopaedia of the Society for the Diffusion of Useful Knowledge* (London: C. Knight, 1833–43), 16:65. (Harvard University Library)

colonial project—evident in *Typee* and *Omoo*—and its desire to capture, possess, and alter both human and nonhuman landscapes, of which Yillah is a composite symbol.[101] In her origin story (chapter 43), for example, Yillah is transformed from an infant into a vine blossom before being swept by the wind into the "valve of a shell" and eventually springing, radiantly, from her "pearly casket" with the "rose colored-pearl on her bosom."[102] She magically condenses from human to vegetable to pearl. Yillah distorts the boundaries of species and stone, mobility and stasis, to remain Taji's ever-elusive and ungraspable phantom. She changes, reconfigures, and can never be fully possessed by Taji's alignment of desire and knowledge, which, Dimock has argued, constitutes the novel's imperial logic.[103] Yillah's transformations can be understood as *Mardi*'s mineral-security reflex, much like the pearl is a product of the oyster's threat response. Again and again, Yillah resists external threats by changing form: to flee the "mystical power" that spirits her from her birthplace, to escape the clutches of the priest Aleema, and finally to evade Taji's impositions.

If Yillah is *Mardi*'s immune reaction to the possessive pressures of "the all-grasping western world," then her presence in the novel transcends individual instances of imperialism.[104] Instead, she embodies the diagenetic resistance of the Mardian isles to all forms of possession. Like the Earth seen from the impossible point of view of deep time, Yillah and her pearl deny the anthropocentric concept of possession itself. The Earth accretes and weathers, erupts and lies dormant, with or without the possessive fantasies of the human. Yillah's conversions from human to pearl and back again model the geophysical processes that lead to sedimentation and erosion, forces that do the actual geomorphological work of dispossession over millennia. Because the novel intentionally keeps Yillah's transformation timeline vague—"in good time" and far from Oroolia where she started, her blossom-shell "was cast upon the beach of the Island of Amma"—her character becomes a narrative projection of sedimentation's slow grind.[105] Yillah is the transverse, diffuse emblem of earthy matter, sharing with *Pierre*'s Isabel a body in transition at different magnitudes (Isabel's ear is "a transparent sea-shell of pearl," her eyes are "meteors," and her hair gleams "like a tract of phosphorescent midnight sea").[106] Isabel, Yillah, and *Mardi* refuse neat categorization. Always in process, *Mardi* can be best understood as a long narrative of slow-motion change that confounds systematic attempts to possess its "vast bulk."[107]

Taji's romantic pursuit of Yillah is thus the superficial plot through which Melville accesses what we can call the *mineral unconscious*: a vague awareness of the shared, inorganic potentiality that transects the living and the dead, animate and inanimate. Yillah's flight forces Taji to perceive this potentiality in the variety and complexity of Mardi's rocky isles. He glimpses his love among the "mosses" and "sea-thyme" and sees her whirling "in the deepest eddies:—white, and vaguely Yillah."[108] Readers of *Mardi* are similarly encouraged to notice the "fractal kinships"—to borrow Dimock's term—produced by the formal resemblances "between shapes with serried outlines" like sea-foam or a human ear. Then, all at once, the cochlear curves of a shell approximate "the wispy puffs of clouds, the lacy fronds of ferns . . . and coiled dimensions inside a ball of twine."[109] Yillah makes Taji, and *Mardi*'s readers, negotiate "between the vague types of form morphology offers and the ideal structures of geometry proper."[110]

To further appreciate how *Mardi* articulates such kinships between human and nonhuman worlds, it is useful to think geometrically about the novel. Consider, for example, how *Mardi* works simultaneously on a spatial-horizontal axis and a temporal-vertical one. The island-hopping characters voyage across Mardi in the nearly two hundred chapters of the novel. But they often pause midchapter to look downward at the many geological features that mark Mardi's lithic prehistory. These gold deposits, pearls, fossils, cliffs, and volcanoes inspire the novel's metamorphic poetics and fluctuating points of view, matching variable magnitudes of planetary history with different syntaxes and literary styles. Transposing the vertical onto the horizontal, Melville generates multiple scales of reading in *Mardi*. The act of reading yields a vision of material contingency—what David Wills calls a "shifting kaleidoscopic or fractal transversality"—that characterizes, simultaneously, the novel's form and the inanimate spheres of existence that it tracks.[111]

But Melville is careful to warn that we should not "seek in nature for positive warranty" of our metaphysical "aspirations" because, again, "if not against us, nature is not for us."[112] This warning is a necessary counterbalance for a book that takes seriously the kaleidoscopic circulation of minerals, reflected at several levels of its narrative structure. Because, ultimately, *Mardi resists* the intolerable allegorizing of the natural. It presents without totalizing. It refuses to dominate the potentiality and emergences it tracks. Melville simply wants to remind us how *ordinary* minerals are, how ubiquitous in our lives and under our feet, even as we tend to imagine minerals exotically isolated in mines or belted to asteroids. For instance, after his discussion of Kolumbo's gold rush, Babbalanja poses an unexpected question:

"What underlieth the gold mines?"[113] A few chapters earlier, in a long lecture about Mardi's mineral soils, he had already intimated an answer: "Deep, Yoomy, deep, true treasure lies; deeper than all Mardi's gold, rooted to Mardi's axis. But unlike gold, it lurks in every soil,—all Mardi over."[114] Melville warily balances a caricature of Emersonian metaphysics—Oro who "is *in* all things, and himself *is* all things"—with Babbalanja's recognition that Mardi's lithosphere contains a diffuse inorganic potentiality, lurking "in every soil."[115] Mardi's subterranean treasures, like Yillah's pearl, deliver the temporary architecture of organic life in mineral arrangements eventually destined for the Earth's crust once again. Babbalanja stresses this "lurking" nature of minerality, withdrawn from view but present in stratigraphic layers rooted to Mardi's axis that generate new patterns from millennial archives of petrified life.

Melville most directly approaches the archival possibilities of the geologic on the "Isle of Fossils," where the crew discovers beaches that resemble "antique tablets . . . crystalized in stone" and etched with fossilized animals like "calcined Herculanean manuscripts."[116] When Media asks Babbalanja to "expound these rocks," he wants their "geological alphabet" deciphered, whether written in volcanic scoria or in the gradual layers of "slaty stone" that disclose "ripplings of some now waveless sea."[117] But, as we've seen, rocks are more than archives to be read by humans. They are the mineral architecture of historicity itself, the porous shells of planetary precedent and futurity. Co-opting New Testament rhetoric, Babbalanja concludes: "These were tombs burst open by volcanic throes . . . All Mardi's rocks are one wide resurrection."[118] On Mardi, minerals rise from the dead. Faith in Oro is faith in stone.

Babbalanja goes on to describe the geological origin of Mardi in terms similar to Cuvier's cataclysm theory, in which primeval volcanoes erupted and "upthrew the ancient rocks. . . . Thus Nature works, at random warring, chaos a crater, and this world a shell."[119] Elizabeth Foster has demonstrated that Melville is parodying early nineteenth-century Plutonian and Neptunian theories of geology here, but Babbalanja also puts forward a competing theory: "the celebrated sandwich System" that explains the slow accumulation of geological strata and fossilization.[120] Melville gently mocks Lyell's "uniformitarianism," which argued, contra Cuvier's catastrophism, for a theory of gradual geological processes unfolding over millions of years. In the 1850s and 1860s, Darwin would incorporate Lyell into his nascent theories of evolution, laying the groundwork for background extinction theory. But in *Mardi,* Babbalanja systematically integrates both cataclysmic and gradual theories of geologic history. "Nothing for us geologists, my lord," he says. "At a word we turn you out whole systems, suns, satellites, and asteroids included."[121]

So what does *Mardi* reveal about Melville's complicated relationship with science? In one sense, as Tyrus Hillway has argued, *Mardi* is a satire of scientific rationalism, particularly the section on the obfuscating Mindarian sorcerers.[122] "In some things," Babbalanja acknowledges, "science cajoles us."[123] But Babbalanja's "doctrine of Philosophical Necessity"—a nod to Joseph Priestley's *Doctrine of Philosophical Necessity* (1777)—posits a philosophy of scientific materialism bound by chains of contingencies in which "all events are naturally linked, and inevitably follow each other, without providential interposition, though by the eternal letting of Providence."[124] Melville's ambivalent pose between literary provocateur and full-on scientific materialist enables him to maintain the pretense of a Providential "eternal letting" while representing the infinitesimal scale of human existence amid deep-time changes on the planet. *Mardi* is in this sense Melville's first engagement with the notion of universal atheistic chance, a view that contradicted the pre-Darwinian continuity of natural history and muddled long-held ideas about the role of inorganic processes in the creation of the planet.[125] In chapter 75, "Time and Temples," Babbalanja observes that Virginia's Natural Bridge was not "worn under in a year; nor, in geology, were the eternal Grampians upheaved in an age. And who shall count the cycles that revolved ere earth's interior sedimentary strata were crystalized into stone."[126] In this remarkable passage, Melville juxtaposes the Natural Bridge against the incomprehensibly slow cycles of mineral time wherein "interior sedimentary strata" are "crystalized into stone."

Similarly, a century and a half later, contemporary mineralogists have proposed an evolutionary history of minerals dating to the earliest phases of our planet's history. Robert Hazen and his colleagues contend that "mineral evolution" is an entirely new field within the geological sciences. In Hazen's reconceptualization of the discipline, "Geologic time becomes a central parameter of mineralogy."[127] Hazen helps us see the histories of planetary minerals as sequences of "irreversible processes that lead from the mineralogical parsimony of the pre-solar era to progressively more diverse and complex phase assemblages."[128] Because planets are "engines of mineral formation," the origin of planetary life "may require that the planet has first achieved some minimal degree of mineral evolution."[129] For example, during the late stages of mineral evolution on Earth, particularly the Paleoproterozoic "great oxidation event" (2.5 to 1.9 Ga), the increased availability of atmospheric oxygen led to the development of multicellular life and the first signs of skeletal biomineralization.[130] In short, the minerality of a planet correlates with its capacity for life. Time, "the mightiest mason of all," fosters the potential for life as increasing magnitudes of mineral clusters assemble in the slow time of planetary animation.[131] "Granite continents," Babbalanja concludes, "seem created like the planets, not built with human hands."[132]

While beginning work on *Moby-Dick* in early 1850, Melville nightly walked the Battery in New York City to contemplate the planets and stars, but he had already outlined a "cosmic allegory" two years earlier, through *Mardi*'s "cosmos-conscious" Babbalanja and Taji.[133] Moreover, *Mardi*'s galactic scope was buttressed by the science of Melville's day, particularly early spectrographic studies of stars that expanded the work of William Herschel to offer evidence that the heavens were indeed made of the same elements as Earth. In 1840, New York University professor John Draper inaugurated celestial photography by taking the first daguerreotype of the moon, and eight years later as Melville was writing *Mardi*, William and George Bond discovered Hyperion, the seventh satellite moon of Saturn. The 1840s brought "stellar photography from second to sixth magnitude stars," Robert Bruce reminds us, by "demonstrating the use of timed exposures as measures of stellar brightness."[134] The linkages between stellar composition, crystalized minerals, planetary formation, and celestial photography explain Melville's consistent transposition of stars onto islands in most of his major works.[135] In *Mardi*, the Milky Way materializes in the "luminous reefs" of the Pacific, glowing bright as "Saturn in its ring."[136] Related astronomical metaphors dot Melville's midcareer fiction, from *White-Jacket; or, The World in a Man-of-War* (1850)—where the Earth is compared to a "world-frigate . . . one craft in a Milky-Way fleet"—to Queequeg's tribal custom of sending embalmed warriors off to a "starry archipelago . . . [where] the stars are isles . . . and so form the white breakers of the milky way."[137]

Mardi's insistence on the similitude between stars, planets, and islands also matches Melville's description of the novel's compositional design. He wrote to Murray that *Mardi* "combines in one cluster all that is romantic, whimsical & poetic" while also forming "a continuous narrative" of science and fiction.[138] In nineteenth-century parlance, "clusters" usually referred to either islands or stars, sometimes interchangeably, and Americans in 1848 would have been primed to think celestially, with the Great Comet of 1843 still lingering powerfully in the public's imagination. Then, as Melville was finishing the manuscript, John P. Nichol lectured rapt New York City audiences about the "infinitude" of our galaxy. Beyond our local "clusters" of stars, Nichol told the crowds, "we should see nothing but constellations after constellations."[139] Melville certainly read about Nichol's lectures in the months of *Mardi*'s composition, and at the very end of the novel, Babbalanja declares that our nebula is "nothing but stars on stars, throughout infinities of expansion. All we see are but a cluster."[140] Today, we know that a local "supercluster" actually contains multiple galaxies, constituting one of the largest structural patterns in the universe and further challenging the capacity of our cosmic imaginations. By the time he wrote *Mardi*, Melville's canvas had become the cosmos, and all its stars were "white, and vaguely Yillah." For mineral Melville, beholding "the white depths of the milky way," like glimpsing the whiteness of the whale, brought science and art together in mesmerizing but terrifying scales.[141]

BABBALANJA'S SKELETON

In the final sections of this chapter, I want to return the claim that *Mardi* provides the skeletal outline of Melville's geologic imagination. Though my use of "skeletal" is figurative, I'm interested in how *Mardi* literalizes this metaphor through the actual human skeletons that appear in the novel, relocating discussions of duration and scale from stars and planets onto femurs and skulls. The most striking example takes place on the island of Juam, where Taji notices the "pavements" surrounding King Donjalolo's house "inlaid" with "the reputed skeletons of Donjalolo's sires; each surrounded by a mosaic of corals,—red, white, and black intermixed with vitreous stones fallen from the skies in a meteoric shower."[142] A three-dimensional relief of bones, coral, and meteoric debris (chondrite minerals of solar nebulae), the pavement triggers Babbalanja's contemplation of his own skeleton: "oh Babbalanja! Thy own skeleton, thou thyself dost carry with thee, through this mortal life; and aye would view it, but for kind nature's screen; thou art death alive; and e'en to what's before thee wilt thou come."[143] Speaking to himself and to his skeleton, a Hamlet-Yorick fusion, Babbalanja accepts the fact that his living body is structured by the physical remainder of his future death. His skeleton is an immanent fossil.

Contemplation of human remains has long been a feature of Western literature, but in the context of nineteenth-century America, Babbalanja's skeleton represents a heightened awareness of the intimacy of the inorganic: what Nathan Brown, following Nancy via Agamben, labels "the *inorganic open*."[144] Both portent and relic of death, the skeleton gives life mobility. It provides complex organisms the vertebral stability and cranial support needed to encounter the world, to look backward or forward, to remember the past or imagine the future. As David Wills observes, "*the inanimate animates*" by imposing upon the animate different "structural credential[s]."[145] "I am dead though I live," Babbalanja muses, "and as soon dissect myself as another; I curiously look into my secrets: and grope under my ribs."[146] Like all bones, ribs are a matrix of salts, collagen, and mineralized tissue called bone mineral. And although scientists of Melville's day did not fully fathom the process of biomineralization, they did understand the anatomy of bones.

The Penny Cyclopaedia explains how the "elaborate structure" of osteological support comes from inorganic "earthy matter," including "salts of lime," "carbonate," and "phosphate."[147] According to the *Cyclopaedia*, ossification is biomineral sculpting or mixing the "calcareous" with the "membranous" to create "ossific matter." The skeleton, then, is a "pyramidal" monument with a "keystone" sacrum, a pelvic "arch," and "pillars" for femora.[148] In our bone monuments, we perceive the minerality that underpins our very understanding of stability as a concept, a narratological point of view from which the human is made visible. A century later, in his influential account of habitation, *The Poetics of Space* (1958), Gaston Bachelard writes that "the inside of a man's body is an assemblage of shells" that, through evolutionary procedures, have over time become skeletal. "A fossil," he determines, "is not merely a being that once lived, but one that is still alive, asleep in its form. The shell is the most obvious example of a universal shell-oriented life."[149]

But let's delve deeper into the phrasing Babbalanja uses to describe his skeleton screen—"Thou art death alive; and e'en to what's before thee wilt thou come." In this passage, Babbalanja gestures at the complexities of the inanimate's relation to life, playing on the double meaning of "before." Read one way, "before" signals spatial orientation: in front of or inside of. Babbalanja's skeleton is "before" his body. Read another, "before" signals orientation in time. The skeleton's composite minerals existed "before" Babbalanja and will endure after him in the former shape of his living body. After death, Babbalanja "wilt come" fully skeletal. He will return to the nudity of his skeletal form, a cluster of bones in the desolate architecture of a dissolving mineral archive.

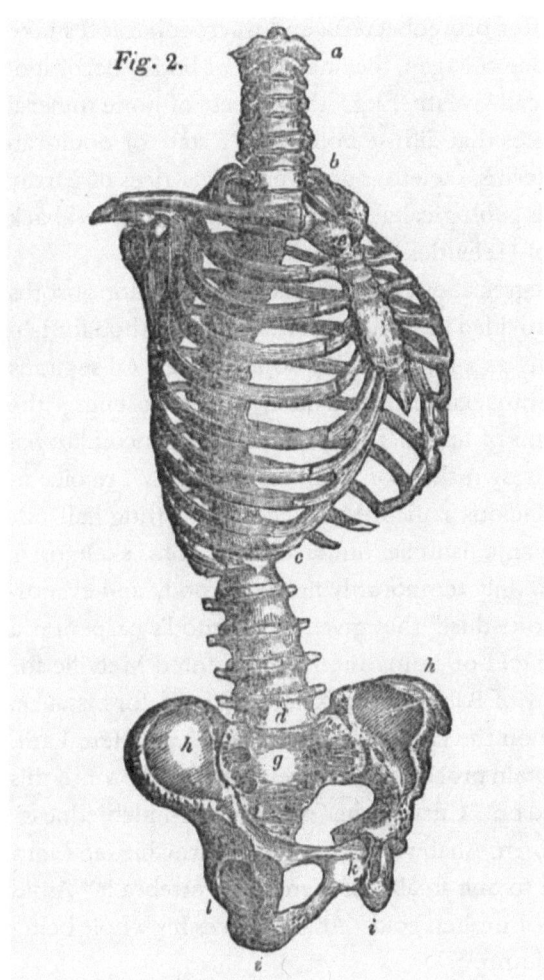

Skeleton, from *The Penny Cyclopaedia of the Society for the Diffusion of Useful Knowledge* (London: C. Knight, 1833–43), 22:73. (Harvard University Library)

This, it seems to me, is the marrow of *Mardi*. Standing on Donjalolo's bone-meteor pavement, Babbalanja foresees the duration of his bones beyond life by peering through "nature's screen," the protective narrative curtain that preserves the illusion of our bodies' spatiotemporal coherence. Like Bartleby's screen in the Wall Street law office, Babbalanja's body offers only an illusory division between self and other, narrator and addressee, animate and inanimate. The dead, Babbalanja concludes, "are not to be found, even in their graves . . . something has become of them that they sought not."[150] Here, and in a number of places in the novel, Babbalanja anticipates the science of *taphonomy*, the study of a living body's transition from biosphere to lithosphere. After proteobacteria and microeukaryotes take carbon and nitrogen from bone collagen, the final stage of bodily decomposition is what taphonomists call "weathering," the process of bone mineral dispersal by geodynamic forces that diffuse bones into a state of nonlocality.[151] In nineteenth-century terms, skeletons are overlaid matrices of earthy matter. They are letters of a geological alphabet eventually scripted back into stone, into a language of "relentless tectonicity."[152]

If *Moby-Dick* is to some degree about how Ishmael's imagination absorbs scientific facts, then *Mardi* provided Melville with a skeletal method for Ishmael's inquiries into anatomy as a form of philosophy. In several sections of *Moby-Dick*, for example, Ishmael investigates the whale by loosening "the hooks and the eyes of the joints of his innermost bones . . . his unconditional skeleton."[153] Reflecting on his own skeleton, Ishmael declares: "I rejoice in my spine, as in the firm audacious staff of that flag which I fling half out to the world."[154] Like Babbalanja, Ishmael understands that his skeleton is only "half out" in the world, only temporarily inside his body and eventually fated to become the "bone-dust" that gives the Pequod's carpenter a sneezing fit.[155] The diffusive end of human remains haunted Melville for the rest of his life. The destiny of Babbalanja's skeleton echoes, for instance, in Ahab's frustrated reliance on the carpenter for his new leg. "Here I am, proud as Greek god," the captain proclaims, "and yet standing debtor to this blockhead for a bone to stand on!" Cursing the "mortal inter-indebtedness" of his spirit to his physical form, Ahab resolves to "get a crucible, and into it, and dissolve myself down to one small, compendious vertebra."[156] Amid a sea shining like "a crucible of molten gold," Ahab reduces his whole being to a single disc in a spinal column.[157]

All of this is to say that Babbalanja's "osseous" reflections reimagine Mardi along a dispersed plane of recycled minerals.[158] Galactic stones, invertebrate shells, and human bones are in *Mardi* the inanimate grammar of deep-time intervals with elemental origins in supernovae nucleosyntheses. Carbonate minerals like silicates ("vitreous stones") constitute the building blocks of Yillah's pearls, Mardi's reefs, Babbalanja's ribcage, and planetary life itself. Babbalanja's skeleton destabilizes the binaries that divide inside from outside, the present time of one's thoughts from the cosmic origins of the elements that generate them. "There is a world of wonders insphered within the spontaneous consciousness," Babbalanja tells Media, "a mystery within the obvious, yet an obviousness within the mystery."[159]

Nutritional neuroscience has even suggested that compounds including iron, zinc, copper, manganese, and magnesium play critical roles in neuroplasticity and the development of the brain.[160] We now know that the brain's "world of wonders" is possible through the interaction of the "earthy" and the "membranous" in our neural networks, an ionic-mineral rhythm of membrane potentials at the cellular level. "Much of the knowledge we seek, already we have in our cores," says Babbalanja. "Yet so simple it is, we despise it; so bold, we fear it."[161] Most minerals are bioavailable simply through a healthy diet, but, in the antebellum South, geophagy—eating soils such as white kaolin for their mineral content—was not uncommon, and Melville mentions these "clay-eaters" in *The Confidence-Man* to critique "mineral doctors" and their dubious tinctures.[162] Melville recognized in *Mardi* the mineral dimension of our bodies' transcorporeality, but by *The Confidence-Man* he had become aware of how quickly a material vision of the body could be co-opted by quacks and confidence schemes.

The notion that "our bodies are our betters" is a recurring theme in *Mardi*, a novel obsessed with the fragmentation, amalgamation, and decomposition of bodies.[163] When Taji is finally entranced by his enemy Hautia—and mutters to his companions, "Here I stand, my own monument"—the reader realizes the true power of Hautia's spell.[164] She enchants Taji with a fantasy of bodily coherence and an ego of monumentality. By the end of this long narrative, we see that Taji is actually more like "grave-yards full of buried dead, that start to life before us."[165] On Mardi as on Earth, the human body is the amalgamated residue of reprocessed minerals. "Nothing, not even the human, is for itself or by itself," Latour reminds us, "but always *by other things* and *for other things*."[166] The material contingency of the mineral universe means that "living is dying" and that "the very mountains melt." "Ah gods!" Babbalanja exclaims, "in all this universal stir, am *I* to prove one stable thing?"[167] The answer that *Mardi* gives is, simply, no.

Yet the authority of Babbalanaja's body over his mind—its "incessant operation of subtle processes" including the regulation of elements like iron—relates to what Graham Harman considers the continuing "allure" of art.[168] For Harman, the artistic impulse originates in the fact that the same materials that compose our bodies are, by their nature, largely inaccessible to us, withdrawn. Art, on the other hand, gives us glimpses of our material selves, apprehensible only through the instability of *other* bodies. Just as Melville's proxy author Lombardo unites "matter and mind" in the "composite" form of his masterpiece "Koztanza," *Mardi*'s labored narrative offers a provisional architecture of stability, an event of reading that in its length, difficulty, and eschewal of plot generates in each chapter appreciation of what Elizabeth Povinelli calls a "quasi-event."[169] For Povinelli, events in the world—materially considered—are only ever "*hereish* and *nowish*," obliging us to look at the "forces of condensation, manifestation, and endurance" that come to bear on the conditions, "rather than on the borders, of objects."[170] In other words, art opens us to unstable quasi-events. The very etymology of Babbalanja's name ("babble-ana") signals Melville's understanding of how literary character is able to capture the essential instability of our embodied experiences of the world. From the French *babil* ("idle or foolish talk, prattle"), *babble* refers to "an indistinct jumble of voices," as well as the "sound uttered by certain birds" and "the murmur of flowing water."[171] Babbalanja's riparian bird-babble throughout *Mardi* mimics the novel's alluvial-sedimentary form and its thematic attention to all sorts of transformations.

MINERAL CRITICISM

By way of conclusion, I'd like to address this issue of instability and its implications for the conceptual difficulties of environmental ethics in the Anthropocene. In previous sections, I've noted the persistence of geological imagery in Melville's works beyond *Mardi*. Take, for example, the karst terrains—unstable limestone formations producing caves, sinkholes, and oil reservoirs—that appear in *Battle-Pieces*, or the several rockslides in *Clarel*.[172] With the exception of *Clarel*, *Mardi* is Melville's most explicitly mineralogical work, but in the later writings, as we will see, Melville's interest in the inanimate finds expression in other, even more volatile forms. *Pierre* is full of lightning bolts, vapors, and foams. *The Piazza Tales* meditate on lived-in and abandoned relics of hermitages: fossils of sociality, memorials to inhabitation. *John-Marr* erodes into "Pebbles" that contemplate flows of dust and dew in weather patterns and endless biogeochemical cycles.

Generally though, the post-*Mardi* writings engage the inorganic as Cole did in *Course of Empire*. An awe of ruins in a posthuman world. Although *Mardi* combines these modes in the most formally elegant way, as early as *Typee* Melville had an eye for the sublimity of derelict terraces, pyramids, and monoliths that clouded distinctions between the human and the geological.[173] Melville routinely imagined a world without the human, one witnessed only by palm trees or crumbling statues. As the Tahitian high priest chants in *Omoo:* "The palm tree shall grow, / The coral shall spread, / But man shall cease."[174] Such visions accentuate the relics of vanished humanity that endure into a future without us. In the following chapter, we will spend time with Pierre's dream of the ancient Greek Giant Enceladus—"that deathless son of Terra"—which captures the anthropocentric terror of the inanimate-as-eternal-witness perhaps better than any other moment in Melville's writing.[175] (The terror resurfaces years later in *Clarel:* "Behold the stones! . . . / No worm—no life; but, all the more, / Good witnesses.")[176]

These moments from *Pierre* and *Clarel* anticipate one of the central dilemmas facing contemporary environmental theorists: How do we witness the Anthropocene? And from what point of view? For Chakrabarty, such questions constitute a real problem: "We humans never experience ourselves as a species . . . [because] one never experiences a concept." Species and planetary thinking necessitate an imaginary of human collectivity, a trope of "the universal" that Chakrabarty believes "escapes our capacity to experience the world."[177] On the one hand, our anthropocentrism inheres in the acts of reading that create geohistorical categories in the first place, figuring the planet in terms of its future legibility and fetishizing what Kate Marshall calls the fantasy of the "posthuman future archeologist."[178] On the other hand, as *Mardi* has shown us, literary texts *do* allow readers to experience a sense of "universal" species-being by defamiliarizing the givenness of the human's relation to the Earth. *Mardi* teaches us that we are our shared minerality. Perhaps the enduring lesson we can draw from *Mardi* is that a robust *mineral criticism* of modern literary traditions exposes new ways of reading literature through science, and vice versa. Viewing our species at different magnitudes of process in the fictional worlds of Mardi, readers of *Mardi* encounter the extraordinary geometries of mineral kinships that correlate sea thyme with the tendrillar splay of human hair.

These kinships are central to *Mardi*'s unfulfilled legacy. Responding to the novel's befuddled reviewers, Melville dismissed his "dunce" critics as frustrated geometry students giving up on "the 47th problem of the 1st Book of Euclid" (the Pythagorean Theorem in *Elements*).[179] Unable to grasp what Dimock terms a "geometry that spills over onto several scales at once," many of *Mardi*'s readers throw up their hands and declare, "There's nothing in it!"[180] Hinting at a relation between reading a novel and tracing the complexities of eco-geometric forms, Melville implies that to truly witness the magnitudes of human creativity and destruction on the planet, we should follow the nonlinear logic presented to us by formally innovative fictions. We should take seriously how fictional form collapses the inherited timelines of Western thought, within and against the pressures of syntax and narrative coherence.

Mardi's pearls and fossils gesture toward an environmental ethic of *sameness* hidden in the scale-curving symmetries of formal correspondence, like the astonishing "universal yellow lotus" Ishmael sees in the Pacific, "more and more unfolding its noiseless measureless leaves upon the sea."[181] The whorled ocean unfolds a lotus that unfolds yet other forms in "layers of concentric spiralizations," spiralizations that, to Ishmael, indicate an "aesthetics in all things."[182] These are symmetries beyond scaling, in which the "delicate geometry" of the spider's "arcs of gossamer" is spun out onto the ocean and into the cosmos.[183] However, thinking about form is a slippery enterprise. As Melville well knew, thinking formally risks naive panpsychism or, worse, falling into "Plato's honey-head."[184] Because, historian David Lord Smail reminds us, even if we need not "assume the existence of a designer when we see the appearance of design," we recognize after Darwin that humans are nonetheless wired to find symmetry.[185] But by shifting the discussion away from archival fiefdoms and toward the geometries of eco-aesthetics, formal criticism's comeback in recent humanities scholarship discloses a potential to upend long-standing divisions of period, genre, and nationality in literary studies. This is a potential I see realized in Melville's major works including *Mardi*, *Pierre*, and *The Piazza-Tales*.

In her recent book *Against Nature* (2019), historian of science Lorraine Daston points out that, in medieval and Renaissance Europe, "nature was understood as a patchwork of regularities of different kinds, jurisdictions, and degrees of strictness," whereas eighteenth-century theology, natural philosophy, and mathematics imposed universal natural laws cloaked in machinic and clockwork metaphors.[186] By the nineteenth century, this "natural" background order generated discourses of "natural" rights, norms, and communities to such a degree that, as Londa Schiebinger phrases it, "inclusion in the polis rested on notions of *natural* equalities, while exclusion from it rested on notions of *natural* differences."[187] Against such naturalized background orders, in *Mardi* Melville veers away from fixed universals toward a more patchwork, agglomerating vision of "local natures" where, out of an evolving mineral foundation, life emerges in mounting complexity ever-woven with mutation, decay, and disaster.[188] In this sense, patient readers leave Melville's earthy and oceanic worlds more attuned to the "ontoaesthetics" of literature, to steal a useful word from Elizabeth Grosz, which encourages the slow labor of reading and welcomes the challenges presented by literature's ductile forms of bearing witness in the Anthropocene.[189] At least Melville thought so, writing confidently to his father-in-law, Lemuel Shaw, that "time, which is the solver of all riddles, will solve 'Mardi.'"[190] So perhaps it is fitting that, in our current era of hypertemporalities and attention deficits, *Mardi* remains unread. As he wrote to his friend and editor Evert Duyckinck, the novel is an ungraspable cypher that should be wrapped in "a bit of old parchment (from some old Arabic M.S.S. on Astrology) . . . & sealed on the back with a Sphynx . . . never to be broken until the aloe flowers."[191]

ALOE-*MARDI*

Over the years following *Mardi*'s publication, Melville continued to speculate on the novel's reception. In the same February 1850 letter to Duyckinck, he elaborated his aloe-*Mardi* metaphor, fancying that *Mardi* might "flower like the aloe, a hundred years hence—or not flower at all, which is more likely by far, for some aloes never flower."[192] On the one hand, Melville's floral tropes for *Mardi*'s legacy suggest an increasing awareness that his most experimental work might not be appreciated in his lifetime. But, on the other, such metaphors extend the mineralogical insights of *Mardi* by aligning literary success with the abhuman timelines and growth cycles of the vegetal world. Like Babbalanja's skeleton and Yillah's pearl, the internal organization of angiosperms (flowering plants) depends on mineral chemistry, but these phytochemical systems regulate spans of blooming and senescence, life and nonlife *together*. And by "aloe," Melville likely meant the American aloe plant, which is actually not an aloe at all but an *agave Americana*, or century plant. Century plants can reach thirty feet tall and thirty years old but will only flower once, right before dying, as an intricate metabolic balance keeps the agave from flowering too early. Melville's offhand botanical-chemical description of *Mardi* seems innocent enough, but read from the perspective of the novels and stories that followed between 1850 and 1856, Melville's retrospective characterization of "aloe-*Mardi*" indicates a shift in ecological emphasis—from the mineral to the vegetal, and from the realm of the inorganic to the organic.

In ways similar to Thoreau, for whom, to quote Branka Arsić, "the slow motion of geological phenomena marks precisely the perseverance and continuity of life," after 1848 Melville began to integrate *Mardi's* geological timeframes into a philosophy of life articulated via three very different literary experiments: *Moby-Dick, Pierre,* and *The Piazza Tales*.[193] Although he continued to think about how life and nonlife share a common minerality, during this period in the early 1850s Melville's attention to vegetable spheres of existence led him to examine how life emerges out of, through, and within nonlife, often at scales and configurations beyond human vision or care. However, this new organic emphasis should be understood as yet one more vantage point—one angle of looking among many—that enabled Melville to better address the persistent questions about creativity, originality, generation, and reproduction that dominate his career.

After *Mardi,* as Melville roved from galactic minerals to country flowers, he looked to botanical worlds for what they might teach us, paradoxically, about ourselves: about the nature of language, literary representation, and human sociality. Peering into the "milky-way of white-weed" and other kinds of vegetal life, Melville began to see creativity not in the traditional sense of the individual human genius but, as cultural ecologist Hubert Zapf puts it, "as a property of life and, to an extent, of the material world itself."[194] To speak of the eloquence of plants seemed to Melville less metaphorical than material, a tight spiral of the semiotic and biotic. We will fully take up the question of *difference* and its many implications for ecology and society when we turn (in chapter 3) to Melville's treatment of animals, but the following chapter argues that the underappreciated botany in *Moby-Dick* and *Pierre* is a pivot point in Melville's ecologies. This is the moment when Melville realizes that time, that "mighty mason," turns out to be an exquisite gardener as well.[195]

Melville's consideration of forests, trees, flowers, vines, and seeds in his midcareer novels uncovers temporal and spatial correspondences between the vegetal and the human, between (a)sexual reproduction and cultural reproduction. We apprehend these correspondences when, all of a sudden, we realize how engulfed we are by worlds that we barely understand and that remain largely hidden from us. For example, in *Moby-Dick,* as Father Mapple recounts the "pregnant lesson" of the prophetic Jonah story—a reminder of the "swallowing" power of God—he also offers a veiled lesson of "engulfment" by concluding his sermon with an image of marine ecology.[196] "We feel the floods surging over us," Mapple bellows, "we sound with [Jonah] to the kelpy bottom of the waters; sea-weed and all the slime of the sea is about us!"[197] Only in the twentieth century did it become clear that marine algae ("sea-weed and all the slime of the sea") produce 80 percent of the oxygen on the planet and that our very breath is linked to the health of the kelpy bottoms around the globe. But even without these lessons in atmospheric biochemistry, Melville's acute sense of being "engulphed" recasts Mapple's Jonah story into a fable for the various layers of human engulfment: being surrounded by animal bodies, weathered by indifferent environments, and dependent on weedy forms of life that are vital for human existence but stay somehow blocked from the dominant views, values, and narratives of our species. Ironically, it is Ahab who recognizes that his breath is an exhalation of once-vegetal life swirled through water, air, and lung: "I am buoyed by breaths of once-living things, exhaled as air, but water now."[198] *Moby-Dick* initiates a network of engulfment imagery that would progressively circle in on plant life over the next six years of Melville's writing career. Was man, he would ask in *The Confidence-Man*, in the end merely the "drifting sea-weed of the universe"?[199] Melville had certainly been attentive to flora and foliage since the opening chapters of *Typee*, but his eccentric emphasis on vegetal and algal imagery between 1850 and 1856 comes to its fullest expression in his most reviled novel, *Pierre; or the Ambiguities*, an eco-gothic classic that unlocks Melville's botanical imagination.

CHAPTER 2

Tendril
Pierre

Think you, my lord, there is no sensation in being a tree?
—*Mardi*

On its surface, *Pierre* is a very human story. A tragic swirl of familial duty and ruinous consequences, the novel's narrative arc exposes the complicated and sometimes dangerous power of desire that Melville saw at the center of social life. Written to redeem the failure of *Moby-Dick* and to cash in on the popular sentimental romance genre, *Pierre* trades in familiar tropes— the drama of marriage and inheritance, light and dark heroines, city and country scenes, and the heartache of splintered families. The novel follows the sheltered artist-idealist Pierre as he discovers a mysterious half-sister, renounces his estate, and flees with her to New York City. It all ends disastrously. Perhaps Melville's bleakest work, *Pierre* nonetheless teases readers with glimpses of the "beautifulness of humanness" that align it with the idealism of the nineteenth-century domestic novel.[1] Most criticism of *Pierre* has worked at the tensions between Melville's ironic gothic pessimism and the sentimental form he deconstructs, putting *Pierre* in conversation with a variety of social, economic, and political contexts in midcentury America.[2] But I'm more interested in what Pierre's all-too-human failures and anxieties distract us from: the novel's "hideous inhumanities," to borrow Evert Duyckinck's term, that lurk in the lush imagery, botanical metaphors, and even vegetal structure of this strange tale.[3]

Duyckinck's phrase is useful in two senses, referring both to the threatening *inhuman* tendencies exposed by the novel (adultery, incest, murder) and to the *inhuman* worlds that threaten our senses of selfhood and security (snakes, storms, rockslides). Although many readings of *Pierre* emphasize the novel's stony imagery, *Pierre* is not primarily about sterility or death.[4] It is instead about forms of life that, precisely because they do not exist for human cultivation or use, remain ignored or obscured from human perspectives. Plants, algae, fungi, and slime—along with phenomena like lightning strikes or cave-ins that unexpectedly reveal them to us—accumulate and flourish in *Pierre*'s tangled syntax. Vines and flowers creep into the novel's metaphors and imagery, creating botanic-gothic textual landscapes that refract the novel's thematic "inhumanities" through a grotesque, feracious background. In *Pierre*, *Mardi*'s geological prophecies about the mineral commonalities among forms of existence are seen in the light of the vegetal "greenness" of Saddle Meadows and the prismatic "fresh-foliaged heart of Pierre."[5]

In other words, *Pierre*'s stones, statues, and cities divert our attention from the abundant descriptions of living matter in the novel, including Pierre's essentially "organic" nature, as the narrator calls it, his persistent "earthliness."[6] The novel's stress on decay and death—the Glendinning name falling "to the mold"—therefore becomes a way to see the obverse, a way into the radicle of Melville's philosophy of life.[7] Because decay, Melville wrote a few years before his own death, "is often a gardener."[8] And if, as Roberto Esposito has recently argued, "sickness and death make up the cone of shadow within which the life sciences carve out their niche," then Pierre's gloomy ruin provides the contrast necessary to see the dawn of modern "life" via biological, botanical, and other protoecological sciences in midcentury America.[9] The "most mighty of nature's laws is this," *Pierre*'s narrator tells us, "that out of Death she brings Life."[10] And so, amid the wreckage of Pierre's life, *Pierre* teems with ferns, bubbles with foams, and explodes with lightning storms. In *Pierre*'s forests, these nonhuman processes generate self-similar patterns and expanding symmetries within Saddle Meadows's local, ordinary ecologies, rather than the faraway, extreme worlds of mineral formation (*Mardi*) or deep-sea whale roads (*Moby-Dick*).

Melville tracks the hidden ranges of organic life by foregrounding a story about failed reproduction—sexual, genealogical, textual—while rendering the narrative in verdant imagery to juxtapose human and vegetal modes of being along the axes of flourishing and decay. This juxtaposition has led most critics to read the novel's vegetality symbolically, and Melville certainly opens the door to those readings by framing the Glendinning clan against the rise and fall of American families more generally. In America, the narrator explains, "the vast mass of families be as the blades of grass, yet some few there are that stand as the oak; which, instead of decaying, annually puts forth new branches."[11] Oak trees and grasses do provide the metaphoric canvas for Melville's critique of American economy and society, but I see a much more material texture in *Pierre*'s botanical worlds that explains the linkages between the novel's notoriously thorny syntax, its hybridization of genres, and its disturbing themes. And, ironically, *Pierre*'s first reviewers were quick to identify these linkages.

Calling the novel "a farrago" full of "utter trash" of "almost infinite" proportions, early critics of *Pierre* get close to articulating the botanical complexity that Melville scrutinizes in the novel (for example, *farrago*, meaning jumbled mixture, comes from the Latin for "corn").[12] So when the *New York Herald* described *Pierre* as "without beginning or end—a labyrinth without a clue—an Irish bog," it unwittingly located a network of marshy relations within *Pierre*'s seemingly chaotic composition: "Word piled upon word, and syllable heaped upon syllable, until the tongue grows bewildered as the mind, and both refuse to perform their offices from sheer inability to grasp the magnitude of the absurdities."[13] Or as the *Springfield Republican* put it: "Of mist-caps, and ravines, and sky piercing peaks, and tangled underwoods, and barren rocks of language and incident, the book is made."[14] Like these critics, I'm fascinated by *Pierre*'s tangled underwoods and grammatical absurdities, its "viscous" style that, according to later critic E. L. Grant Watson, repelled readers "like some alien particle."[15] But my interest runs exactly counter to the disgust of initial reviewers. In this chapter, I map the viscous dynamics of *Pierre*'s "repellingness" in order to read those dynamics as ecologically generative, to show how *Pierre*'s repellent grammars enable Melville to explore in writing obscure ranges of life that fall between Linnaean categories.[16] These unseen patches of "cunning purpleness," as Melville calls them, are resistant to human contact or representation. Within such hidden, boggy, abjected worlds, Melville finds compelling bonds between vegetal life, the origin of writing, and the progress of human history. For example, it is not lost on Melville that the very ink used to write and print *Pierre* was composed of turpentine distilled from the drained sap of pine trees—crucially, it should be noted, by southern slave labor—so that Melville's writing and *Pierre*'s pines coalesce, materially and metaphorically, in the "tear-mingled ink" of Isabel's letter.[17]

In this wider sense, Melville's novels and stories of the 1850s show a deep appreciation for what anthropologist Anna Tsing terms the "historical force of plants" like pine and oak in shaping the development of human economies. Plants provide the material basis for human nutrition, agriculture, and civilization itself.[18] Just as "Nature planted our Pierre" in the sylvan worlds of Saddle Meadows, Melville planted *Pierre* in the growing protoecological discourses of antebellum America.[19] By the 1850s, for example, the Melville family had many sources on vegetal life at hand in their personal library: Frances Sargent Locke Osgood's *The Poetry of Flowers and the Flowers of Poetry* (1841), Sarah Carter Edgarton Mayo's *The Flower Vase; Containing the Language of Flowers and Their Poetic Sentiments* (1844), and James Andrews's *Floral Tableaux* (1846), to name a few.[20] And the Melville family's not-uncommon interest in plants fits in the broader history of the popularization and dissemination of nineteenth-century American science. Asa Gray's botany textbook *Elements of Botany* (1836), for instance, helped professionalize American science at midcentury. Almira Phelps's *Familiar Lectures on Botany* (1836) educated generations of women readers and amateur botanists. And, as noted in the introduction, Maxwell Masters's *Botany for Beginners* (1872) provided a way for budding scientists to understand the interrelations between plants, animals, and environments.

In the twists and turns of Melville's midcareer—between novels and sketches and poems, between oceans and cities and deserts—the plant emerges as a central figure for Melville's ecological imagination. Understood this way, Melville's description of "the god-like population of the trees" lining Saddle Meadows, which seem to Pierre "a nobler race than man," makes more sense. Pierre hopes that these trees' "high foliage shall drop heavenliness upon me; my feet in contact with their mighty roots, immortal vigor shall so steal into me."[21] A reversal of the taphonomic processes that allow plants to absorb the minerals of decaying organic life, Pierre wants to steal the "immortal vigor" of vegetal life, an energy he later identifies with the creative impulses of writing and music. Struggling to write at the Church of the Apostles, for example, Pierre "resolved to plant his head in a hot-bed of stove-warmed air, and so force his brain to germinate and blossom, and bud, and put forth the eventual crowning, victorious flower."[22] And much earlier in the novel, after hearing Isabel's guitar for the first time, Pierre becomes "a tree-transformed and mystery-laden visitant, caught and fast bound in some necromancer's garden."[23] Brain-blossoming and tree-transforming, Pierre finds his match in Isabel, for whom happiness is feeling like a "plant, absorbing life without seeking it, and existing without individual sensation." "I feel that there can be no perfect peace in individualness," she exclaims, "Therefore I hope one day to feel myself drank up into the pervading spirit animating all things."[24] Affiliating Pierre's literary ambitions and Isabel's pantheist desires with the rhetoric of germination and flowering gave Melville license to imagine how the processes of literary creation might be conceptualized in vegetal cycles of growth, blossoming, and decay.

But, most importantly, the luxuriant style of Melville's literary imagination ran counter to the popular trends of antebellum novel writing. In particular, the tidy norms of the sentimental novel—arranged around the consequences of desire, the meaning of duty, and the restoration of family—seemed to have little room for the formal experimentation and heterodox thematic risks of Melville's overgrown literary sensibility. As Jeffrey Nealon has argued at length, this kind of "plant desire" is seen as fundamentally unproductive in modern Western society, associated with "masturbation, queer desire, prison, the thief's underworld, [and] cathection onto the mother."[25] Understood in its socio-rhetorical milieu, for Nealon the plant becomes a metonym of all the nonnormative, unlabeled *stuff* that constitutes the uncontrolled parts of society. It stands for the "emergent undocumented material that needs to be rendered meaningful, negated, and raised" to expand the territory of capital and (agri)cultural progress.[26] This may partially explain the common pretense in antebellum women's writing of dismissing their compositions as falling "leaves" randomly "gathered," as Fanny Fern phrased it, to strike a pose of gender humility and botanical decorum.[27] In Melville's case, *Pierre* provided the vocabulary to enunciate his extravagant growth as a writer in the post–*Moby-Dick* period, a period when his writing about plants dovetailed with his writing about runaways, outlaws, prisoners, revolutionaries, and con men: the excesses of human life cast aside, isolated, repressed, or ignored. In short, life beyond the state, the law, or the margins of the ledger. Life whose spatial and temporal frames—like plants themselves—did not always coordinate with the legal or agrological development of capitalist society, just as Melville's writing in "aloe" *Mardi* or "maple-sap" *Moby-Dick* could not be fully recognized in the span of his lifetime.[28]

Pierre wrestles with his vegetal desires throughout the novel, visible to the reader through gravid metaphors of a vibrant wilderness where "infinite inhumanities" moan from "profoundest forests." Channeling Pierre's desires into his mother issues and incestuous longing for his sister, Melville ultimately directs them into the murderous rage that leads to

Pierre's imprisonment and death. But Pierre's desire *does* find expression, only not at the level of plot. Instead, Melville absorbs it into the novel's pulsating landscapes: the "rain-shakings of the palsied trees, slidings of rocks undermined, final crashings of long-riven boughs, and devilish gibberish of the forest-ghosts."[29] The spontaneously creative, inhuman wilderness of Saddle Meadows generates life even as it destroys, initiating spirals of ecological reproduction that Pierre—with his sexual frustrations and writing blocks—simply can't match.

This is how Melville approaches the sentimental romance form. He makes Pierre a reader and writer of bad novels, an impotent artist incapable of reproduction. Bad novels are Melville's ironic targets in *Pierre,* and his attacks on writing, publishing, and literary originality concentrate on how writing reduces the emergent complexity of ecological relations by compressing the "web of life" into familiar narrative structures and Procrustean tropes. The narrator lambasts novels for "their false, inverted attempts at systematizing eternally unsystemizable elements; their audacious, intermeddling impotency, in trying to unravel, and spread out, and classify, the more thin than gossamer threads which make up the complex web of life."[30] And yet, of course, Melville is himself writing a novel, an audacious investigation into the meaning of literary and sexual "impotency," the sign of "sterility" against which "fertility" is judged. Melville resists systemizing "the complex web of life" by staying rooted in vegetal rhetoric that deviates from the traditional style of the sentimental romance and from the dominant, patriarchal norms of heterosexual reproduction. Instead, Melville creates a novel of "mutilated stumps," as he puts it, whose attention to decay and partiality makes visible the interstitial spaces where life and nonlife intersect, deform, and mutually inter-merge.[31] *Pierre* is Melville's attempt to move beyond what he calls "common novels" that "laboriously spin veils of mystery, only to complacently clear them up at last." *Pierre* reaches for the "profounder emanations of the human mind" that "never unravel their own intricacies, and have no proper endings, but in imperfect, unanticipated and disappointing sequels (as mutilated stumps), hurry to abrupt intermergings with the eternal tides of time and fate."[32]

This chapter of *Magnificent Decay* is organized around the idea that, in *Pierre,* Melville's botanical fascinations specifically appear in the form of the *spiral,* a distinguishing feature of plant life for nineteenth-century scientists. The spiral—a slow-lapse image of growth made visible—unfurls for Melville the contours of his philosophy of *bios* and embeds *Pierre* in a long

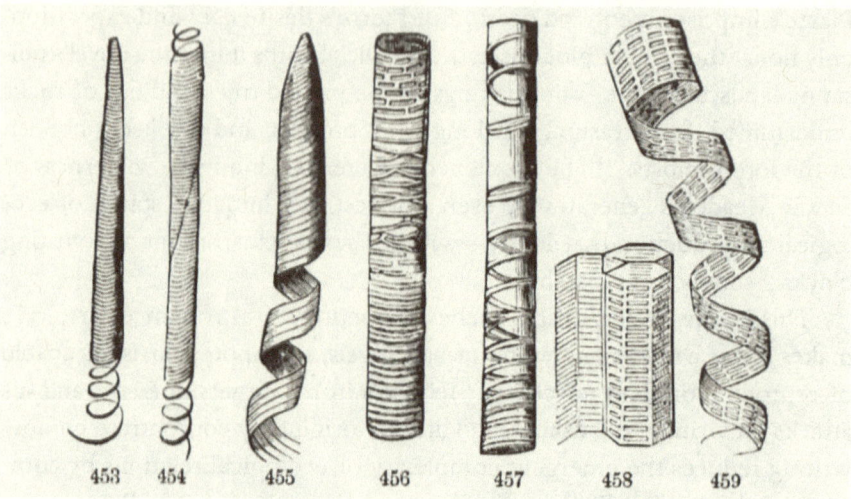

Spiral and scalariform ducts, from Asa Gray, *The Elements of Botany for Beginners and for Schools*, rev. ed. (New York: Ivison, Blakeman, and Co., 1887), 135. (University of Michigan Library)

history of Western ecoformalism with particular resonance for transatlantic Romanticism. The "spiral tendency in plants," as Goethe called it, provides a fundamental tie between *Pierre* and nineteenth-century European science, figuring Melville's ecologies into the wider pre-Darwinian debates over plant life, vitalism, and recurring aesthetic patterns in Romantic philosophies of nature. But Melville's relationship to Romantic and transcendentalist philosophy is complicated. While he proudly rejected much of the vitalism in Goethe and Emerson, both writers' deep dives into what Emerson termed the "occult relation between man and vegetable" remained subtly influential on Melville.[33] As we will see, botanical spirality becomes an icon of "ever-shifting Nature," as Melville phrased it in *Pierre*, whose cross-scale geometries reflect the patchy, "shifting steady-state mosaics" of ecological processes.[34] *Pierre*'s awareness of morphological change in the forests and fields of Saddle Meadows materializes Melville's lifelong interest in the mosaic qualities of literary inheritance, composition, and reproduction at the center of the practice of writing itself.

The spirals of vegetal life in *Pierre* take their most dramatic form in the image of "moss-turbaned," flower-encrusted Enceladus rising from the Earth before Mount Greylock, but they are equally apparent in the novel's emphasis on more subtle, even microscopic movements—marks, turns, spins—that characterize the most elemental units of ecological patterning.[35] Recent ecologically oriented criticism in the humanities and social sciences has started to think more deeply about how modern emphasis on (and access to) knowledge about planetary spatiality has become decoupled from an emphasis on micro-movements over time. "What if our indeterminate life form was not the shape of our bodies," asks Anna Tsing, "but rather the shape of our motions over time?"[36] This is the ghostly question that Melville answers in *Pierre*'s spiraling imagery and syntaxes that layer and accumulate in the text like "the profuse aerial foliage of a hanging forest."[37] But other questions quickly follow. Is Pierre's downward spiral self-generated? Is it a problem of internal character or external social conditions? Melville takes on classic problems of free will by locating them in the bidirectional ambiguity of the spiral, carving *Pierre* into a form that approximates the "agglutinated fractal universe," as Benoit Mandelbrot would describe it a century later, within the paradoxical simultaneity of the spiral's "ascending" and "descending" cascades.[38]

In the following sections, I trace *Pierre*'s ascending and descending spirals to the novel's most important character, Isabel. Isabel is a woman whose mental life is "all one whirl," a woman whose backstory poses the primary questions of *difference* that preoccupy *Pierre*.[39] Isabel is the epicenter of *Pierre*'s vortex, the vanishing point of what we might call *Pierre*'s spiral ecologies. To create Isabel's character, Melville borrows ideas from Goethean science and European vitalism—with nods to Mary Shelley's *Frankenstein; or, The Modern Prometheus* (1818)—by filtering Isabel's history through imagery of lightning bolts, atmospheric hazes, and the geometric complexities of weird biochemical structures like foam. Isabel, as with Yillah before her and Marianna and Hunilla after, is one of only a handful of female characters in Melville's writing, but these women embolden Melville to integrate his insights on mineral and plant ecologies into larger models of human ecology. As *Pierre*'s botanical focus clarifies Melville's spiral philosophy of organic life—inextricably bound to his philosophies of writing, memory, and difference—readers begin to recognize how Western attention to our species' latent animality might mask not just our minerality or vegetality but also the extent of our relations to the far ranges of nonhuman phenomena. Beyond whales, stones, trees, cats, or snakes, *Pierre* shows us how lightning, vapor, and foam impinge on human dwelling—or "abiding" as Melville calls it—on this multi-existential whirl of a planet.

THE IMMORTAL VIGOR OF PLANTS

Pierre was written after a particularly challenging financial period for the Melville family. Melville freely admitted that the two novels that quickly followed *Mardi*—*Redburn* and *White-Jacket*, both written and published in less than a year—were "done for money" rather than out of "heart" or purely creative drive.[40] These novels were composed under duress. They were not outgrowths of a free-roaming, "organic" imagination. They lacked the complex "metaphysics" and "conic-sections" of *Mardi* that Melville described to British publisher Richard Bentley in 1849.[41] In other words, *Redburn* and *White-Jacket* were not *plant-like* in the Greek sense of the word *psukhe*, meaning "growth itself," blind and purposeless, both promise and danger.[42] Quite the opposite, Melville specifically described the process of writing these two novels as plant *destroying*. He was by economic necessity "forced into it, as other men are to sawing wood" (he later complained that he had written *Redburn* just "to buy some tobacco with").[43] So, after the failure of science-rich *Mardi*, it is not surprising that *Redburn* and *White-Jacket* contain comparatively few references to scientific ideas at all.[44]

But by 1850, Melville had secured enough money to feed his family and buy Arrowhead Farm in western Massachusetts, finding once again "the silent grass-growing mood in which a man *ought* always compose."[45] Returning to the compositional mood of *Mardi*, Melville was free to contemplate how human and ecological creativity converged, how literary and environmental forms outgrow the molds of narrative convention or geometric idealism in which we seek to contain them. After 1850, Melville's arboreal rhetoric appears more often and in denser, tangled configurations. In *Moby-Dick*, for example, Ishmael compares his narrative to an oak tree: "Out of the trunk, the branches grow; out of them, the twigs. So, in productive subjects, grow the chapters."[46]

Although there are plenty of references to plant life in the early novels—such as the "wilderness of vines" in *Typee* or the conservation and sustainability of the Tahitian "cocoa-palm" in *Omoo*—the midcareer triad of *Moby-Dick*, *Pierre*, and *The Piazza Tales* represent Melville's most sustained interrogation of plant life until the unpublished *Weeds and Wildings* at the very end of his life.[47] Staying with *Moby-Dick* for a moment, it is hard to ignore how descriptions of flora sneak in amid the novel's famous homages to charismatic megafauna including whales, squid, and octopi. Ahab's beard, for instance, is gnarled as "unearthed roots of trees blown over, which still grow idly on at naked base, though perished in the upper verdure."[48] In the transformative, "soggy, squitchy" world of *Moby-Dick*, right whales turn into oak trees, and paddles of whaling boats are reduced to their composite material: "white ash" oars that propel the hunt.[49] On the *Pequod*, it takes plants to make humans more animal than animals. Then there's Fedallah—described as a "gamboge ghost," pigmented yellow from the resin of Southeast Asian evergreens—who sees the right whale's oaken form in his own tree-tinted hand: "Fedallah was calmly eyeing the right whale's head, and ever and anon glancing from the deep wrinkles there to the lines in his own hand."[50] (Fedallah also delivers to Ahab his mortal botanical prophecy: "Hemp only can kill thee.")[51] Slipping from tree to man to whale, Ishmael's depictions of the *Pequod* and its crew find correspondences between foreheads and flora, palms and plains, human bodies and grasslands. American prairies become vast seas of "flowery earth," and upon them "you will often discover images as of the petrified forms of the Leviathan partly merged in grass, which of a windy day breaks against them in a surf of green surges."[52] The latent symmetry between America prairie and Pacific wave unexpectedly appears in the *greenness* of organic life, the color of vegetal growth that entombs ancient whale fossils yet bends to the slightest afternoon breeze.

Writing to Hawthorne in 1851, Melville described himself growing to that same "greenness" as his literary life matured from seed to flower: "I am like one of those seeds taken out of the Egyptian Pyramids, which, after being three thousand years a seed and nothing but a seed, being planted in English soil, it developed itself, grew to greenness, and then fell to mould . . . I feel that I am now come to the inmost leaf of the bulb, and that shortly the flower must fall to the mould."[53] This revealing passage offers a way to understand the pervasive "greenness" of Melville's thinking during the early 1850s, and it also parallels the narrator's depiction of Pierre after reading Isabel's letter: "But though through many long years the henbane showed no leaves in his soul; yet the sunken seed was there: and the first glimpse of Isabel's letter caused it to spring forth, as by magic."[54] In both cases, the "magic" of germination activates dormant desires and hidden insights that blossom into novels or restore familial bonds. Twinning literary activities (reading and writing) with ecological ones (germination and flowering), Melville allies time with growth in the "flowering" of complex phenomena. Subtending our animal natures, the spiraling botanical world showed Melville a more pliable and capacious model to represent the complexities of inter- and intra-human patterns of meaning that shape life, ecologically and socially. And if we track our botanical entanglement back to its ultimate source, we realize that all our linguistic metaphors and literary forms are, at root, analogies that enable us to accept the incomprehensible luminescence of our sun. By extension, every metaphor is also a metaphor for the vegetal origins of life made possible by solar illumination. Metaphor is (photo)synthetic; story is (phyto)metaphoric. Plants absorb sunlight and reflect near-infrared light; metaphors absorb two semantic fields and reflect a new, synthetic meaning. The paradigm of vegetation is the paradigm of metaphor and storytelling: in a word, greenness.

In fact, the word "green" appears more than thirty times in *Pierre*. The very first sentence of the novel describes a city-sojourner "wonder-smitten with the trance-like aspect of the green and golden world" of Saddle Meadows, foreshadowing a longer meditation on the color green a few pages later: "nothing can more vividly suggest luxuriance of life, than the idea of green as a color; for green is the peculiar signet of all-fertile Nature herself."[55] Jennifer Greiman has argued that Melville's reading of Goethe's *Theory of Colours* (1810)—translated into English by Charles Locke Eastlake in 1842—before writing *Moby-Dick* influenced the various color motifs in that novel, most dramatically in the "Whiteness of the Whale" chapter. Greiman notices the color green present as far back as the first paragraph of *Typee* and claims that, for Melville, green is correlated with bodily comfort, "fellow-feeling," natural freedom, and democratic liberty.[56] Green, she writes, is "the color that links revolution to its repetitions and reversals."[57] The spiraling "greenness" of ecological life is therefore a window into eighteenth- and nineteenth-century Euro-American political upheavals over freedom, luxury, and fertility that, at the same time, carry over into the literary domain. Because we live amid nearly infinite "photochemical intra-actions" that regulate how we perceive one another, Heather I. Sullivan reminds us that color and light unexpectedly illuminate discourses of politics, ethics, and even literary narrative.[58]

But if we conclude that the greenness of *Pierre* fits neatly with Melville's description of his "greening" literary talent, we miss a crucial part of the metaphor. After germination and flowering of the seed, though "the inmost leaf of the bulb" remains, the decay begins. Once-blossoming life starts falling "to the mould." Melville's senescent characterization of a writing career falling "to the mould" opens an entirely new bond between ecology and writing in the mysterious world of mycology, the study of fungi. Melville's invocations of "mould" in his letter to Hawthorne and in other places between 1851 and 1856 should not be dismissed as a simple analogies for Melville's dwindling popularity. Fungi play fascinating, albeit minor, roles in Melville's major works, usually as signs of the processes of decay that are entwined with greenness and that, in fact, make greenness possible.

In nineteenth-century America, mycology was barely studied—the field as a whole was developing almost exclusively in Europe in the late decades of the nineteenth century—and when it was taken seriously, the science of fungi was relegated to a minor subfield of botany. So, in Melville's day, "mould" became a catchall category for fungi, moss, and slime. As Melville writes in "The Encantadas," all kinds of "fungous things" could be easily collated as one "sooty moss."[59] Today we recognize that fungi are actually less plant-like and more animal-like than we ever imagined. But Melville's mention of fungi is significant because most plants *do* have some association with fungi, whether endophytic or endomycorrhizal. As Anna Tsing puts it, "fungi and plant roots become intimately entangled. . . . Neither the fungus nor the plant can flourish without the activity of the other."[60] A fungus "makes worlds for others" by forming underground networks between plants and providing calcium, nitrogen, potassium, phosphorus, and other minerals.[61] The fungus resists classical Linnaean forms of Enlightenment taxonomy and, in this way, becomes a perfect representation of the "purpleness of hidden life" that haunts the celebrated greenness visible to us. The intimacy between the "purpleness" of buried fungal networks and the greenness of vegetal and social life is apparent in Melville's references of fungi in *Moby-Dick* and *Pierre*. In *Moby-Dick*, "the smitten tree gives birth to its fungi," while in *Pierre*, American landowners are perishable "as stubble, and fungous as the fungi, those grafted families successively live and die on the eternal soil of a name."[62] Fungi's challenge to taxonomy makes that which rots, decomposes, and deforms much more important in the ecological schemes that fill Melville's midcareer writings. In *Mardi*, Taji points out that the ocean ebbs and flows with "decomposed animal matter" and that the luminous "phosphorescence" of the sea may be caused by "myriads of microscopic mollusca" that "kindle fire in the brine."[63] In *Moby-Dick*, the "slobgollion" Ishmael describes in the "Squeeze of the Hand" chapter is "an ineffably oozy, stringy affair," inviting us to look at "the wonderously thin, ruptured membranes" of the world, always bursting and "coalescing."[64]

Melville's attention to spiraling, bursting, coalescing ecologies that cross plant-animal-fungal divisions also produces his most trenchant critiques of American society and the increasingly intrusive regimes of biopolitical power that molded it in the nineteenth century. In this sense, we are only now catching up with the implications of Melville's visionary political ecologies. Indeed, recent scholarship working at the intersection of biopolitics, critical plant studies, and new materialism has begun to reimagine the ways in which the philosophical frameworks of modernity from Foucault onward have relied almost exclusively on animality as the paradigm of the biopolitical. For example, Cary Wolfe's *Before the Law* (2013), Jeffrey Nealon's *Plant Theory* (2015), and Francesco Vitale's *Biodeconstruction* (2018) offer fresh looks at the material conditions of biopower in order to account for the multiplicity of organic and inorganic spheres that shape our conceptions of *bios* and *polis*. Nealon, for example, argues that plant life is essential for understanding the biopolitical discourses that scaffold and support structures of power precisely because it has, historically, been excluded and neglected. Somehow, we can't easily think about our relations to plants as easily as we can to animals or other humans.

Melville's enduring contribution to biopolitical critique may not appear in his more obvious commitments to mapping the etiology of slavery ("Benito Cereno") or short-circuiting the logic of capitalist labor regimes ("Bartleby"). What if, instead, Melville's ecoformalist techniques—the mineral cluster in *Mardi*, the plant spiral in *Pierre*, the honeycomb in *The Piazza Tales*—more incisively diagnose the interfaces between sameness and difference that organize ecological complexity, literary creativity, and biopolitical discourse? In the following sections, I examine how Melville's interest in the intersection of the organic and the inorganic in *Pierre* constitutes an extended contemplation of the aesthetic patterns that result from the residues of these intersections. For Melville, a transorganic philosophy of life is discernable in the curvilinear arcs of the spiral: a model of the biosocial and biopolitical complexities of planetary ecology across numerous subfields and areas of study.

SPIRAL TENDENCIES

Today we understand that ecological systems work in ever-evolving sequences that cannot be perfectly conceptualized in tidy phases. Instead, open geometrics like spirals more accurately represent how river nutrients cycle or how extinction itself occurs in a kind of "vortex" accelerant pattern of contingent factors.[65] In *Pierre,* the figure of the spiral functions narratively in exactly this way. The spiral provides the novel a network of "open" geometries, operating at several levels simultaneously. This includes the environmental imagery of Saddle Meadows—whose summer fields "spin themselves green carpets"—as well as Melville's frustratingly snarled syntax and the confusing plot.[66] At the same time, the spiral also captures the experience of reading the novel, the feeling that chasing *Pierre's* convoluted mysteries might only "lead us on in barren mazes."[67]

Like many nineteenth-century intellectuals, Melville recognized that spirals featured prominently in the long history of human fascination with recurring patterns in nature. From Plato, Pythagoras, and Empedocles to Fibonacci and Leonardo Da Vinci, distichous (corn), whorled (mint), and spiral (ivy) patterns have sparked philosophies of life and art all the way back to antiquity. As Nico Israel reminds us in his book *Spirals: The Whirled Image in Twentieth-Century Literature and Art* (2015), the Latin *spiralis* is "cognate with the Greek *speira,* an everyday word describing anything wound, coiled, or wrapped around," and from the pre-Socratics to the Romantics the spiral was "the organic principle par excellence."[68] But in the eighteenth century, the spiral took on new meanings to symbolize the anxieties of modernity and the unintended consequences of early globalization pathways. A sign of the elegance of nature, sure. But the spiral also became more and more freighted in the revolutionary discourse of late eighteenth-century politics. At first, Descartes's equiangular spiral was adopted as a model for symmetry in nature and art. Then it offered a model for the cyclical nature of history. By the early nineteenth century, the spiral had transformed into both metaphor and mode for various strands of European philosophy. Thought itself was theorized as "an organic spiral-shaped striving on the way to resolution," an idea that features in Hegelian dialectics, gets deployed much differently in Marx's thoughts on capital, and operates within Nietzsche's critique of metaphysics.[69] And sometimes, as in the case of Goethe, the repeating spiral patterns in the natural world provided the basis for a romanticist philosophy of growth.

Goethe's attempt to characterize plant morphology via the spiral was one of the first projects in modern life sciences to see the aesthetic beauty of plant life as more than mere ornamentation. Writing to botanist E. H. F. Meyer on June 21, 1831, Goethe exclaimed that he was obsessively "absorbed by the vortex of the spiral tendency."[70] We now know that more than 80 percent of the 250,000 species of higher plants—99 percent of the eukaryotic planetary biomass—demonstrate "spiral phyllotaxis," repeating spirals called *parastichies* that can be mathematically modeled by the Fibonacci series ($F_n = F_{n-1} + f_{n-2}$). But even more importantly, spiral phyllotaxis relates to a decisive concept in ecological theory. According to complexity theorist Brian Goodwin, phyllotaxis can show us how "spatial order arises with temporal order," and how "similar patterns of activity can arise in systems that differ greatly from one another in their composition and in the nature of their parts."[71] The same spiral phyllotaxis is visible, for example, in the muscle formation of the human heart and in the patterning of cellular slime mold colonies like *dictyostelium discoideum*. Exactly a century after *Pierre* was published, mathematician and computing pioneer Alan Turing struggled to produce a more refined mathematical basis of phyllotaxis in "The Chemical Basis of Morphogenesis" (1952), and a year earlier, Soviet chemist Boris Belousov theorized the basis for non-equilibrium thermodynamics by showing how some chemical systems can evolve chaotically without achieving equilibrium by maintaining spiral patterns (known as Belousov-Zhabotinsky reactions). These systems create complex self-organizing spiraling arrays that resemble phyllotaxis at the molecular level.

Part of our continued attraction to the spiral is its ambivalent direction, at once a representation of descent as much as ascent. The spiral resists quick attempts to capture its trajectory, forcing the viewer to shuttle between coiling to a point (death) and expanding into infinity (life). It is not surprising, then, that the descending/ascending ambiguity of the spiral reproduces the affective experience of gothic literature, trafficking as the genre does in extreme states of mind and the unsettling, ambiguous sensation of being between two conditions at once. The "feelings frequently associated with the spiral—flying, falling, drowning, or being smothered—are the anxieties of limit," Israel writes, "psychical and perceptual."[72] Similarly, Jeffrey Jerome Cohen has argued that limits are thresholds to the monstrous: to the grotesque figure in art, literature, and film that "offers an escape from [the human's] hermetic path, an invitation to explore new spirals, new and interconnected methods of perceiving the world."[73]

As revolutionary turmoil in late eighteenth-century Europe expressed itself in narratives of ruined abbeys and other crumbling sites of religious and political authority, American gothic writers experimented with anxieties of the limit while also thinking about the linkages between historical consciousness and natural patterns in the burgeoning life sciences. This is why we see spirals so often in early American writing, particularly in writers such as Charles Brockden Brown and Edgar Allan Poe. Most famously, Emerson relies on circular and spiral imagery to craft his transcendentalist subject. For Emerson, "Man is a self-evolving circle," a mere part of nature's "subtle chain of countless rings" that appear in "spires of form."[74] But early American literature even draws on the spiral for narrative *structure*. Think, for instance, about the circular organizations of Brown's *Edgar Huntly* (1799) and *Arthur Mervyn* (1799) or Poe's mysterious chasms and whirlpools at the end of *Arthur Gordon Pym* (1838) and "A Descent into the Maelström" (1841). In Brown and Poe, the spiral operates as plot device and trope for the limits of human-nonhuman relations. Antebellum readers were thus already prepared for the ending of *Moby-Dick,* when the Pequod yields to "one vortex" that sucks the ship, the sailors, and the casks of oil into the depths of a rolling, endless sea.[75]

In *Pierre*, the spiral is the organizing principle of the entire narrative. At the level of plot, Pierre's primary decision is whether to uphold the name of his dead father and preserve the secret of his half-sister Isabel. But this local family crisis soon gets larger, affecting networks of characters and communities so that Pierre's "vertigo" begins to stand in for wider patterns.[76] These patterns depict "history in incremental spiral, the generations past preparing a context for generations future," Milton Stern writes, that equally applies to literary genealogies and artistic influence.[77] As Melville unfolds Pierre's story, he melds scenes of painting (Pierre Sr.'s portrait) and sculpture (the marble descriptions of Isabel and Lucy) alongside literary allusions that reduce Pierre to a blend of classical Greek myths, Dantean visions of hell's spirals, and Hamletian dead-ends. More explicitly, the narrator compares the reader's descent into Pierre's dark heart with the "spiralness" of a staircase: "Deep, deep, and still deep and deeper must we go, if we would find out the heart of a man; descending into which is as descending a spiral stair in a shaft, without any end, and where that endlessness is only concealed by the spiralness of the stair, and the blackness of the shaft."[78] Echoing Emerson in "Experience" (1844)—we find ourselves in "a series, of which we do not know the extremes, and believe that it has none"—this passage can be read as a synecdoche for *Pierre*, a novel that conceals the "endlessness" of our species' ecological relations by foregrounding a twisty domestic plot that distracts us with "the spiralness of the stair."[79] In this sense, Sam Otter has argued, *Pierre* is not a parody of a sentimental novel; it is "a sentimental text taken to the nth degree."[80] Here Otter draws on polynomial mathematics to describe how *Pierre* magnifies the sentimental genre, but as he does, he outlines the logarithmic spiral structure of the novel as a whole. Read in terms of Pierre's itineraries, the novel spatially maps its internal spiral form. In the early chapters, for example, Pierre shuttles between familiar local sites of Saddle Meadows—back and forth from Pierre's mansion to Lucy's house or the sewing party—while in later chapters he moves in wider circles through the forest, to Isabel's house, and eventually to lower Manhattan and the ne plus ultra of the subterranean prison cell.

But if "spiralness" organizes the geometric forms of Melville's midcareer, I read *Pierre* as an investigation into what motivates the curve of the spiral itself: the more fundamental movement of rotation or spin, *turning* or *spinning*. The word "turning" has multiple valences in the novel, especially in Isabel's story. In the dense textual landscape of *Pierre,* the plot turns on ambiguous words and unspoken secrets, but Melville usually uses "turn" to mean *transform*—for example, when Pierre imagines how Isabel's face "might turn white marble into mother's milk"—or *eventuate,* as in the narrator's rebuke of Pierre early in the novel: "how sheepish now will ye feel when this tremendous note will turn out to be an invitation."[81] Then again, "turn" can also indicate temporal *sequence* ("it is my turn, sweet Isabel, to bid thee speak to me") as well as spatial *movement* ("Why turn thy face from me?").[82] Thinking spatially and geometrically about *Pierre,* the reader is suddenly struck by the simplest movements of the novel. Turns become spins and then spirals. *Pierre*'s turns approximate the psyche of a literary character's descent into poverty and death *and* the transformative qualities of organic life more generally.

Because Pierre's story is one of entangling revelations—"complicating knots" and "inextricable twist[s] of fate"—*Pierre*'s calamitous plot unstitches other meanings of entanglement with implications not just for literary expression but for the material relations that make them possible.[83] Meeting the universe halfway, as Karen Barad would have it, means thinking less vaguely about Deleuzean becoming and more precisely about *turning* and *spinning* as movements of entanglement, both of which are fundamental to the poetics of *Pierre*. Furthermore, Richard Grusin reminds us that "turn" comes from the Greek word for *rotation*—of a wheel or a planet—which carries ethical implications. The movement *of* the turn corresponds with waiting *for* one's turn, one's "obligation to serve."[84] Finally, of course, in a literary sense "turn" means to swerve away from the literal into the figurative. Turning is the principle of metaphor in the (green) origin of storytelling. As in the photosynthetic operations of a leaf, literary fiction reveals a world turned and made otherwise. *Pierre*'s plot turns, and its readers become more attuned to its botanical poetics of spiraling growth, the elemental movements through which we apprehend ecological difference.

From our vantage point in the twenty-first century, *Pierre*'s spirals also prompt us to speculate about how vegetal spiral tendencies resemble the spin that characterizes the strange quantum world beneath all forms of matter. At the quantum level, contemporary physics has shown that matter must be understood in dynamic geometric positions, in elusive patterns of rotation that appear, for example, in vector spaces called *spinors*.[85] Obviously, Melville and his contemporaries could never fathom the advances of Euclidean geometry—based on the development of linear and multilinear algebras in the late nineteenth century—that would lead to our understanding of how geometric position relates to the properties of matter. It is worth noting, however, that American mathematics made significant strides in Melville's lifetime, often with bearing on Melville's favorite literary themes (Harvard mathematician John Farrar once called math "God's grammar").[86] Melville scholar Zachary Turpin has gone so far as to suggest that Melville's "direct engagement with the philosophy of mathematics" is visible in his use of mathematical variables as emblems of ambiguous unknowns, as metaphors "for signs that seem to offer meaning even as they remain impenetrable."[87] For example, *Pierre*'s narrator describes Pierre as "an algebraist," who "for the real Lucy" had "substituted but a sign—some empty x—and in the ultimate solution of the problem, that empty x still figured; not the real Lucy."[88] But if this passage is about how we too easily abstract tidy signs from the messiness of social relations (Lucy hollowed into an empty variable, some "empty x"), it is equally about how equation and metaphor are unnervingly similar operations. What if mathematical phrases and literary tropes only *seem* like incommensurable idioms but are, in fact, grounded in the same analytics of opposition and translation? Perhaps it is only a matter of position, of which variables we solve for and which ambiguities we leave open. Perhaps in *Pierre,* as one critic mused in his 1852 *Literary World* review, Melville "may have constructed his story upon some new theory of art to a knowledge of which we have not yet transcended."[89] Might the emphasis on force, drive, and spin in geometry and physics disclose certain essential movements and differential matrices that undergird both ecology and literary form? Recent work in neuroscience appears to bear this idea out, posing a geometric basis of thought that provides a "continuous map of experience" in multidimensional cognitive spaces via grid cells in the Hippocampus.[90]

Relatedly, some of the most staggering advances in nineteenth-century American science were possible through the application of mathematics to physical phenomena. For instance, Tennessee schoolteacher William Ferrel's "Essay on the Winds and Currents of the Ocean" (1856)—a debunking of Matthew Maury's slipshod *Physical Geography of the Sea* (1855)—proved that the Earth's rotation was a key driver of wind patterns and ocean currents. Ferrel went on to found the field of geophysical fluid dynamics and used mathematical physics to advance meteorology.[91] Ferrel and others recognized that *force* could be modeled, that phenomena are driven and whirled into existence, and that ecological patterns divulge nature's "schemes" as the residues of force, spin, and spiral. Or, as Melville would phrase it in his poem "Conflict of Convictions" from *Battle Pieces*:

> The Ancient of Days forever is young,
>   Forever the scheme of Nature thrives;
> I know a wind in purpose strong—
>   It spins *against* the way it drives.[92]

While *Mardi* and *Moby-Dick* remind us of Nature's forever thriving schemes—the persistent "aesthetics in all things"—*Pierre* suggests that there is a limit to what literary form can capture. In *Pierre*, life resists representation.

Pierre examines the places where life turns away from capture, where the geometric complexity of ecological truth evades our species' grasp and where, as Max Planck would later phrase it, science "cannot solve the ultimate mystery of Nature . . . because in the last analysis we ourselves are part of the mystery we are trying to solve."[93] This is why, at times, Pierre's narrator verges on absolute relativism in his descriptions of "Nature." "Nature" becomes simply "the mere supplier of that cunning alphabet, whereby selecting and combining as he pleases, each man reads his own peculiar lesson according to his own peculiar mind and mood."[94] Yet this blurring of the natural and the textual surpasses naive relativism and moves in the direction of early twentieth-century physics à la Heisenberg, Schrodinger, Dirac, and Bohr. These trailblazing physicists pushed the field toward a theory of *complementarity*, the idea that "there is no reality until that reality is observed, and there are as many realities as observers."[95] If reality resists representation, then we must displace questions about it from domains of knowledge to domains of position.

In the twenty-first century, quantum physics has forced us to accept this elemental ambiguity of existence. We must admit the fact that quantum superposition characterizes a world of "ghostly matter," Karen Barad's phrase for the hauntological materialism that pervades the universe.[96] Is it possible that our contemporary understanding of (super)position is perceptible in the structural asymmetries of *Pierre,* in the profusion of passages about haunting and grief, and in the irregular narrative logic that has frustrated readers for a century and a half? I'm thinking here of how *Pierre*'s narrator circles back in time like a "merry dance," acknowledging to the reader his is an "irregular sort of writing."[97] Working with the slippery rhetoric of absence and presence, Melville crafts a narrative world in *Pierre* where everything is fluid, in process of being converted from one state to another: marble to milk, molten liquid to cast metal, human to plastic. "'Thy hand is the caster's ladle, Pierre,'" Isabel cries, "which holds me entirely fluid. Into thy forms and slightest moods of thought, thou pourest me.'"[98] (In a strikingly similar phrase, earlier in the novel, Isabel proclaims her love to Pierre so strongly that she becomes mere "plastic" in his hands.)[99]

Milk, molten metal, plastic. These fluid conditions oblige us to think not just about transformation but also about containment, forms, and positions. The mother's breast, the caster's ladle, Pierre's molding hands. I'm using "mold" here to mean both molding structure and molded material: the structure used to create certain shapes and the shapes themselves, as when Ishmael compares his first glimpse of Ahab's "high, broad form" to a bronze statue "shaped in an unalterable mould, like Cellini's cast Perseus."[100] And as we saw earlier, "mould" was also a word for fungus in Melville's day, so that "mold" and "mould" double across formal and ecological domains in homonymic elasticity. My reading of *Pierre* starts with the elasticity that typifies reproductive, transformative, creative processes: the tendency to double, turn, and spiral in ecological and literary worlds alike. As *Pierre*'s narrator declares, "This history goes forward and goes backward, as occasion calls. Nimble center, circumference elastic you must have."[101]

ALL IS LEAF

And so we must go back. In this next section, I take a circuitous route, returning to *Mardi* with Goethe's spirals in mind before proceeding to *Moby-Dick* and then, finally, to my reading of *Pierre*. Because, while emphasizing

Melville's geo-mineral imagination in the previous chapter, I intentionally neglected *Mardi*'s abundant references to vines, flowers, and weeds. Babbalanja argues, for example, that man "may be said to be an inferior species of plant" since plants "elegantly inhale nourishment, without looking it up: like lords, they stand still and are served; and though green, never suffer from the colic.... Plants make love and multiply; but excel us in all amorous enticements, wooing and winning by soft pollens and essences. Plants abide in one place, and live: we must travel or die. Plants flourish without us: we must perish without them."[102] "Enough Azzageddi!" cries Media: "Open not thy lips till to-morrow."[103] Beyond the topical jab at Harvard biologist Louis Agassiz, Babbalanja's comments on plant life are significant because they crystalize the origin of Melville's thoughts on vegetal-human relations. When Babbalanja observes the differences between humans and plants—plants flourish without us, whereas our flourishing depends on vegetal life—he contrasts the rooted fertility of plants with the mobile impotence of humans. Plants simply "abide in one place, and live." Although plants do "travel" as species disperse and respond to environmental conditions (which scientists like Humboldt and Asa Gray demonstrated in their work on plant geography), Babbalanja's attitude toward botanical flourishing discloses a more eco-philosophical notion of "abidingness," of dwelling in place.

The relation between flourishing and abiding is precisely what interested Goethe about vegetal life, particularly in *The Metamorphosis of Plants* (1790) and in his botanical journals of Italy between 1786 and 1788 (later published as *Italian Journey* in 1816). Instead of Newtonian abstractions, Goethe wanted a science—most famously, of color—grounded in everyday observation: a science that emphasized *"dwelling in the phenomenon* instead of replacing it with a mathematical representation," to quote Goethe scholar Henri Bortoft.[104] Bortoft writes that "Goethe's approach was to avoid reducing the phenomenon to the mere effect of a mechanism hidden behind the scenes," so that plants, for instance, were understood as holistic and irreducible to their petals, stamens, or roots.[105] Goethe even mused in his *Autobiography* (1811) that perhaps "all plant forms can be derived from one plant."[106] Or as he phrased it in his Italian journals: "All is leaf... and through this simplicity the greatest diversity becomes possible."[107]

Goethe's influence on scientists and artists in the nineteenth century was enormous. In volume 1 of *Cosmos,* Humboldt references Goethe's concept of metamorphosis, glossing it as "that inextricable net-work of organisms by turns developed and destroyed."[108] Goethe pushed the methodologies and languages of Romantic science past the static and the organismic into the processual and the aggregate with phrasings like "being-complex" that would echo in Humboldt's idea of a protoecological "ensemble" (from his 1807 *Essay on the Geography of Plants*).[109] To make sense of these complexes and ensembles, Goethe and Humboldt focused on the abhuman spatiotemporal cycles of plant life, the places and phases away from human spheres of vision, influence, and dominance. In the same *Essay on the Geography of Plants*, Humboldt is fascinated by the "immense space occupied by plants, from the regions of perpetual snows to the bottom of the ocean, and into the very interior of the earth, where there subsist in obscure caves some cryptograms that are as little known as the insects feeding upon them."[110] Though Humboldt's anthropocentric characterization of plants' unreadability circumscribes them within human systems of writing, this idea of cryptogrammatic, obscure plant (and insect) life is something that Melville plays with constantly in *Pierre*. For if the unreadable, secret writing of plants unites the vegetal and the literary—the biotic and the semiotic—then nonhuman writing in not-for-human places demands new ways of reading. Here, Melville and Humboldt align. Both thinkers create their own systems and styles of writing that they then consistently destabilize and undermine, deforming established conventions and genres into new modes of environmental thought.

In his own edition of *Goethe's Autobiography* (1849), Melville underlined Goethe's entry on March 25, 1787, where Goethe reports that, in Naples, "a good insight into botanical matters opened on me. Tell Herder that I am very near finding the primal vegetable type."[111] Goethe's stress on the "primal vegetable type" would have appealed to Melville for a number of reasons, but prominent among them was Goethe's novel way of thinking about "morphology," a term he famously coined from the Greek *morphe*, meaning "shape." For Goethe, *morphe* captures how the multiplicity of difference in vegetal life nonetheless pointed to a "continuity of form" that he called *Urorgan* or *Urpflanze*.[112] But by *Urpflanze*, Goethe didn't have in mind a literal master species in a proto-evolutionary sense. Instead, *Urpflanze* was meant to emphasize *morphe* as the key into the "abidingness" of plants, the spiraling growth of plant ecology. Goethe believed in the "coming-into-being of the plants so deeply that he saw all plants as one plant," Bortoft notes, so Goethe's botanical philosophy centers on the "'possibility of plant' . . . forming itself according to itself" in a process he called "entelechy," with all respect to Aristotle.[113]

Having spent *Mardi* considering change in terms of the gradations and stratifications of geologic time—acknowledging catastrophic events that puncture such periodization—it was not until *Moby-Dick* that Melville turned his attention explicitly to defining change as *growth* or *morphe*. Hershel Parker has claimed that during the composition of *Moby-Dick*, Melville had a rich psychological realization about the power of "morphing" in life, the way that identity and history and place were ceaselessly woven together.[114] Although there is no evidence that Melville read Goethe's botanical masterpiece, *Metamorphosis of Plants*, he owned many of Goethe's major works, and references to Goethe appear throughout his writings.[115] In his copy of Matthew Arnold's *Poems* (1856), for example, Melville wrote: "of Goethe it might also be said that he averted his eyes from everything except Nature, Intellect & Beauty."[116] (The *Penny Cyclopaedia*—so important for Melville's composition of *Mardi*—also contains several pages on the "Spiral Structure in Plants" that reference Goethe and Henri Dutrochet.)[117]

However, Melville's relationship with Goethean ideas was thorny. Melville often mocked "the all-permeating principle to which Goethe and others have subscribed."[118] Most famously, in an 1851 letter to Hawthorne, Melville derided Goethe's supposed pantheism of universal transformation. He rejected the Goethean ethos to *"live in the all"* and its subsequent directive to "get outside of yourself, spread and expand yourself, and bring to yourself the tinglings of life that are felt in the flowers and the woods, that are felt in the planets Saturn and Venus, and the Fixed Stars."[119] "What nonsense!" Melville concluded, for even if there is "some truth" in the *"all feeling,"* the problem is that "men will insist upon the universal application of a temporary feeling or opinion."[120] Ironically, Melville paraphrases Emerson's "The Poet" here, which he had read the year before in Hawthorne's house in Lenox, Massachusetts: "Mysticism consists in the mistake of an accidental and individual symbol for a universal one."[121]

In any case, for Melville metaphysical systems like transcendentalism were untenable because they masked the problem of evil and the persistence of cruelty that signaled irreconcilable differences in human character. Melville pressured the transcendental idealist—"thou inconceivable coxcomb of a Goethe"—to explain the "darkness" that features so prominently in human history and its legacies of violence, destruction, and injustice.[122] In *Pierre*, Melville lampoons Goethe as one of the vain "imposter philosophers" who "pretend somehow to have got an answer," when the only real truth is "profound Silence, that only Voice of our God."[123] "For—absurd as it might seem," the narrator concludes, "men are only made to comprehend things which they comprehended before (though but in the embryo, as it were)."[124] Melville rejected Goethe's vitalism—"the tinglings of life that are felt in the flowers and the woods"—as well as any wholesale "universal" metaphysics that attempted to speak for the absolute "Silence" that pervaded the universe. He heartily believed that there were no new ideas, no truly original thoughts. Only increased awareness, a thought's "embryo" to its flowering, might enable a person to "suddenly become conscious of [Nature's] own profound mystery, and feeling no refuge from it but silence" slowly sink "into this wonderful and indescribable repose."[125]

And yet Melville deploys the rhetoric of Goethe's botanical philosophy in that same critique of the all-permeating "tingling." Discarding its vitalism and metaphysics but retaining its attention to thought as "embryonic"—a term applied to all multicellular eukaryotic organisms, including plants—Melville finds himself subtly directed by Goethe's morphological theory of life. Faced with Goethe's "flummery," Melville admits that "in proportion to my own contact with him, there is a monstrous deal in me."[126] He grants that when "lying on the grass on a warm summer's day," one's "legs seem to send out shoots into the earth. Your hair feels like leaves upon your head."[127] We can see here, from *Mardi* to *Pierre*, how Goethean *morphe* becomes delicately infused in Melville's thinking. It becomes the germ that would embryonically develop Melville's metaphors for literary creation. In "Hawthorne and His Mosses," Melville erotically exclaims: "Hawthorne has dropped germinous seeds into my soul. He expands and deepens down, the more I contemplate him; and further, and further, shoots his strong New-England roots into the hot soil of my Southern soul."[128] America, he counsels, should eagerly await the "full flower" of Hawthorne's genius.

All of this is to say that, between *Mardi* and *Pierre*, Melville was simultaneously working out his relationship to plants, to Hawthorne, and to Goethe. Melville was attracted to the vegetal Goethe, a philosopher not of the "all" but of the "embryo" whose vision of post-Linnaean nature must be seen in formation, in all its living contours. Following Melville scholar Michael Jonik, we should think of Melville's ecological vision similarly: "a multifarious state of conflicting imperatives, a 'not-all' of partialities, emphermeralities, and incompletenesses."[129] Though Melville remained suspicious of metaphysics and binaries, all-permeating principles and easy distinctions, he kept musing, in the 1850s and beyond, about the relations between forms of life and the "worlds" that arise from their contact.

Returning briefly to *Mardi*, we can see one of Melville's earliest meditations on the ecological relations that link various organisms and their environments: an issue that would become central to post-Heideggerian philosophies of nature in the late twentieth century. Deep into the novel, Babbalanja asks Media: "Think you, my lord, there is no sensation in being a tree? feeling the sap in one's boughs, the breeze in one's foliage? think you it is nothing to be a world? one of a herd, bison-like, wending its way across boundless meadows of ether?"[130] This is a decisive moment in *Mardi* and in Melville's career, a moment when Melville takes *Mardi*'s mineral worlds and magnifies them into new vegetal scales and chronologies through the vocabularies of "sensation" and movement that structure domains of life, from pine trees to bison herds to humans. Babbalanja directly asks Media a critical question for the philosophy of ecology: "think you it is nothing to be a world?"

In environmental philosophy, the problem of "worlding" has been, at least since Husserl and Heidegger, designated as an exclusively human enterprise, a lynchpin in discussions of species difference and distinctions between stone, tick, and human.[131] But for Melville, "being a tree" is indeed "being a world." Tree-being is dwelling within and among "wending" forms of "ethereal" life. Tree-sap boughs sensationalize for Melville the abidingness of being *of* and *in* the herd, becoming "herd-like." Melville is not using "herd" here in the negative sense of blind mob-think (as in Kierkegaard and Nietzsche) but instead in its ecological dimension, where herd stands for the aggregation of bodies, movements, crossings that constitute the "boundlessness" of life. "Wending" is how life becomes organized, takes form, is driven and spun. And this articulation of Being's living contours is morphological, Goethean, and Melvillean all at once. "All existence is possible only because bodies are organized," Goethe writes in his "Preliminary Notes for a Physiology of Plants" (1795), and thus bodies "are capable of being organized and preserved in activity, solely through the state we call life."[132] To "world" is to take form, to wend, to cross, and to become animated from within *or* without. Babbalanja continues:

> In the sight of a fowl, that sees not our souls, what are our own tokens of animation? That we move, make a noise, have organs, pulses, and are compounded of fluids and solids. And all these are in this Mardi as a unit. Daily the slow, majestic throbbings of its heart are perceptible on the surface in the tides of the lagoon. Its rivers are its veins; when agonized, earthquakes

are its throes; it shouts in the thunder, and weeps in the shower; and as the body of a bison is covered with hair, so Mardi is covered with grasses and vegetation, among which, we parasitical things do but crawl, vexing and tormenting the patient creature to which we cling. Nor yet, hath it recovered from the pain of the first foundation that was laid . . . To exist, is to be; to be, is to be something: to be something, is—[133]

Babbalanja advocates that life be understood through its "tokens of animation," the movements that make bodies function—pulses, flows, circulations—that are the selfsame motions of the planet writ large: "And all these are in this Mardi as a unit." A quick reading might conclude that Melville is offering anthropomorphic Gaian body-Earth metaphors (river-veins and rain-weeps), but his use of the term "unit" takes this familiar trope into new territory.

In Melville's day "unit" was understood less as vague harmonious whole and more in its mathematical sense: "An instance of oneness or singularity . . . a magnitude of one."[134] Per the *Oxford English Dictionary*, a unit designated an "individual person, thing, or group regarded as single and complete," or, to put it differently, "each of the (smallest) separate individuals or groups into which a complex whole may be analysed."[135] In this sense, the antebellum understanding of "unit" approximates the way twentieth-century complexity theory would model a variety of patterns and behaviors in ecological systems. For complexity theorists, scale—the spatiotemporal dimensions of an object or process—is characterized by *grain* (the smallest homogenous unit of study) and *extent* (the area or time period). Melville's use of "unit" in *Mardi* matches the procedural definition of scale, parametrically determined by grain and extent.[136] The unitary nature of Mardi—its "oneness"—does not mean "wholeness" but instead, strangely, the *obstinacy of difference* as a kind of resistance to wholeness: an "active absence" that characterizes the unit.[137] Mardi's "unit" is a series of thresholds. Distributed "throbbings" through which objects and patterns appear at the boundaries of chaos. I use "chaos" here not in its colloquial meaning but in its technical sense. Chaos, complexity theorist Melanie Mitchell tells us, describes a feature of "dynamical systems with sensitive dependence on initial conditions," producing "mathematical order" that is nonetheless still unpredictable and can generate random behavior.[138]

But representing the objects and patterns that appear in chaotic systems is extremely difficult because, instead of direct correspondences or familiar equations, ecological units are more like "networks with loops."[139] These loop networks are best visualized in four-dimensional "fractal geometries of nature," as Mandelbrot would describe them, that materialize at the outer limits of our perceptive abilities.[140] When Babbalanja claims that Mardi's "rivers are its veins," he directs us to the edges of those fluid images, to the boundaries that determine their form. Babbalanja encourages readers to imagine, as Mandelbrot would do in the 1970s, a "geometry of arteries and veins" that follows the patterns by which "every point in nonvascular tissue should lie on the boundary between the two blood networks."[141] Mardian nature is all geometries, points, boundaries, rivers, and veins. The migratory whales of Mardian seas, "like the silver ore in Peru, run in veins through the ocean."[142] Babbalanja's arterial rhetoric slips between parts and wholes, deconstructing the logic of wholeness that organizes traditional visions of "Nature" and the associated linguistic regimes that make a figure of speech like synecdoche possible. Instead, Melville creates an image that seems anthropocentric but actually glides among forms of life (bison to grassland, artery to whale pod) and among forms of ecological dwelling (from organ to lagoon, human body to mineral seam): a vision of abidingness that maintains the obstinacy of difference.

But, and this is critical, by extending relations, tracing veins, and collapsing wholeness, Melville is not flattening all differences into a monadic ontology, a trap that new materialism—in its exuberance for a corrective disanthropocentrism—sometimes falls into. Melville wants to remind us of the uneven distribution of agency in ecological systems. Sidestepping the tendency toward leveling all differences, ecocritic Hannes Bergthaller has drawn on twenty-first-century systems theory to distinguish between allopoietic systems (systems that cannot reproduce, as in mineral clusters) and autopoietic systems, wherein reproduction depends on *"self-organization . . . predicated on self-limitation."*[143] Autopoeisis refers to an *"operationally closed"* system that reproduces itself by differentiating "between itself and its environment, between inside and outside."[144] But operational closure is simultaneously *"complementary* to energetic or material openness" and thus larger systems of complexity.[145] In other words, Bergthaller argues, the system "creates a boundary between itself and the environment that shuts out the undifferentiated complexity of the environment and allows it to build up ordered complexity within."[146] At their most ecological, Melville's fiction and poetry work at the boundaries, edges, verges, and margins of life forms *while at the same time* being hyperaware of how the creative, energetic, open practice of fiction writing is precisely complementary to the ecological complexity of operationally closed systems. Melville maps ecological autopoiesis through literary poiesis.

Via veins and skins, verges and confines, Melville draws out the parasitic relations among the living and nonliving: the ways that environments and bodies reciprocally invade and remake one another. The human species—"parasitical things . . . vexing and tormenting the patient creature to which we cling"—has permanently altered our bison-Earth by occupying, building, and extracting. The Earth has never "recovered from the pain of the first foundation that was laid," but neither has the human "thing" recovered from its "thingness." Despite our attempts to repress or abject our "thingness," we are nonetheless objects, hosts, and invaded skins. And this is how Melville brilliantly concludes the passage: "To exist, is to be; to be, is to be something: to be something, is—."

Such an obtuse, faux-Hamletism seems at first tautological, silly, pretentious. It intentionally resists paraphrase. It resists summary. Yet its tautological, triadic form calls for us to interpret it, reproduce it, and say it again differently. So let's paraphrase. To exist is to take form, to be *something*. But the result of being some*thing* is inaccessible to language, cut off from it, and in that abrupt severance of syntax we glimpse an openness beyond inscription. This is the ecological open, the dehiscent range of life. A threefold consciousness, wherein formal pattern (*some:* adjective), material part (*thing:* noun), and processual unit (*being:* verb) are grasped together as the paradigm of the ecological. Melville's genius is the construction of the sentence that tries to do the grasping. It is iterative and incomplete, each phrase retaining part of the last. More precisely, this retentional iteration—apparent in both Melville's syntax and his meaning—*takes the form of the spiral.* It constitutes the "germ-life," as Pierre puts it, of Melville's philosophy of *bios*.[147]

In Babbalanja's description, Melville's grammar modulates Mardi's "pulses" with commas and extends its "throbbings" with semicolons, guiding the reader through the grasses and vegetation that cover Mardi just like "the body of a bison is covered with hair." Life on Mardi, like the writing of *Mardi,* exists by repetition and retention, or what Derrida would famously term "trace" through "différance," both difference and deferral.[148] Barad would later elaborate on how différance operates in the quantum realm, concluding that "diffraction patterns—as patterns of difference that make a difference—[must] be the fundamental constituents that make up the world."[149] What distinguishes Melville's philosophy of ecology from twentieth-century work by Husserl and Heidegger is the emphasis on literary form as a mode of thought, on fictionality as a kind of superposition that gives glimpses into the hauntological reality of matter. Nowhere is this idea more present than in *Moby-Dick*, when, at the end of chapter 114 ("The Glider") an ambiguous voice that seems to be Ishmael and Ahab together offers the pervading ethos of the novel: "mingled, mingling threads of life are woven by warp and woof: calms crossed by storms, a storm for every calm. There is no steady unretracing progress in this life; we do not advance through fixed gradations."[150] Unsurprisingly, the master tropes of *Moby-Dick* are ropes, threads, looms, lashings, and mats that come together in the spatial complexities of the *Pequod*'s whale-line. "Spirally coiled . . . [in] layers of concentric spiralizations . . . the whale-line folds the whole boat in its complicated coils," Ishamel tells us, "twisting and writhing around it in almost every direction."[151]

What unites Goethe and Melville (and eventually Derrida and Barad) is the emphasis on spinning and driving, twisting and writ(h)ing: on unsteady, retracing différantial *movement* as the condition for both life and literature. For Goethe, the "spiral tendency" is constantly "expressing itself in windings, crooks, and twists."[152] For Melville, the "tokens of animation" that characterize Mardi's ecology are "slow, majestic throbbings." For Derrida—building on Freud's sense of inertia or "drive" as he called it in *Project for a Scientific Psychology* (1895)—structures in nature and language must not be understood statically but as ongoing magnitudes of "force."[153] Spiral, throb, force. Metamorphosis cannot be properly comprehended by looking at singular organisms in a given space. Instead, *morphe* can only be seen as force registered in transorganismic movement. Wendings, spirals, throbs. For Goethe, the "true Proteus" is the plant, which "is nothing but leaf," absolute *morphe*.[154] Goethe concludes that "a general spiral tendency . . . in combination with a vertical force" creates "all plant structures" through "vertical and spiral systems."[155] Referencing *oscillaria* (or *oscillatoria*, microscopic flowering algae) and *convolvulus* (a flowering weed "climbing in spirals"), Goethe translates Dutrochet's principle of *"vital incurvation"* into a full-blown theory of nature.[156] When Darwin took up the spiral tendency in his own treatise *The Power of Movement in Plants* (1880)—he called it "circumnutation"—he reconciled morphological spin with the drive of evolutionary progress, endlessly unsteady and retracing.[157] As Robert Richards phrases it, by the end of the nineteenth century, Darwinian "evolutionary theory was Goethean morphology running on geological time."[158]

Looking back at Goethean morphology through the prism of Darwinian evolution, we can see how Goethe's spiral-botanical vision widens to accommodate *abiotic* influences and the weathering processes that lead to destruction, ruin, and decay. In Goethe's example, the birch tree "grows spirally upward," but "weather, wind, rain, and snow have great influence on the development of the spiral movement."[159] The principle of spiral-*morphe* thus represents not just the persistence of *bios* but also the disintegrating force of *abios*. On this generalized spiral form of a/biotic metamorphosis, Goethe notes its tensions specifically in terms of *force:* "The concept of metamorphosis is a highly estimable gift from above, but at the same time a highly dangerous one. It leads to formlessness, destroys knowledge, disintegrates it. It is like centrifugal force and would lose itself in the infinite if a counterweight were not provided. I am referring to the specification force, that tenacious capacity for persistence inherent in whatever has attained existence, a centripetal force that cannot be disturbed in its deepest nature by anything external."[160] Goethe's language here—the "centrifugal" and "centripetal" spiral forces of metamorphosis—anticipates Darwinian evolution by suggesting that, on the one hand, life is "development *from within toward without*," but on the other, is also development "*from without toward within*."[161] Life is not just the product of random mutations or natural selections that solve particular environmental problems. Daniel Smail explains that this view gives the "illusion of teleology" because "ongoing selection pressures, coupled with biochemical and morphological constraints, squeeze adaptations down relatively narrow and often converging pathways."[162] Rather, the elegance of life demands that we account for multiple solutions converging at once, in what Wendy Wheeler terms *"repetition with difference,"* or the spiral structure of evolutionary capacitance.[163] Evolutionary robustness—Conrad Waddington called it *canalisation* in epigenetic landscapes—is in this sense a measure of Goethean metamorphosis: the forces spiraling life centripetally, adaptatively ordered, in concert with the forces spiraling life centrifugally, mutatively disordered.

Might we characterize the language and imagery of *Moby-Dick*, for instance, in precisely this way? When "death whirls round the corpse" of a rotting whale or when Ishmael notices a sea hawk "spiralize downwards" to steal Ahab's hat, Melville turns to the spiral to align disparate ecological phenomena—rotting whale corpse, diving sea hawk—across the same geometric movements.[164] This is also how Ishmael describes whales throughout the novel. Their tails are "scroll-wise coiled," their intestines involuted like "great cables and hausers coiled" under deck. All the while, above deck, the *Pequod*'s crew stand ready to cut into the whale, ready for "spiralizing" and "coiling" its blubber.[165] Observing the "crescentric" form of whale pod in the Java Sea, Ishmael watches how these stunning creatures make "vast irregular circles" and quickly become "a delirious throb . . . in more and more contracting orbits."[166] Even the word "whale" itself has a spiral etymology, derived from the Danish *hval*, or "rolling."[167] Method and metonym for philological history, the spiral can be ultimately understood as a kind of "*ur*-writing," that, for Melville, connects the etymologically haunted practice of composing novels with the spiral movements of the organisms that metaphorically populate (and materially compose) their pages.[168]

At the most general level, then, spirals recur in philosophy, science, and design because they enact the motion and symmetry necessary to understand the "natural" within geometric forms. In the twentieth century, spirals appeared in the greatest scientific advancements of modernity: the discovery of spirochaete bacteria that causes syphilis, Hubble's observations of the swirling Milky Way, and Watson and Crick's double-helix model. Way back in the 1850s, Melville was representing the complexity of life in fiction by posing a conceptual ecology of emergence that bound biological reproduction to the reproductive impulses of art and technology. To explore this astonishing project in more depth, we need to retrace our steps back to Pierre's dream of "American Enceladus." The phrase is a reference to the Greek myth of the Giant who fought the Olympian gods, lost, and was buried under Mt. Etna. Enceladus, so the story goes, is eternally struggling to free himself from his earthy prison so he can ascend to his rightful spiritual plane once more. In "American Enceladus" Melville brings together two terms—one national and one mythic, one modern and one ancient—that conjure a bizarre image of a Greek god crawling out from the rocky landscape of upstate New York. Like Isabel, Enceladus is a vanishing point for many of *Pierre*'s spirals, and critics have argued that "the novel's central figures can be arranged in concentric circles emanating from the hub of the Enceladus vision."[169] The Enceladus dream—"the *mise en scene* of Pierre's emotional life," according to Jonik—is the most concentrated example of how Melville uses plants, metamorphosis, and (a)biotic force to approach the immensity of ecological relations, or what he calls the "cunning purpleness of hidden life."[170]

AMERICAN ENCELADUS

The image of "American Enceladus" appears at the end of *Pierre,* when, reduced by fate and fortune to an "iron-framed fiery furnace of a body," Pierre stumbles through the streets of New York City and eventually passes out in a gutter. The next day, he enters a "state of semi-unconsciousness," wherein "a remarkable dream or vision came to him." Pierre dreams of a "phantasmagoria of the Mount of the Titans" amid "the grand range of dark blue hills encircling his ancestral manor" at Saddle Meadows.[171] All of a sudden—taking the past tense, second-person point of view—the narrator addresses the reader directly: "You saw Enceladus the Titan, the most potent of all the giants, writhing from out the imprisoning earth;—turbaned with upborne moss."[172]

Enceladus rising from the American landscape can be read at several levels. Most obviously, Enceladus is Pierre. Both are ambitious and then shamed for it; both are undone by their desire to reorder the given state of their birth. Enceladus is also a dark double of Prometheus who, like Pierre and Ahab, is punished for his overreach, and the "natural" order is restored. But in *Pierre,* Melville does not draw on Prometheus, whose punishment for stealing fire from the gods is the daily torture of a liver-eating bird. Instead, Melville uses Enceladus, the "tiger-passion'd, lion-thoughted" Enceladus of Keats's *Hyperion* (1820), a figure with fierce eyes that inspire the courage of resistance. Still, in the end, Enceladus is defeated. He is left a statue of disgrace and helplessness, incest and loss. His punishment is to be stuck in the rocky earth, covered with moss, and defecated on by passing birds. Compared to Prometheus's daily pageantry, the struggle of Enceladus is hidden, forgotten, derided, excremental.

In *Pierre,* Melville translates the social disarray that follows from the revelation of Pierre's mixed genealogical heritage into the material disarray of Enceladus's body (rock, moss, bird shit). As Pierre becomes conscious of his incestuous, genealogical impurities, he becomes conscious of his Enceladean nature: of the inorganic and organic materials that make up his body, undermining all noble endeavors to fully transcend his "earthliness" or make his way out of "the slime."[173] At its core, the myth of Enceladus speaks to the fact that we are all chained to our physical being, despite our constant striving to outlast the inevitable decay of our bodies by having children, by creating monuments, or by writing books. And Pierre completely fails at each of these activities. Procreation becomes incest. Monuments disintegrate into ruins. Books turn to ashes. To forestall these disappointments, Pierre aspires to the "monolithic permanence" of stone, which explains his interest in the Memnon Stone, his identification with Enceladus, his petric proper name, and the opening dedication to a Mount Greylock (the only true "sovereign lord").[174] But these aspirations fail too, and by the end of the novel, Pierre's identity and family structure are totally inverted. His kinship networks are reordered, and the rural geographies of country landscapes (Saddle Meadows) are paved over by cities (New York).

If Enceladus is a metaphor for early America's sense of itself, its developing character and shifting genealogies, it also reflects American anxieties over changes to the physical landscapes wrought by new energy paradigms (coal, oil, electricity) that, as we saw in chapter 1, heralded the manufacturing age and America's rise to global power. In American Enceladus, the shift from ancient Titans to the modern world of Olympian gods parallels the shift from European models of governance to the "democratic," increasingly corporatized political economies of post-Jacksonian America. And Americans, like Enceladus, are always fighting to rise from the dust and ascend to riches: "For it is according to eternal fitness, that the precipitated Titan should still seek to regain his paternal birthright even by fierce escalade. Wherefore whoso storms the sky gives best proof he came from thither! But whatso crawls contented in the moat before that crystal fort, shows it was born within that slime, and there forever will abide."[175] Enceladus is the American resistance to one's given station, a sign of ferocious ambition to move upward in "fierce escalade" toward "that crystal fort" of economic and spiritual ideals. Ancestor to the American mythos of self-reliant individualism, Enceladus remains "unconquerable" and ever struggling in spite of the odds against him. He is a geological manifestation of the American spirit, a bridge between rock and character, ecology and economy. More succinctly, the narrator seems to summarize a certain strand of American libertarianism by saying, basically, "if you're content to be in the slime, you'll abide in the slime."

Winking at a long tradition of Franklin-cum-Emerson bootstrapping and market faith in "merit," as Pierre puts it, Melville fashions his critique of American success myths in writhing stone.[176] The immobilized statue of Enceladus is a monument to the power of American ambition seeking an ancient, paternal birthright in a new world. In the 1840s and 1850s, America needed a reproductive legacy amid political turmoil, shaky markets, and swiftly degrading environments. Enceladus is a representation of how the "uncrystalizing Present," as the narrator of *Pierre* phrases it, is vulnerable to democratic "acid" that oxidizes the past and prohibits a clearly defined future, "forever producing new things by corroding the old."[177] In America, "Death itself becomes transmuted into Life," while in the necropolitical world of *Pierre*, even "Death itself" becomes commoditized, controlled, and made to foster new forms of property relations at the service of a corporate economic system.[178] After his mother dies and leaves her estate to Pierre's cousin Glen, for instance, Pierre is converted from rural landholder to "propertyless renter" in a spiral of property loss that characterized the variable tides of capital exchange in the industrial age.[179]

This was the pattern Marx described in the first volume of *Capital*, where he shows how the logic of capital accumulation moves "on a progressively increasing scale," turning into a "spiral" that shifts the magnitude of capitalist exchange to new scales of exploitation.[180] Capitalist accumulation "passes from the circular to the spiral form" with the rise of joint-stock companies that marked the rapid transformation of the American political economy in Melville's lifetime.[181] For Marx and other radical economists of the nineteenth century, spirals offered a conceptual figure for the ever-productive tendrils of capitalist expansion, linking local communities to global markets and reducing rural New York ecologies to their resource value in international exchanges. In this sense, American Enceladus is a representation of how economic systems fragment individual subjects into commoditized parts, into bits of data given over to corporate entities in spirals of capital accumulation at a global scale.

THE CUNNING PURPLENESS OF HIDDEN LIFE

Despite Enceladus's many meanings in *Pierre* and in antebellum American culture, the real heart of Melville's ecological philosophy takes place elsewhere in Pierre's dream. It coalesces not in the intense image of Enceladus rising but in the earlier descriptions of Mount Greylock and its "hill-side pastures" of amaranth and catnip. In true ecological fashion, Melville's more profound environmental visions are buried in a series of unnecessary and overwrought passages about flowers, rocks, and goats that readers easily skim past. The hiddenness of Melville's ecological project in *Pierre* is, in other words, precisely the hiddenness of planetary ecological relations writ large.

For example, as he contrasts the flora that grow on the hillsides of the mountain, *Pierre*'s narrator observes that the "continually multiplying" growth of wild amaranth was "irreconcilably distasteful to the cattle" and had become the "bane" of the "disheartened dairy tenants" who lived there.[182] But catnip—"that dear farm-house herb"—was continually celebrated by the dairy farmers for its usefulness and beauty. The farmers adore the "green solicitudes of the un-emigrating herb." Catnip is resourceful. It takes root in "old foundation stones and rotting timbers of log-houses long extinct" and flourishes symbiotically with deserted human structures. "Though all that's human forsake the place," the narrator says, "the plant will long abide, long bask and bloom on the abandoned hearth."[183] "The catnip and the amaranth!" he concludes, "man's earthly household peace, and the ever-encroaching appetite for God."[184] For Melville, this casual botanical contrast between catnip and amaranth reveals kinships between plant and human, between abidingness and appetite, between the comfort of the hearth and suicidal Enceladean ambitions.

Critics have usually read the amaranth symbolically, noting similarities in the descriptions of Lucy and Isabel or the amaranth's various economic, political, and religious resonances.[185] In Christian iconography, the amaranth's white flowers are always in bloom, reminders of the immortal flourishing of life in Eden. As Milton phrased it in *Paradise Lost*—a passage that Melville marked in his edition of *The Poetical Works of John Milton* (1836)—"Immortal amarant, a flower which once / In paradise, fast by the tree of life, / Began to bloom."[186] The amaranth has a long history in Anglo-American literature, from Milton and Cowper to James Fenimore Cooper, who references amaranth in a misquotation of Spenser on the title page of the *Littlepage Trilogy* (1845–46): "The only amaranthine flower on earth / is virtue: the only treasure, truth."[187] Paul Royster has pointed out the parallels between the amaranth, an ideal "image of the perpetuity of families and their estates," and the crumbling reality of the Littlepage and Glendinning families in Cooper and Melville's fictionalized 1840s worlds.[188] But considered ecologically, the contrast between the amaranth and the catnip is more complex than mere symbolic binary.

To the human residents of Mount Greylock, the short-lived perennial blooms of amaranth are wild and unproductive, actively retarding the development of agriculture and the tenant economy that depends on it. Whereas catnip is cultivated, pliant, and benign, amaranth flourishes to spite the human population. Because amaranth signifies uncontrollable growth

(growth-not-for-human-benefit), it becomes the ironic, vegetal double of human Enceladean appetites. The anti-human amaranth is thus, paradoxically, a most appropriate icon of the human species: flowering, spreading, covering, altering, making unusable. The amaranth's wild appetite exposes a similar parasitical drive in our species. We make "progress" over the earth in ways that are ultimately against our own species' interest. We hate amaranth because it *is* us. Melville summarizes this weedy prosperity in "Conflict of Convictions" from *Battle-Pieces:*

> The People spread like a weedy grass
>   The Things they will they bring to pass,
> And prosper to the apoplex.[189]

Catnip, on the other hand, is seasonal and predictable: "every autumn it died but never an autumn made the amaranth wane."[190] Catnip is finite, knowable, calendared, domesticated. We cultivate catnip for the security of the domestic that safeguards "man's earthly peace" and our cats' enjoyment. We love catnip because it is not us, yet, like domesticated a cat, relies upon us. In Melville's telling, catnip depends on human dwellings, springing forth from rotting walls, cracks in stone foundations, and fissures in abandoned hearths. The image of a hearth riven with catnip articulates an enduring human fantasy of one-way ecological dependence, a tamed and romanticized symbiosis between plant (or more generally, growth) and human dwelling that stands for broader, exceptionally self-centered relations between human civilization and the planet in the Anthropocene.

But this image is, crucially, positioned on the abandoned hearth. The hearth is the center of the home, the stone alcove for eating, warmth, and gathering in household peace. It is the spatial origin of storytelling. Its disuse and abandonment means the ruin of story that, in the catnip, becomes revived again. Catnip makes life from the death of human story, turns a new leaf, tells a new story of vegetal becoming. Remarkably, in the foothills of Mount Greylock, Melville sees the semiotic and the biological converging in the material space of the hearth, in the space of cinders that constitute the remainder of the Promethean fire. If the "biosphere and the semiosphere are co-extensive," Wendy Wheeler writes, then that co-extensivity becomes only fully visible in the vegetal arrival after the human, in the hearth awaiting the catnip that would never be visible to us, that would remain always hidden.[191] Again, it is this hiddenness—of biosemiotic realities that resist human observation—that characterizes the entire ecological range of Mount Greylock. Contemporary biology is only now catching up with Melville's insight here, as advances in biosemiotics and sensory ecology show the incredible, hidden visual landscapes of animal life (of, for instance, bees that perceive flowers in ultraviolet patterns of rings and starbursts).[192] In an astonishing concluding passage, the narrator tells us: "all here lived a hidden life, curtained by that cunning purpleness, which, from the piazza of the manor-house, so beautifully invested the mountain once called Delectable, but now styled Titanic."[193] Viewed from the piazza of the manor-house, Mount Greylock is a picturesque tableau of "Delectable" beauty. But up close, in all its asymmetrical ecologies, it appears "Titanic" and frenzied, hidden behind curtains of "cunning purpleness." The visual method here is classic Melville, playing perspectives against one another—as he does in more elaborate terms in "The Piazza"—to highlight the instability of human points of view, perspectives reliant on relatively tiny scales subject to constant misjudgments.

In one sense, Pierre's dream of Mount Greylock shows us how little difference there is between our "modern" world and the "mythic" Titanic world of pure transformation and chaos. The narrator explains that the very rocks of Mount Greylock are, Etna-like, constantly in motion. The mountain "insensibly changes its pervading aspect within a score or two of winters . . . annual displacements of huge rocks and gigantic trees were continually modifying its whole front and general contour."[194] Enceladus, who appears soon after this passage, is the ultimate example of the Titanic radiance and power of a world before humans. But such a Titanic world is simply too "violently pitched alive in constant flow to ever be seen by men directly," as Thomas Pynchon would write a century later. We are meant "only to look at it dead, in still strata, transputrified to oil or coal. Alive it was a threat: it was Titans, was an overpeaking of life so clangorous and mad."[195] *Pierre* is Melville's Titanic project, an attempt to truly look at a world alive, throbbing in constant flows that resist direct representation. This is what makes the novel so difficult and complicated, particularly at the level of the sentence where Melville tries to get at the "overpeaking of life" by *overspeaking* life.

To see how he accomplishes this, we have to take account of a persistent and weird phenomenon in Melville's grammar in *Pierre*: the use of words like "purpleness" to describe Mount Greylock's ecologies. Michael Jonik has brilliantly observed that, seen as a whole, *Pierre* has a strangely abstract syntax. "Swarms of '-ness' words hang in the air," Jonik writes, "creating a dense affective fabric" that permeates the novel.[196] I see Melville's reliance on making abstract nouns ("purpleness" or "spiralness") from adjectives ("purple" or "spiral") as a way of addressing through poetics a key problem of language that relates to ecological complexity. Expressing in words the complexity of biological relations and inheritances over space and time would become a major problem for Darwin, but in *Pierre*, I'm fascinated by how "ness" phrases like "vital realness" correspond with the "ambiguousness" of the novel as a whole. In other words, how does Melville's very grammar generate the internal spin of his driving philosophy of ecology?

Linguistically, "-ness" is a suffix that gestures at a transient state of being, related to what are called "nonce words," or neologisms invented for a single occasion. The "purpleness" of hidden life is a fleeting, vivid, irreducibly original experience only partially glimpsed in language or thought. It remains obscured in its distance, scale, or transience. Not *despite* but *as a function of* our attempts to know it. This is a key point around which the entirety of *Magnificent Decay* turns, and I can't stress it enough. The material entanglement of the human in the world—as quantum theory has demonstrated—must be taken seriously in the realm of ecology as much as in the modes of perception that we have available to apprehend it (vision, language, narrative, technology). This is what Melville has to teach us about ecology's "purple promise," its veiled spirals of throbbing life that recoil from our presence.[197]

By now, the human species has become the ultimate driver of ecological complexity. From nuclear waste to microplastics, we are the spiral. We have created literal and figurative weather patterns that mark our presence on the planet. Like enormous configurations of weather (called Kármán vortex streets), we human-spirals only occasionally and always partially discern the arc of our eco-historical flight. "We see the cloud, and feel its bolt; but meteorology only idly essays a critical scrutiny as to how that cloud became charged, and how this bolt so stuns," says *Pierre*'s narrator. The cloud is, in the end, "the product of an infinitely involved and untraceable foregoing occurrences."[198] In our century, the cloud has become both a functioning nucleus and opaque metaphor for the dispersed nature of technological progress—and thus agency and responsibility—in the age of the internet. Perhaps by practicing what technology critic James Bridle terms "cloudy thinking," a slow, critical "embrace of unknowing" we can begin to trace our perpetual involvement within the cloudiness of techno-dwelling and the concurrent vanishing purpleness of ecological life.[199]

To put it directly, "purpleness" is Melville's literary approximation of emergent complexity. Melville needs the purple haziness of grammatical spirals to properly represent botanical life. This is because, to paraphrase Deleuze via Nealon, a single "tree" is always a metaphor, an abstract noun that sublates the "swarm of differences" that actually constitute the biological totality of the network of processes and organisms we call "tree."[200] The metaphor "tree" renders invisible the ecologies that maintain the tree by linguistically transforming differential processes into the bounded category of a singular organism. Similarly, as Melville put it in *Mardi*, the very possibility of coherent, individual human subjectivity is possible only by ignoring "the incessant operation of subtle processes" in our physical bodies: "of vessels lacteal and lymphatic, of arteries femoral and temporal; of pericranium or pericardium; lymph, chyle, fibrin, albumen, iron in the blood."[201] But Melville's "-ness" words in *Pierre*—all those weirdly a-metaphoric metaphors—keep everything ambiguous, blurry, purple, hidden, and obscure. They maintain an emphasis on the unfinished and untotalizable processes that create complexity.

Moreover, Melville's flowers and flowery style crossed nineteenth-century gender lines. Dorri Beam explains that as antebellum women were asked to "cultivate flower-like qualities"—"essentially to *be* a flower"—they were also encouraged to study botany as a way of knowing themselves and their "ideal" state.[202] Despite the prevailing belief that women had no "inherent sexual desire," flower writing in botany textbooks, journals, or novels could code for "transgressive sexualities" and alternate sociosexual forms of expression.[203] *Pierre*'s unkempt vines and excessive blossoms recover these messy, affective states of transgressive gender roles and sexual desires in fluid, purple syntax that, as Beam puts it, revises "grammar of relation" between people and between organisms and their environments.[204]

Lastly, of course, "purpleness" has for centuries been associated with bad writing, with flowery styles whose images and metaphors distract from clarity and argumentative concision. Purple prose designates elaborate, excessively ornate and sometimes sexually explicit writing. Ironically, this has been a constant criticism of Melville's work, from the earliest reviews of *Typee*'s irreligious immodesty and *Moby-Dick*'s "purposeless extravagance" to unlucky undergraduates struggling through *Pierre* for the first time.[205] Part of the discomfort with Melville's digressive prose is that it spreads past the boundaries of logic and narrative coherence. It deforms the contours of what a thought should be, where it should stop, and where excess begins.

Melville follows Pierre's "infinitely involved and untraceable" motivations in a vegetal style of writing that breaches the boundaries of good taste, productive discussion, useful time, and good old American efficiency.

The deepest irony, then, is the fact that the rhetoric of American democracy has been saturated with vegetal metaphors from the start, deployed to clarify the differences and distinctions of the young Republic from other nations. So when Melville draws on arboreal language in *The Confidence-Man* to survey sociality on the decks of the *Fidèle,* he does so with an eye toward the functional but imprecise nature of arboreal metaphors. "As pine, beech, birch, ash, hackmatack, hemlock, spruce, bass-wood, maple, interweave their foliage in the natural wood," the narrator observes, "so these varieties of mortals blended their varieties of visage and garb."[206] Translating the sensory experience of a crowd of strangers into a more intelligible ecological image (variation of trees in a forest), Melville suggests that while metaphor illuminates the world—makes it intelligible and available to abstraction and logic—it simultaneously "makes it impossible for intelligibility to fully escape its dependence on these flowers of rhetoric," to quote Jeffery Nealon, "which are always already overgrown."[207]

In *Pierre*'s scandalously coiled syntax—full of semicolons and dashes that elongate thoughts and string together dozens of images in a single sentence—Melville builds complexity at a level that is, at first, veiled from the reader who sees only from the piazza of the manor-house. But as sentences spiral into long paragraphs, then chapters, then books, then the novel as a whole, emergent patterns come into partial view. The terror of American Enceladus throws into sharp relief the cunning purpleness of hidden ecological complexity *within* the cunning purpleness of hidden literary complexity: simultaneous emergences made possible by the reader's interaction with the nonlinear design of *Pierre*'s narrative form. In this way, *Pierre*'s amaranthine prose becomes an integral part of its meaning. A thicket of purple complexity irreducible to its component parts—spirals of sentence and plot and theme and character—the novel's ambiguousness is a recovery of literature's essentially ecological character, its catnip origins in the abandoned hearth, its "repellingness" to the formal logic of capitalist-industrial-imperial-military grammars.

Pierre demonstrates that, in the end, we have only the *partial* approximation of geometric forms like spirals to apprehend ecological relations. This speaks to what Daniel Dennett called "Darwin's dangerous idea," the notion that "the algorithmic level" best "accounts for the speed of the antelope, the wing of the eagle, the shape of the orchid, the diversity of species, and all the other occasions for wonder in the worlds of nature."[208] But while Dennett might celebrate the algorithmic as a triumph of rationalist anti-metaphysics, Melville's algorithms and geometries are necessarily incomplete, open, and resistant to pretenses of mathematical certitude that supplant one metaphysical system with another. This is why, like Ishmael, who often admits the limits of his ability to express himself in sentences, the narrator of *Pierre* runs up against the limits of language again and again. The "feelings of Pierre were entirely untranslatable into any words that can be used," he laments at one point. Another time he muses: "Who shall put down the charms of Lucy Tartan on paper?"[209] At significant moments in the novel, the narrator is forced to "draw a veil" between the narrative and the reader: "Some nameless struggles of the soul can not be painted, and some woes will not be told. Let the ambiguous procession of events reveal their own ambiguous-ness."[210] Whereas Humboldt saw the impenetrable, "rich luxuriance of living nature, and the mingled web of free and restricted natural forces" as obstacles to the clarity of science ("shrouded in a vapory vail"), Melville sees their "ambiguous-ness" as essential.[211] Humboldt wants to "lift the vail that shrouds [Nature's] phenomena," but Melville wants to "draw" it in all of its purpleness.[212]

In this way, *Pierre*'s purple plant rhetoric is rhizomatic—to invoke Deleuze and Guattari's oft-misunderstood category—as a way of thinking (vegetally) about life beyond the organism. For Deleuze and Guattari, an organism is not a *form* but chain of variations, an assemblage whose differential compositions are often hidden from view. Although Deleuze and Guattari opposed characterizing lifeworlds as "hidden" to avoid the anthropocentric implications, Melville reminds us that, in fact, much *is* hidden from organisms of all kinds and that "hiddenness" is an index for the multiperspectival complexities of planetary life. Something is hidden from everything. Thus Melville's method in the period from *Moby-Dick* to *The Piazza Tales* is to work within this hiddenness or "patchiness," to quote Ana Tsing, in order to model the "mosaic of temporal rhythms and spatial arcs" that typifies ecological complexity.[213]

The multiscalar slipperiness of ecological phenomena, combined with our relative lack of precise data about these phenomena, produces an ironic humility at the heart of Melville's eco-sophy. Irony is everywhere in Melville, but seen through the green and purple lenses of *Pierre,* irony is above all an essential destabilizer that calls into question our assumptions about environmental systems. If "ecological posthumanism must be ironic," to quote Heather Sullivan, then Melville is its fully, ecologically ironic poster boy.[214] Mocking the metaphysical self-assurance of Emerson's avatar Mark Winsome in *The Confidence-Man*, for instance, the Cosmopolitan laughs: "What are you? What am I? Nobody knows who anybody is. The data which life furnishes, towards forming a true estimate of any being, are as insufficient to that end as in geometry one side given would be to determine the triangle."[215]

The Cosmopolitan's sardonic comments about data insufficiency replicate a more earnest narrative arc in Pierre: the strange story of Isabel. After obliquely hearing of her father's (Pierre Sr.'s) death—"they said the word *Dead* to me"—Isabel asks the driving questions of the entire novel: "What was it to be dead? What is it to be living? Wherein is the difference between the words Death and Life? Had I been ever dead? Was I living?"[216] These questions summarize Isabel's traumatic childhood, a childhood that, in her narrative recounting to Pierre, culminates in the discovery of what it means to be human in relation to nonhuman forms of existence. Because Isabel's memory of the past is characterized by double ambiguities—she calls it a "vacant whirlingness of the bewilderingness" she had felt as a child—her involute history creates a spiral within a spiral that disorients both Isabel's and the reader's sense of species boundaries.[217] That is to say, while Isabel motivates the tragic plot of *Pierre* and provides a character double for Pierre, her backstory also allows Melville to investigate phenomena that operate between the boundaries of death and life. Isabel makes us look at Pierre anew, through lightning strikes, vapor clouds, and residues of foams that are, on first read, easy to disregard. But these abiotic constellations of matter become difficult to ignore as Pierre becomes increasingly stormy, vaporous, and foamy when Isabel enters his life.

THE ELECTRICALNESS OF ISABEL

Isabel has long been read as a representative of the "primitive mind" in eighteenth-century ethnography.[218] She asks the all-too-obvious questions, the simple and silly ones. For example, she wonders if she was "something different from stones, trees, cats." To arrive at "the sweet idea of humanness," Isabel has to work through "the fancy that all people were as stones, trees, cats."[219] In its attention to the child-like perceptions of a confusing adult world, Isabel's story duplicates the narrative dynamics of another well-known story of developing self-awareness, Mary Shelley's *Frankenstein*.

Like Isabel, Victor Frankenstein's "monster" wonders what features of "humanness" distinguish humans from other creatures. He famously concludes that instead of discovering those features, human knowledge actually creates them: "Of what a strange nature is knowledge! It clings to the mind, when it has once seized on it, like a lichen on the rock. . . . Who was I? What was I? Whence did I come? What was my destination?"[220]

Melville owned the 1849 edition of *Frankenstein*, and *Pierre* and *Frankenstein* tell similar stories about the biological, genealogical, and social boundaries that define the human species. Narratologically, *Frankenstein*'s structure coils inward from Robert Walton's letters and Victor's narrative to the Creature's story and ultimately to the novel's core—Safie's story in the DeLacy's cottage—before spiraling outward to its Arctic conclusion. Working in the other direction, *Pierre* spirals outward from Saddle Meadows and then coils inward when Pierre reaches New York City. If we put aside the obvious parallels between dark-haired and blond-haired romantic archetypes—Safie and Isabel, Elizabeth and Lucy, respectively—the more significant doubles in the novel become clearer. Both Isabel and the Creature ask the reader the same question: how do I weigh an abstract "humanness" against the materials and forces of which the human body is composed? Working within the conventions of the sentimental gothic tradition, both novels test the bounds of sympathy, an influential eighteenth-century concept rooted in European philosophies of social progress. Both novels let their motherless, abandoned heroes tell their own stories, and both share similar rhetoric of decay and disaster in narratives full of wrecks, blasts, and storms. (Early in *Frankenstein*, for example, Walton describes frozen Victor as a "wreck," and, in his own narrative, Victor recounts seeing lightning splinter an oak into a "blasted stump" before his scientific ambition carried him onward like a "hurricane.")[221]

Though Victor's scientific ambition does not exactly parallel Pierre's literary ambition, Shelley and Melville both engage eighteenth-century vitalism and its precursors to address Romantic-scientific questions about matter, vitality, and the possibility that death may not be such a settled state after all. For Melville, Spinoza and Goethe are the key figures. For Shelley, Erasmus Darwin and Sir Humphry Davy offer the novel's scientific-philosophical contexts.[222] Erasmus Darwin, for instance, believed in spontaneous generation of life out of decomposition.[223] In his poem *The Temple of Nature* (1803), he writes that the "wrecks of Death are but a change of forms; / Emerging matter from the grave returns."[224] *Frankenstein*'s central conceit steals from Darwinian materialist biology to pose questions about how death and decay simply engender a "change of forms" that could be reproduced to create life once again. But *Frankenstein* specifically measures the risks of this kind of *asexual* reproduction, punishing Victor for his inventiveness and reinscribing a heteronormative regime of sexual reproduction as the paradigm of creativity. We will return to Pierre's (a)sexuality in the next section, but the point is that both *Frankenstein* and *Pierre* deal with the consequences of nonnormative human creativity by associating it with stormy, destructive forms of abiotic creativity like lightning and hurricanes.

In perhaps the novel's most famous passage, Victor describes his creative breakthrough in specifically luminous terms: "I beheld the corruption of death succeed to the blooming cheek of life; I saw how the worm inherited the wonders of the eye and brain. I paused, examining and analysing all the minutiae of causation, as exemplified in the change from life to death, and death to life, until from the midst of this darkness a sudden light broke in upon me—a light so brilliant and wondrous, yet so simple . . . I became dizzy with the immensity of the prospect which it illustrated."[225] Unpacking the role of vitalism in *Frankenstein* is beyond the scope of this book, but here I want to briefly highlight the imagery of light and lightning that signal, simultaneously, the rewards and the costs of creativity. Just as Victor describes his discovery as a "sudden light," he sees his Creature in a "flash of lightning" after little William's murder.[226] And, late in the novel, Victor compares himself to "a blasted tree" fissured by the lightning bolts that had "entered my soul."[227] Like Ahab—who likewise describes himself as "blasted" and whose body is scarred like the "lofty trunk of a great tree, when the upper lightning tearingly darts down it . . . greenly alive, but branded"—Victor's genius is associated with the greenness of trees while his Promethean penalties take the form of lightning strikes that destroy that greenness.[228]

Scientifically, lightning is the result of an electrostatic discharge inside or between clouds, or between cloud and ground, resulting from some pressure differential. In *Pierre,* Isabel is consistently identified with lightning strikes that result in "rot" or "decay." Most dramatically, a flash of lightning finally enables her to differentiate between human and nonhuman: "When the lightning flashed, and split some beautiful tree, and left it to rot from all its greenness, I said, lightning is not human, but I am human. And so with all other things. I can not speak coherently here; but somehow I felt that all good, harmless men and women were human things, placed at cross-purposes, in a world of snakes and lightnings, in a world of horrible and inscrutable inhumanities."[229] For Isabel, lightning illuminates what it is to be human by momentarily flickering light on the purpleness of ecological relations. Although Isabel "can not speak coherently" about it or fully explain the overpowering insight, for her lightning functions as a flash between states of pressure and memory: the origin of creativity, a moment "wherein what-has-been comes together in a lightning-flash with the now to form a constellation" of thought, as Walter Benjamin would phrase it.[230] Lightning dominates many of the scenes in *Pierre*, especially descriptions of Isabel, around "whose wondrous temples the strange electric glory had been playing," revealing "flashes of her electricalness."[231] When Pierre visits Isabel the second time, the narrator tells us that to "Pierre's dilated senses Isabel seemed to swim in an electric fluid," and "the vivid buckler of her brow seemed as a magnetic plate." Pierre "could not help believing [there] was an extraordinary physical magnetism in Isabel."[232]

Initially, Isabel's electricity produces clarity for Pierre: "Against the wall of the thick darkness of the mystery of Isabel, recorded as by some phosphoric finger, was the burning fact, that Isabel was his sister."[233] From a Christian standpoint, the whorled fingerprint of a human being is an imprint of the immortal hand of God, a sign of God's "all permeating wonderful-ness" that brings light amid the darkness of sin and the mysteries of the wilderness.[234] But soon, Pierre finds himself shrouded in more and more ambiguities as he gets to know Isabel. "For over all these things, and interfusing itself with the sparkling electricity in which she seemed to swim," the narrator intones, "was an ever-creeping and condensing haze of ambiguities." Isabel's magnetism makes Pierre more confused, entrancing him from that "first magnetic night" when she "had bound him to her by an extraordinary atmospheric spell—both physical and spiritual." Pierre is entranced by the same "Pantheistic master-spell" that attracts "heat-lightnings and the ground lightnings" to Isabel. He meshes with the electro-chemical throbbings of atmospheric ecology. Isabel is an elemental mixture of fire and air "vivified" in the thunderclouds and made electric: "This spell seemed one with that Pantheistic master-spell, which eternally locks in mystery and in muteness the universal subject world, and the physical electricalness of Isabel seemed reciprocal with the heat-lightnings and the ground-lightnings nigh to which it had first become revealed to Pierre. She seemed molded from fire and air, and vivified at some Voltaic pile of August thunder-clouds heaped against the sunset."[235] Isabel's "physical electricalness" has reciprocity with ground lightnings and August thunderclouds, as energy cycling through human and nonhuman forms molds her into a light-image vivified to the point of photographic simulacrum. Melville also suggestively compares Isabel to the "Voltaic pile"—the first electric battery invented by Alessandro Volta in 1800—which, as Humboldt pointed out in *Cosmos*, "taught us the intimate connection existing between electric, magnetic, and chemical phenomena."[236]

Throughout the nineteenth century, electricity possessed what Sam Halliday calls "an almost inestimable charisma," partly because it was used in technologies like the telegraph, but also because electricity seemed to be deeply invested in organic life (which explains the interest in animal magnetism, galvanism, and other pseudo-electro-sciences of the century).[237] Halliday observes that, for some antebellum thinkers, electricity was "the source of life itself, a kind of *urkraft* from which all organisms were ultimately derived," which was to varying degrees supported by science of the day, most substantially Hans Oersted's work on electromagnetism in the 1820s.[238] Lightning and electricity make their way into many early American literary texts, including Emerson's description of truth as "rough electric shocks" in "Self-Reliance" (1841), Hawthorne's use of "electricity and other kindred mysteries of Nature" in "The Birth-Mark" (1843), Poe's electrical "principle of the universe" in "Eureka" (1848), and Whitman's paeans to the "body electric" in *Leaves of Grass* (1855).[239] In *Moby-Dick*, Ishmael compares Kant and Locke to "thunder-heads," or lightning clouds, while Ahab, with "clouds piled upon his brow," seems to be opening "a chasm" from his very body "from which forked flames and lightnings."[240] (A few years later, Bartleby's passive resistance would leave the lawyer-narrator "thunderstruck," feeling like a man killed by "summer lightning.")[241]

Pierre's lightning reveals the initial inklings of a new paradigm for Melville's later writings, one that imagines how human "nature" is actually a metaphor for our response to natural disasters like lightning storms (or pandemics). Lightning represents the catastrophic suddenness of death that interrupts our lives and reminds us of the powerful interpenetrations of nonhuman forces in our familiar, routine economies and ecologies. Seen this way, *Pierre* is about human responses to loss and the cultural processes of grieving and mourning, processes specifically described in the rhetoric of lightning, electricity, and fire. In these "flashing revelations of grief's wonderful fire," the narrator tells us, "we see all things as they are."[242] Like the beautiful tree split by lightning in Isabel's account, Pierre is "transfigured" from "a green foliaged tree into a blasted trunk" by the revelations that his father did not exactly match the "long-cherished image" he had of him. The "storm" of these shocks left him with both "electric insight" and "infinite mournfulness."[243] Though *Pierre*'s lightning imagery fits neatly within Melville's satire of the clichéd tropes of the sentimental genre, the persistent *over*use of lightning in the novel suggests a different angle of interest. By aligning Pierre's sudden self-awareness with lightning, Melville dilates Pierre's personal, genealogical, and biological obsessions into a wider circle of concerns. What does it mean, after Darwin, to feel loss, to grieve in a world of porous boundaries, abiotic ruin, and spiraling vegetal growth that carries on indifferently to human lamentations or arts that eloquently protest a single species' finitude?

LYRICS OF FOAM

There are certainly moments of grieving in *Mardi, Redburn,* and *Moby-Dick,* but the lightnings, vapors, and foams of *Pierre* generate a fizzy, abiotic matrix that gives Melville space to contemplate the paradoxical nature of grief in the age of Darwin. Melville will extend these meditations in later works like "The Encantadas" and *Clarel,* but *Pierre* introduces readers to the eco-spiritual nature of mourning that Melville will more fully elaborate on in his postnovel writings, especially his poetry. At first, Pierre achieves lucidity in "grief's wonderful fire," but after his decision to abandon Saddle Meadows and preserve his father's secret (and Isabel's paternity), he burns every letter, heirloom, and trace of familial mourning so that the Glendenning "all" becomes nothing but "ashes": "Hitherto I have hoarded up mementoes and monuments of the past . . . [But now it] speaks merely of decay and death, and nothing more; decay and death of endless innumerable generations; it makes of earth one mold."[244] Instead of memorializing and monumentalizing, Pierre wants to "Let all die, and mix again!" The Goethean vitalist "all" is, in Pierre's mind, a necrological leveling. Pierre urges readers to return to "old Greek times, before man's brain went into doting bondage," a time when men "cheated the glutton worm, and gloriously burned the corpse; so that the spirit up-pointed, and visibly forked to heaven!"[245] Pierre sees cremation as superior to burial because it is a process of reverse lightning, a funeral pyre "visibly forked to heaven."

Pierre's anti-mourning rant, made at the decisive moment when he leaves his ancestral home, recalls an earlier scene in the novel when Pierre sits among the "half-bared roots" of a "primeval pine-tree" in Saddle

Meadows and thinks about the "mournful" character of this "mighty tree." Noticing "the mighty bulk and far out-reaching length of one particular root, which, straying down the bank, the storms and rains had years ago exposed," Pierre hears "the pyramidical and numberless, flame-like complainings of this Eolean pine . . . the wind breathes now upon it:—the wind,—that is God's breath! Is He so sad?" [246] He continues:

> Oh, tree! so mighty thou, so lofty, yet so mournful! This is most strange! Hark! as I look up into thy high secrecies, oh, tree, the face, the face, peeps down on me!—'Art thou Pierre? Come to me'—oh, thou mysterious girl,—what an ill-matched pendant thou, to that other countenance of sweet Lucy, which also hangs, and first did hang within my heart! Is grief a pendant then to pleasantness? Is grief a self-willed guest that will come in? Yet I have never known thee, Grief;—thou art a legend to me. I have known some fiery broils of glorious frenzy; I have oft tasted of revery; whence comes pensiveness; whence comes sadness; whence all delicious poetic presentiments;—but thou, Grief! art still a ghost-story to me. I know thee not,—do half disbelieve in thee. . . . The face!—the face! . . . It visibly rustles behind the concealing screen.[247]

Pierre sees correspondences ("pendants") between the tree's face, Lucy's, and his own. But he also perceives the "face" of "Grief" in the Eolean pine, visibly rustling "behind the concealing screen." Through this arboreal screen, he discerns Isabel and, through Isabel, a deeper grief. Visible ecology becomes a "concealing screen" for the rustling of death amid the abundance of life. In the pine-face of universal grief, Pierre connects the botanical growth of Saddle Meadows to his own story of disrupted genealogies. But rather than abandoning grief as an outdated relic of pre-Darwinian cultures, Melville frames the second half of Pierre's narrative around the seemingly archaic and even absurd practice of mourning. In a revealing metanarrative flourish, Pierre acknowledges that grief motivates the narrative logic of all "ghost-stories," all gothic tales. The hauntedness of living on in the absence of those you love is channeled, deferred, and made present in the traces, marks, and signatures of writing *and* in the lofty mournfulness of wind-swept pines whose high secrecies are the untold stories of storms and the ruin of abiotic forces. But despite the gloomy mood of the passage, there lurks in this pine-Gothic scene whispers of spiritual hope.

For example, Pierre calls the wind "God's breath," a pantheist spirituality built from the "fleetingess" of ecological life. Yet Pierre has, at best, uneven spiritual progress over the course of the novel. In opening pages, Pierre resists the "insensible sliding process" of passively inheriting "a venerable Faith, which the first Glendinning had brought over sea, from beneath the shadow of an English minister."[248] He cannot see that "this world hath a secret deeper than beauty."[249] But then the genealogical and ecological spirals he discovers in Isabel and in his wilderness walks through Saddle Meadows hint at something more: a spiritual life perceived in the secrets of hanging tree canopies whose expanding symmetries we might compare to the bronchial branching of human lungs. In our century, religious historian Clayton Crockett has pondered the possibility of a postmodern "ecological becoming of philosophy of religion," a possibility that *Pierre* and nineteenth-century scientists like Humboldt took seriously. (Humboldt wrote that there is a "spiritual essence manifested . . . in unfolding the flower and maturing the fruit of the nutrient tree, in upheaving the soil of the forest, or in rending the clouds with the might of the storm.")[250] And Babbalanja urges his companions to let their theological frustrations rest with the patterns of the botanical: "Let us be content with the theology in the grass and the flower, in seed-time and harvest."[251]

Melville explores such spiritual pensiveness in the epigraph to his late poem "Buddha," which appeared in *Timoleon, Etc.* (1891) only a few months before his death. The epigraph, taken from James 4:14, speaks to the reader in explicitly evaporative terms:

> *"For what is your life? It is*
> *even a vapor, that approacheth for a*
> *little time, and then vanisheth away."*[252]

The speaker of the six-line poem that follows suggests that each of us is an "Aspirant to nothingness."[253] "Aspire" here carries the double meaning "to breathe" and the Enceladean ambition "to rise," to "spire" like a flame, or to "grow upwards" like a plant.[254] "Buddha" reminds us that we are, to quote Heather Sullivan, "vibrant bodies pulsing *without harmony,*" influenced by the many flows of air, streams of light, and invisible toxins the engulf us.[255] Pierre often resorts to a vapory diction of breath, wind, and nothingness, especially when talking to Isabel. For example, he tells her: "'a nothing should torment a nothing; for I am a nothing. It is all a dream—we dream that we dreamed we dream.' . . . Swiftly he caught her in his arms:—'From nothing proceeds nothing, Isabel!'"[256] Clearly, the influence of *King Lear* is strong here—a tragedy built on the word "nothing"—but equally present is *The Tempest,* a play that lingers in the background of this entire 1852–56 period of Melville's career.[257] In particular, Melville seems to have had in mind Prospero's metafictional speech in Act V, when he tells the audience: "These our actors / . . . were all spirits and / Are melted into air, into thin air: / . . . like the baseless fabric of this vision."[258] Pierre adopts Prospero's atmospheric metaphors for the transitory nature of artistic creation, at one point admitting that writers "are paid for our breath." A "thing of life, was, after all," Pierre concludes, "a thing of breath."[259]

The relation of breath to reading and writing—Thomas Ford labels it the "Romantic poetics of air"—is a common trope in transatlantic Victorian fiction from Austen and the Brontës to Hardy and Yeats. According to Ford, the airy poetics of Victorian literature is even visible at the level of punctuation marks that create "grammatical forms to the exclusion of spoken and respiratory rhythms."[260] Melville's atmospheric description of *Pierre*'s environs and characters exemplifies the broader "novelization of Romantic lyric atmosphere," in which atmosphere didn't mean milieu or context metaphorically but instead *actual* air, linking words to their spoken formation in breath and exhalation.[261] And Thoreau, anticipating Derrida's deconstruction of the speech/writing binary, famously saw writing as "the work of art nearest to life itself" because it may be "actually breathed from all human lips;—not to be represented on canvas or in marble only, but be carved out of the breath of life itself."[262] Like Thoreau, Melville was fascinated by the contradictory *absent presence* of breath in writing. He studies this dynamic in his portrayal of characters like Pierre and Ahab who are distinguished from other characters by, as Jonik phrases it, an "interplay of atmospheric and material forces" wherein the "ontological and meteorological merge."[263] Pierre and Ahab are always threatened with "becoming undone" by their environments.[264] They are perpetually vulnerable to weathering and forces of "Dissipation, Evaporation, Exudation," a phrase that provided the title of Goethe's 1820 essay (and which Amanda Jo Goldstein has recently retranslated as "Going to Dust, Vapor, Droplets").[265]

The confusion and "whirlingness" of *Pierre* are the consequences of a world where all is atmospheric haze, without clear relations of cause and effect. After reading Isabel's letter, for instance, Pierre slips into the miasmatic confusion of "whirling rack and vapor . . . mist . . . and fog."[266] Melville extends this whirling fog to the Church of the Apostles by mocking the "Vaporites" who live there, taking "vapor-baths" that "steamed their lean ribs every morning" so that smoke "issued from their heads, and overspread their pages."[267] The Vaporites are as confused as the navigators of "The Encantadas," who get lost in the "fogs" and "vapors" shrouding the isles of Massafuero.[268] The alignment of vapor and fog with confused thought also appears in *The Confidence-Man,* where Indian hating becomes meteorological as much as metaphysical. For Indian haters, prejudicial thoughts develop "such attraction, that much as straggling vapors troop from all sides to a storm-cloud, so straggling thoughts of other outrages troop to the nucleus thought, assimilate with it, and swell it."[269] In all three texts, Melville associates fog and mist with tragic situations. The accumulation and attraction of "straggling vapors" collectively generate a disastrous outcome without clear causality or figurehead, as in the "vapory fleece" that shrouds Billy Budd's hanging.[270]

But the oddest and most fascinating nonhuman material that appears in *Pierre* is *foam.* Chemically, foam is created by pockets of gas in a liquid or solid: a closed cell, multiscale system of dispersed media. Foam is the result of gasses and liquids that cannot fully mix. As they accumulate in increasingly complex forms, bubbles become small sheets called *lamella* governed by Plateau's laws (from Belgian physicist Joseph Plateau, who realized in 1873 that every vertex of a soap bubble is close to 109.47 degrees, the tetrahedral angle). Today we recognize that lamellae create *Weaire-Phelan structures,* structures that approximate, in Mandelbrot's words, *"triadic fractal foam."*[271] In recent years, the unusually complex, multiscale geometric structure of foam has garnered increased attention across scientific fields. For example, in cell biology, foam is now understood to be a matrix for the origin of life out of the primordial ooze. Peter Sloterdijk writes that the earliest bacterial fossils, *Swaziland microspheres,* demonstrate that life depends on "the ability to adopt a position through opposition to something external . . . folding into oneself" to generate foamy arrangements of the living among nonliving.[272] This insight is spookily similar to what Robert Chambers—in *Vestiges of Natural Creation* (1844), an important source for Melville in the 1850s—identified in the "nucleated vesicle," which he called "the fundamental form of all organization . . . the meeting point between the inorganic and the organic."[273] By the mid-twentieth century, John Wheeler had coined the phrase "quantum foam" to model micro-fluctuations of spacetime within quantum mechanics.[274] Quantum foam visualizes the persistent instability of observation that has become the hallmark of quantum worlds, a term that has also been adopted by loop quantum gravity as *"spinfoam."*

But what does foam have to with *Pierre*? A few pages into the novel, the narrator tells us: "In the country then Nature planted our Pierre . . . She blew her wind-clarion from the blue hills, and Pierre neighed out lyrical thoughts, as at the trumpet-blast, a war-horse paws himself into a lyric of foam."[275] Here, equine-Pierre's lyric of foam reorganizes language into an ecological film or membrane, in which matter seems to be marking the human, not the other way around. Nature plants and blows; Pierre neighs and foams. Even more provocatively, we could say that Melville transforms Pierre into a lyric excretion, a body indistinguishably horse and human, whose presence over time in Saddle Meadows can be best represented in congealed, foamy, fractal sheets. In *Mardi*, Yillah's sedimentary body gave Melville a way to conceptualize deep time. In *Pierre,* Pierre's foamy thoughts offer a way to conceptualize the human from an abiotic point of view, from the "wind-clarion" processes of Saddle Meadows that interface with organic bodies to create sound and to shape the ephemeral socialities that define our species.

Along these lines, Sloterdijk has written about foam as a paradigm for modern social organization, specifically because foam is more properly a *process* than a structure. "The processual dynamic of foam," he writes, "provides the empty form for all stories dealing with immanently growing spaces of inclusion" based on their "internal tension, or tensegrity."[276] For Sloterdijk, "aphrology"—from the Greek *aphros*, "foam"—is "the theory of co-fragile systems," and the "lively thought-image of foam serves to recover the premetaphysical pluralism of world-inventions post-metaphysically."[277] Foam is a useful emblem for theorizing contemporary sociality because it is so disappointing, fleeting, and dream-like. In *Moby-Dick*, foam becomes a metaphor for human-ocean interfaces, from the "scud" (or sea foam) in Father Mapple's chapel painting to "poor Pip," who, after drowning, "came up all foaming."[278]

According to Sloterdijk, the opposition of immiscible elements in foam stands for the challenges of the democratic *polis*, but a number of nineteenth-century writers had already thought about foam in this exact way. Take Hawthorne's "Celestial Railroad" (1843), where people in society appear and "vanish like a soap bubble."[279] Or *The Confidence-Man,* where the penultimate scene concerns a "cunning barber" named Bill Cream who lathers the Cosmopolitan "with so generous a brush, so piled up the foam on him, that his face looked like the yeasty crest of a billow."[280] Bill Cream's foam silences the Confidence Man for the first time in the novel.

The ultimate swindler was as "vain to think of talking" under the foam, "as for a drowning priest in the sea to exhort his fellow-sinners on a raft. Nothing would do, but he must keep his mouth shut."[281] Foam shuts us up, shuts us in together. Like the "lather" of Benito Cereno's shaving scene or the "ceaseless sea" that "pours a fury of foam" upon the rocky coasts of the Encantadas, foams defy the organismic logic of individuality and relocate the human to a place of humility and silence.[282] Only then are we able to hear the clarion winds sweeping through blue hills as they give us, like Taji mourning Yillah, a sudden "rush, a foam of recollections!"[283] Foams remind us, in short, of our vulnerability to ruin and loss. How quickly the "gay foam" of socializing humpback whales turns into a scene of "clotted red gore"![284] Like Nature-planted-Pierre, we too neigh lyrical foams (art! literature! criticism!) that reproduce and multiply our transient, foamy natures.

VITAL REALNESS

In this section, I want to return to the theme of reproduction we've tracked in *Pierre*'s botanical worlds to draw a number of conclusions about the spiraling, vegetal creativity of Melville's midcareer. During the spring of 1852, as *Pierre* was going to press, Melville was on his knees, planting a row of saplings along the road to Arrowhead Farm. He was putting into practice the "greenness" that pervaded *Pierre*.[285] And the short stories that followed between 1853 and 1856 continue Melville's greening trajectory. In "The Tartarus of Maids," for example, Melville explores the relationship between trees, writing, and political economy by shadowing his narrator to a Massachusetts paper factory where he picks up envelopes for his agricultural seed business. Manufactured from rags made of hemp, linen, and cotton, these botanico-textile-envelopes would carry seeds to farmers across growing postal networks of antebellum America. In fact, in the nineteenth century seeds were the third most popular enclosures in letters, after money and photographs; a three-cent stamp could send a letter three thousand miles.[286] Read through the greenness of *Pierre*, "The Tartarus of Maids" clearly develops Melville's interest in how producing paper, inking an envelope's address, and sending a seed are ghostly extensions of botanical life cycles. These epistolary activities supplement dead and processed plants with writing. While seed enclosures might produce a new generation of plants, herbs, and crops, the acts of writing and receiving letters are themselves haunted by vegetality. The envelope's paper and its ink signatures signify doubly.

Biosemiotic traces of previous organic life produce the marks that facilitate a seed's journey from Massachusetts distributor to Carolina farmer. Biological, political, and transportation economies blur within the vegetal economy of writing. Plant and human geographies merge.

In addition, as Robert Bruce notes, the expansion of paper manufacturing during Melville's lifetime created America's market for industrial chemicals like sulfuric acid, bleaching powder, and sodium phosphate.[287] In "The Tartarus of Maids," Melville explores the ways in which writing has facilitated—and been facilitated by—the agrologistical and chemical demands of expanding techno-agricultural societies in the West. To put it bluntly, "The Tartarus of Maids" and other stories in Melville's magazine writing period like "Bartleby" show Melville's mounting interest in human ecologies. By human ecologies, I mean a historical-environmental accounting of human dwellings, structures, cities, and transportation/energy networks, plus more invisible or obscured phenomena like the chemical, toxic, and epidemiological traces of our species that have overwhelming ecological implications for both nonhuman and human spheres of life. Human ecology is the primary focus of the next chapter, but to conclude my reading of *Pierre*, I want to stress how, through *Pierre*'s spirals and foams, Melville joins the detailed attention to biogeochemical forms with the theme of reproduction, contrasting the novel's incest and sterility motifs with the abundance of Saddle Meadows and the flowery rhetoric that saturates the narrative. Such contrasts allow Melville to target the linkages between sexual reproduction and the reproduction of experience and memory that writing promises: the traces that constitute both the structure of life and of writing.

Shuttling between biological reproduction and linguistic reproduction, in *Pierre* Melville contemplates the meaning of *inscription* in the broadest possible sense (what Derrida would eventually term *grammè*). This is why so much reading and rereading happens in the novel. Isabel, for instance, comes to consciousness by learning to read the name *Isabel* gilded inside her guitar and the "talismanic word" *Glendinning* in Pierre Sr.'s handkerchief.[288] Unexpectedly, these instances of inscription provide a way to conceptualize the organizing principles that underpin plant life and systems of writing, both of which get deeply entangled in *Pierre*. Thinking the botanical and the literary together enables us to glimpse "the most general structure of life and of its evolution," to quote Francesco Vitale, "of which writing in its restricted sense would be only a moment." For post-Derridean theorists like Vitale, the principle of difference that is disclosed through writing (and that makes writing possible) is at the same time the "genetico-structural condition of the life of the living and of its evolution."[289] As in Victor Frankenstein's creature, reading and inscription coalesce the very idea of "humanness." The emergence of the human species thirty thousand years ago coincided, not incidentally, with the repetition and iterability of markings on cave walls (over twenty thousand years before conventional writing systems develop). Thus a literary text like *Pierre*, seemingly the most obscure and challenging form of writing, becomes the clearest way to see the converging, differential origins of life and species through the differential conditions of inscription that re-presents that life and that species. In this sense, literature, Hubert Zapf tells us, is the "paradigmatic cultural form representing the play of similarities and differences that make up the ecosemoitic processes of life itself."[290] Because literatures and oratures produce spaces that emphasize the "creative" over the "functional," and indeed smear those distinctions entirely, their exuberant excesses let writers like Melville access questions about sex, reproduction, pleasure, and creativity by translating the biological into the literary. In literature, life is not strictly functional but creative, not strictly purposeful but playful. In literature, we see the evolutionary principles of play, difference, chance, and accident generate their elegant designs.

Isabel's bond with Pierre, the major twist of the novel, hinges on exactly these (meta)textual issues: the failure of genealogical reproduction that culminates in Pierre's death and the experiments with literary reproduction that culminate in Melville's creation of *Pierre*. At first, Isabel seems to be a kind of anti-Eve, a counter-figure to the ultimate symbol of creation in the Romantic era, of which Lucy is obviously an avatar. (In *Paradise Lost*, Milton describes the "wanton ringlets" of Eve's hair waving as "the vine curls her tendrils," while at the end of *Pierre*, Isabel's "long hair ran over" Pierre's corpse and "arbored him in ebon vines.")[291] In Melville and Milton, coiled hair and spiraling vines intermingle with montages of (in)fertility and (surrogate) motherhood. This is established early on by the novel's insistence that Pierre and his mother are, indeed, incestuous. Pierre the "son," the narrator wryly observes, "seemed lover enough for this widow [Mrs. Glendinning].... This romantic filial love of Pierre seemed fully returned by the triumphant maternal pride of the widow ... they were wont to call each other brother and sister."[292] Over the course of *Pierre*, Isabel becomes Pierre's only sibling, replacement wife, and substitute mother. All of this despite the fact that Lucy and Mary Glendinning are very much alive and, Melville hints, both reproductively fertile: "litheness had not yet completely uncoiled itself from [Mrs. Glendinning's] waist, nor smoothness unscrolled itself from her brow."[293] Mary Glendinning's still-coiled "litheness" appears in stark opposition to Isabel, who "seemed as dead" to Pierre even as the "death-like beauty of her face" entranced him.[294] However, as the novel goes on, Mrs. Glendinning does die, Lucy accepts a subservient role, and death-like Isabel assumes more and more creative powers. When she asks Pierre if she has a "Gorgon's" face for delivering the stone-cold news of her paternity, he responds: "Nay, sweet Isabel, but it hath a more sovereign power; that turned to stone; thine might turn white marble into mother's milk."[295] Isabel's face turns marble into breast milk. She produces life from rock—is *mater* to *matter*—and calls songs from her guitar. It is this guitar that bears inside it her "secret name," the maternal trace that "whirls" her into Pierre's life:

> I am called woman, and thou, man, Pierre; but there is neither man nor woman about it. Why should I not speak out to thee? There is no sex in our immaculateness. Pierre, the secret name in the guitar even now thrills me through and through. Pierre, think! think! Oh, canst thou not comprehend? see it?—what I mean, Pierre? The secret name in the guitar thrills me, thrills me, whirls me, whirls me; so secret, wholly hidden, yet constantly carried about in it; unseen, unsuspected, always vibrating to the hidden heart-strings—broken heart-strings; oh, my mother, my mother, my mother! . . . *mother, mother, mother!*[296]

In this fascinatingly manic passage, Isabel's uses the word *immaculateness* to describe her relationship with Pierre, a word with multiple meanings in the novel.

"Immaculateness" first appears in the satire of Mr. Falsgrave's "napkined immaculateness" as a way to mock the reverend's masquerade of piety and "sinlessness." But Isabel's use of the word clearly connotes the "immaculate" womb of the Virgin Mary, with further resonances in nineteenth-century zoology ("Without contrasting spots or marks; unspotted") as well as literary publishing (a manuscript "completely free from textual errors").[297] *Immaculateness* is the asexual conception of life, religiously and biologically and textually pure: a condition of theological-hermaphroditic propagation that counters Pierre's fantasy of an incestuous, sexual union. Instead, immaculateness reveals a deeper fantasy of literary-material kinship, the revelation that writing must be understood materially, as a fabric of traces anterior to concepts like Nature or ecology, life or thought. Pierre cannot handle this insight. The immaculateness of Isabel's spontaneously generative, maternal materiality cannot be assimilated by Pierre's male mind.

This is further evident in one of the most ambiguously sexual moments of the novel, where Pierre concludes that Isabel longs for his "vital realness." As Pierre "tremblingly" holds Isabel, his mouth "wet her ear" and then "imprinted repeated burning kisses upon her." (Remember, too, how Victor Frankenstein "imprinted" a kiss on Elizabeth's lips in his psychosexually rich, postcreation dream.)[298] But, suddenly, the passage comes to a mysterious end. Pierre and Isabel "changed; they coiled together, and entangledly stood mute."[299] The sexual energy of this scene—Isabel's wetted ear and their erotic coiling—exposes and then immediately represses Pierre's incestuous yearning. (Remember, too, Ishmael's pansexual delight in "The Squeeze of the Hand" chapter as his "serpentine" fingers "spiralize" with other sailors' hands.)[300] By having Pierre imagine what Isabel wants of *him*, a fantasy of "vital realness," Melville projects Pierre's desire for patriarchal stability onto mother Isabel. This whirling transference of reproductive anxiety is delivered in syntax so disrupted by semicolons that it moves beyond a staccato rhythm into a looping spiral. The sentence coils to a close as the coiled characters stand, "entangledly," mute.

Pierre has repeatedly imprinted incestuous kisses on Isabel—he has "written" her with his desiring lips—but the result is, improbably, the immaculate conception of something genealogically original. Pierre upholds the name of his father by concealing Isabel and abandoning Saddle Meadows. Yet the cost is sacrificing his own Glendinning name. As Pierre dies in prison, his cousin Glen Glendinning takes over, a double of the family name and an autoreproduction of patriarchal lineage, genetically and linguistically. Pierre's vital realness is found only outside of this lineage, in the fugitive verse he composes, in the arms of his mother-sister-wife Isabel, in the slums and prisons of the city, and in the ecological excesses of vapory, foamy, lightning-stricken Saddle Meadows. Pierre cannot be seminally foamy, only lyrically foamy. His queerness sets him outside the patriarchy, outside regimes of human sexual reproduction, and into the pansexual, spontaneously generative worlds of ecological purpleness. And he must die for it.

Remarkably, critics of *Pierre* described the novel in the very terms of reproductive failure that run through it. In January 1853, for instance, the

New York *National Magazine* called *Pierre* "the late miserable abortion of Melville," and a year earlier the *New York Herald* had already declared that "Melville has written himself out."[301] Melville wrote himself out in *Pierre*, pushing himself to the limits of what interrelations writing could represent. And this is why Pierre is such a bad writer, a copycat. Nevertheless, Pierre *does* produce one set of original writings. His signatures. The narrator tells us that Pierre's signature is so inconsistent, so iteratively original each time, that his signature undermines his "supereminent name," and "posterity would be sure to conclude that they were forgeries all."[302] Like Bartleby's, Pierre's signature is an original forgery. Unable to reproduce sexually, genealogically, or literarily, Pierre produces an immaculate Glendinning signature: a series of turns and spirals that accumulate into the foamy lyric of a creative life. Pierre into *Pierre*.

Near the end of the novel, the narrator teases Pierre for his inability to see "that there is no such thing as a standard for the creative spirit; that no one great book must ever be separately regarded, and permitted to domineer with its own uniqueness upon the creative mind."[303] Rather, "all existing great works must be federated in the fancy; and so regarded as a miscellaneous and Pantheistic whole."[304] This becomes obvious when we remember that we read *Pierre* as Pierre reads Isabel's letter. The letter even speaks directly to Pierre: "Read, Pierre, though by reading thou may'st entangle thyself, yet may'st thou thereby disentangle others."[305] The grieving Eolean pine, the talking letter, and the lyrically foaming human-horse are each objects given faces that speak through the veil of ecological hiddenness. This incredible moment in the novel models the phenomenon of *orientation entanglement*, a term used in contemporary physics to describe how spatial vectors cannot fully approximate the complexity of quantum geometric forms like spinors. The act of reading *Pierre* alters us readers irreversibly by changing the conditions of our orientation to the text and to "the infinite entanglements of all social things," as the narrator puts it.[306] We cannot but be changed by reading *Pierre*, at the quantum level as much as at the level of meaning. Reading Pierre reading his fate reminds us how precariously poised our lives really are, just like a lightning-blasted pine, a curling vine, or a foamy cell. Biota is, in the end, shaped by abiotic caprice: "the minutest event—the falling of a leaf, the hearing of a voice, or the receipt of one little bit of paper scratched over with a few small characters by a sharpened feather."[307]

Yet the falling leaf, the speaking voice, and the written text *are* significantly different. The human is not a plant. The plant's stance toward the world is "the promise of life and growth, not the avoidance of death or loss," to quote Elaine Miller, an avoidance that characterizes both the individual human's experience of the world and our species' evolutionary trajectory.[308] In the next chapter, we look at the avoidance of death and the memorialization of loss, twin activities that appear to distinguish animals from humans but actually conjoin the two categories of being—animal and human—within shared rituals of sociality like the construction of dwelling places or funerary memorials. From a strictly evolutionary perspective, reproduction and survival align human and animal instincts in the persistent drive of adaptation. But plants, animals, and humans survive and adapt very differently. It is not a question of differential access to the world but, rather, a question of differential inhabitation. As we've seen in the first two chapters, a new materialist emphasis on the material *sameness* of existence is necessary but not sufficient for a rigorous ecological philosophy. Andreas Malm reminds us that it is equally important to "maintain the analytical distinction" between forms of existence *as forms of difference* in order to "tease out how the properties of society intermingle with those of nature" and thus consider the ecologies of a multiple, differential *anthropos*.[309]

To conclude my digressive, spiraling reading of *Pierre*, it is useful to summarize where we have been and what environmental insights we can take away from a novel that so resists reductive or pat endings. I began by reading vegetal life in *Pierre* against nineteenth-century transatlantic botanical sciences before tracing the figure of the spiral (and Pierre's dream of "American Enceladus") back to Isabel and the lightning, vapors, and foams that interrupt the novel's green imagery. But above all else, *Pierre*'s ecologies provide at least one critical term for ongoing conversations in the eco-humanities: *purpleness*. Whereas my reading of *Mardi* understood that novel's form within a wider history of nineteenth-century geology and astronomy—one example of what I called historicized *mineral criticism* for the environmental humanities—my analysis of *Pierre* emphasized sentence-level syntax and grammatical style to suggest that purple passages in Melville and other environmentally attuned writers might be indexes of ecological thought-in-and-as-writing. Melville teaches us that, in the most tangled and experimental environmental writing, we glimpse the ways in which the limits of human expression dovetail with the complexity of ecological relations. *Pierre*'s lesson for eco-literary studies is to linger on such purple passages in order to more carefully track the convergences of syntax, thought, and ecology.

MORTAR SECRETS

After considering the power of plants and reproduction in *Pierre*, after 1852 Melville turned to the sketch and short story forms familiar to readers of monthly magazines popular in the 1840s and 1850s. The six stories collected in *The Piazza Tales* reflect Melville's shift toward thinking about the differential ways of surviving, adapting, and dwelling among animal species instead of plant ones. Melville was not entirely convinced by those who tried to crudely apply Darwinian paradigms to all domains of human and animal endeavor, as some have tried to do with art and literature in the twentieth century. To quote Rolfe in *Clarel,* reducing the world to its material substrata only leads so far:

> Tell Romeo that Juliet's eyes
> Are chemical; e'en analyze
> The iris; show 'tis albumen—
> Gluten—fish-jelly mere. What then?[310]

What then? Melville had a more pragmatic understanding of human beings' capacities for expression (including being vicious as much as being artistic) than narrow channels of adaptation could account for. After *Pierre,* Melville takes up the post-Darwinian project of living with others—which Derrida glosses as *sur-vivance,* or *living with*—by concentrating on human spaces of sociality like ships, offices, and towers.[311]

The varied, globally dispersed stories in *The Piazza Tales* continue the themes of desire we saw in *Pierre*'s pansexual botanical play, but in these tales Melville contemplates another, more rudimentary need: human shelter as a means for survival. The architectural impulse has defined the visible landscapes of human ecology, first by generating huts, then walls, prisons, and cities. Whereas plants thrive by maximal exposure to sunlight and oxygen—what Emanuele Coccia calls "the most intense, radical, and paradigmatic form of being in the world"—humans need to be shielded from the world, to resist exposure.[312] When *Pierre*'s motley crew first arrives in New York City seeking shelter, Lucy asks Pierre about the urban ecologies she sees for the first time. Will the time ever come, she cries, "when all the earth shall be paved?" Pierre replies: "Thank God, that never can be!"[313] Although the planet remains less than 1 percent paved, in the twenty-first century, 40 percent of the earth's ice-free land has been zoned for agricultural use, and 70 percent of all freshwater for human use is routed for irrigation. Isabel's sheepish innocence ironically frames the sensory consequences of human ecologies, the felt inhabitation of a globally dominant species. She tells Pierre that the silence of New York City "is unnatural, is fearful. The forests are never so still." Pierre knowingly responds: "Because brick and mortar have deeper secrets than wood or fell, sweet Isabel."[314]

CHAPTER 3

Honeycomb
The Piazza Tales

. . . truth sometimes is sheepish.
—*The Confidence-Man*

In his 1859 copy of William Hazlitt's *Lectures on the English Comic Writers*, Melville checked a passage on the famous Greek fabulist Aesop, who, according to Hazlitt, "saw in man a talking, absurd, obstinate, proud, angry animal."[1] Melville wrote at the bottom of the page: "One more adjective wanting—cruel." For Hazlitt, in traditional fables—short tales of talking foxes or thirsty, tech-savvy crows—we encounter a truth about our animal selves that cannot be ignored. "The invention of a fable," Hazlitt writes, "is to me the most enviable exertion of human genius: it is the discovering of a truth to which there is no clue, and which, when once found out, can never be forgotten."[2] In the fable, we realize that the capacities of the human that we so assuredly designate to our species alone—the ability to invent tools, for example, or build homes and mourn loss—are not restricted to or even fully reached by us humans.[3] In the fable, we discover that "the human animal is," as the narrator of the *Confidence-Man* phrases it, "for most work-purposes, a losing animal."[4]

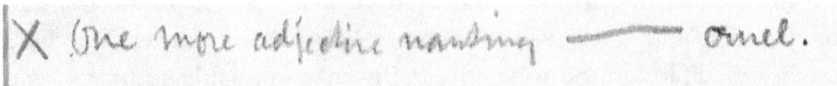

Melville's marginalia, in William Hazlitt's *"Lectures on the English Comic Writers" and "Lectures on the English Poets,"* 3rd ed., vol. 1 (New York: Derby & Jackson, 1859), 25, from Melville's Marginalia Online, ed. Steven Olsen-Smith, Peter Norberg, and Dennis C. Marnon (14 November 2019). (Collection of Mr. William Reese; photograph by Melville's Marginalia Online)

But Melville's addition of *cruelty* to Aesop's characterization of "angry animal" man provides a different valence for reading ancient fables as well as for reading *The Piazza Tales,* Melville's only published collection of sketches and short stories. Circulated individually in the newly launched *Harper's New Monthly Magazine* and the more established *Putnam's Monthly Magazine* between 1853 and 1855, these stories were collected as a single volume by Dix & Edwards in 1856. Together, they represent Melville's most intensely focused look at the distinctions between humans and animals. These stories were also, along with *Typee* and *Omoo,* his best-received works in the nineteenth century and, in the twentieth and twenty-first centuries, his most-often anthologized. Writing anonymously for the magazines, Melville made more money than the combined lifetime sales of *Moby-Dick, Pierre,* and *The Confidence-Man,* and he reached more readers than he had in a decade. Moreover, readers of *Harper's* and *Putnam's* would have been familiar with mixtures of literary, artistic, and scientific writings—especially Darwin's—that jostled in the pages of the magazines and that swirl in the stories that make up *The Piazza Tales.*

Drawing on recent work in critical animal studies, architecture, and the field of human ecology, this chapter repositions *The Piazza Tales* within Melville's broader ecological imagination. *The Piazza Tales* are a series of modern fables about dwelling among, and as, animals in the Anthropocene. Each story in *The Piazza Tales* offers a different grand narrative of human accountability for our species' animal imprint on the planet, ranging from the optimism of an eco-technological future to the pessimism of inevitable eco-eschatology driven by the long history of human cruelty, narcissism, and short-sightedness. To think the human-as-and-more-than-animal, Melville departed from the romances and novels he had written for the first ten years of his professional writing life. Instead, he picked up the literary sketch, a provisional and intentionally ragged form that enabled him to consider how, over time, both humans and animals aggregate into social orders concentrated in structures of inhabitation like nests, monasteries, and honeycombs. With particular attention to religious sanctuaries, Melville's sketches meditate on the ways that the human animal *keeps time* within these inhabited social spaces. The human, for Melville, is thus a mode of *being-in-time.* The temporal consciousness of the human differentiates it from other species and opens an accounting of the future that bears on our social and environmental responsibilities. Ultimately, after closing *The Piazza Tales,* readers are left with the most unexpected ecological thought of Melville's career—a series of reflections on the meaning of grief in the age of Darwin.

After the failure of *Pierre* and the rejection of the now-lost 1853 manuscript for *The Isle of the Cross*, something profound happened to Melville's writing.[5] At a formal level, with the exceptions of *Israel Potter: His Fifty Years of Exile* (1855) and *The Confidence-Man* (1857), Melville began to move away from the novel toward shorter fictions, sketches, lectures, and, eventually, poetry. At a thematic level, his writing from 1853 to 1876 is much more overtly about social issues, from labor and slavery in "Bartleby" and "Benito Cereno" to economic corruption and spiritual despair in *The Confidence-Man* and *Clarel*. *Israel Potter*, also serialized by *Putnam's* in 1854 and 1855, satirizes the American national mythos to its origins, following the homeless wanderings of a Revolutionary veteran across Europe and back. In *Battle-Pieces*, Melville takes on the trauma of the Civil War by anatomizing the hope of reconstruction in a postwar democracy trying to cope with the meaning of failed promises, large and small (the "Supplement" to *Battle-Pieces* is Melville's most overtly "political" work). Although I will touch on *Battle-Pieces* and *Clarel* in chapter 4, I see these works, alongside *Israel Potter* and *The Confidence-Man*, motivating a different, theo-political path of Melville's writing that is less attentive to—but nonetheless built on—the philosophy of ecology developed in *Mardi*, *Moby-Dick*, *Pierre*, and *The Piazza Tales*. Contrary to some critical accounts of Melville's career, I argue that it is in *The Piazza Tales* that Melville most completely addresses the question of the animal and therefore the questions of technology, cruelty, and collective dwelling that converge at the dawn of the Anthropocene.

HUMAN ANIMAL ARCHITECT

In the past fifty years, anthropologists and behavioral ecologists have determined that animals have what could be called, anthropomorphically at least, *culture:* tool use, for instance, or episodic memory and the transmission of social meaning in songs. In the avian world, crows demonstrate working memory and even meta-tool use—using tools to get other tools—while chickadees, science writer Jennifer Ackerman observes, have "one of the most sophisticated and exacting systems of communication of any land animal," including flexible syntactical structures that alert birds to predators so reliably that other species listen for the chickadees' unique sonic signatures for their own protection.[6] Animals have also been spotted giving gifts and punishing cruelty, leading some anthropologists and writers to consider whether the "moral lives of animals" might offer new ways of conceiving species difference.[7] How do we reckon with scrub jays and crows that mourn their dead by placing twigs or grasses on the corpses of fellow birds? Or the cats, dogs, rabbits, goats, horses, birds, dolphins, whales, buffalo, bears, elephants, and turtles that have all exhibited degrees of ritualized grief for members of their own, as well as other species?[8]

While none of these questions are new—especially to scholars and activists concerned with animal studies and animal rights in recent decades—Hazlitt's comments about the blurred human-animal divide remain significant in the context of Melville's writing because Hazlitt emphasizes the power of the fable to disclose ancient insights that are slowly being confirmed by modern science.[9] In *Mardi*, for example, Melville describes the mutualism—he calls it "reciprocal understanding"—between shovel-nosed sharks and pilot fish, a mutualism so profound that when a shark is killed, the fish evince "their anguish by certain agitations, otherwise inexplicable."[10] If it is meaningful to say that the pilot fish mourn the shark, then it is meaningful to say that, beyond physiology, species difference takes the form of provisional affiliations and disaffiliations between living beings. This, it seems to me, is precisely the motivation of storytelling itself. At base, every fiction is really about the relative differentials or kinships that persist between humans and animals. Aesop and Hazlitt remind us that in the fable we face these kinship networks directly. In the fable awaits the realization that we have often "seen the animal without being seen by it," as Derrida would later put it.[11] In the fable, the reader grasps the fact that the animal "surrounds me. . . . It has its point of view regarding me."[12] And this recognition is what Melville offers his reader in his most animal-centered texts like *Moby-Dick:* where, for example, Ishmael and his crewmates are faced with the point of view of young whales "looking up towards us, but not at us, as if we were but a bit of Gulf-weed in their new-born sight."[13]

Melville was thoroughly fascinated by the "animal form," and particularly the "bond 'tween man and animal," as he wrote in *Clarel*.[14] So thinking the animal through Melville offers yet another way to consider the shifting fields of ecological-literary sameness and difference that we've been following in the previous two chapters. On the one hand, Melville is most famous for his declaration in *Moby-Dick* that the "universal cannibalism of the sea" and the "horrible vultureism of earth" extend to the human species as well.[15] The human is, it seems, the most animal animal, the maximal expression of animality. "White civilized man," Melville claimed in *Typee*, is "the most ferocious animal on the face of the earth."[16] A century later, Foucault and Derrida would argue that this attitude structures modernity not by "abjecting animality but rather by fully incorporating animal desire into our definition of the human."[17] Remember Ahab's enraged confession to his crew that the white whale had "dismasted" him, a speech delivered with an "animal sob, like that of a heart-stricken moose."[18] Or the hermit Oberlus in "The Encantadas," who is only superior to the tortoises he hunts because he has "larger capacity of degradation" and "an intelligent will to it" (what the narrator describes as a "pure animal sort of scorn for all the rest of the universe").[19]

Contemporary posthumanist thought—which Stacy Alaimo tracks back to Darwin's *Descent of Man* (1871), calling it "the founding text of posthumanism"—is also based on the insistence that the human is an animal, but one specifically "composed of the vestiges of other creatures."[20] This has long been established by evolutionary biology, microbiome science, and virology, but the vestiges of our premodern creaturely being also haunt our brain physiology and motivational psychology. Post-Darwinian biology tells us that we are wired as prey, still neurobiologically terrorized by former predators to be conditioned for flight or fight responses that echo threats from thousands of years ago. But Darwin himself did not fully address the more foundational and vexing question of what, exactly, constitutes a species.[21] Posthumanists would note that although Darwin was influenced by Lyell and Malthus to see evolution as design without a designer, after Mendelian genetics was integrated into evolution in the 1930s and 1940s, we began to see a different picture of evolution, one that depicts genetic mutation as a mode of navigating the chromosomal microscale within the macroscale of species change.[22] Today we understand that the unit of evolution cannot just be the individual species but, rather, the coevolution *between* species, a collective unit of evolutionary conjunction or "quasispecies."[23] Cutting-edge evolutionary developmental biology, for instance, has explored the roles of genetic switching and nonconvergent evolution whereby humans share common genes (like *PAX6*) with octopi and flies.[24] Adding in viruses, parasites, and the trillions of microbes in our digestive tracts, we must admit we are creatures of such organismic admixtures that, as the Cosmopolitan declares in *The Confidence-Man*, "You can conclude nothing absolute from the human form."[25]

However, Melville's animal fables only superficially reveal our similarity with animals; in fact, they disclose our deeper differences from them, not by posing absolute ontological distinction but by highlighting how humans and animals are different *inhabitants* in the world. Instead of hardening the difference between animal and human, the fable multiplies differences to expose its readers more directly to the variegated fields of life, to magnitudes of inhabitation and cohabitation that elude all systematic human approximations of sameness or difference. Consider the squid Ishmael sees from his whaleboat: an "unearthly, formless, chance-like apparition of life," so mysterious and differently inhabiting the world that no human knows its "true nature and form."[26] Or think about "brit," the tiny crustaceans Ishmael describes as "bulky masses of overgrowth" that appear so distant "in instinct" from "the same sort of life that lives in a dog or a horse."[27] After long cetological taxonomies and exhaustive inquiries into Enlightenment reason, Ishmael's descriptions of squid and brit offer a view of animals that resist category names. They present, instead, the unbounded abidingness of ecological life. In Melville's writing, apprehending species difference demands "acceding to a thinking, however fabulous and chimerical it might be, that thinks the absence of the name and of the word otherwise, as something other than a privation," to quote Derrida.[28] Derrida's solution—the zoontological-linguistic phrase *"Ecce animot"* (a portmanteau of *l'animal* and *le mot*: homophone for *les animaux*)—signifies neither "a genus nor a gender nor an individual" but "an irreducible living multiplicity of mortals."[29] In this chapter, I'm interested in how Melville's midcareer short stories might be read as fabular meditations on *being-animal*, materially and linguistically: *fables animot*.

Predictably, *Moby-Dick* has been taken as the centerpiece of animal life in Melville's writing.[30] The novel's immense biodiversity magnifies the central plot and primary philosophical tension, both concerning a single human and a single animal. In the opening "Extracts," Melville cites early zoologists like Cuvier and Darwin, whose *Animal Kingdom* (1827–43) and *Researches* (1839) he owned alongside Robert Chambers's *Vestiges of the Natural History of Creation* (1846) and Thomas Beale's *Natural History of the Sperm Whale* (1839).[31] Marine life dominates *Moby-Dick*, including an abundance of fish, whales, dolphins, sharks, and porpoises, leading at least one critic to call Melville an early "marine biologist."[32] But throughout Melville's fiction, in and beyond *Moby-Dick*, terrestrial megafauna run wild too. Elephants stomp, tigers prowl, and lions hunt. We've already seen more familiar animals in *Pierre*—cats, snakes—and the writings of the 1850s feature roosters ("Cock-A-Doodle-Doo!," 1853), bugs ("The Apple-Tree Table or Original Spiritual Manifestations," 1856), donkeys (*The Piazza Tales* and *Clarel*), and a wide variety of dogs: the "monstrous bull-dog" in *Israel Potter,* the Newfoundlands in "The Piazza" and "Benito Cereno," and Hunilla's "soft-haired, ringleted" puppies in "The Encantadas."

But the most prolific animals in Melville's writings are birds. The seed dispersal of "tropical birds" is vital to the development of *Omoo's* coral reefs; *Israel Potter* opens with an extended description of hawks, crows, and robins; and *John Marr* concludes Melville's career with a menagerie of haglets, black hawks, and gannets.[33] *Moby-Dick's* many albatrosses, eagles, and other seafowl seem to have migrated to *Pierre's* New York City buildings, as the artists who live in the attic of the Church of the Apostles are "storks," "magpies," and "pelicans."[34] The poems in *Battle-Pieces* are full of eagles, crows, orioles, and robins, and—flitting among camels, scorpions, slugs, and snails—owls and other birds roam *Clarel*. Birds also soar through *The Piazza Tales*, most famously in "The Encantadas," where "hermit-birds" and seafowl like "sea-gulls" and "cormorants" cohabit Rock Rodondo with penguins, iguanas, lizards, snakes, spiders, anteaters, salamanders, and tortoises.[35] Tortoises have a particularly special place in Melville's imagination, which he indulges in "The Encantadas," describing the "crowning curse" of the tortoise that is the selfsame jinx of the human: the "drudging impulse to straight-forwardness in a belittered world."[36] Melville was so inspired by tortoises—which brought together in a single creature many of the mineral, vegetal, and animal motifs we've worked through so far in *Magnificent Decay*—that he wrote a three hundred-page book, now lost, which he called in an 1853 letter to Harper Brothers "The Tortoise-Hunters."[37] This book was never published and apparently contained much more material than appears in the tortoise sections of "The Encantadas," which I discuss below.

But this chapter is not about Melville's literary and philosophical relation to animals per se. That important literary and philosophical project is beyond the scope of this book and remains to be undertaken in full. My brief, noncomprehensive list of Melville's animals here is less an attempt to catalog the species Melville mentions for zoological accuracy than a way to figure animals within Melville's environmental vision. This is, above all, because our familiar questions of difference and sameness inevitably turn on the *discourses of species,* as Cary Wolfe phrases it, since "our stance toward the animal is an index for how we stand in a field of otherness and difference generally."³⁸ Similarly, writing about Derrida's final lectures on animality and power, *The Beast and the Sovereign* (2011, 2017)—lectures whose themes of solitude, castaway dwellings, and islands bear on *The Piazza Tales* in important ways—Michael Nass observes that "philosophical discourses are never made up of discrete, unrelated claims but always of a network or configuration of analogically established and hierarchically ordered relations."³⁹ Therefore it is impossible to "think the animal in relation to the human without also thinking the relationship and putative affinity between the animal, women, children, and slaves, on the one hand, and the human and free adult male, on the other."⁴⁰ Here we are again reminded of the hermit Oberlus, a man who tried to create his own kingdom through violence and slavery, a man who delighted in "tyranny and cruelty."⁴¹ Oberlus enslaves sailors with the help of his "blunderbuss" (a homemade shotgun) before converting them "into reptiles at his feet," into absolute "animals" that are forced to serve his every whim.⁴²

Following this line of thought—in which cruelty is a key intervening term between animal and human—Melville's writings on animals show us how species difference must be seen not only biologically or materially, but in terms of sociality, which orients our attention toward language, social orders, and technologies. In the case of language, for example, we must appreciate that language, as we usually conceive it, never remains fully within the territory of the human but, as a field of semiotics, spreads to animals and plants (as in *Pierre*'s thickets of spiraling botanical life). Cary Wolfe has done much in animal studies to move beyond language as the sole differential matrix between humans and animals and plants in order to "theorize the *disarticulation* between the category of language and the category of species."⁴³ And yet the complexity of human language does enable several unique modes of inhabitation, particularly because language yokes humans together in collective dwellings by bringing to consciousness the imminence of one's individual death and the persistence of one's community/species after one's death. Such consciousness, in short, founds the human impulses toward monumentality and architecture.

Writing a decade before Melville, Marx used this insight to underpin his theory of alienated labor: "it is only because [man] is a species being that he is a Conscious Being, i.e., that his own life is an object for him."⁴⁴ Shadowing Marx through Melville, in the following sections I'm concerned with the forms of objectification that human sociality makes possible through an awareness of species-being. By objectification I mean the practices of human domination and cruelty—like slavery, kidnapping, torture, and rape (all of which feature in *The Piazza Tales*)—that are more extreme and elaborate forms of the ecological objectification that takes place in resource extraction. More precisely, Melville's short stories of the 1850s are about the impulse *to objectify* and thus make human dwelling possible: the desire to construct homes and human habitats that initiates architecture and organizes the *polis* around issues of precarity and homelessness. For, without a dwelling space, a human would be a "dispersed being."[45] Without a home, humans would be at risk, so the story goes, of being more animal than human. This leads, ultimately, to fantasies of belonging within national communities that, as Baudelaire phrased it, are but "vast animals whose organization is adequate to their environment."[46]

One reviewer of *The Piazza Tales* called Melville a "wizard" who wrote "strange and mysterious things that belong to other worlds beyond this tame and everyday place we live in."[47] But careful readers of the *Putnam's* stories would have noticed an equal emphasis on lived-in and everyday places that are made invisible by modernity. Melville ponders animality, human ecology, and democracy by creating stories set in common, familiar spaces of inhabitation. This is how he advances a subtle but piercing critique of technology, by painstakingly depicting the materials—screens, bricks, walls—required by *techne* to build monuments and living spaces and prisons. By the same token, in *The Piazza Tales* Melville hollows out the fullness of domestic scenes that filled nineteenth-century sentimental romances. He depicts invisible and abandoned inhabitations that mark an opposite, though still Romantic, asocial tendency. He studies the hermitic withdrawal from social life. With help from Bachelard, Bataille, and Agamben, I read Melville's chimneys, ships, and tombs as interrogations into broader discourses of vulnerability and security that have structured human political ecology through practices of dwelling.

Human ecology, as defined by Stanford biologist Paul Ehrlich, studies the "intersections of two complex adaptive systems," a technoeconomic one and a biogeochemical one.[48] Methodologically, human ecology relies on systems dynamics to explore how biotic and abiotic systems intervene in our species' lifeworlds, lifeworlds that are then looped into extraordinarily complex feedback spirals shaped by our own environmental interventions. This transdisciplinary field peels back the layers of inhabitation—the "nests upon nests" Melville describes on Rock Rodondo—that characterize multispecies practices of collective knowledge and dwelling related to the ever-shifting dynamics of food consumption, agriculture, and technology. Marx is especially useful for human ecology because he identifies capital as *value in motion* and therefore shows us how *"property relations are emergent properties of societies,"* to quote Andreas Malm, developing at the boundary between human sociality and nonhuman ecologies in which the human is entangled and from which, via *techne*, the human seeks to stand apart.[49] In sum, humans want shelter. Property is birthed—through Lockean individualism and a Smithian theory of labor—from this dwelling desire.

House building, real and imagined, has been a profound theme in human history, featuring in all world literary traditions. While architecture poses interesting philosophical implications for literature, especially in terms of originality and creativity in the long *durée* of architectural theory, I want to bypass this mammoth topic to see dwelling against the wider networks of nonlife and life that we've traced in chapters 1 and 2: to see dwelling in a more strictly ecological sense. For if architecture "participates in the construction of meaning through the ordering of spaces and social relationships," as architectural theorist Sophia Psarra argues, then architects understand meaning "not exclusively in the morphological properties of space themselves, nor in the cultural processes of its formation and interpretation," but both, simultaneously.[50] Architecture and literature construct experience, respectively, through *"structure* and *sequence* in a text" and the "conceptual and perceptual in architecture."[51] The emphasis on literary architecture has been a familiar theme in Melville, starting with the descriptions of island villages in *Typee* and *Omoo*, continuing in *Mardi*'s monumentality and the consistent depictions of temples and pyramids in *Redburn*, *Moby-Dick*, and *Pierre*. In *Moby-Dick*, Ishmael unequivocally compares writing to architectural design. "I am the architect," he declares, "not the builder."[52] In *Pierre*, as the rocky streets of New York City give way to the Church of the Apostles, readers encounter an "ancient edifice, a relic of a more primitive time" that stands in stark contrast to a neighboring law office building.[53] Walking past this "fearful pile of Titanic bricks" is like walking through an "avenue of sphinxes."[54] Melville's architectural motifs resume in "The Two Temples" (written in 1854 but unprinted in his lifetime), in *Israel Potter*'s famous bricklaying scene (chapters 23–24: "Israel in Egypt"), and in the ancient monuments of *Timoleon*. In one of *Timoleon*'s last poems, "Greek Architecture," the speaker distills Melville's eco-architectural theory of composition by emphasizing the formal corollaries between poetics and place: "Not magnitude, not lavishness, / But Form—the Site."[55]

The Piazza Tales also foregrounds architectural sites, and reading the collection as more than a sequence of individual sketches hinges on the central word of title: *piazza* tales, from the Latin *porticus* or "porch," which also carries the Italian word *piazza,* meaning "public place" or "square." Wyn Kelly has suggested that the "piazza tale" is a "narrative that provides literary space for cultural conflict" by inverting public/private spaces: Marianna's wooded "abode," Bartleby's "hermitage" in the Wall Street office, the "deserted château" of the *San Dominick,* the Albanian "cottage" in "The Lightning-Rod Man," and the "metallic aviary" of Bannadonna's bell tower.[56] In these dwellings, Melville crosses the thresholds that delineate the public from private, animal from human. This exploration comes to its fullest expression in "The Encantadas," where tortoise shells are "citadels," undersea grottoes are "honey-combs," and the earth itself is a "monastery."[57] However, among the many structures in *The Piazza Tales,* the religious abbey and the monastery stand out above all others. These places, where one's withdrawal from society means a lifelong dedication to absolute spiritual rules, indicate Melville's attraction to spiritual solitude and its meaning for socio-ecological life.

Etymologically, the word "monastery"—from the postclassical Latin *monasterium* or "monk's cell"—comes from Hellenistic Greek μονάζειν "to live alone."[58] In *The Highest Poverty: Monastic Rules and Form-of-Life* (2013), Agamben argues that the monastery, which originates in fourth- and fifth-century Europe, is best understood as "a field of forces run through by two intensities" he identifies as *rule* and *life.* For Agamben, without these two concepts, "the political and ethical-juridical rationality of modernity would be unthinkable."[59] In the monastery, rule and life are conjoined in monastic *rules for living* to create what Agamben terms "form-of-life," or "a life that is linked so closely to its form that it proves to be inseparable from it."[60] In the cloistered community—as in the first monastery at Monte Cassino founded by Benedict of Nursia in the sixth century—work, technology, and religion were integrated to such a degree that the monks took on a historically unprecedented stance toward the environmental inhabitation. (It might be useful to note here that the pioneering geneticist Gregor Mendel, who published his landmark theory of genetic inheritance in the 1860s, seventy years before it was fully appreciated, was himself an Augustinian monk.)

The monastery is prominent in Melville's writing because it unites his lifelong quest for spiritual meaning with his interest in human-animal dwellings. Repeatedly comparing spaces and characters to monasteries and monks, Melville's major works are dotted with religious recluses, from the "man-hunting" but pious hermit at the end of *Typee* to *Clarel*'s "Syrian monk"—"a true recluse, an anchorite."[61] As we will see, life in the monastery and life at the writing desk depend on *rules* that give form to existence. But why should we ecologically sensitive readers care about architecture or monastic rules? What then? This is the question that Bartleby's narrator poses to readers of *The Piazza Tales* more generally: "What then will you do?"[62] How can we not just observe the intriguing discourses that underwrite the Anthropocene but *witness* and *respond* to it?

The central argument of this chapter is that *The Piazza Tales* outline the four primary human responses to the Anthropocene—the eco-conscious response, the eco-technic response, the economic response, and the eco-pessimistic response. Each of *The Piazza Tales* historicizes the Anthropocene, repeating over the course of the collection the lesson that there is no single *anthropos*, no single way of (species) dwelling. In *Moby-Dick*, and *Typee* and *White-Jacket* before it, Melville had begun to shift his readers' attention to the long history of human subjugation and cruelty in the West, directed both toward animals and, especially, toward nonwhite humans like Tashtego, Dagoo, and Queequeg. In *Pierre*, such conflicts remain largely hidden but present themselves in subtle ways, like the original deeds to Saddle Meadows that bore "the cyphers of three Indian kings, the aboriginal and only conveyancers of those noble woods and plains."[63] These suppressed histories of indigenous dispossession, slavery, and imperialism rehearse Melville's midlife conclusion that we are cruel animals, and cruel to animals of all kinds. The fish on Rock Rodondo in "The Encantadas," for instance, have too much "confidence" and "trust" in humans, for they "do not understand" the intrinsic cruelty of human nature (an observation Darwin made in *Researches* regarding the initial "tameness" of Galapagos birds that eventually became a learned fear of man).[64] Moreover, we are cruel to, imprison, and destroy our own species. "How unlike are we made!" Captain Delano ironically puts it in "Benito Cereno."[65]

Melville shows us that the seemingly diffuse culpability for the Anthropocene can be made visible by tracing its origin to certain actors at certain times: Britain and America in the eighteenth and nineteenth centuries, a period in which the two countries alone produced the vast majority of carbon emissions and were largely responsible for the ecological footprint of settler colonialism in North America. Juxtaposing the Global North—western Massachusetts in "The Piazza" and Wall Street in "Bartleby"—to the Global South—the Chilean coast in "Benito Cereno" and the Ecuadorean islands in "The Encantadas"—Melville makes an oblique commentary on the uneven distribution of resources and consumption in the world systems of planetary modernity. This is made even more explicit in other diptychs of stark inequality that Melville composed in his magazine period, like "Poor Man's Pudding and Rich Man's Crumbs" (1854) or "The Bachelors of Paradise and the Tartarus of Maids" (1855). *The Piazza Tales* seem to say that flattening ecological agency and stressing material sameness may obscure the guilty actor systems of the Anthropocene: white, male, imperial, capitalist, Anglo-American.

For example, the title story in *The Piazza Tales*, "The Piazza," is a simple fable of species-consciousness, a staging of the initial *aha!* moment produced by seeing animals, plants, and other humans from a nonhuman, ecologically informed perspective. The narrator of the story glimpses his home from the point of view of another, a cottage inhabited by a hermit named Marianna. The dance of perspectives in "The Piazza" cultivates awareness of alternate vantage points, a process that haunts the narrator long after he returns home. On the one hand, this is the basis of ecological thought. But, on the other, Melville's ironic distinction between the narrator's romanticized, touristic realizations and Marianna's ongoing, lived experience of ecological dwelling points to the conclusion that sudden ecological insight is fleeting and insubstantial (a process often troped as blindness-to-illumination, which we saw in *Pierre*'s lightning). These lightning flashes may seem profound and hopeful, but, more often than not, they merely repackage myths of progress within a fantasy of ecological consciousness that hopes, somehow and magically, that the Earth will be saved without collective action or radical changes to the rules that govern human dwelling.

Such magical thinking organizes a second conceptual approach to human-ecological relations: an abiding faith in future technology to manage risk and solve environmental problems. This attitude has many names and faces—from Promethean myths to Italian futurism to Elon Musk—but whatever we call it, eco-technical optimism is inextricable from the assurance of limitless economic growth that promises to manage limitless population growth on a planet with absolutely limited resources. Melville addresses techno-optimism in two closely related stories about security and mastery titled "The Lightning-Rod Man" and "The Bell-Tower." Together, these stories are inquiries into precarity, the condition of being vulnerable that motivates the technologist and that is, in the modern era, no longer limited to the space of home or village but extends to the nation and the very political order of the planet. In these stories, Melville asks: "where and how one may be safe in a time like this?"[66]

"The Lightning-Rod Man" considers the human capacity to manage risk and anticipate "danger-time." This capacity is at once underdeveloped—in the case of environmental impact and future planetary flourishing—and overdeveloped—in the case of national security or the proliferation of increasingly abstract financial instruments. At a less abstract level, "The Bell-Tower" deals with the practical management of resources and risk by recounting the final project of the eco-technical master builder Bannadonna. Signor Bannadonna is a "practical materialist" inspired "not by logic, not by crucible, not by conjuration, not by altars; but by plain vice-bench and hammer."[67] Bannadonna's aim is "to solve nature, to steal into her, to intrigue beyond her, to procure some one else to bind her to his hand . . . to rival her, outstrip her, and rule her."[68] For Bannadonna, as Melville put in a late poem, "Apollo's bust / Makes lime for Mammon's tower."[69] Bannadonna creates an automaton to ring the bells of his newly built tower, an "iron slave" who ends up murdering its master. After Bannadonna's death, an earthquake levels the tower, but the true legacies of his creations—tower, bell, and iron robot—are their environmental imprint. The production of iron, for example, depends on deforestation and the charcoal energy of fir trees (the production of one ton of iron requires more than twelve hectares of forest). However, the failure depicted in both of these stories—of the lightning rod man's security con and the unexpected consequences of Bannadonna's experimental iron slave—remain singular and local, easily dismissed anecdotes of historical pasts consigned to the mists of Italy or unnamed Albanian villages, where the stories are set.

By contrast, geographically precise stories like "Bartleby" and "Benito Cereno" update and expand the scope of environmental risk and technological fixes for modernity, attending to global systems of capitalism, slavery, and empire that, taken together, offer a third history of the Anthropocene. This is a history of cruelty, motivated by the possessive impulses toward property and money. If, as Ishmael put it in *Moby-Dick*, "man is a money-making animal," then any honest story of human ecology must trace the history of property and economic regimes that administer our relationships to nonhumans.[70] I read Bartleby and Babo as visionaries who see these truths when others, like the lawyer and Delano, cannot. Bartleby and Babo are figures of resistance that indict capital and slavery, respectively, as the systematic, global human interventions that have driven not just ecological change but changes within the human species that radiate out into sociality and ethics.

In "Bartleby," for example, the lawyer-narrator—an avatar of liberal kindness and its attendant blindness—is drawn to Bartleby through a "bond" of "fraternal melancholy." But soon, after Bartleby's insistent preferences "not to" create problems for the lawyer's practice, "that same melancholy merge[s] into fear, that pity into repulsion."[71] Because he resists the work of Wall Street and therefore blocks the pathways of property and capital lubricated by the law, Bartleby remains an "unaccountable" hermit, a monastic presence in the office. He prefers to "remain stationary." Similarly, after his revolt, the former slave Babo remains silent and unaccountable. His head a "hive of subtlety," he is a honeycomb builder of revolutionary structures that violently de-glove the body of empire to reveal its skeletal form. Nietzsche understood that this cruelty, embedded in the will to power, had no opposite. Attempts to address cruelty inevitably fail because we can only negotiate less cruelty within the same economy that will continue to produce it. The lesson of Bartleby and Babo is that to escape from the system is to die, imprisoned or executed. But Melville does not end there. He continues beyond Bartleby and Babo into a far darker and troubling set of conclusions in his brilliant meditation on the most famous ecological sites in the world, the Galapagos: "an archipelago of aridities, without inhabitant, history, or hope of either in all time to come."[72]

"The Encantadas"—a set of ten interlinked "sketches" set in the Galapagos and serialized in *Putnam's* in three parts (March, April, and May 1854)—comprise Melville's most incisive philosophy of animal-human dwelling. "The Encantadas" bring together understanding of global systems with a fourth, more temporally dispersed outlook on the Anthropocene that anticipates an eco-pessimistic future of inevitable dystopic collapse. "The Encantadas" are full of "solitary abodes, long abandoned to the tortoise and the lizard," now tenanted by various human "refugees" who find themselves searching for water, "building a hut," and "preparing for hermit life."[73] Over time, these abodes and huts are abandoned as well, becoming mere "relics of hermitages and stone basins" that read like ghostly "signs of vanishing humanity."[74] "The Encantadas" provide a microcosm of the desertification that accompanies a warming world, where, amid the "parched growth of distorted cactus trees," tangled "thickets of wiry bushes, without fruit and without a name, sprin[g] up among deep fissures of calcined rock."[75]

On the Galapagos, Darwin and Melville meet. Not just in their shared fascination with the mysteries of the islands, but in the specific form of the literary sketch that both use to make sense of the stark solitude and inhuman beauty of the "Enchanted Isles." Describing his sketch method in *Researches,* Darwin explains that because the naturalist stays "but a short space of time in each place, his descriptions must generally consist of mere sketches."[76] In this regard, both Darwin and Melville find a kindred spirit in Goethe, who once wrote: "We talk too much. We ought to talk less and draw more. I personally should like to renounce speech altogether and, like organic nature, communicate everything I have to say in sketches."[77] Darwin's archive at the Cambridge University Library suggests that his writing life was indeed supported, and perhaps supplanted, by a trove of visual materials including photographs, magazines, sketches, etchings, woodcuts, lithographs, and drawings.[78] Even though Melville once wrote that "scientific drawings . . . are about as correct as a drawing of a wrecked ship," he too was attracted to the paradoxical nature of literary sketches, a mode of writing that sought to capture the limits of visual perception as much as the temporal ephemerality of human experience in the geologically sensitive era of Darwin.[79] For example, in a number of his stories from the mid-1850s, Melville combines the sketch form with the comparative visual effect of the diptych in painting. Graham Thompson maintains that the multipart structure of "The Encantadas" may have been influenced by Melville's viewing of multipart paintings in London in 1849 or, as we saw in chapter 1, the Boston exhibition of the *Course of Empire* paintings in 1847.[80] This helps explain why the ostensible author of "The Encantadas"—"Salvator R. Tarnmoor"—appears to be a double reference to the landscape painter Salvator Rosa and to Tarnmour, Iceland (another desolate island).

"The Encantadas" place Melville in the pseudonymous sketch-writing tradition of Irving, Dickens, and Thackeray, a tradition established by the eccentric, itinerant narrator-guide. But unlike Dickens's novels, for example, or even the other stories in *The Piazza Tales,* part of the interpretive difficulty of "The Encantadas" is that they do not form a coherent whole. They have oblique, ragged, and sometimes nonexistent relations to one another; they remain unfinished and incomplete. Further, as Thompson has explained, in their original magazine contexts each serialized sketch referred readers back to the previous one, with headings like "(Continued from page 319)" or "(Concluded from page 355)."[81] "The Encantadas" are in this sense intentional failures, for all sketches by design fail to completely capture their subjects. In "Sketch Eighth," the narrator is explicit: "I wish I could but draw in crayons" the grieving Hunilla, for "tracing softly melancholy lines, would best depict the mournful image of the dark-damasked Chola widow."[82] It is not surprising that two of Melville's other sketches for *Putnam's*—"The Happy Failure" and "The Fiddler" (both published in 1854)—deal with themes of failure, partiality, and incompleteness at a time when Melville was coping with the perception that he had largely failed as a novelist after *Pierre*. But in "The Encantadas," the theme of partiality is visible in the Galapagos Islands themselves, islands (along with others like the Marquesas or Hawaiian Islands) that had been so formative for Melville's developing environmental imagination.

Faced with the desert islands of "The Encantadas," Melville's response is ultimately not one of pessimism or nihilism but of grief, a condition of mourning that, at first, appears selfish or evasive or meaningless. But on closer examination, grief actually carves the space and time in which the memory and preservation of life are made, finally, paramount. This is most elaborately developed by Melville in "Sketch Eighth," which ostensibly follows the castaway widow Hunilla but quickly transcends the specific case of her mourning to contemplate mourning as a condition of evolutionary adaptation and persistence. The emphasis on mourning in Hunilla's story was also deeply personal for Melville himself. Melville's life was marked by influential moments of grief: his father's death in 1830, his son Malcolm's suicide in 1867, and then the deaths of both his brother Allan and mother Maria in 1872. At the end of *Pierre*, we're left with the ashes of Pierre's family archive. At the end of "The Encantadas," we're left with cinders on a deserted beach, the hollowed-out remnants of fire that become—like *Mardi*'s mineral clusters and *Pierre*'s plant spirals—emblems of ecological iterability. In *Moby-Dick*, Melville wrote that "the ancestry and posterity of Grief go further than the ancestry and posterity of Joy," for even "the gods themselves are not for ever glad."[83] Like grieving gods in the sooty haze of the Anthropocene, we withdraw into "The Encantadas" to learn the lessons of the "great general monastery of earth," whose absolute rules we must absorb to better dwell on this "melancholy sphere."[84]

MARIANNA'S PRIORY

The first story in *The Piazza Tales*, "The Piazza" was the only one not previously published in *Putnam's* between 1853 and 1855. Melville wrote it early in 1856, specifically to provide the varied tales that followed a coherent introductory frame. Set in western Massachusetts "not long after" the year 1848, "The Piazza" takes the first-person point of view that had characterized all of Melville's novels before *Pierre* and that organizes the majority of the *Piazza Tales*.[85] The story opens with a lush description of the Berkshire countryside, which the narrator notes "was such a picture" that it drew painters who filled the hills with easels on summer days. Summer in the Berkshires was the "very paradise of painters."[86] The narrator then compares the "limestone hills" to "galleries hung, month after month anew, with pictures ever fading into pictures ever fresh."[87] We've appreciated how the Enceladus sequence in *Pierre* blends literary pictorialism with the ancient dream vision, but *Pierre*'s emphasis on visuality and perception becomes even more fabular in "The Piazza." The narrator stands on the piazza porch of his country manor and notices some "uncertain object" that glints like "glass" or perhaps, the narrator muses, a "roof newly shingled."[88] Whatever it is, it looks "dazzling like a deep-sea dolphin," and the narrator is irresistibly drawn to investigate.[89]

Upon reaching the house, after following a "sheep-track" and being piloted there by a number of "yellow-birds," he discovers this dazzling dolphin is actually a "little, low-storied, grayish cottage" with a "fly-specked window, with wasps about the mended upper panes."[90] The house is unfenced, standing alone with "no inclosure." The narrator surveys the scene: "Near by—ferns, ferns, ferns; further—woods, woods, woods; beyond—mountains, mountains, mountains; then—sky, sky, sky. Turned out in aerial commons, pasture for the mountain moon. Nature, and but nature, house and all; even a low cross-pile of silver birch, piled openly, to season; up among whose silvery sticks, as through the fencing of some sequestered grave, sprang vagrant raspberry bushes—willful assertors of their right of way."[91] Without "inclosure," this dwelling is open to the ferns, ferns, ferns, woods, woods, woods, mountains, mountains, mountains, sky, sky, sky. By contrast, the house brings its dense, multiple surrounding environments to the present consciousness of the narrator. The house discloses an "aerial commons" that envelops everything: "nature, house and all." Even the "low cross-pile of silver birch, piled openly," is part of this commons, "among whose silvery sticks, as through the fencing of some sequestered grave, sprang vagrant raspberry bushes—willful assertors of their right of way." The birch firewood, gathered to heat the cottage hearth, is at once funerary fence and raspberry bush. It divides house from wilderness but also provides the *techne* that can bridge the two. And this is precisely how the narrator sees the "small abode." It is a "mere palanquin, set down on the summit, in a pass between two worlds, participant of neither."[92]

The woman who lives in the house, Marianna, sees herself similarly caught between two worlds, human and animal, and the raspberry bushes that spring among the cross-piles serve as reminders of seasonal transience that Marianna measures in solitude. But the turn of the story occurs when the narrator looks through Marianna's window at his own house. "I hardly knew it," he murmurs, "though I came from it."[93] At first, the lesson of "The Piazza" seems to be the narrator's newly found awareness of perspectives beyond his own. However, Marianna's awareness goes far past the narrator's, even to the point of hallucination. Living so long, alone in "the vastness and the lonesomeness" of the wilderness, Marianna has absorbed its "oceanic" silence and its enduring "sameness, too."[94] The "stillness was so still," the narrator says, that "deafness might have forgot itself, or else believed that noiseless shadow spoke." Indeed, to cope with her solitude, Marianna sees shapes in those noiseless shadows outside her door. As the midday sun and clouds turn shade into figures, she discerns "black Newfoundland" dogs in the forest light. For Marianna, passing "clouds and vapors" become "things," and "these lifeless shadows are as living friends." Marianna stays in her house, "knowing nothing, hearing nothing—little, at least, but sound of thunder and the fall of trees—never reading, seldom speaking, yet ever wakeful." She concludes that "this is what gives me strange thoughts—for so you call them—this weariness and wakefulness together."[95]

Marianna's wakefulness and weariness are at once effects and affects of ecological consciousness. Being attuned, patient, and silent enough to hear falling trees requires an exhausting form of emotional and intellectual labor. The labor of solitude. Marianna's wakefulness holds her in the gulf between the human world and the wilderness; she dwells between dwellings. And the abundant plants and animals in "The Piazza" mirror Marianna's double dwelling, as when the narrator describes the various scales of inhabitation in the "Chinese creeper" he plants outside his manor. By summer, this vine had "burst out in starry bloom," but as the narrator looks deeper into the foliage, he uncovers "millions of strange, cantankerous worms . . . worms, whose germs had doubtless lurked in the very bulk which, so hopefully, I had planted."[96] This multiplication of habitation—the worms inhabit the vine that inhabits the wall of the narrator's home, which he inhabits—signals the nested, ecological nature of dwelling: always in the dwellings of other beings.

But the most captivating example of habitat ecology in "The Piazza" is a brief reference to the "snail-monks" who "founded mossy priories" on Marianna's roof.[97] These snails inhabit their shells and the roof, building attics upon Marianna's single-story cottage in their slow life of double dwelling. The "snail-monks" are part of a series of religious cloisters that appear throughout *The Piazza Tales*. The entire Berkshire countryside is described as a "monastery of mountains," and Melville's juxtaposition of ecology with monastic life will, over the course of the collection, suggest how rules for living spiritually might double as rules for living ecologically.[98] In "The Piazza," Marianna's solitude affiliates her with a certain type of monk, an anchorite who lives alone in the wilderness (versus other kinds of monks like cenobites who live in a common *habitus,* Sarabites who live without affiliation, or religious itinerants who wanderer the countryside). The solitude, destitution, and poverty of Marianna's hut seems the very opposite of the collective life of a monastery, yet it is made monastic by the sails' shared life in their "mossy priories." Marianna's cottage, a trans-species communal space of monastic existence, has the potential to show us, in Agamben's words, how "to think life as that which is never given as property but only as a common use."[99] Life, in other words, as the "aerial commons."

"Yours are strange fancies," the unsettled narrator tells Marianna at the end of the story. She replies: "They but reflect the things."[100] Marianna's response to the world is to withdraw, to slow down, to await Newfoundland shadows. This bizarre and "nonfunctional" decision troubles the narrator, who walks his piazza deck, "haunted by Marianna's face, and many as real a story."[101] The narrator is haunted by Marianna who is, in turn, haunted by the immensity of the engulfing woods that are so "lonesome, because so wide."[102] As mentioned earlier, the narrator's preoccupation with Marianna is the first step in an ecological awareness of the Anthropocene. Being haunted by another being is to allow her to interrupt and affect one's private, individual economy. But "The Piazza" is just the initial story in *The Piazza Tales*. Simple awareness of our embeddedness, our inhabitation of other forms of dwelling, is not enough. For mere consciousness of ecological relations might actually accelerate complacency, dehistoricization, or, worse, a re-romanticization of "Nature." Melville recognizes this and places the tale first, following it with his most famous, de-romanticized and specifically urban tale, "Bartleby, the Scrivener: A Story of Wall-Street." We will take up "Bartleby" in a moment, but first, we need to detour through another form of nature re-romanticized. We need to delight in the fetish of the technological.

BANNADONNA'S STONE PINE

One of the most obvious differentials between human and animal is the capacity to create and develop complex technologies. Originally published in *Putnam's* in 1854 and 1855, respectively, "The Lightning-Rod Man" and "The Bell-Tower" are the two stories in *The Piazza Tales* that directly investigate the ways in which technology intervenes in modes of human dwelling. Both stories are set in Europe ("The Lightning-Rod Man" in Albania and "The Bell-Tower" in Italy); both concern the fashioning of copper metals (lightning rods and tower bells); and both focus on the environmental dimensions of risk, security, and technology. Most crucially, both investigate the meaning of what could be termed *eco-futurism,* the idea that technology provides the management of future risk and a means of problem-solving large-scale relations between humans and environments.

Take, for example, "The Bell-Tower," the final story in *The Piazza Tales.* It follows the master builder, "great mechanician," and "architect" Bannadonna. Sometime in the distant past, during some "forgotten days," Bannadonna is commissioned to create a tower, a "stone pine" column in the Italian forests capped with a "metallic aviary," or clock-belfry, "in its crown." This "Titanic" structure is as upright and god-defying as "Babel."[103] "Stone by stone, month by month, the tower rose," until, in "one erection, bell-tower and clock-tower were united." The bell is cast from melted "tin and copper" out of a "mammoth mould," dented all over with "with mythological devices."[104] But everything does not go smoothly in the construction of the tower. As the metal workers pour the molten mixture, the "unleashed metals bayed like hounds," and the laborers shrink back from the heat. Charging through them, Bannadonna smashes one of the workmen with a "ponderous ladle" so that the poor man "was dashed into the seething mass, and at once was melted in." As a result, the bell now has "one strange spot," a "flaw"—like the one in *San Dominick*'s "forecastle bell"—that betokens the "homicide" of the laborer: Bannadonna's sacrificial lamb.[105] In Bannadonna's bell, labor is subsumed, literally, in the product of technology. The metalworker is an unfortunate martyr at the altar of techno-progress.

But the story is really about Bannadonna's creation of a mechanical creature that automatically rings the tower's "clock-bell."[106] Bannadonna's "experimental automaton," as the narrator calls it, represents the apotheosis of technology as it moves from human supplement to human replacement.[107] Melville visually depicts this replacement effect when, seen from below the tower's belfry, Bannadonna's machine cannot be distinguished from a human figure. But upon closer inspection, and though it seems to possess "animal vitality," the automaton is without "human pattern, nor any animal one." It is *autohuman*. It has the appearance of "intelligence and will" but is, instead, wholly determined by its programmed circuit, its mechanics, and its rules. "Instead of bespeaking volition, its gestures rather resemble the automatic ones of the arms of a telegraph."[108] And metaphorically, this proto-robot is not just "Talus, iron slave to Bannadonna," but also "through him," a slave "to man" more generally.[109] The notion of animals as automata, as self-driven machines, comes (via Descartes) from the French zoologist Henri Milne-Edwards, whose *Dictionnaire classique d'histoire naturelle* (1822–31) argued for the deterministic, machinic nature of animal life. Milne-Edwards's animal-automaton theory echoes in the climax of "The Bell-Tower," when the automaton ends up killing Bannadonna. The builder accidentally interrupts the robot's "well-oiled route" and gets brained by the automatic arms of his creation. Melville concludes with an arresting image of the murder scene, where the automaton, standing over Bannadonna's corpse, "seemed clad in scaly mail, lustrous as a dragon-beetle's." "It was manacled," the narrator reports, "and its clubbed arms were uplifted, as if, with its manacles, once more to smite its already smitten victim. One advanced foot of it was inserted beneath the dead body, as if in the act of spurning it."[110] The manacled, beetle-automaton has successfully revolted against his master. The artificial animal has spurned its human creator in the ultimate act of resistance.

To make sense of what Melville is trying to articulate here, we should look to the description of Bannadonna's theological faith in machinery: "With him, common sense was theurgy; machinery, miracle; Prometheus, the heroic name for machinist; man, the true God."[111] A modern Prometheus like Victor Frankenstein, Bannadonna is at once monster and god, destroyer of old systems and creator of new ones, short-sighted experimenter and sacrificial visionary. He is the architect of a stable tower whose automated bell-tolling makes possible a temporal world apart from the rhythms of sunrise and sunset. At the same time, this Promethean architect introduces the technological paradigm that will eventually destroy him and the worlds he makes possible. Bannadonna, inflictor and sufferer, feels the inhuman mercilessness that he created. This is the "metallic necessity, the unbudging fatality which governed . . . the autocratic cunning of the machine" that Melville described in "The Tartarus of Maids."[112] Like the narrator of that story, in "The Bell-Tower," Bannadonna is confronted with the "inflexible iron animal" whose "machinery" strikes "dread into the human heart, as some living, panting Behemoth might."[113] The terror of the machine is its "metallic necessity," its complete governance by inflexible rules. The *auto-human* reintroduces to advanced civilization the unvarying instinct that we fear in wild animals, their untamable violence. Bannadonna's automaton reinjects the animal into a world of technological fantasy characterized entirely by control.

Throughout Western culture, the Promethean myth endures because it is so malleable and adaptable, capacious enough to register every century's anxieties over creation and destruction. As Emerson put it: "What a range of meanings and what perpetual pertinence has the story of Prometheus!"[114] But the Promethean myth is, finally, about our willingness to sacrifice central aspects of humanness in the name of (technological) progress. Ahab, for example, is an intellectual Promethean, a man whose "thoughts have created a creature" in him, a man "whose intense thinking thus makes him a Prometheus; a vulture feeds upon that heart forever; that vulture the very creature he creates."[115] In *Mardi*, Taji invokes Prometheus as a figure for responsibility. "In all the universe is but one original," he proclaims, "and the very suns must to their source for their fire; and we Prometheuses must to them for ours; which, when had, only perpetual Vestal tending will keep alive."[116] Vesta, the Roman goddess of the hearth, reminded citizens to tend the fire in the home, to take responsibility for cultivating the fiery source of our difference from animals. Bannadonna ignores this responsibility in his theurgical drive for construction. He starts by sacrificing the worker, exposing the first logic of environmental-economic relations under capitalism by which resource and labor collapse into identical objects of exploitation. The first logic then masks a second. Spirals of human ecology produce feedback loops in wider ecological networks so that substituting stone pines for wooden ones constitutes not merely a singular event in southern Italy in some remote past but a general, diachronic consequence of the human species. The automaton's creation is an abdication of Vestal tending. Technologies are not solutions, Melville seems to say, but are instead formal procedures for asking questions of human "nature" by magnifying its biases, prejudices, and cruelties. Experimental automatons only make the human more fully visible by ratcheting up the scale of philosophical problems—like agency or determinism—without addressing the underlying structural social relations that frame those problems, whether in artificial intelligence or climate engineering.

In his Promethean creations, Melville identified how technologies had become progressively integrated and internalized in humans' daily schedules and experience of the world. This is why he repeatedly describes processes of *timekeeping* in *The Piazza Tales*: from the seasonal "berry-time" of the Berkshire mountains in "The Piazza" and the lawyer's detailed description of his clerks' daily schedules in "Bartleby" to the ringing of ten and two-o'clock bells on the *San Dominick* and Hunilla's "labyrinth" of castaway grief-time in "The Encantadas." Importantly, Gerard M. Sweeney reminds us that Melville based "The Bell-Tower" on one of Hawthorne's *Tanglewood Tales* (1853), a collection of Greek myths for children that, in 1854, was given to Melville's five-year-old son Malcolm by his brother-in-law John Hoadley.[117] In "The Minotaur," Hawthorne retells the story of Theseus and the labyrinth, including a description of "Talus, the Man of Brass," the fabled giant automaton whose thrice-daily patrols protected Crete from pirates.[118] In Hawthorne's story, Talus "moved like clockwork," but in "The Bell-Tower," the automaton ("Talus, iron slave to Bannadonna") *is* the clock. Bannadonna's iron slave is created to ring the bell, to measure time. Melville wanted his readers to keep in mind that *techne*—Greek statuary to Bannadonna's automaton to Apple Watches—was deeply related to Western conceptions of time, a tradition that dates to the medieval Christian monastery and the doctrine of *horologium vitae,* or "clock of life."[119] The ringing of bells, and thus the consistent awareness of time in the monastery, began when certain monks (*vigigalli*) would awaken their monastic brothers at specific times based on their standing in the order, commencing a day synced by, and dedicated to, unceasing prayer. For Agamben, the intensely regulated horological life of the monk aims at the "spiritualization of the work of the hands" that might eventually culminate in "a sanctification of life by means of time."[120]

We will return to monastic life and its meaning for *The Piazza Tales* in later sections of this chapter, but it is significant that, in "The Bell-Tower," Bannadonna essentially creates an automated monk. Specifically described wearing a "domino"—the hooded cloak worn by French priests—Bannadonna's enslaved automaton is "manacled" to his labor, fulfilling the function of a monk without the spirituality of *horologium vitae*. Melville understood the deep irony here. Monastic life, in its attempts to sanctify life and resist the temptations of fleeting material pleasure, anticipates and gives temporal form to the Protestant work ethic that would be, by the nineteenth century, secularized in capitalist modes of production to produce mass quantities of consumer goods aimed to crudely and briefly satisfy those very desires. Further, the automation and commodification of time extended to forms of governmentality organized around precarity in the modern West, creating states of exception, permanent security threats, and counterinsurgent governance. In the twentieth century, Foucault would link the ideal of the Christian pastorate and parish—a flock of synchronized and devoted sheep—to the ideal of modern governance based on the synchronicity of consumption and risk management. This pastoral power is eventually marshaled by the institution of the police, reinstalling within the state a "theological program of sacrifice," to quote contemporary security theorist John Hamilton, "whereby one secures life by putting one's life at risk," and therefore security becomes "the basis for the state's rationale."[121] But a century before Foucault or Hamilton, in stories like "The Bell-Tower," Melville was already thinking about how discourses of sacrifice and risk intersect with modern temporal paradigms. What, in "The Lightning-Rod Man," Melville calls "danger-time."

"The Lightning-Rod Man" concerns a stranger who arrives at the narrator's house during a thunderstorm to sell copper lightning rods. Allegedly, these rods reduce the risk of catastrophic lightning strikes. The stranger tells the narrator to "get off of the hearth!" because the chimney has conductive powers that only the stranger's "specimen-rod" can divert to save the house and family.[122] The lightning-rod man claims that, "by nature, there are no castles in thunderstorms" and that any failures of the rods are the result of a faulty installer: "Not my fault, but his."[123] He further points out that "man is a good conductor" and urges the narrator to imagine "being a heap of charred offal, like a haltered horse burnt in his stall;—and all in one flash!"[124] "The Lightning-Rod Man" is a fable of *securitas*, of caring so deeply about being free from care that one actually generates more insecurity produced by the anxiety of becoming *se-cura*, without care. The lightning-rod man's con capitalizes on a vision of human vulnerability built from the phantasm of a self-contained Lockean self. The grifter promises security for the narrator and his family that can forestall the fear of stormy nature's violent reductions: man to animal flesh, charred offal, burnt horse. To sell his scam, the lightning-rod man manufactures fear, not only of storms but of other people—"avoid tall men" in a thunderstorm, he advises the narrator—and this fear can only be logically abated by isolation from, and replacement of, people by technologies like lightning-rods. "Do I dream?" asks the narrator incredulously, "Man avoid man? and in danger-time too?"[125]

The key word in the story is "danger-time," a time of unmanageable risk that has underwritten Western political philosophy for two centuries.[126] The lightning-rod man is, essentially, an investor in a sham technology, a financed confidence man whose practice has historical roots in the expansion of sea trade and the rise of insurance in the eighteenth century. This period of economic history is characterized by what Arjun Appadurai calls "actuarial thinking," or the management of risk by statistical calculations that attempt to counter natural uncertainty like storms or hurricanes.[127] But the narrator sees through the scam. "Something you just said, instead of alarming me," he tells the lightning-rod man, "has strangely inspired confidence."[128] The stranger pitches his rods as "reverse-lightning," but the narrator understands the faulty logic. The more we want security, the more we want to "reverse" lightning, the more insecure we become. Eventually, the narrator curses the lightning rod man: "you mere man who come here to put you and your pipestem between clay and sky. . . . False negotiator, away!"[129] After comparing the lightning rod man to "Tetzel"—a reference to the Dominican friar Johann Tetzel who sold indulgences in the early sixteenth century and subsequently motivated Martin Luther's theses—the narrator throws the "dark lightning-king" out the door.[130]

Despite the failure of the lightning-rod man, though, the commodification of risk continues. The "Lightning-rod man still dwells in the land," the narrator sighs, "still travels in storm-time, and drives a brave trade with the fears of man."[131] Anticipating the many faces of *The Confidence-Man*, the "Lightning-Rod Man" demonstrates how actuarial thinking shapes attitudes toward ecological relations, how an accounting of "danger-time" might culminate, a century later, in what Appadurai calls the "financialization of everyday life."[132] From rudimentary insurance instruments like lightning rods to highly abstract insurance instruments like credit default swaps, contemporary finance has altered the very category of a person by registering human beings through "the empire of probability" and risk management.[133] The operation of power has moved from the prison to the credit score so that "man is no longer a man confined but a man in debt," as Deleuze put it.[134] And the themes of security, risk, and time that we see in "The Lightning-Rod Man" play out, to different effect, in the law offices of "Bartleby, the Scrivener." Amid the New York City "turbulence" of midcentury America, the narrator of that story considers himself an "eminently *safe* man." Turbulence—which, in fluid dynamics, means irregular, chaotic flow—is a shrewd tag-word for the story, establishing the narrator's emphasis on the perceived safety and security of the law office, its precisely delineated spatial divisions and autohuman workday schedules.

BARTLEBY'S HERMITAGE

"Bartleby" and "Benito Cereno" are Melville's most read and most theorized short stories. They both emphasize, in remarkable ways, how practices of accounting—legal, financial, racial—have come to define modern life. The lawyer-narrator of "Bartleby," for example, cannot give a "satisfactory biography" of "unaccountable" Bartleby, nor can he precisely identify his duty to the clerk beyond the employer-employee relationship.[135] When Captain Delano encounters the *San Dominick* in "Benito Cereno," he cannot account for the odd relationship between Benito Cereno and Babo, or between the other sailors and slaves acting strangely aboard the ship. The reader of these stories—a proxy for the lawyer and for Delano—only gets the true story of Bartleby from "rumor" and the "true history" of the *San Dominick* from the partial translation of Benito Cereno's deposition (taken from the real Amasa Delano's 1817 *A Narrative of Voyages and Travels*).[136] Yet these two narratives are about more than mediated storytelling, (mis)perception, and accounting. They are about how the human species has inhabited the planet, not just by way of Promethean technological innovations but also in terms of economic exchange and the circulation of value. Modern human ecology in the past three centuries is inextricable from the abstract systems of accounting that organize technologically transformed labor and resources into capital flows and the traffic in bodies, nonhuman and human alike. In turn, these forms of techno-accounting shape new forms of modern sociality that have quickened our appropriative relation to nature and, ultimately, the global imprint of the Anthropocene.

Much has been made of the figure of Bartleby, a character so open to interpretation that he has become everything, a blank slate for creative interpretation that reveals more about the interpreter than the interpreted. Bartleby's "pale form" is "laid out, among uncaring strangers," like a "shivering winding sheet" that calls to be written.[137] And so philosophers and critics have written Bartleby through political, philosophical, gendered, and other lenses, emphasizing the story's economic and legal settings, its attention to the reproduction of documents, and the ethical complexities of Bartleby's preferences. But within the broader argument of *Magnificent Decay*, I read "Bartleby" as one of several stories in the mid-1850s where Melville addresses politics through a *negative* emphasis on dwelling: privation, homelessness, and eventually vagrancy. For example, in stark contrast to "The Piazza," which immediately precedes it in *The Piazza Tales*, "Bartleby" is full of whiteness, bleaching, and the absence of life. Unlike the painterly Berkshires, the narrator's "chambers" on Wall Street are "deficient in what landscape painters call 'life.'"[138] Bartleby appears to be a "lean, penniless wight," "a ghost" whose "cadaverously gentlemanly nonchalance" would leave the narrator "unmanned" as he imagines Bartleby's "horrible" solitude.[139]

Bartleby's solitude is crucial to the story and its wider implications for human ecology in *The Piazza Tales*, particularly as Bartleby deconstructs the meaning of dwelling (to the horror of the narrator and to the confusion of many readers). For, more radical than his preference "not to" perform the duties of the law office, Bartleby begins to *occupy* the narrator's office at night, making it his "hermitage," a word used seven times in the story.[140] The narrator defines Bartleby through the narrow vocabulary of accounting related to property and living space—mentioning, for instance, rent, taxes, and property—and he fears being "held to the terrible account" for Bartleby's preferences.[141] The narrator even offers to take Bartleby to his private "dwelling," if he would just leave the public one.[142] After this conditional hospitality is rejected, he pleads with Bartleby: "will you do any thing at all?" As an answer, Bartleby "silently retired into his hermitage."[143]

From the Latin *erēmīta*, the secluded dwelling of a hermit, "hermitage" connotes withdrawing from society for spiritual reasons, but the term has also been used to characterize anyone living in solitude. More generally, "hermitage" conveys the "condition of a hermit," a hermitic state of being. Importantly, the word "hermitic" is etymologically distinct from "hermetic," as being hermitic is not about controlling knowledge but being *withdrawn from the knowledge of others*. As Emerson once phrased it: "The poets who have lived in cities have been hermits still."[144] A hermit is in this sense an anti-Hermes—the messenger to the gods who actively interpreted the divine for humankind—because hermits remove themselves from the world, take up solitary habits, and to some degree become less socially human and more socially animal. Bartleby appears to be a hermit animal whose single preference is "to be stationary."[145] Like the masthead watchers in *Moby-Dick,* who are compared to "Saint Stylites, the famous Christian hermit of old times," Bartleby remains at his post, stationary, even after the office empties at night.[146]

But, in truth, Bartleby only appears to be solitary. Yes, Bartleby is absolutely withdrawn, the hyperbolic consequence of an individualist, capitalist system. At first. The state's perfect, passively reproducing subject, Bartleby slowly transforms the space in which property laws are put into practice, written, signed, copied, and disseminated. The law office on Wall Street becomes the dwelling for a dissident who "prefers not to" work, refuses the logic of private property, and short-circuits the linguistic, economic, and legal wiring of modern sociality. Similar to vegetal Pierre, Bartleby looks like some strange "gentleman forger," a man with no original claim who eventually dies in prison, presumably by starvation, in the ultimate poverty that reduces him to "wasted Bartleby."[147] But Bartleby's originality is, like Marianna's snails, his *dwelling within dwelling.* Interrupting the ceaseless accumulation of value that guarantees capitalist exchange, Bartleby makes capitalist infrastructure, and its status *as* human ecology, visible. Within the highly abstracted and largely invisible infrastructure of capitalist production, Bartleby's ghostly nothingness can be read as a consequence of being screened off from his environment. The lack of direct feedback signals from Bartleby's inhabited environments—the blank walls, the screens, the mass-produced ginger cakes from unknown sources—typifies modern life under urban techno-capitalism. "Bartleby" lets us inside a system that captures the energy of such alienation and redeploys it into new assemblies—better windows, green products, local parks—thus repackaging that alienation under the rubric of limitless economic growth that shields consumers from ethical guilt by rehearsing a triad of libertarian fantasies: free market choice, individual freedom, and personal responsibility. Bartleby, however, becomes the embodiment of the *limit* to economic growth-as-progress, an emergency brake in the momentous speed of unevenly beneficial capitalist trade.

Bartleby is most haunting to the narrator because he is not completely hermitic like Marianna. Bartleby is *fully* social. He is philosophically communal; *"he was always there."*[148] In precisely this way, we can read Bartleby's occupation in the context of Agamben's "form-of-life." Bartleby is the exemplum of the "monastic ideal, born as an individual and solitary flight from the world" that actually becomes the origin of a "model of total communitarian life."[149] Agamben notes that monastic rules aim to lead monks toward "cenoby" or "*koinos bios,* the common life."¹⁵⁰ Communal habitation is therefore "the necessary foundation of monasticism," based around *habitus,* ways of acting that become virtues expressed through modes of dress and, over time, dwelling.¹⁵¹ Agamben's argument is that because monastic life so closely followed certain rules—to the extent that life and rule merged—it was incomprehensible to the secular Roman law of the time. Nonetheless, monastic life created an example of order that would eventually be adopted by modern law in the West after the twelfth century, maturing into regimes of time, rules, and consequences. But the monastery is exceptional because it cannot be reduced to purely legal or religious bases. On the contrary, the monastery shows us new ways of thinking about the intimacy between human life and rules or laws. The idea of *form of life* or *forma vitae* predates monastic life, back to Cicero—a bust of whom hangs over the law office in "Bartleby"—but *forma vitae* achieves its peak only in the monastery. Bartleby's hermitage is a relic of a monasterial form of life, in which Bartleby's "monastic exile from the world could be conceived as the foundation of a new community and a new public sphere," to borrow from Agamben again.¹⁵² Bartleby's preferences, deferences, and occupations become a formula for ecclesiastical practice. In exile at home, Bartleby lives the perfect life of a philosopher-monk who, being alien amid his countrymen, is able to speak the truth of sociality. He has claimed the slow time and monastic space to see it clearly.

Bartleby resists capitalism's obsession with time—what Marx dubbed the "petty pilfering of minutes"—whereby individual moments are translated into "the elements of profit" in the attention economy.¹⁵³ Bartleby's preference, then, is a deferral of time that also functions like the monastic promise, the vow that joins the monk to the order and separates him from wider society. When monks took vows, they became *homo sacer,* bare life beyond the law, killable without legal recourse, so that the novitiate monk occupied the threshold between life and death (in some orders, new monks had to live by the entrance of the monastery for a whole year).¹⁵⁴ The monastic vow is not directed toward this or that behavior, like a law would be, but is rather the *obligation of obligation,* obligation toward dwelling in a general sense: "a vow of the vow," as Agamben calls it.¹⁵⁵ Bartleby's phrase, "I would prefer not to," is a vow of preference without grounding in the binary logic of the law. Bartleby's *forma vitae,* his occupation and (non)preference, renovates the meaning of dwelling, time, and obligation that have structured the *polis* in the West for seven hundred years.

Agamben writes that the monastic condition reaches its fullest expression in Franciscan monks, those so fully devoted to monastic rules and the achievement of spiritual work that their lives become "something that cannot be named."[156] This lack of naming is precisely the narrator's problem with Bartleby. Bartleby cannot be properly named for he is not "ordinarily human."[157] He is less human, animal, or vegetal and more mineral, mute and stony. Bartleby, like Yillah's pearl, is a sign of death-in-life, a monastic figure who slows time and takes a full "three days to meditate" on the lawyer's suggestion to leave the law office, before refusing it.[158] In the monastery, meditation (*meditatio*) meant the recitation of Scriptures from memory, rather than the contemporary sense of the word. This is noteworthy because Bartleby refuses to read, copy, and write, and Bartleby is himself unreadable and unwritable. It is impossible to "write the complete life" of Bartleby, and "nothing," the narrator claims, "has ever been written" of him.[159] However, the monastery was also a place of silent reading, the modern form of reading so ingrained in us but so unfamiliar to the ancients and even to Augustine who, in the fourth century, was astonished to see Bishop Ambrose of Milan reading without speaking. (Ambrose's "voice was silent" and his "tongue was still").[160] In monastic traditions, the "perfect life" coincided with "the legibility of the world," while sin became associated with "the impossibility of reading" the world: the terror of the world becoming illegible.[161] To the narrator, Bartleby is the becoming-illegible of the world. He is simply "air." He is "nothing."[162] As with Pierre and Babo—who likewise declare themselves "nothing"—Bartleby's meditations and form of life appear to others as absence, privation, withdrawal.

And, in the end, like Pierre before him and Babo after, Bartleby winds up in prison. Shifting from the law office to the prison, Melville's conclusion of "Bartleby" is remarkable for its architectural implications alone. Famously, Bataille and Foucault both argued that the prison is the origin of modern architecture because the architectural edifice, once a general emblem of social order, now enforces order on the cellblock. Within the arc of *The Piazza Tales*, the art galleries of "The Piazza" have been transmuted into the "massive cell-galleries" of the Bartleby's honeycomb prison. "The cumbersome stone ceiling almost rested on his brow; so that the long tiers of massive cell-galleries above seemed partly piled on him."[163] Tritely, the narrator tries to lighten the mood by appealing to the aesthetics of the prison yard: "Look, there is the sky, and here is the grass." Bartleby replies, "I know where I am."

In the final analysis, "Bartleby" is about how any ecological politics requires a philosophy of dwelling, of knowing where you are. Genuine eco-politics must originate in the home, which presupposes having a home. Ecological politics depends on not being homeless and not being in a state of enforced dwellings like the prison or the plantation (or a condition of permanent indebtedness). This is the political starting point for living in the Anthropocene. The root obligation of human society must be founded not in value accumulation but in the hermitage that promises the silence of privacy and the dignity of occupation. In this sense, Bartleby's occupation anticipates a number of twenty-first-century "housing first" movements, and the "high green folding screen" that separates narrator from seeing Bartleby in the law office, so often taken as an emblem for alienation, might better be seen as a symbol of ethical cohabitation. The screen does not completely "remove" Bartleby from the narrator's "voice" but makes it so that "privacy and society were conjoined."[164]

All of this is to say that Bartleby makes us rethink the close alignment of *eco-logy* with *eco-nomy*. Ecology, or the law of dwelling (*oikos-logos*) concerning the *relation to* human and nonhuman others, has historically been inseparable from economy, or the law of household (*oikos-nomos*) concerning the *relation from* human and nonhuman others. Bartleby asks us to separate these terms and reimagine them, for in the modern world "economy authorizes us to speak about dwelling while forgetting what it means to dwell," to quote Michael Marder.[165] Marder notes that our conceptions of dwelling shuttle "undecidedly" between economy and ecology like a house divided, as Lincoln would phrase it in 1858. "Bartleby" demonstrates that neither absolute possession nor absolute nomadism is acceptable. We must reframe dwelling through Bartleby to avoid replicating the same logics of economic alienation in other, seemingly radical political formulations, socialist and communist alike. Calling to us from a century and a half ago, "Bartleby" asks how, or if, economy might coexist with ecology.

But Bartleby's form-of-life is even more incomprehensible on today's Wall Street, where high finance has seized the monastic promise, the sacred vow, and reassigned it according to the logic of *liquidity* in the derivative market, which Appadurai explains is essentially "a market in promises, each of which leverages a prior promise" in a world without a sovereign or state to guarantee the promises are kept.[166] In the realm of derivatives, the inevitable collapse of promise chains finds its source in the house, the mortgage-backed security whose bundling into derivative forms caused the

2008 financial crises and left more than a million Americans without homes. Yet we have allowed the system to continue. We continue as *autoghosts*, less Bartleby and more the narrator-lawyer, quietly contributing to the haunting specter of economically driven planetary destruction.

Still, the last image we have of Bartleby in the "eternal pyramid" of the Tombs concludes Bartleby's story with an ecological tableau, and perhaps a hopeful one. The narrator notices that amid the "soft imprisoned turf" and "through the clefts" in the stone walls, "grass-seed, dropped by birds, had sprung."[167] Although he would not publish it for another six years after "Bartleby," in chapter 3 of *The Origin of Species* Darwin offers a related parable of ecological dependence: "As the mistletoe is disseminated by birds, its existence depends on the birds."[168] Melville's genius here, as with the Chinese creeper and snail-priory in "The Piazza," is to remind us of the dwelling-within-dwelling that ecology ensures, despite our anxieties over human individuality and the economic systems that threaten our habituated forms of life. Ecology persists, adapts, and overspills all walls, with or without us. The opening of the subsequent story in *The Piazza Tales*, "Benito Cereno," continues the same imagery of birds darting in and out of human dwellings. But instead of slipping across prison walls, flights of "troubled gray fowl" circle Captain Delano's ship off the coast of Chile, before skimming "low and fitfully over the waters, as swallows over meadows before storms."[169]

BABO'S HONEYCOMB

Unlike the greenness of *Pierre* or the whiteness of Bartleby, all is gray during the action of "Benito Cereno." Even at high noon the narrator is disturbed by the ambiguous "grayness of everything."[170] As the story unfolds, the gray uncertainties of Delano's encounter with the slave ship *San Dominick* and its mysterious captain Benito Cereno eventually come into black and white focus. The slaves have revolted; to avoid detection, they force Benito Cereno to put on a masquerade for Delano. Following the thematic of misperception readers encountered in Marianna's glittering dolphin-house, "Benito Cereno" tracks Delano's growing awareness of the "lurking significance" in the strange scenes he witnesses on the *San Dominick*. "What was that which so sparkled?" he ponders. And readers of the story are stuck pondering why Delano can't see the truth until it is too late.

"Benito Cereno" hinges on the inability to see difference, and, paradoxically, the tendency to see *too much* difference. Initially, for example, Delano perceives the "faces" on the *San Dominick,* especially its slave cargo, like "every other object" on board.[171] Because they are property, slaves are as much objects "as crates and bales" and are therefore largely "untroublesome."[172] But then Delano starts to doubt his perceptions, toying with the notion that Benito Cereno might be weirder than he originally thought, that Cereno might be an "imposter" or "trickster."[173] Still, Delano can't fathom the "plot" because, he reminds himself, whites "by nature, were the shrewder race." To imagine a white captain plotting with black slaves would be "to apostatize from his very species almost, by leaguing in against it with negroes."[174] For a brief moment, Delano considers the situation from a species level (one in which race is a determinant of species-being) to show readers the difficulty, for antebellum white Americans, of considering the species *without* differences like race. But Delano quickly gives up on this line of thought, for it is anti-theological. Entertaining the potential subversion of racialized species identity promptly gives way to "atheist doubt of the ever-watchful Providence above," the ultimate transgression of theological logic.[175] And really, Delano shrugs, "Who would murder Amasa Delano? His conscience is clean."[176]

Like the narrator of "Bartleby," Delano is the paradigmatic open-minded liberal subject: well intentioned but completely egocentric, so privileged that the systematic rules that structure and benefit his life have become invisible. And this is where Melville introduces a host of animal metaphors that police the category boundary between human and nonhuman, making visible the distinctions that support the institutions of property that prop up slavery. For example, Delano calls himself a "donkey" for mistrusting Benito Cereno and Babo, because "like most men of a good, blithe heart, Captain Delano took to negroes, not philanthropically, but genially, just as other men to Newfoundland dogs."[177] Moreover, before he is even named in the story Babo is compared to "a shepherd's dog."[178] The practice of aligning animals—especially dogs—with slaves in social and legal discourse has a very long history, as detailed by Colin Dayan's masterful *The Law Is a White Dog* (2011), which references a number of Melville's works, including "Benito Cereno."[179]

But the slaves on the *San Dominick* are not just dogs, they are "wolf-like," "pilot-fish," "black sheep," and "cawing crows escaped from the hand of the fowler."[180] When Delano inspects the "slumbering negress" and her child on the decks of the *San Dominick,* he identifies her as a "doe" with a "wide-awake fawn," before proclaiming the family of slaves "naked nature," full of "pure tenderness and love. . . . Unsophisticated as leopardesses; loving as doves."[181] Delano's naive, racist, *animot*-interpretive schemata recode enslaved African women as deer, leopards, and doves. And this transposition occurs throughout the narrative. As Delano approaches an old sailor, a "Barcelona tar," he remarks that the sailor seems be a "grizzly bear" hidden by "sheep's eyes" so that the sailor's "urisne air was somehow mixed with his sheepish one."[182] Another sailor with skin like a "pelican's" ties "gordian knots" for "someone else to undo."[183] In all three cases, Melville depicts the masquerades on the *San Dominick*—white and black—as forms of *performative ecology*. This is the definitive form of species-difference: the ability to rehearse the point of view of another species, where the relation to another transcends race, gender, and class and moves to an avant-garde inhabitation of trans-species distinctions.

Although this may seem outlandish, the climactic scene of the story is rendered in exactly these theatrical, spectacular terms. What duped Delano sees in Babo and Benito Cereno—"the black upholding the white" in a beautiful "spectacle of fidelity . . . and confidence"—becomes literalized when Delano is about to leave the *San Dominck*.[184] At that decisive moment, Babo "formed himself into a sort of crutch" for Benito Cereno and, "walking between the two captains . . . would not let go the hand of Captain Delano, but retained it in his, across the black's body."[185] This striking instance of convincing-but-fake racial sociality gestures at the "unnatural" relations that organize the Anthropocene's dependence on slave labor: global capital flows and enforced homelessness. Melville's virtuosity in "Benito Cereno" is clear when Delano ironically express the obvious—"Ah, this slavery breeds ugly passions in man"—without seeing the network of economic abstractions and environmental degradations that truly debase forms of sociality into "ugly passions."[186] Again, and also ironically, Delano perceives Benito Cereno as a hard-nosed commander who must obliterate "every trace of sociality" from his crew, hence "transforming the man into a block, or rather a loaded cannon, which until there is call for thunder, has nothing to say."[187] Yet this is exactly what the institution of slavery does, supported by the passive consent of consumer blocs that accept slave-produced goods and accede to a militarized philosophy of security that preaches the narrative of "loaded-cannon-precarity" to every citizen. These human ecologies are organized by economic relations that replace kinship relations. Abstract networks of global consumption supplant familial and ethical ones. As is made evident aboard the *San Dominick,* the economies that depend on cycles of extraction and slavery inevitably generate cycles of revolution and revenge that only more firmly entrench the systems as they seek to protect themselves against further threats and risks. Delano's "singularly undistrustful good nature," which sees "the benign aspect of nature," is embarrassing because the narrator sees "what humanity is capable"—the role Babo has been pushed to perform.[188]

All of this is unmistakably present in the story's final reveal. After Benito Cereno jumps for freedom in Delano's whaleboat, Babo's revolutionary slaves break performance and, in a "sooty avalanche," jump over the bulwarks of the *San Dominick*. Suddenly, with "involutions of rapidity," the "past, present, and future seemed one."[189] Cereno's jump and the slaves' reactions allegorize, in a single second, the eco-catastrophic consequences of black chattel slavery. "Benito Cereno" is about racial revolt, certainly, but it is portrayed in terms of an ecological disaster that is indescribable *without* the racial dimension. Is not the Anthropocene precisely a "sooty avalanche" in which rapid "involutions" blur past, present, and future, and in which race and ecology are indissolubly linked?

And if Melville's sooty avalanche metaphor neatly describes accelerating spirals of extinction and predatory human practices, then the final image of Babo, Delano, and Cereno fighting on the unsteady whaleboat is even more compelling. At last comprehending the situation, Delano holds Benito Cereno in his left hand "while, with his right foot, on the other side, ground[s] the prostrate negro," Babo. This moment obviously recalls the earlier description of the *San Dominick*'s "stern-piece," painted with "a dark satyr in a mask, holding his foot on the prostrate neck of a writhing figure, likewise masked."[190] The *San Dominick*'s emblem of Spanish heraldry offers a visual paradigm of domination and the networks of human ecology that support it. If we make prostrate other humans, the dark woodland gods punish us writhing humans with avalanches and catastrophes. Melville extends this allegory even more obviously in the description of Captain Aranda's stripped skeleton. When the "bleached hull swung round towards the open ocean," Delano finally understands that Babo had substituted "death for the figure head, in a human skeleton" and "chalked words below, 'Follow your leader.'"[191]

In the excerpted legal documents appended to the story, Melville multiplies the "prostration" effects of slavery to account for the centuries of colonial exploitation dating to its earliest figurehead—and metaphor for Western cartographic-colonial domination—Christopher Colon. The "official" account that splits the narrative continuity of "Benito Cereno" reveals that Aranda's skeleton "had been substituted for the ship's proper figurehead, the image of Christopher Colon, the discoverer of the New World."[192] Then there are, of course, the historical parallels between Babo's revolt and the widely reported revolts on the *Amistad* (1839) and the *Creole* (1841), plus Melville's decision to redate "Benito Cereno" from Delano's original 1805 encounter with the *Tryal* back to 1799, setting the story during the Haitian Revolution and against the wider backdrop of slave traffic, revolts, and naval commerce in the eighteenth-century Atlantic world.[193]

But this is fairly well-worn territory. I want to return to the rhetoric of habitation that we've pursued in *The Piazza Tales* so far because it is hard to overstate the persistent emphasis in "Benito Cereno" on human houses and animal dwellings. For example, the narrator tells us that entering the odd world of the *San Dominick* is like "entering a strange house with strange inmates in a strange land."[194] It all feels "unreal," and the ship itself "seemed the charred ruin of some summer-house" or "some deserted château."[195] Further, Melville packs on description after description of dwellings so densely layered that it is difficult to separate forsaken château from fox den, slave vessel from beehive. Recall the famous shaving scene between Babo and Benito Cereno. It takes place in "the cuddy," which at first looks like "the cluttered hall of some eccentric bachelor-squire in the country" but then dissolves into a multifunctional space without discernable rules: "a dormitory, sitting-room, sail-loft, chapel, armory, and private closet all together."[196] The story is also peppered with pronouncements of hospitality, as when Delano offers Benito Cereno "hospitality" by "stepping" from one ship to another as if moving freely from "room to room."[197] But, like Bartleby's lawyer, Delano is rebuffed. Consequently, Delano thinks Cereno's questions are similar to the creep of a "burglar" who "reconnoiters the walls of a house."[198] This security metaphor quickly slides into a fearful fantasy of human cunning and cruelty: "On heart-broken pretense of entreating a cup of cold water, fiends in human form had got into lonely dwellings, nor retired until a dark deed had been done."[199] But nowhere is human cunning more explicitly depicted in "Benito Cereno" than inside Babo's head itself, "that hive of subtlety."[200]

Babo's hive mind aligns slave rebellion with the sociality and cooperation of bees. The *San Dominick,* taken over by mutinous slaves, has been reinhabited, occupied, and, as Benito Cereno describes it, "every inch of ground mined into honey-combs."[201] Babo is its hive queen. He orchestrates his drones—like the slave Francesco who is described as "creature and tool

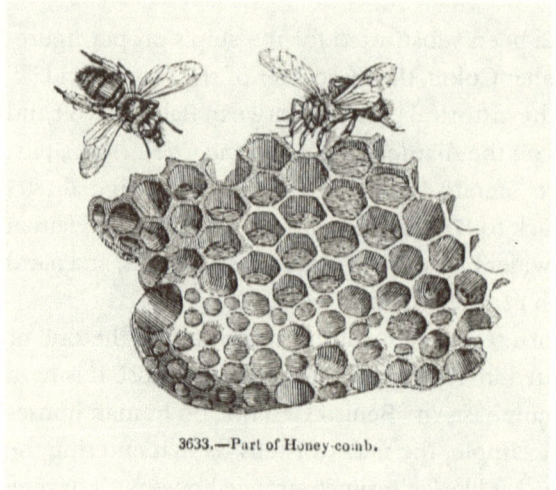

3633.—Part of Honey-comb.

"Part of Honey-comb," from *Pictorial Museum of Animated Nature*, vol. 2 (London: George Cox, 1844), 373. (University of Toronto Library)

of the negro Babo"—to create entomological sociality, a performance of dwelling that he has long been denied.[202] In the eyes of the law, "Babo is nothing"—a husk of a body, to be used and discarded, like an abandoned honeycomb—but Babo reinhabits his body, his "nothingness," via the reclaimed body of the ship. This moment is echoed in *Clarel*, where the Palestinian desert appears to the nonnative pilgrims as dead, "honey-combed," and "dumb," whereas the "true natives of the waste abode, / They moved like insects of the leaf."[203] Like the native Palestinians, Babo not only accepts and dwells in "that sacred uncertainty which forever impends over men and nations," to quote Melville in *Battle-Pieces*, but he also seizes the opportunity to create eco-revolutionary art from the violent dis-inhabitation of slavery.[204]

The *San Dominick* has been hived. It has been transformed into an insect dwelling, stripped of the techno-capitalistic abstractions and nationalist-patriarchal heraldry that support slavery. In "Benito Cereno," Melville does not re-animalize the slave but, instead, emphasizes the true nature of habitation: always reinhabitation, the temporary occupation of a previous occupant's place, the double dwelling of human and/as animal. This is the lesson Delano cannot learn but is one that haunts Benito Cereno to his death. Inhabiting the house of another former being makes us "hover between awareness of being and loss of being," as Gaston Bachelard delicately phrases it, producing awareness of our inhabited bodies as we nest upon nests.[205] Formerly merely a ship made of trees (lumber, tar), minerals (iron, copper), and animal products (hair, fat) carrying enslaved humans, the *San Dominick* metamorphoses into layers of nested animal dwellings, literal

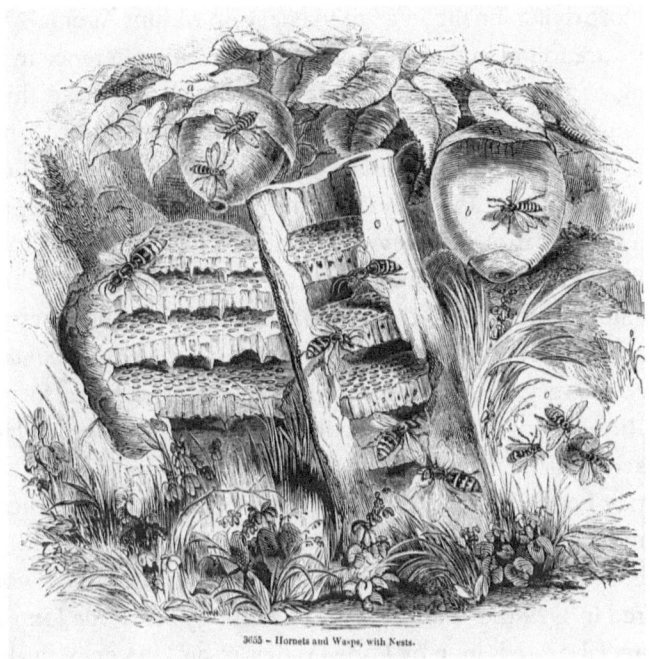

"Hornets and Wasps, with Nests," from *Pictorial Museum of Animated Nature*, vol. 2 (London: George Cox, 1844), 376. (University of Toronto Library)

and imagined. Early on, the narrator muses that the *San Dominick*'s topsails seem "like three ruinous aviaries," with a "white noddy" (or white tern) perched on the rigging.[206] Families of slaves peer out at Delano like "bats" in a "den" from the depths of the ship, while a Spanish sailor likewise reconnoiters the scene "from a porthole like a fox from the mouth of its den."[207]

But when Delano initially glimpses the *San Dominick*, he sees an altogether different form of inhabitation. To Delano, the *San Dominick* "appeared like a white-washed monastery after a thunder-storm," with "a ship-load of monks" milling about like "Black Friars pacing the cloisters."[208] (Even the ship's decks are monastic, littered with "melancholy old rigging, like a heap of poor friars' girdles.")[209] This strange crossing of metaphors to describe the *San Dominick*—at once honeycomb and monastery—is the crux of Melville's ecological thinking in "Benito Cereno." Why is Benito Cereno described as an "abbot," an "anchoritish" recluse whose demeanor suggests the devotion of religious piety? And why, at the very end of the story, does Cereno end up in the "hospitable refuge" of the "Hospital de Sacerdotes" in Lima before dying, finally, in a "monastery on Mount Agonia"?[210] Perhaps the answers are found in the most obvious monastic reference in the story, the naming of the *San Dominick* itself. Melville changed the ship's name from his source material to bring to his readers' minds Saint Dominic, the founder of the Dominican Order in the thirteenth century. The original "black friars," Dominicans conjoined monastic traditions with a lifelong dedication to education. However, a number of Dominic's followers participated in the medieval Inquisition after Dominic's death, which led to anti-Dominican sentiment in the West lasting well into the nineteenth century, six hundred years later. In "Benito Cereno," the *San Dominick*, once a metonym of slavery, becomes reoccupied by new black friars, former slaves who have hived from monastic practice a honeycomb of *koinos bios*: structural rules for collective dwelling.

This may be why Babo himself is not identified as Dominican but as "a begging friar of St. Francis."[211] The most recognizable Catholic saint worldwide, St. Francis of Assisi gave homilies to birds, tamed wolves, and was declared in 1979 the "Patron Saint of Ecology" by Pope John Paul II (a declaration elaborated upon by Pope Francis in his 2015 encyclical "*Laudato Si'*: On Care for Our Common Home").[212] From their inception as an order, Franciscan monks leveled the distinctions between the spiritualization of human and animal life by preaching to animals, liberating sheep, and loving even the lowliest worms. This had the effect, according to Agamben, of flattening the divisions between monks and animals: "If on the one hand animals are humanized and become 'brothers' . . . conversely, the brothers are equated with animals from the point of view of the law."[213] (Similar blurrings of animal and human recur throughout "Benito Cereno" and, as we will see, in "The Encantadas," where pelicans are taken to be "sea Friars of Orders Gray.")[214] Allying Babo with the Franciscan "grayfriars," Melville counterpoises the celebrated poverty and *horologium vitae* of monastic life against the compulsory poverty and timelessness of the slave. For, as Henry Louis Gates writes, "A 'slave' was he or she who, most literally, stood outside of time."[215] Slavery was, in other words, temporally infinite, enforced homelessness: a state of permanent exile and anti-dwelling. This is evident when Delano, naive to the synchronized conspiracy on the ship, calls the slave Atufal Benito Cereno's "tall man and time-piece" because "every two hours he stands" before Cereno, who dumbly awaits his apology.[216] But Babo recovers time, forcefully reclaims it, and creates a synchronized honeycomb of the *San Dominick*. The Franciscan focus on poverty culminates in *altissima paupertas,* the "highest poverty," which Agamben maintains is *"the attempt to realize a human life and practice absolutely outside the determination of the law."*[217] Babo's performance is similarly outside of the law. When he cannot act or live by his rules of inhabitation, he must remain silent. "Since I cannot do deeds," the narrator imagines him saying, "I shall not speak words."[218] Monastic poverty was an attempt to resist private property but retain use, *usus,* available to all. This is what Babo does on the *San Dominick.* He separates the economic from the democratic by uniting human dwelling (monastery-ship) with animal dwelling (aviary-honeycomb).

Religion has long been an interpretive avenue for Melville criticism, with one critic going so far as to say that Melville's writings offer a "deconstruction of religion" in which religious belief becomes associated with "claustrophobic architectural interiors" (like prisons or abbeys) that need to be escaped.[219] But rather than thinking of the monastery as an oppressive structure, "Benito Cereno" guides us to think of its philosophical openness, its encouragement of *communitas.* In the consistent deployment of monasteries and religious temporal ideals in *The Piazza Tales,* I see Melville deconstructing the Western monastic tradition—a tradition directly and indirectly complicit in the history of imperialism and environmental degradation, in addition to fostering regressive attitudes toward gender—in order to realign the value of spiritual life along an animal plane.

This is, however, exactly what Delano still cannot see. At the story's conclusion, the irrepressible captain tries to console Benito Cereno in much the same way the lawyer tries to console Bartleby, by emphasizing the persistence and beauty of the blue sky and sea. Mixing environmental metaphors, Delano counsels Cereno that "the past is passed; why moralize upon it? Forget it. See, yon bright sun has forgotten it all, and the blue sea, and the blue sky; these have turned over new leaves."[220] Benito Cereno replies that this is simply because these ecological realms "have no memory . . . because they are not human." Cereno identifies human memory—the capacity to be haunted, to achieve Marianna's "weariness and wakefulness"—as the differential between human and nonhuman forces. It is the foundation of the temporal life, the grievable life, the monastic life. "The negro" has "cast such a shadow" upon him that Benito Cereno perceives the force of Babo's eco-inhabitation everywhere, especially in his own "silver-mounted sword, apparent symbol of despotic command," which had become but the "ghost of one. The scabbard, artificially stiffened, was empty." Cereno's consciousness of his impotence, the failure of his "despotic command," is not just a consciousness of the artificiality of racial hierarchy but of the artificiality of the rules of *formae vitae* that have thus far driven the Anthropocene. He comes, at last, in the monastery on Mount Agonia, to a deeply pessimistic conclusion: that Babo's Franciscan form of life will be visible only at the eco-eschatological end of the world, a time at "the end of all lives . . . when all the West's forms of life have reached their historical consummation."[221] Babo heralds a revolutionary form-of-life motivated by a deep despair over human cruelty that, ironically, carries hope for our species, but only when we are forced to think beyond the Anthropocene, beyond the end of the world *as we knew it*.[222]

THE UNIVERSAL COPE

Babo's ghostly prophecy, foreseen by Benito Cereno at the end of his life, is magnified in the arid futurity of "The Encantadas," a series of sketches whose diagnosis of human life on the Galapagos can only be described as a mourning-in-advance, a collective species *memento mori*. The first two sketches—"The Isles at Large" and "Two Sides to a Tortoise"—for example, depict the "desolateness" and "solitariness" of the islands, permanently stuck in what appears to be a static condition ("change never comes") exacerbated by "everlasting drought" that produces "emphatic uninhabitableness."[223] The "spellbound desertness" of the rocky outcroppings presents to the narrator "a most Plutonian sight. In no world but a fallen one could such lands exist."[224] "The Encantadas" collapse past, present, and future visions of the earth, emphasizing an imminent desertification that some scientists have warned might be the ultimate consequence of the Anthropocene: not just the destruction of ecosystems but the unimaginable elimination of biotic sound from the world. This "Eremozoic Era," as Edward O. Wilson calls it, would rightly be deemed "The Era of Loneliness."[225] A silently enforced monastic world. The narrator confirms this experience of soundlessness on the islands: "Little but reptile life is here found:—tortoises, lizards, immense spiders, snakes, and that strangest anomaly of outlandish nature, the iguana. No voice, no low, no howl is heard; the chief sound of life here is a hiss."[226] (Melville clearly borrows from Darwin here, as both "The Encantadas" and *Researches* note the "hiss" of "antediluvian" tortoise, among other parallels.)[227]

If the Anthropocene is a time of great future suffering, sensitive planetary dwellers grieve in advance what will come. We participate in collective trans-species mourning. For even the naming of the Anthropocene is itself confirmation of the expectation of grief. Derrida teaches us that each act of naming is precisely "a foreshadowing of mourning," and, accordingly, the majority of "The Encantadas"—especially sketches 4, 5, 6, 7, and 9—deal with the traces of human society that linger in abandoned dwellings: residues of suffering and loss.[228] "Mixed with shells," we discover on these human-haunted islands "fragments of broken jars." Take Barrington Isle in "Sketch Sixth," designated a "harbor of safety" for pirates who "tarried here for months at a time" but never "erected dwelling-houses upon the isle."[229] Instead, the pirates made "seats" in the landscape, "symmetric lounges of stone and turf" that are "singular monuments" to the buccaneers' "kindly fellowship with nature."[230] These "ruinous green sofas," crafted by murdering outlaws, remind the narrator of the "vacillations of man"—how a person might be a robber one moment and "rural poet" the next.[231] But many of the sketches in "The Encantadas" are less sanguine about the human potential for persistence, often recording the *failure* of settlement, which critics have usually read as signs of Melville's latent political philosophy.[232] For instance, the "Creole" José de Villamil in "Sketch Seventh" (a man who was, historically, the first mayor of Galapagos in the early nineteenth century) attempts to populate Charles' Isle with eighty colonists, plus cattle, goats, and dogs. His experiment ends in "permanent *Riotocracy.*"[233]

But what binds the sketches of "The Encantadas" together is the ecological endurance of the Galapagos Islands themselves, visualized by Melville over centuries like a replayed time-lapse camera. These *"islands,"* the *Faerie Queene* (1590, 1596) epigraph to "Sketch First" notes, *"Are not firme land, nor any certein wonne, / But stragling plots which to and fro do ronne."*[234] The following sketches veer from the interiorities of "Bartleby" and "Benito Cereno" toward the cinematic quality achieved by multiple takes of a single space. In what might be called *literary rack focusing,* Melville oscillates his attention in "The Encantadas" between the foreground and background, between human ecologies and aquatic, avian, and reptile ones. The sketch form provided Melville a way to represent the double dwelling that characterizes ecology. By modeling human perception on the provisional, protophotographic form of the sketch, Melville approximates how human beings actually perceive ecology: sketchily. The failure of perception is a motif in all of *The Piazza Tales,* but "The Encantadas" contains the most extreme, even overwhelming examples.

Let's consider the celebrated tortoises that skulk about the Enchanted Isles. According to naval legend, tortoises were once "wicked sea-officers" who, in death, have been "transformed into tortoises; thenceforth dwelling upon these hot aridities, sole solitary Lords of Asphaltum."[235] The narrator is reminded of these sailor-turned-tortoises during dinner parties far from the equatorial sun, where "candle-light" makes shadows that "look of haunted undergrowth of lonely woods." He continues: "I have seemed to see, slowly emerging from those imagined solitudes . . . the ghost of a gigantic tortoise, with 'Memento ****' burning in live letters upon his back."[236] Much has been made of this "Memento Mori" tortoise, with its urgent reminder to "remember (that you must) die" as well as the typographical hiddenness of "death" behind asterisks that reduce the phenomenon of dying to absent language, a cinder of a word. But the narrator also notices that the tortoises' bodies are as "black as widower's weeds." These tortoises are mourners whose shells—"slimy with the spray of the sea," covered in "furry greenness" and "dark green moss"—are grieving amalgams of minerals, vegetables, and animals.[237] They are, at once, terrestrial and aquatic, geological and atmospheric, animal and human.

Subsequently, the narrator describes the haunting "affect" of the tortoises on him as they crawl the decks of his ship: "These mystic creatures suddenly translated by night from unutterable solitudes to our peopled deck, affected me in a manner not easy to unfold. They seemed newly crawled forth from beneath the foundations of the world. . . . They expanded—became transfigured." As the tortoises are translated from ancient, dead, geological relics to present, living beings, they become transfigurations of Melville's spiritual-environmental vision. They are exalted figures of the long duration of dwelling sustainably within their own habitus. The narrator extols the tortoise for its sovereignty of dwelling inside its shell: "pray, give me the freedom of your three walled towns" of "magnificent decay." In the tortoise shell, the narrator sees "a citadel wherein to resist the assaults of Time," and he becomes "inspired" by their "dateless, indefinite endurance."[238]

The tortoise sequence concludes with the strangest and most mysterious moment in "The Encantadas," and perhaps all of Melville's writing. The narrator recounts a dream—a hallucinogenic reversal of Pierre's dream of Enceladus—in which three Galapagos tortoises crawl through the "volcanic mazes" of the Enchanted Isles, "century after century": "crawling so slowly and ponderously, that not only did toadstools and all fungous things grow between their feet, but a sooty moss sprouted upon their backs. With them I lost myself in volcanic mazes; brushed away endless boughs of rotting thickets; till finally in a dream I found myself sitting crosslegged upon the foremost, a Brahmin similarly mounted upon either side, forming a tripod of foreheads which upheld the universal cope."[239] Like the "monstrous tortoise drear" in *Clarel* whose "ancient shell / Is trenched with seams where lichens dwell," these tortoises are mixtures of mushroom, moss, and "all fungous things."[240] Following the tortoises, the narrator gets lost in endless rotting thickets, eventually finding himself "sitting crosslegged" upon a tortoise alongside two Hindu high priests "similarly mounted" on their tortoises. The three humans-upon-tortoises form "a tripod of foreheads" that upholds a planetary ecclesiastical vestment: "the universal cope" of cloistral dress. This striking image is the culmination of Melville's monastic imagery, in which the entire planetary atmosphere becomes a surplice textured by ecological patterns, seamed and stitched by the uneven agencies of a multiplex world.

Even more remarkable is the fact that the word "cope" also means "canopy" and the "covering of vaulted form" that doubles as "sky," as well as the "outer mold" used to cast a bell (think of Bannadonna's eco-technical disaster).[241] Collating all of these definitions, the cope becomes a figure of encounter—whether vestment or canopy or vault—that simultaneously exposes as it covers and shelters. Melville's "universal cope" is shorthand for all planetary encounters between and among spheres of existence: the outer layer of a monastic habit, the tree-line limit of vegetal life, and the atmospheric immensity beyond. The tendril's reach, the foamy smear, the honeycomb. At the same time, the "universal cope" is a bell and a memorial tomb, double emblems of human time that hold hope for coping with the planet, for cooperation. The dream of "The Encantadas" is, in the end, about stopping time and interrupting our mundane work to glimpse the universal cope that engulfs us. Although eco-eschatological narratives tend to make the present hollow as we imagine the terrors of future dystopias, the narrator's dream rediscovers the present, a "tripod of foreheads" that, collectively, maintain ecological thought and the fragility of optimism. Then another tripod of foreheads—writer, narrator, and reader—reproduces that dream architecture as future generations write, live, and read in the Anthropocene.

But wait! In the following paragraph, and with delicious irony, the narrator forgets these lessons and proceeds to *eat* the tortoises. This is a genius move on Melville's part, reminding readers seduced by the buoyant eco-mysticism of the universal cope that humans are still cruel, storytelling animals who eat other animals. These transcendent tortoises are simply one link in a global maritime economy. Yet, a few pages later, Melville returns for the last time to the mysterious eco-promise of the tortoise in the most troubling story of the series, "Sketch Eighth: Norfolk Isle and the Chola Widow." About to depart from Norfolk Island after two days "hunting tortoises," the narrator of that sketch and his fellow sailor glimpse an "object" on the island that appears to be a "white-winged bird." The bird turns out to be the "handkerchief" of an exhausted castaway on the island, "a half-breed Indian woman of Payta in Peru" named Hunilla.[242] "Sketch Eighth" continues the paradigm of counter-visuality we examined in "The Piazza" and "Benito Cereno." However, the focus on Hunilla revises the paradigm by dramatically expanding the scale of narrative time beyond days, weeks, and years to introduce what could be called Melville's eco-philosophy of mourning.

MONASTERY OF EARTH

Hunilla is marooned on Norfolk Isle while hunting for valuable tortoise oil with her husband Felipe and her brother Truxill. In some ways, Hunilla is a stock character, an example of a popular subgenre of antebellum sea narratives that centered on grieving widows and female castaways. For instance, a significant source for the "Chola Widow" sketch came from an article published in the *Albany Evening Journal* on November 3, 1853, titled "A Female Robinson Crusoe," one of many such Robinsonades in the eighteenth and nineteenth centuries that allowed readers to ruminate on human solitude in alien and defiantly nonhuman places. In *Redburn*, for instance, Melville references Charles Ellms's popular *The Tragedy of the Seas* (1841), a book with illustrations of forlorn castaways and maritime disasters and whose frontispiece shows the genuflection of the shipwrecked. Also of note is the opposite panel, which cites Shakespeare's *The Winter's Tale* (1623), "The art itself is Nature," and Pope's "Essay on Man" (1734), "Art is but nature better understood." Ironically, these two excerpts on the intersection of art and nature summarize the primary thrusts of *Magnificent Decay*, though in their fuller contexts, they rapidly deviate from Melville's post-Darwinian ecologies (Pope, for example, deistically concludes that "whatever is, is right").

After being rescued aboard the narrator's ship, Hunilla tells the crew her story, beginning with her account of her husband's and brother's drownings while they fished off the island's rocky coast. The narrator recounts the tale: "Before Hunilla's eyes they sank, as some sham tragedy on the stage." He

Frontispiece to Charles Ellms, *The Tragedy of the Seas* (New York: Collins, Keese & Co., 1841). (Library of Congress)

continues: "Hunilla had withdrawn the branches to one side, and held them so. They formed an oval frame, through which the bluely boundless sea rolled like a painted one. And there the invisible painter painted to her view the wave-tossed and disjointed raft, its once level logs slantingly upheaved, as raking masts, and the four struggling arms undistinguishable among them, and then all subsided into smooth-flowing creamy waters, slowly drifting the splintered wreck, while, first and last, no sound of any sort was heard."[243] From her "balcony" Hunilla watches the "bluely boundless sea"—"the invisible painter" of wave-tossing hydrodynamic force—kill her loved ones. The narrator proceeds to interpret Hunilla's trauma: "Death is a silent picture; a dream of the eye; such vanishing shapes as the mirage shows."

Frontispiece to Charles Ellms, *The Tragedy of the Seas* (New York: Collins, Keese & Co., 1841). (Library of Congress)

The strange way that the narrator renders the scene as a *painting being painted*, a sketch within a sketch, is a double reference to the techniques by which death was made visible in the nineteenth century, particularly in the development of photography. At the heart of the photographic impulse is the desire to look at and memorialize the dead. The success of antebellum commercial photography businesses, for example, often depended on requests for funeral portraits. The final image of the loved one's body, especially a child, was a cherished object for nineteenth-century Americans, functioning as both prosthetic memory and a reminder of the specific time dedicated to mourning a loss. By the 1850s, when Melville was writing "The Encantadas," expensive posthumous memorial paintings had been supplanted by daguerreotypes affordable to a wider range of customers, sometimes for as little as fifty cents. But, marooned on the island, Hunilla has no images but those of her own memory. Only brushstrokes of an invisible painter whose hand moves with the same dispassionate fatalism as the sea that drowned her family.

Hunilla's depiction as a "dark-damasked Chola widow" thus embeds "Sketch Eighth" in a broader history of American mourning rituals dating to the colonial period. American writing has always been concerned with grief and mourning, from the Puritan sermon onward. But after the American Revolution, the meaning of mourning and commemoration became linked to national sovereignty and U.S. identity. Remember, for instance, Daniel Webster's orations on George Washington's death or Whitman's elegy for Lincoln in "When Lilacs Last in Dooryard Bloom'd" (1865). By Melville's time, the material cultures of mourning—dresses, flowers, handkerchiefs, fruit, and pocket-sized daguerreotypes—were tied to performances of mourning: objects to be worn, carried, wiped, eaten, and gazed at. In the early twentieth century, Freud would argue that the time of grief should be limited for the psychological health of the mourner because society relies on mourning "being overcome after a certain relapse of time, and we look upon any interference with it as useless or even harmful."[244] This is necessary, Freud argued, because "when the work of mourning is completed the ego becomes free and uninhibited again."[245]

Checking "excessive" grief is a theme that runs through Western culture, from Shakespeare and the Puritans all the way to nineteenth-century American conduct manuals and women's magazines. When Claudius famously reprimands Hamlet for "unmanly grief" over the death of Hamlet Sr., for instance, he reminds the young Dane that disproportionate grief is against heaven and nature. It is inhuman, animal.[246] To mourn too long is to be unaware of dates and thus obligations to the larger social sphere. But later scholars like Derrida and Judith Butler have shown that the egological rhetoric of individual freedom and the linear conception of time that underpin commands to stop mourning are part of a wider tissue of Western biopolitical hegemony that, through its rules for practices like mourning, sutures over wounds of loss with anesthetizing patriarchal, militarized, and capitalist norms. From Sophocles's *Antigone* to the September 11th attacks, we've seen how grief can be co-opted, commodified, and made the grounds for political or military action under the banner of security. (Hamlet Sr.'s ghost tells Hamlet to resolve his grief by avenging the patriarch's death, while Claudius warns that Fortinbras, thinking Denmark "disjoint and out of frame," sees the opportunity to invade.) Writing about George W. Bush's post-9/11 speeches, Judith Butler argues that when grieving is something to be feared, we have the impulse to "resolve it quickly" and act in a way that seems "to restore the loss or return to the world to a former order, or to reinvigorate a fantasy that the world formerly was orderly."[247] The desire to restore order—to get back to work, to move on from the acute pain of loss—is therefore symptomatic of a deeper anxiety over our planetary future. This anxiety is registered, as we have seen, in the eco-technics of risk management manifested in security measures that foreclose communal experiences of mourning. In Hunilla's case, however, Melville reconfigures the scene of mourning in a number of ways that allegorize the seemingly imperceptible ties between ecology and grief.

For example, Hunilla's burial of her husband was a ritual not possible for her brother Truxill, whose body remained forever lost at sea. Truxill's body never returned to Hunilla. "Her hands fresh from the burial earth, she slowly went back to the beach, with unshaped purposes wandering there, her spellbound eye bent upon the incessant waves." These waves "bore nothing to her but a dirge," endlessly returning to the beach and maddening her "to think that murderers should mourn."[248] The Pacific "murders" and "mourns" in a field of temporalities incommensurate with the anthropocentric fantasies of human time, a moment would have reminded Melville's readers of "The Chapel" chapter in *Moby-Dick*, in which family members of lost sailors like Truxill—sailors whose bodies were never recovered from the sea—sit alone "as if each silent grief were insular and incommunicable." These families, Ishmael observes, were "silent islands of men and women."[249] In "The Encantadas," Melville offers a poignant scene of Hunilla's insular labyrinths of grief, alone on her island:

> Day after day, week after week, she trod the cindery beach, till at length a double motive edged every eager glance. With equal longing she now looked for the living and the dead, the brother and the captain, alike vanished, never to return. Little accurate note of time had Hunilla taken under such emotions as were hers, and little, outside herself, served for calendar or dial. As to poor Crusoe in the selfsame sea, no saint's bell pealed forth the lapse of week or month; each day went by unchallenged; no chanticleer announced those sultry dawns, no lowing herds those poisonous nights. . . . What present day or month it was she could not say. Time was her labyrinth, in which Hunilla was entirely lost.[250]

Hunilla is the anti-Antigone. Without her brother Polynices's corpse, without the political regime of Creon, and without the space and time of Thebes. Hunilla's isolated island mourning is specifically articulated through a vocabulary of time loss: "Little accurate note of time had Hunilla taken under such emotions as were hers, and little, outside herself, served for calendar or dial." Hunilla has no clock or monastic bells on the island, only herself, without even animals like roosters or cows to regulate the hours of the day. Her mourning is outside of human time *and* outside of animal time. Her plight, marooned and doubly mourning, directs readers to think about loss in the largest possible frames of the indifferent seas, leading us to consider human grief meaningless against enormous scales of time and space that, through Darwin, the Galapagos have come to represent.[251]

And yet mourning practices date to prehistory, to the origin of our species and even to the Neanderthals, who, as Elizabeth Kolbert notes, did bury their dead.[252] So maybe, instead of being the most marginal of human activities, Hunilla's grief provides a primary clue to species difference, not in binary terms—for animals, as we've seen, do mourn—but rather as a measure of given species's capacity to handle "increased temporal complexity," Cary Wolfe's phrase for global ecologies-in-time, in which "organisms constantly adjust to each other."[253] For Wolfe, temporal complexity leads to a "supersaturation of chronicities that in turn generates a scarcity of time that drives the evolutionary process," but it also opens the capacity to think of loss from the perspective of planetary inhabitation, of communal dwelling amid death.

In this way, Hunilla's rituals of burial, mourning, and wave watching are screens through which the reader of "The Encantadas" reads another's grief. Like the narrator, we care for Hunilla as we bear witness to Hunilla's own caring. The word "care," from the Old Saxon *kara* (sorrow), appears in the modern German *karg* (gaunt, meager), an adjective that marks "the frugality that accompanies mourning."[254] And if Hunilla's mourning bears within itself the condition of reading—the address to the absent other—then this ethics of mourning is triangulated between Hunilla, the narrator, and the reader and replicates the universal cope upheld by the triad of foreheads in sketch 7. The endlessness of Hunilla's grief is a permanent rupture that reminds us readers of our own losses and our own impending deaths in such a way that it connects us, as grievers, to all loss, in all times, over the great arc of planetary life. Hunilla teaches us that grief cannot be exchanged; it can only be witnessed. Grief is in this precise sense *koinos bios*, life mourned collectively and thereby made communal. In *Clarel*, Melville understands that such a communal coping is beyond the reach of language; "ties may form where words be not" because "spiritual sympathy / Transcends the social."[255] This spiritual sympathy is the effect that Hunilla's story has on the narrator of "Sketch Eighth," who claims that Hunilla's suffering remakes Norfolk Isle into "a spot made sacred by the strongest trials of humanity."[256] "Humanity, thou strong thing, I worship thee," the narrator cries, "not in the laurelled victor, but in this vanquished one."[257] To Hunilla, "pain seemed so necessary, that pain in other beings, though by love and sympathy made her own, was unrepiningly to be bourne."²⁵⁸

In Hunilla's story, Melville salvages the meaning of mourning for the Anthropocene. Hunilla's story suggests that grief—affiliating pain with memory and emotion—can be understood as part of the wider evolutionary project, cultivating the species potential for communities of care that, through shared liturgies and literatures of mourning, interrupt the security of our private, ego-driven domestic economies. This is the import of the "post-offices" on "The Encantadas," which consist of letters in bottles whose writers are dead and whose addressees will never read them, alongside the epitaphic "grave-boards" that list names that will remain forever unrecognized. The origin of architecture is not, Melville seems to say, the hut, the prison, or the temple, but the grave. The unread grave-boards of "The Encantadas" are literary acknowledgments and epitaphic covers, encounters and shelters. Copes. This leads the narrator to remark that "the Encantadas too should bury their own dead, even as the great general monastery of earth does hers."²⁵⁹ In *Mardi*, "Oro, the supreme, had made a cemetery of the sea," but in "The Encantadas," the Earth is figured as the ultimate monastery.²⁶⁰ Melville's "monastery of earth" is an orientation toward ecological mourning, a becoming-conscious of the Earth as, like the monastery at Mar Saba in *Clarel*, a "place for discipline and grief."²⁶¹ But while the monastery was always known a place of discipline, Agamben has shown that, more properly considered, a monastery was a *workshop* and the monks artists. The monastery is "the first place in which life itself . . . was presented as an art . . . life itself in relation to a never-ending practice."²⁶² And if art in the conditions of planetary geotrauma is necessarily "grief-work," to quote Tim Morton, then Melville's detailed attention to our earthly monastic potential in "The Encantadas" resolves into an environmental requiem for the future dead.²⁶³

However, Melville does not advocate for some enforced set of rules that might cultivate the monastic life and reduce us to compulsory drones in an eco-fascist nightmare. This is the fate of the sad friar in *Clarel* who "toiled as in employ / Imposed, a bondsman far from joy."²⁶⁴ Whereas *Clarel* is about the possibility that faith might mitigate the universal condition of grief—"To believe, / Belief to win nor more to grieve!"—Melville had already arrived at the answer in Hunilla's story.²⁶⁵ We, like Hunilla, must give up trying to maintain the coherence of a singular world, for, as Derrida phrases it, "There is no world, there are only islands."²⁶⁶ Only the ecological open and its transient forms: clusters and spirals and foams and cinders.

Cinders, which appear in both Darwin's and Melville's characterizations of the Galapagos, are the ur-residues of planetary life. Generally, cinders are combustible substances burnt of their volatile constituents (as in the ashes of a body after cremation), but in physical geology, cinders are millennia-old remainders of thermodynamic processes like the phreatomagmatic eruptions of Galapagos shield volcanoes.[267] These shield volcanoes—so named for their resemblance to a warrior's shield—are formed by eruptions of magma-driven gas that create small fragments that fall in cinders around the vent: volcanic scoria, pyroclastic igneous rocks. For Darwin, cinders are material markers of geologic time. For Melville, they constitute a "convenient Potter's Field," full of "doggerel epitaph[s]."[268] Taking Darwin and Melville together, as "The Encantadas" invites us to do, cinders are deposits of the thermodynamic cycling of states of matter—what dissolves, burns, and persists—as well as metaphors for the residues of language that constitute the act of writing.[269] Cinders remind us of the common conditions of dwelling in a shared "Potter's Field," a cemetery-planet where strangers lie together in death. Readers of "The Encantadas" undertake the work of grief-reading, responding to the fact of death without succumbing to the politics of anti-mourning.

And yet, one chapter of Hunilla's story remains untold: her implied rapes by other passing sailors before the narrator came upon her. These events the narrator refuses to tell. They "shall remain untold," he says firmly, for the "two unnamed events which befell Hunilla on this isle, let them abide between her and her God. In nature, as in law, it may be libelous to speak some truths."[270] At the end of Hunilla's story, we are again reminded of the cruelty of the human animal. We face in the lacunae of her story the sexual violence, enforced servitude, and torture so deeply engrained in the history of our species. This might also explain the brief mention of the *San Dominick*'s "negresses" in the "official account" of the revolt that Melville interjects into "Benito Cereno." These newly liberated women "would have tortured to death, instead of simply killing, the Spaniards slain by command of the negro Babo," the document explains. For, "in the various acts of murder, they sang songs and danced—not gaily, but solemnly . . . they sang melancholy songs."[271] Ready to avenge their cruel treatment with torture, instead the female ex-slaves mourn through melancholy song and solemn dance the very *fact of cruelty*, the cycle of violence that they desire to perpetuate but do not. They grieve instead the violence that has been perpetuated on them, and upon the earth. Such violence and suffering will, only five years after *The Piazza Tales* was published, come to the hearths and dwellings of millions of Americans during the Civil War, burning through the South and leaving cinders of devastation in its wake. War turns men "loose," as Melville put it in "The Armies of the Wilderness," loosening ever further the elastic distinctions between human and animal:

> *Turned adrift into war*
> *   Man runs wild on the plain,*
> *Like jennets let loose*
> *   On the Pampas—zebras again.*[272]

The Piazza Tales tell the story of the humanimal origins of the Anthropocene, a story of accounting, objectification, and cruelty that nonetheless contains within it an often-obscured narrative of hope for generating human communities of care through collective practices of mourning that are—as shared rituals of surviving with others in suffering—deeply linked to environmental concern and the evolutionary arc of our species. The hope is that we may indeed turn "zebras again," not adrift in endless war but congregating to grieve: to see individual, kinship loss as collective, ecological loss. For zebras do mourn. Melville's *fables animot* dissolve species boundaries and enable us to apprehend, if only in the ephemeral moment of reading, the monastery of earth and the universal cope.

CHAPTER 4

Pebble
John Marr

If you find any *sand* in this letter, regard it as so many sands of my life, which run out as I was writing this.
—Letter to Hawthorne, October 25, 1852

In 1859, at the age of forty, Melville turned to poetry. After a visit to the Holy Land two years earlier and the unspectacular season on the lecture circuit that followed, Melville began to reread the poets of his youth, especially Spenser and Milton, with renewed attention to craft, or what he called "poet-problems."[1] He would continue to write poetry for more than thirty years, by far the majority of his writing life. In his struggles to compose verse—his poems sometimes ran "hard as sap from a frozen maple tree," as he put it to Richard Dana—Melville extended his engagements with "Nature," testing how poetic form might generate new modes of protoecological thinking.[2] In his well-worn copy of Hazlitt, for example, Melville checked a passage about poetry's ability to penetrate the egocentrism of modern life: "If poetry is a dream, the business of life is much the same."[3] Poetry enabled Melville to think rigorously beyond the logic of consistence—"Reason's arid law," to quote *Clarel*'s Rolfe—that, to some degree, is the very basis of narrative structure and literary character.[4] Poetry freed Melville from the strictures of narrative order, and he fell headlong into the rules and rhythms of the poetic line. Accumulating meaning line to line, stanza to stanza, poem to poem, and collection to collection, Melville's poetry reconsiders the linguistic procedures that shape how ecological insights are expressed.

Although Melville's poetry has long been neglected and remains today the least-studied aspect of his work, poetry was not a luxury for Melville. It was the most sustained business of his literary career, the definitive way to contemplate "the skeleton architecture of our lives," as Audre Lorde would phrase it a century after the publication of *Clarel*.[5] Studying his poetic contemporaries in the 1860s—especially Wordsworth, Tennyson, and Browning—Melville's annotations reveal a man in transition: a sailor-turned-novelist-turned-magazine-writer now contemplating the philosophical implications of poetic forms, forms that would have been very familiar to Americans of the period. In Melville's day, spoken poetry was woven into everyday life. Even illiterate citizens could recall memorized poems and songs, and the reading public generally thought that the great American literary artists of the nineteenth century would be poets, not fiction writers. As far back as *Mardi*, through the voice of the Mardian poet Yoomy, Melville had tried his hand at writing verse, but his first publishable collection of poems—composed in 1858–59 and titled simply *Poems*—was rejected by Scribner in June 1859 and subsequently lost.[6] *Battle-Pieces* and *Clarel* followed in 1866 and 1876, respectively, and then *John Marr* (1888) and *Timoleon, Etc.* (1891), the latter published four months before Melville's death. Melville's final collection, *Weeds and Wildings Chiefly: With a Rose or Two*, remained unpublished in his lifetime and was only restored in 2017 to its original form in the final volume of the Northwestern-Newberry edition of *The Writings of Herman Melville*.

As I will detail below, *Battle-Pieces*, *Clarel*, and *Timoleon* contain numerous references to ecological phenomena, often rehearsing the mineral, vegetal, and animal ecologies developed in *Mardi*, *Moby-Dick*, *Pierre*, and *The Piazza Tales*. But in general, these important works take an alternate course, a much more figurative one, by sublimating ecology into political or spiritual or historical meaning instead of dealing with the materialities of the ecological per se. In part 2 of *Clarel*, for instance, the Dominican friar invokes an image of botanical persistence—"how thrive the ferns / About the ruined house of prayer"—to make a theological claim: "Science but deals / With Nature; Nature is not God."[7] For many of the devoted characters in *Clarel*, science brought "Enlargement" of one's ecological consciousness, but so what? "[W]here's the change? / We're yet within the citadel" of human affairs.[8] Clarel himself cuts to the chase and asks the primary question of the entire poem: "Science and Faith, can these unite?"[9] *Clarel* leaves this question unresolved and in the process seems to abandon the ideas that Melville developed in his earlier fiction: *Pierre*'s spiraling purpleness, for example, or the universal grief of "The Encantadas."

But at the very end of his life, Melville published *John Marr and Other Sailors*, a slender volume of poems that does something remarkable at the twilight of his career. *John Marr* compresses a lifetime of ecological thought into a single collection of linked poems. In the process, *Mardi*'s geologies and *Pierre*'s plants, as well as *The Piazza Tales*'s ruminations on human-animal dwellings, mingle in the varied poetic forms of *John Marr*, crossing one another in wider and wider systems that capture the dizzying effect of "the wide world's swarm," as Melville put it in a late poem.[10] In *John Marr*, Melville networks various ecologies in a concentrated swarm, a final eco-signature of sorts. Hershel Parker notes that in the final years of his life, Melville regularly took long walks with his son-in-law Harry Thomas, and the two talked in depth about the theories of "Nature" that had preoccupied Melville for so long.[11] This last stage of Melville's ecological vision—in which the most evanescent planetary phenomena (storms, weather, atmospheres) are understood in terms of biogeochemical pathways—is a fitting culmination of Melville's decades-long entanglement with protoecology: a ragged multispecies ending, squally and windswept like the "hurricane-fire" of "The Haglets," where, in the "rigging's howling wilderness . . . Like bees the clustering sailors cling."[12]

This chapter highlights the presence of storms and weather in *John Marr*, atmospheric wonders that feature in many of Melville's most famous scenes (for example, "The Try-Works" and "The Candles" chapters of *Moby-Dick*) but signify differently in *John Marr*. This is in part because, by 1888, it was clear how big a role meteorology played in the history of nineteenth-century American science, from Elias Loomis's creation of isobaric and isothermal lines in weather mapping to William Redfield's research into the circular movements of wind around a storm center. (Then there was James P. Espy—known widely as "The Storm King"—who discovered principles of convection in storms and crafted the earliest synoptic weather charts.)[13] As we will see, in *John Marr*, Melville ponders whether a "Clerk of the Weather," or meteorologist, can ever distill the chaotic turbulence of atmospheric patterns into a coherent "weather-law." Nonetheless, meteorology provided a lively interface between scientific advancement and the general public in midcentury America. But after the Civil War, the relationship between the reading public and meteorologists changed substantially. As they became fully professionalized, all scientific disciplines became increasingly specialized in the postwar period. University faculty played larger and less publicly transparent roles in research, especially after the Morrill Land Grant College Act of 1862 that put science and the "mechanic arts" (like engineering) on par with traditional education. So, by the mid-1880s, publications on scientific topics in popular American newspapers and magazines like *Putnam's* slowed. At the close of the nineteenth century, the rising mathematical difficulty of cutting-edge science had largely alienated the American public, a public now conditioned to identify science with the wonders of technological innovation alone.

Yet the last three decades of the nineteenth century saw key developments in earth sciences, chemistry, and physics, particularly the work of physicist Josiah Willard Gibbs, who, building on the efforts of Lord Kelvin, provided an integrated theory of thermodynamics and a mathematical system (vector calculus) to describe it. Gibbs's two-part, landmark paper "On the Equilibrium of Heterogeneous Substances" (1876, 1878) created the field of physical chemistry as we know it today. In her biography of the man, *Willard Gibbs* (1942), Muriel Rukeyser has a chapter linking what she calls the "Three Masters: Melville, Whitman, Gibbs." Reading the *Pequod* as a symbol of "the conflicting energies of existence," Rukeyser understands Ahab and the whale as Gibbs might have: *thermodynamically*, flows of energy working in wider systems.[14] Although there is no direct evidence that Melville read, or knew of, Gibbs's work, he had clearly been attentive to the force, drive, and spin underlying "schemes" of physical phenomena since *Moby-Dick* and *Pierre*. These dynamics—how bodies move under applied force—lead the later Melville to think in terms of the circulation of "aggressive energy," as he put it in *Clarel*.[15]

In twenty-first-century parlance, this means tracing feedback systems' interactions in energy ecologies, especially the processes of *accumulation* central to contemporary questions of sustainability that confront the general energetics of complex systems. In his poetry, beginning with *Battle-Pieces*, Melville emphasizes the forces that drive weather events, tracking their implications for human-nonhuman feedback interactions. The fractal forms of clouds, wakes, and jets unexpectedly take on novel, ecological meaning in a soon-to-be-globalized world where energy flows are increasingly the mode by which planetary effects are most visible. In the poem "Misgivings," for instance, Melville intuits that "storms are formed behind the storm we feel."[16] Or when describing the aurora borealis, his speaker muses: "What power disbands the Northern Lights / After their steely play?"[17] But *John Marr* goes even further than *Battle-Pieces* or *Clarel*, following the interlinked energetic pathways of sharks, kelp, dust, and wind all the way to the seven poems that conclude the collection, each grouped under a single title: "Pebbles."

Largely ignored by Melville critics—even those who have concentrated on *John Marr,* a text itself dismissed as a "book of scraps" by Melville's early biographer Leon Howard—I see in these aphoristic, enigmatic lyrics Melville wrestling with the meaning of endurance and erosion, and with the correspondences between geomorphology and poetry.[18] A kind of envoi, "Pebbles" marks the end of *John Marr,* a collection that begins with a prose headnote and nautical elegies before dissolving into a series of shorter "sea-pieces" that ultimately fracture into epigrammatic, pebbly fragments. *Mardi* had its geomorphologic focus (on minerals), and *Clarel* is full of stones—as are Melville's journal entries of the Holy Lands—but "Pebbles" signal a dispersive expansion of Melville's geo-atmospheric imagination. In "Pebbles," Melville overlaps geology with religion, technology with storms, and chemistry with the breath of speech.

Geologically, pebbles are clastic rocks. Amalgams of detritus left by weathering and wave erosion, pebbles primarily end up on shingle beaches, but pebbles also appear further inland, where they indicate the presence of ancient seas formed millions of years ago. In "Pebbles," Melville taps into the ecological energetics of planetary systems: the flows of energy from sun to plants to more complex organisms whose digestion and respiration, body heat and excretion eventually lead to death, decomposition, and the return of energy to the soil as dust and sand. Scientists in Melville's day were arriving at this very conclusion, that all nutrients come from minerals and atmospheric gases. And in a biogeochemical sense, the diffuse circulation of dust and dew in "Pebbles" might be relevant for contemporary attempts to represent *"the warming condition,"* as Andreas Malm terms it, of our social existence.[19] In *The Progress of This Storm* (2018), Malm argues that thinking with heat—and other forms of energy that characterize thermodynamics—can clarify the temporal complexities of our current crisis, for "the excess of heat in the earth system is the sum of all those historical fires, of the cumulative emissions" of the Anthropocene. *"We can never be in the heat of the moment,"* Malm reminds us, *"only in the heat of this ongoing past."*[20] Human influence on energy systems is evident even in the most humdrum economic activities, like paving a road or building a home. Gravel, for instance—composed of natural pebbles formed from alluvial geological debris (usually old streams and lake beds)—is the major ingredient for concrete used in the industrial network of dams and roads that has characterized late nineteenth- and twentieth-century modernity. The aggregate industry, which produces crushed gravel, rock, and sand, is currently the largest mining industry in the United States. Moreover, the planet is actually running out of the industrial grade sand used for concrete and the quartz used for silicon chips, prompting mineral moguls and economic advisers to wish: "Were Niagara but a cataract of sand."[21]

Even though Melville was not completely finished writing after *John Marr*—*Timoleon, Weeds and Wildings, The Burgundy Club* sketches, and, of course, *Billy Budd* all remained on Melville's writing desk during this period—*Marr* is the proper end to Melville's ecologies. Proper because it is an ending that is not an ending at all; nor is it even a beginning, as the compound temporalities of the poems in *John Marr* are multiplied by the compound compositional history of the poems themselves. Melville began writing versions of the verses that would appear in *John Marr* and *Timoleon* as far back as 1860, and both collections must be understood as a lifetime accretion of poems.[22] Melville was drawn to the plasticity of poetry for precisely these reasons. Poetry offers more than singular endings. To some degree, poetry's interpretive "incompleteness" accounts for the enormous range of environmental poetry in world and American literatures, from Basho and Emerson to Juan Felipe Herrera and Juliana Spahr. But Melville's poetry is singular in this tradition, not because he was uniquely attuned to mineral, plant, animal, and energies ecologies but because he experimented with such an array of poetic forms.[23] Think, for example, of the elegies and martial chants of *Battle-Pieces*, the buckling iambic tetrameter of *Clarel*, the sea ditties and epigrams of *John Marr*, and the Attic fragments of *Timoleon*. In "Pebbles" alone, Melville tests the limerick, the ballad, the rhyme royal, the terza rima, and the aphorism to create a hybrid, ecological poetics in which the poems' petric forms match the aggregate biogeochemical objects they describe.

In my reading of "Pebbles" that follows, I focus on what I take to be poetry's essential difference from prose. The line break. Spatio-temporal pivot and syntactical gap, the line break acts upon an image to challenge, expand, distort, or prolong. To change, in other words, the duration of thought. Specifically because poetry is highly patterned language—whether in free verse parallelism, fixed rhyme, strict meter, or syllabic forms—its reading depends upon disruption, the interruption of rhythm that makes its form visible. The line break interrupts our accounting of the poem, just as the poem unsettles our finished calculations of the world by giving us new grammars for nameless thoughts. (The word "calculate" itself comes from *calculus*, "a pebble used for reckoning," and some linguistic histories understand human language as an extension of early accounting practices.)

Mapping mountain ranges onto massive waves, traversing hemispheres from the Appalachians to the Andes, "Pebbles" contemplate the measuring of weather and dust (from which the Hebrew word *abacus* is derived: קבא, āvāq, dust).[24] At the end of Melville's career, we are left with the incalculable endurance of our planet. As we've seen in Hunilla's tale, "endure" means to bear pain and hardship, to suffer long and to have patience. But the word also means to "indurate," or harden, as in stone. In "Pebbles," the practices of writing and mourning converge in rocklike poetic forms. They endure, to be taken up again like pebbles in a palm or a book in a hand.

DUST, KELP, SHARK, MARR

On a sea voyage to San Francisco in 1860, with his first collection, *Poems*, under review at Scribner's, Melville witnessed the accidental death of a sailor named Ray.[25] In his journal, Melville concluded that "death is indeed the King of Terrors." But, he pointed out, the terror is directed "not to the dying or the dead, but to the mourner—the mother.—Not so easily will his fate be washed out of her heart, as his blood from the deck."[26] Melville's contemplations of mourning and the epitaphic tradition that we examined at the end of "The Encantadas" carried well into the 1860s, finding their first poetic elaborations six years later. *Battle-Pieces and Aspects of the War*, like "The Encantadas," is full of widows, burial mounds, graves, and monuments, especially in the "after-quiet" of the "Verses Inscriptive and Memorial" section.[27] During the war, exhausted soldiers improvised camps on cemeteries, where a "head-stone" could be "used for a hearth-stone."[28] The space of death became the space of living. But, as Melville well knew, the grim inhabitation of death-in-life laid bare on the battlefield is a microcosm for the decay/growth ecologies that engulf us at all times. Melville's geo-temporal realism in *Battle-Pieces*—setting his poems in the Shenandoah River Valley or at the Battle of Shiloh, for example—translates universal Darwinian mourning on the Galapagos to Confederate and Union grief across war-torn U.S. geographies.

But *Battle-Pieces* is also an important laboratory for Melville's experiments with *atmospheric* imagery. For instance, the horrors of "Donelson" are matched by the "dark weather's sleety spleen." And the "livid Antarctic storm-clouds" glowing in "The Fortitude of the North" seem ominous corollaries to the war itself.[29] Then there are *Battle-Pieces*'s famous meteors, comets, and volcanoes. Trading in geo-environmental images, Melville imagines the meteoric, long-lasting impacts of human conflicts in the specific battles of the Civil War as much as in the more generalized war on the planet. Whether John Brown, "the meteor of the war," or the "plain mechanic power" of the "great Parrott gun" that bombarded Charleston, Melville sees in the lingering consequences of human-technological violence kinships with the collisions of earth-bound asteroids (like the one that contributed to the Fifth Extinction 65 million years ago).[30]

Battle-Pieces is most significant, however, because during its composition Melville reached a number of conclusions about the capacities and limits of newly mastered poetic forms he would deploy with even more complexity in *Clarel*. In Melville's Civil War poems, "entangled rhyme" can only hint at the "maze of war":

> None can narrate that strife in the pines,
>   A seal is on it—Sabaean lore!
> Obscure as the wood, the entangled rhyme
>   But hints at the maze of war.[31]

Obscure as the purple, hidden life on Mount Greylock, the woods in "The Armies of the Wilderness" remain shrouded in the fog of war that none can narrate fully. Similarly, and like the War itself, Melville's *Clarel* is so enormous—in sheer length and volume of allusions—that it may be outside the capacity of one reader to think it completely. Although a more comprehensive reading of *Clarel* is beyond the scope of this book, I want to note that, apart from its deserts, camels, and scorpions, *Clarel* is ecological precisely because its formal density and digressive, branching structure create intervallic hiccups in the reading process. *Clarel* is a self-described "interrupted tale," the proper form of an ecological network.[32] The regularity of *Clarel*'s iambic tetrameter establishes a rhyme rule that is consistently broken. Inaugurated in *Mardi*, the themes of endurance and fragmentation—knotted with questions of originality, inheritance, and copying—carry through *Pierre* and *The Piazza Tales* to their most elaborate poetic expressions in Melville's engagements with poetic rules and traditions: poet-problems. At the very end of his life, such problems took on more freighted significance as Melville anticipated his own personal and literary legacies.

When he wrote his last will and testament in June 1888, for instance, we can imagine that, like Ishmael's, "a stone was rolled away" from Melville's heart.[33] Melville's voice would, in some form, survive his body. His final wishes would endure. This was also the time when, a few months earlier,

Melville had composed *John Marr*. Published in a run of only twenty-five copies, *John Marr* is set of poems deeply concerned with the memory of friends long past, the aftermath of sickness, and the burial of loved ones. Unsurprisingly, then, it begins with a funeral. About "the year 1838" (when Melville was nineteen and about to begin his seafaring adventures), the title character John Marr, a retired seaman, settles in the plains of the Midwest. Soon, however, his malarial wife and young child are "committed with meager rites to the earth," not far from "where the Mound-Builders of a race only conjecturable had left their pottery and bones, one common clay, under a strange terrace serpentine in form."[34] Recalling *Israel Potter*—"what is a mortal but a few luckless shovelfuls of clay"—the narrator draws our attention to the mineral sameness of our sedimentary bodies, much as Babbalanja's skeleton had done forty years earlier.[35]

Marr buries his family on the prairie, likely in present-day northwest Illinois on the edge of the Mississippi River and Missouri Territory, where in 1840 a young Melville traveled to Galena to see his uncle Thomas Melvil Jr. The town of Galena was named for the lead ore found in the surrounding hills, ore that was originally a resource for indigenous peoples, including Havana Hopewell, Sioux, and Winnebago. The narrator describes how these native peoples were forced out of the area to the "wilds not very far beyond the Mississippi" after mining began in Galena during the 1820s. Likewise dispossessed, the "companionless sailor" John Marr is an exile from his sea-faring life, "an absentee from existence" lost in the American grasslands.[36] The provinciality and ruggedness of the neighboring wheat farmers—likely immigrant Norwegians who settled Illinois in the 1830s—seemed "of a piece with the apathy of Nature herself as envisaged to him here on a prairie where none but the perished Mound-Builders had as yet left a durable mark."[37]

A grieving stranger on the frontier, John Marr is suddenly awakened to his place in geologic time, a temporal scale in which human settlements, burial mounds, and writings are but momentary scratches in the "blank stillness ... of that immense alluvial expanse."[38] Looking at this American prairie-desert, Marr, who is admittedly "no geologist," concludes: "It is the bed of dried-up sea." Melville could have been referring to what is now known as the Driftless Area, a region stretching from present-day southwestern Wisconsin to northwest Illinois that was not glaciated during Pleistocene Epoch and is therefore characterized as a Paleozoic Plateau, full of karst terrain, caves, and sinkholes. These are landmarks "upon whose flanks Time leaves its traces, like old tide-rips of diluvian seas," as Melville put it in *Mardi*.[39]

From *Mardi* to *John Marr*, sponsored surveys of the American West had unearthed a massive quantity of geological knowledge, and the exploration of territories west of the Mississippi drove American field science after the 1840s. Most notably, this exploration included John S. Newberry's work on river erosion and Fielding Meek's and Ferdinand Hayden's careful reconstruction of the Cretaceous Sea that once covered the northern plains. And in his meticulous studies of peak erosion, William P. Blake theorized that wind-blown sand might be a shaping force in the maturity of mountains. The mind-boggling power of erosion thus became a crucial concept in American geology, which was confirmed and extended in a series of expeditions in the 1870s. For example: Clarence King's 1878 survey of the fortieth parallel, which included microscopical petrography, and George Wheeler's 1879 survey of the southwest. And we cannot overstate the interest in John Wesley Powell's famous 1876 survey of the Rockies that examined physiographic geology, or geomorphology, and figured erosion into the magnitudes of continental creation. Powell's tribological approach—"tribology," from the Greek "to rub" or "grind"—solidified the science of wear and friction in geological formations. This may help explain Melville's shift in focus from the relative stability of Mardi's mineral clusters to the erosive, ambient, and diffusive grit of sand and dust in *Clarel* and *John Marr*.

A residue of ecological interfaces, dust covers nearly all of the landscapes in Melville's later writings. In *Clarel*, for example, a rocky cliff at Petra appears to be a "sea-face," smoothed and "worn / Through long attrition of that grit / Which on the waste of winds is borne."[40] Later, the speaker notes that "sun and rain, and wind, with grit / Driving, these haste to cancel" any inscriptions humans make in rock.[41] This "flying grit" thickens like foam so that the desert "seems to enter in with us—/ At home amid men's homes [it] would glide."[42] Melville's observation that the desert "enters in with us" is an awareness that dust crosses all boundaries, "between the domestic sphere and the cosmos, between frazzles of artifice and byproducts of plants, animals, and humans."[43] Dust provides the gritty basis of an atmospheric ecology that Melville advances in *John Marr*'s "Pebbles" and in late poems like "Rosary Beads" from *Weeds and Wildings*. (In that poem, the speaker watches as "Grain by grain the Desert drifts / Against the Garden-Land," warning the reader to "Hedge well thy Roses" and "heed the stealth / Of ever-creeping sand.")[44] But, amid the arid despair of *Clarel*, Melville begins to envision these desert-drifts as generative, geo-atmo-ecologies that create immanent matrices for new life while simultaneously eroding it:

> ... see, day and night
> The sands subsiding from the height;
> In time, absorbed, these grains may help
> To form new sea-bed, slug and kelp.[45]

Faced with the seemingly barren expanses of *Clarel*'s deserts, Melville recognized that sand grains are markers of future potential for flourishing and greenness. Sand is the material foundation for new constellations of life in yet-to-be-formed seabeds that, in turn, may foster slugs and algae. A decade later, in *John Marr*, Melville proposes a more pessimistic future for planetary life in his short poem "The Tuft of Kelp," where the speaker addresses the kelp directly:

> All dripping in tangles green,
>   Cast up by a lonely sea,
> If purer for that, O Weed,
>   Bitterer, too, are ye?[46]

At first, the word "bitter" appears to personify the kelp's resentful reaction to being "cast up" into terrestrial spheres, but Melville's readers would have known that kelp was often burned into soda ash—another name for the bitter alkaline sodium carbonate—to make glass and paper. That process, called "kelping," "purified" green tangles of kelp into chemical compounds that then enabled the production of microscopes and paper, technologies that helped readers better see and write about kelp. Further, in a nautical sense, a ship is "brought up to a bitter" when the anchor cable is allowed to run out completely, becoming taut to the bitter (the sturdy ship-post that marks the "bitter-end").[47] Well-versed in ship jargon, Melville puns on the bitterness of shore-cast kelp, suggesting that alga's ability to extend human knowledge means it will inevitably be used unsustainably, to extinction, to the bitter end. Read from a twenty-first-century perspective, Melville's beached kelp is a potent emblem of end times, the bitter end of an ecologically diverse planet in which, as mentioned at the end of chapter 1, some 80 percent of breathable oxygen comes from marine algae severely threatened by climate change.[48] But "Tuft of Kelp" is also noteworthy for its point of view. The speaker is speaking to the marine alga, acknowledging it, seeing it, and letting it, in a sense, see him. The speaker's address to the kelp is an apostrophe to the oxygenated environment that makes human life possible, a fabular articulation of inter-species dwelling that bridges human and algaeic spheres of bitterness.

Even more dramatically, in *Weeds and Wildings,* Melville dedicates an entire volume of poems to floral perspectives on the world. He takes the point of view of the aster flower, lets the aloe plant speak, and listens to a ground vine converse with a rose: "O Rose, we plants are all akin. / Our roots enlock."[49] Here Melville examines the mutualisms between plants—their enlacing roots and shared mycorrhizal networks—which have historically extended to mutualisms between plants and humans. For example, corridors of "kelp highways" provided food and passageways for early humans as they navigated Pacific coasts of North America over thousands of years. Such kinships between species—now violently and permanently disturbed by modernity, as in the feared extinction of many of the world's kelp forests—is echoed a few pages after "Tuft of Kelp" in *John Marr*'s most anthologized poem, "The Maldive Shark." Somewhere in the Indian Ocean, "sleek little pilot-fish, azure and slim" dart about the "saw-pit" of an oceanic whitetip shark's mouth and "liquidly glide on his ghastly flank." They are "friends; and friendly they guide him to prey."[50] The oceanic whitetip, whose populations have declined by as much as 80 percent in the past thirty years, is similarly threatened with extinction. And on John Marr's desert-prairie, the narrator describes other extinctions: of bison and the forced migration of the indigenous populations. "Such a double exodus of man and beast left the plain a desert, green or blossoming indeed," he notices, "but almost as forsaken as the Siberian Obi."[51]

After the deaths of his wife and child, John Marr is a relic of a past age, a "kinless man" who "resolves never to quit the soil that holds the only beings ever connected with him by love in the family-tie." He rents out his log house and "dwells with the household" of new tenants.[52] Now with time to reflect on the onrush of modernity—the roads, railroads, telegraph wires that crisscross the landscape—Marr imagines how a simple mailbox, "in the unintermitting advance of the frontier, would perhaps decay into a mossy monument, attesting yet another successive overleaped limit of civilized life."[53] *John Marr* continues Melville's fascination—unmistakable in *Mardi* and "The Encantadas"—with reading the decayed monuments of human civilizations. In "The Haglets," the speaker recalls the image of a "carved memorial stone . . . decayed and coral-mossed" outside a sea chapel.[54] Addressing the stone in hopes that it will speak back and reveal "the cenotaph's intent," the speaker is rewarded with the story beneath the stone. This is the mode of most of *John Marr*'s early poems. They are recollections of old sailors (for example, "Bridegroom Dick," "Jack Roy," "Tom Deadlight," and "To Ned") whose memories have become less "phantoms of the dead" than lively "spiritual companions."[55] Memories, like "tides that enter creek or stream," put John Marr in "shadowy fellowship" with the dead.[56] Marr's reminiscences are in one sense a final retrospective of a sailor-novelist in the sunset of his life, but these poems do more than ebb on memory-tides. They inspect those creeks and streams in which the tides enter, carefully accounting the pebbles that comprise the streambed and the dust inside them. As John Marr's memories flood back and then erode over the course of *John Marr*, the forms of the poems themselves begin to erode. From prose beginnings to epigrammatic ends, *John Marr* abrades itself, becomes halves and halves again, descending into the self-dividing forms of Cantor dust.

ON PEBBLES

The first edition of *John Marr*, published in 1888 by De Vinne Press in close collaboration with Melville, organizes the final seven poems under the heading "Pebbles." (note the period, itself a pebble), each subtitled with a roman numeral, "I." to "VII." In the 2017 Northwestern-Newberry edition of Melville's *Uncompleted Writings*, the editors give individual "Pebble" poems their own page, and while this seems like a minor distinction, Melville had in 1888 carefully arranged the layout of *John Marr* to guide the reading of his pebble poems. Coming in at a total of thirty-two lines, "Pebbles." is purposefully designed to create a specific effect in the reader, so I have reproduced the entire sequence below as it was originally printed.[57]

I.

Though the Clerk of the Weather insist,
    And lay down the weather-law,
Pintado and gannet they wist
That the winds blow whither they list
    In tempest or flaw.

II.

Old are the creeds, but stale the schools,
    Revamped as the mode may veer,
But Orm from the schools to the beaches strays

And, finding a Conch hoar with time, he delays
    And reverent lifts it to ear.
That Voice, pitched in far monotone,
    Shall it swerve? shall it deviate ever?
The Seas have inspired it, and Truth—
    Truth, varying from sameness never.

III.

In hollows of the liquid hills
    Where the long Blue Ridges run,
The flattery of no echo thrills,
    For echo the seas have none;
Nor aught that gives man back man's strain—
The hope of his heart, the dream in his brain.

IV.

On ocean where the embattled fleets repair,
Man, suffering inflictor, sails on sufferance there.

V.

Implacable I, the old Implacable Sea:
    Implacable most when most I smile serene—
Pleased, not appeased, by myriad wrecks in me.

VI.

Curled in the comb of yon billow Andean,
    Is it the Dragon's heaven-challenging crest?
Elemental mad ramping of ravening waters—
    Yet Christ on the Mount, and the dove in her nest!

VII.

Healed of my hurt, I laud the inhuman Sea—
Yea, bless the Angels Four that there convene;
For healed I am ever by their pitiless breath
Distilled in wholesome dew named rosmarine.

Unevenly metered, irregularly rhymed, and with varying number of lines, the poems do not, at first, seem to have coherence at formal or thematic levels. But this desire for coherence—and the poems' intentional decoherence—is the first clue to the meaning of "Pebbles."

The reader must take up each poem individually, yet because of the poems' sequential numbering and close proximity on the page, the reader is urged on to the next. The reading experience is thus intentionally fast (contrast this effect with the page turning required of the Northwestern Newberry edition). For most students of *John Marr*, reading "Pebbles" means rereading them, perhaps out of order. Each poem defers to the next, refers back to an earlier one, and foreshadows a future one. "Pebbles" are thematic iterations of similar motifs and images—wind, time, suffering, wrecks, force, and the "inhuman Sea"—with different rhymes, line lengths, and meters. "Pebbles" are a geological condensation of the paradigms of sameness and difference we've been tracking throughout this book: of difference installed in similarity. Just as each pebble on a beach is a unique supplement to the taxonomy of pebbles, each pebble-poem is a unique supplement to "Pebbles." A single pebble gestures beyond itself to another. Each pebble marks the end of an energy pathway, but pebbles also signal the potential beginning for new, *very* slowly generating forms of life. In "Pebbles," we can finally appreciate Derrida's insight that all life "undergoes the opposition between *physis* and *techne*. As a self-relation, as activity and reactivity, as differantial force, as repetition, life is always in habited by technicization."[58] The *physis* ("nature") of the pebble is at the same time the foundation of *techne* ("craft"). But just looking at the "Pebbles" as a whole, we can visualize "differantial force" in the constant repetition of pebble-poem after pebble-poem, each with a unique, numerical-temporal tag (I. to VII.). A given pebble-poem's number provides the basis of difference from—and deferral to—the next one. This sequencing, or spacing, mimics the erosions and flows that happen through biogeochemical pathways, reassembling from nonlife the matrices of life once again.

The dynamic geo-atmospheric architecture of the "Pebble" poems speaks to Melville's final perspective on causality. The poems might remind vigilant readers of a moment in *Mardi*, when, meditating on drowned sailors whose bodies are now dissolved elements of Pacific currents, the narrator registers the magnitude of his grief as a squall with the power of a fallen asteroid: "For as a pebble dropped into a pond ruffles it to its marge; so, on all sides, a sea-gale operates as if an asteroid had fallen into the brine; making ringed mountain billows, interminably expanding, instead of ripples. . . . Every wave in my eyes seems a soul."[59] The sea-gale becomes an asteroid, which becomes expanding ocean mountains, which become waves and then drowned sailors. Pebbles and asteroids initiate the endless expansion of abiotic effects, from pond ripples to billowing waves to the gritty cadences of erosion and weathering.

This is the accumulating poetic effect of "Pebbles," visible, for example, in the third "Pebble" poem. A six-line sestain (ababcc), one line short of a Chaucerian rhyme-royal (ababbcc), the lyric speaker collapses imagery of oceanic waves onto mountain ranges:

> In hollows of the liquid hills
>   Where the long Blue Ridges run,
> The flattery of no echo thrills,
>   For echo the seas have none;
> Nor aught that gives man back man's strain—
> The hope of his heart, the dream in his brain.

The "liquid hills" in line one are the blue crests of immense open ocean waves, so large that Virginia's Blue Ridge Mountains fit neatly in their valleys. Melville's first line break holds the image of the cresting waves in suspension before introducing the mountains in their "hollows" on the next line. But by superimposing mountain chain upon wave, Melville does more than indicate scale. The image suggests a shared time frame in which rock becomes liquid: the lapse of millions of years of sedimentation, erosion, decomposition, and diagenetic erasure. In such a frame, nothing echoes in the pelagic hollows. There is no human ear to be flattered by the sound. Nothing "gives man back man's strain." "Strain" here means voice—as in the seraphim's harmonious "strain" above the thunder of *Clarel*—but also physical or mental *labor*, the hopeful strain of building monuments or writing down dreams in books. In this poem, the desire for a full accounting of one's life is denied by the molten hills of geologic time. Here, calculating the compensation of strain and reducing duration to an algebra of human rewards fails completely. But "strain" can also mean *offspring* (in humans, animals or plants) as well as, zoologically, the "germinal vesicle in the yolk of an egg."[60] Taken this way, force triumphs over species, abiota over biota, which diminishes humankind to a "thread" or "line"—the tertiary definitions of "strain"—across the stratified history of the planet.

The power of the liquid hills is similarly depicted in the sixth "Pebble," where Melville uses a four-line (abcb) quatrain to contrast elemental and theological visions of an Andean peak:

> Curled in the comb of yon billow Andean,
>   Is it the Dragon's heaven-challenging crest?
> Elemental mad ramping of ravening waters—
>   Yet Christ on the Mount, and the dove in her nest!

As in the third "Pebble," the speaker merges sea and mountain. A distant sea wave ("yon billow") blurs with a deep valley ("comb") at the foot of the Andes. Throughout Melville's writing, the "snowheaded Andes" conjure fear of losing "oneself in such inhuman solitude," as Ishmael describes it, which generates distrust of such an "unwaning clime that knows no autumn."[61] In this poem, the word "comb," which first reads as "valley," also suggests "coombe" or "coombe rock," a deposit of flint within chalk that indicates ancient glaciation. Apparently versed in physical geology, the speaker then shifts to a theological question about his scientific worldview: might such geological features be emblazoned with "the Dragon's heaven-challenging crest?" (Milton describes Satan as a "dragon" in Book IV of *Paradise Lost* and later uses the phrase "the proud crest of Satan" to describe the hubris of fallen angels.)[62] A crest, of course, can be mountain peak and wave, but here it is ironically figured as a battle shield for science's secular valorization of nature's power.

In the following two lines, the elemental "ramping of ravening waters" is counterbalanced by the mercy of Christian beatitudes and the peaceful dove that endorsed Noah's territory after the flood. While "ramping" carries the association of an animal rearing on its legs and, sometimes, the flourishing of plant growth, "ravening" refers exclusively to the voracious hunger of an animal, as in *Moby-Dick*'s open-mouthed "ravening sharks."[63] Swirling together glaciated flint, ramping vine, and ravening shark, Melville condenses the mineral-vegetal-animal ensembles of Andean ecologies into two paired lines that dispute the tranquil theology of doves. Recalling the many nests in *The Piazza Tales* and the doves at St. Saba in *Clarel*, here the dove's serene nest-dwelling is a sign of cooperation and religious piety that seems to contradict the (Satanic) cruelty of natural forces. But Melville's line break in line three provides the dash that dramatically separates ravening waters from Christ on the Mount. The dash defers the water and dams the uncontrolled "ramping" of hydrological energy. The poem arbitrates force and mercy. But the exclamation mark that concludes line four betrays the satirical tone of the poem, mocking biblical dogma that cannot account for the "brutal claims" and indifferent intensities of material "Nature." "Matter in end will never abate / His ancient brutal claim," as Melville would write three years later in *Timoleon*.[64]

This is the sentiment of the second "Pebble," again taunting hackneyed creeds and "stale" schools, which are merely revamped versions of older ideas "as the mode may veer." The poem follows a mysterious figure named "Orm," who "from the schools to the beaches strays / And, finding a Conch hoar with time, he delays / And reverent lifts it to ear." The narrator wonders what Orm hears in the conch:

> That Voice, pitched in far monotone,
>   Shall it swerve? shall it deviate ever?
> The Seas have inspired it, and Truth—
>   Truth, varying from sameness never.

This nine-line poem assumes the guise of a ballad's traditional rhyme scheme (abcb defe), but with the difference (abccb defe) of an additional double rhyme in lines four and five ("strays" / "delays"). The extra rhyming line disrupts the ballad form, delaying it as Orm defers from familiar schools and creeds to wander the coast, reverently lifting ancient conchs to his ear. In the conch, Orm hears not the sea but the resonance of the ambient environment around him and the rhythms his own body. The "voice, pitched in far monotone," is his embodied, acoustic signature as he inhabits and disrupts the soundscapes of a windswept beach.

The identity of "Orm" is ambiguous. Some have suggested the eighteenth-century British painter Daniel Orme, but more likely it is a reference to the twelfth-century Augustinian monk Orm, author of *Ormulum:* a collection of homilies on the Bible that served as companions to the liturgy.[65] The word *orm* itself is Old Norse for "dragon," which anticipates the sixth pebble-poem, but the title of Orm's *Ormulum* probably played homophonically on *speculum,* Latin for "mirror." A mirror of the gospels, the *Ormulum* was meant to be repeated and chanted, unswervingly and without deviation. The unvarying sameness of the *Ormulum*, like the conch's ambient-environmental "Voice," models the unswerving truth of ever-swerving ecological relations. To complicate things even further, Melville's rarely reprinted "Story of Daniel Orme," written around 1886 as Melville was composing *Billy Budd,* can be read as an intertext here.[66] Unlike the painter or the monk, Melville's fictional Orme is explicitly unknowable. He appears "like a meteoric stone in a field" from some "unimaginable sphere."[67] This is a man who, after a life at sea, dies alone by the ocean and is buried by strangers. The only human character unambiguously identified in "Pebbles," Orm is a mirror of Orme is a mirror of John Marr. Both Marr and Orme are craftsmen of a sort; Marr is a "rough-bench carpenter," and Orme is a sea captain, possibly a gunsmith, and definitely a "salt philosopher."[68] Likewise, in "Pebbles," Orm's engagement with the conch is a kind of primal staging of *techne,* where object and human merge to produce insight into inter-species dwelling. Technology, then, is the covert theme of "Pebbles," one that extends our discussion of animals, humans, and architects from *The Piazza Tales.*

Take, for instance, the fourth and most concise pebble poem. With only two rhyming lines (aa), this terse lyric describes embattled, sunken ships returning to the sea: "On ocean where the embattled fleets repair, / Man, suffering inflictor, sails on sufferance there." The key word of line one is "repair," meaning, simultaneously, retreating (to patch up) and dissolving (to deteriorate into oceanic immensity). A fast engineering fix is shadowed by a slow descent into unknown depths. The balance of this poem, amid a series of jagged poems dominated by images of fragmentation, can be deceiving. Its neat imagery of parts and wholes—embattlement and reparation—is undermined by the technological subtext that lurks in line two, which introduces the ambiguity of "suffering." Man is cruel. He inflicts suffering with his tools, his weapons of war, his fleets sent into battle. There is a beautiful symmetry here, at the exact center of a series of "Pebbles," between this shortest of all of Melville's poems and the history of *techne* itself, for pebbles provided man with his earliest tools and his first weapons. "The stone," Rolfe solemnly tells us, "was man's first missile."[69]

The pebble is at once rudiment and remainder of the tools that—so the argument goes from Heidegger to Latour and Harman and Wills—make us "properly human" through their prosthetic extensions of our "natural" bodies.[70] Latour writes that technology is "the art of the curve" that projects human agency onto the world, pebbles to warships.[71] Grasping a pebble, using it intentionally to carve a symbol, light a fire, or bash a skull, is an exteriorization of self and species. But human civilization did not "invent" the tool. Rather, the tool coevolved with life in what Bernard Stiegler calls the "double plasticity" of thought, memory, and language.[72] We realize today that our pebble-techs have given us the planetary power of abiotic force, but Melville had already reached this conclusion in *Mardi*, in one of his very first published poems: Yoomy's war song. "The pebbles they hurl, have been hurled before,—" Yoomy cries, "Hurled up on the beach by the stormy sea!" She urges the soldiers to pick up those "Pebbles, buried erewhile in the head of the shark," for they shall be "buried erelong in the heads of our foes!"[73] Forty years later, armed with pebbles of various scales and complexities, the humans in "Pebbles" inflict suffering. We have become, the poems seem to say, a species "suffering inflictor."

Yet this enigmatic phrase can also be read in reverse. It is equally the case that Promethean man is himself suffering from an affliction or "infliction." The infliction is the acceleration of man's cruelty through technological progress, as compensation for—or distraction from—the inevitable wear of time on the short duration of human life. Technology, as much as cruelty, is a cover for the terrifying reality that all of our thoughts and memories will be liquidated by our deaths, all our "durable" marks effaced by the general energetics of tide and time. Facing this infliction, at sea, man sails "on sufferance" because, in the end, no tool can repair his fate. And in the context of the Anthropocene, we sail on with the knowledge that we will certainly become one more of the planet's extinct strains. Ships unrepairable, we must repair to the intensities of our suffering made visible in artistic forms like "Pebbles." This quasi-Buddhist sentiment has its antecedents in *Clarel*, where in part 4 the speaker ruminates on Buddha's consciousness of human suffering:

> . . . How Buddha pined!
> Pierced with the sense of all we bear,
> Not only ills by fate assigned,
> But misrule of our selfish mind,
> Fain would the tender sage repair.[74]

Our irreparable suffering—borne of both "fate assigned" and "misrule of our selfish mind"—is precisely what makes us human, and thus cannot be repaired. Our myriad mistakes, our collective wreckage, are the basis for a communal life, a life of shared suffering and mourning.

I use the word "wreckage" intentionally here, leading us to the fifth "Pebble," a three-line terza rima (aba) and the most widely recognized of the pebble poems. It is usually read as a satire on the desire to personify the forces of the natural world:

> Implacable I, the old Implacable Sea:
> > Implacable most when most I smile serene—
> > Pleased, not appeased, by myriad wrecks in me.

First granted a "voice" in Orm's conch shell, the environment is now given a serenely smiling face, a point of view on the world. While this *prosopopoeia*—giving a face to the sea—appears to be a silly or even child-like anthropomorphism, it is better understood as an inversion of the "Tuft of Kelp" poem we looked at earlier. In that poem, the speaker addresses the bitterness of the kelp, whereas here, the sea *speaks to itself*. Although Melville did think about calling the pebble-poems "epigrams"—a form usually reserved for satire, irony, and punning—the poem is less a satire on anthropocentrism and more a poetic archeology of the "face" and the act of "facing" environments of all sorts. It poses a reverse-projection of the face of the sea onto the face of the human. Remember that "face" comes from the Latin *facere*, "to make," a philology buried in the etymology of "facts" themselves: pure actions and indisputable forces that make up the "face of the deeps" (*facies abyssie*) in Genesis 1:2. We are confronted with the facticity of the sea's face, its making and unmaking, through the faces of pages that constitute the surface of a book. This interpretation helps us read the many fantastical images of stormy faces and landscape foreheads in Melville, as in "Ahab's brow" described by Ishmael to be "gaunt and ribbed, like the black sand beach after some stormy tide has been gnawing it, with out being able to drag the firm thing from its place."[75] In the fifth pebble-poem, the ancient sea makes a cruelly human face that is only a mask for tidal forces. The sea is pleased (as in "having one's way") rather than appeased (as in "settling disorder" or "relieving suffering") by its "myriad wrecks," the residue forms of its fact making.

At first, the word "wrecks" refers to ships wrecked at sea, like the embattled fleets of the previous pebble-poem that have become deep-sea monuments to the hubris of human technologies. But, in Melville's day, shipwrecks more often happened on rocks close to shore. Recall the "Lee Shore" chapter of *Moby-Dick* or "The Haglets," both of which harken back to the Sirens' rocky coastlines in *The Odyssey*. The littoral confluence of sea and rock thwarts man's strain against nature, his hopes of security and homecoming. Shipwrecks feature in nearly every one of Melville's major works, but they seem to proliferate in his later writings, especially in *John Marr*, where Melville integrates shipwrecks into his marine ecologies with figurative implications for the collection as a whole. In "The Aeolian Harp at the Surf Inn," for example, the wreckage of some storm-tossed ship "drifted till each plank / Is oozy as the oyster bank."[76] Read another way, a "wreck" signifies a "broken-down, debilitated, or emaciated form of a person," as in the narrator's description of Bartleby, "a bit of wreck in the mid Atlantic."[77]

All bodies are in various stages of wreckage, wracked by the pressures of time and the forces of aging, decay, and disease. In an evolutionary sense, we are wrecks from the sea—as in "that which is cast ashore by the sea in tidal waters"—since our bodies contain some of the same bacteria and minerals as marine vegetation: the "wrack" that attaches to the pebbles of estuaries where fresh and saltwater meet.[78] Serial wrecks with oversized brains that contemplate cruelty, suffering, and death, humans are the most sophisticated formulations of material, thermodynamic contingency. We are always embedding and impacting and overlaying ourselves. Or as Melville puts it in *Clarel*:

> . . . serial wrecks on wrecks confound
> Era and monument and man;
> Or rather, in stratifying way
> Bed and impact and overlay.[79]

The serial wreckage of *John Marr* circles us back to the oozy, foamy, spiraling growth of *Pierre* and finds resonance in the immovable weeping willow of the unpublished prose sketch "Rip Van Winkle's Lilac," written in large part in 1888 when *John Marr* was going to press. In Melville's telling of the classic Irving tale, after Rip's mysterious disappearance, several attempts were made to cut down Rip's favorite willow tree. But the "venerable tree" resists all efforts and "long remained a monument of the negative victory of stubborn inertia over spasmodic activity and an ineffectual implement."[80] Then one day, after a summer storm, the willow eventually falls, creating an "ever-crumbling monument . . . an umber-hued mound of yellow punk, mossed in spots, with wild violets springing from it."[81] The narrator of "Rip Van Winkle's Lilac" finds new layers of ecological complexity and splendor in a fallen, mossy willow tree just as Melville exhumes new layers of literary meaning from Irving's familiar, time-worn tale. Out of the impact of the tree's fall, out of the wreckage and magnificent decay of the willow, comes the overlaid "umber-hued mound of yellow punk" and the unpredictable beauty of the lilac that grows on top.

The ecological effects of unpredictability, cast earlier in Melville's career in nondeterministic terms, are manifest at the end of *John Marr* in imagery of oncoming storms and meteorological forecasts. As stated earlier, the first pebble-poem—a five-line quintrain with an abaab rhyme scheme that echoes the limerick in its use of anapests—is about man's attempts to predict and regularize ever-changing atmospheric phenomena. The predictions of the "Clerk of the Weather" are weighed against the instincts of birds:

> Though the Clerk of the Weather insist,
>   And lay down the weather-law,
> Pintado and gannet they wist
> That the winds blow whither they list
>   In tempest or flaw.

The birds here are the Pintado petrel (Spanish for "painted, spotted") and the gannet, both of which feed on fish by "surface seizing," or skimming the sea for prey "like pebbles sent skipping from the shore," as Melville put it in *Mardi*.[82] The speaker announces that petrels and gannets "wist" (or discern) atmospheric conditions far better than humans. They intuit weather instinctually. They expect it. (Though sometimes storms do decimate bird populations, and the term "wrack" can refer to the "death of a large number of pelagic birds, usually as the result of a storm.")[83] In "tempest or flaw," the petrel and the gannet "list" from side to side, rolling this way or that for more efficient flight dynamics. "Flaw" likely derives from the Old Norse *flaga* (squall), but the phrase aptly echoes John 3:8 on the limitations of human knowledge: "The wind bloweth where it listeth, and thou hearest the sound thereof, but canst not tell whence it cometh, and whither it goeth: so is every one that is born of the Spirit."[84] Adapting the biblical mystery of the windy Holy Spirit to the avian behavioral ecology of petrels, Melville emphasizes how we humans only "hearest the sound thereof" the wind. One never apprehends wind directly, only *across* surfaces like skin or flags or *through* objects like conches or harps (the latter featuring, significantly, in *Pierre*'s pines, the Aeolian opening to *Battle-Pieces*, and *John Marr*'s "Surf Inn"). Ahab, for his part, spends a long time in *Moby-Dick* musing on the wind: "'tis a noble and heroic thing, the wind! . . . run tilting at it, and you but run through it . . . all the things that most exasperate and outrage mortal man, all these things are bodiless, but only bodiless as objects, not as agents . . . there's something all glorious and gracious in the wind."[85] The bodiless agency of the wind—like the energy ecologies we've seen throughout this chapter—is a helpful way to conceptualize environmental pathways that are not purple but hyaline, hidden from human view but with enormous impacts on human life, like "dry tempests" where "viewless and intangible winds make a shipwreck," as Melville phrased it in "Daniel Orme."[86]

Although to Ahab it is noble, gracious, and even healing, wind has long been figured as the force of wreckage and end times. In Revelations 7:1–3, for instance, four angels hold back "the four winds of the earth" that would "hurt the earth and the sea" until they have "sealed the servants of our God in their foreheads."[87] Melville clearly had this passage in mind for his seventh and final pebble-poem in "Pebbles":

> Healed of my hurt, I laud the inhuman Sea—
> Yea, bless the Angels Four that there convene;
> For healed I am ever by their pitiless breath
> Distilled in wholesome dew named rosmarine.

Healed by the "pitiless breath" of the same four angels of Revelations, the speaker lauds the "inhuman Sea" because it convenes phenomena not cruelly but pitilessly: pitiless not in the sense of without mercy, but pitiless meaning not an *object* of pity. The speaker identifies with the brute, material realism of atmospheric pitilessness that heals his anxieties, his hurt, his suffering, and his anxieties over death. Some critics have argued that this final pebble is about the restorative aims of art. We might see the poet, for example, as "healed by his very power to figure and refigure" with a literary power akin to wind erosion.[88] In this reading, the speaker's healing comes from rituals of *poeisis* that reconfigure our senses of time and order, channeling Ben Jonson's call for ritual purification in *Masque of Queens* (1616):

> You shall . . . steep
> Your bodies in that purer brine,
> And wholesome dew, call'd ros-marine . . .
> So that, this night, the year gone round,
> You do again salute this ground . . . [89]

But in Melville's poem, the wind's breath is "distilled" from the ethereal sphere of angels into an earthy one. And following Dickinson's famous description of the poet as one who "Distills amazing sense / From ordinary

Meanings," Melville's poem distills from all of the previous "Pebbles" the final image of "wholesome dew named rosmarine."[90]

Rosmarine, sea dew or sea spray, derives from *ros marinus,* a reference to the plants growing near the sea and an emblem of memory that echoes Ophelia's gift of rosemary to Laertes, "for remembrance."[91] As Jonson conceives of it, rosmarine's healing capacity is a reminder to "salute this ground," to acknowledge the material grounds of our bodies. But in contemporary marine ecology, rosmarine is the term for *sea salt aerosol,* aerosolized ocean particles that contain dissolved organic matter and inorganic salts. Dissolved organic carbon is critical for marine biogeochemical cycling of carbon and the bioavailability of metals on the planet.[92] Sea spray is therefore, to quote marine chemist John I. Hedges, "an important component of the aerosol–cloud–climate feedback system involving marine biota."[93] Ahab—wind-philosopher and atmo-conscious captain that he is—*feels* this feedback system in his lungs: "I am buoyed by breaths of once-living things, exhaled as air, but water now."[94] Even Ishmael's epitaph to the all-but-forgotten Bulkington contains rosmarine spiritual hope: "Up from the spray of thy ocean-perishing—straight up, leaps thy apotheosis!"[95]

In the last lines from *Timoleon*'s "Buddha," the speaker pleads for a similar, final absorption into the atmosphere: "Nirvana! absorb us in your skies, / Annul us into Thee."[96] "Annul," from the Latin *annullare,* means "to make to nothing," but at the conclusion of "Pebbles," we have more than nothing. We have rosmarine. Standing at the sea's edge, pebble in hand, inhaling the sea spray, we breathe dissolved organic matter. Rosmarine reconstitutes a kind of molecular memory that invests our bodies with myriad wrecks of previous forms of life. Rosmarine is grounded in us, becomes us, suffers us, and provides the grounds for future wreckages. Melville's pebble poetry, in its iterative wreckage form, leads us, finally, not to dust but to sea spray and the atomized, organic potentiality of future life.

This final image of Melville's ecological imagination is, appropriately, *spindrift*: continuous, driving spray. Like the "celestial" spray Ishmael glimpses one night from a whale's "Spirit-Spout"—a "silvery, moon-lit jet" arcing exhaled, condensed water vapor—and the "pillars of sand which whirl about" *Clarel*'s deserts ("True kin . . . to the water-spout"), rosmarine is a misty condensation of ecological relations.[97] Although much remains unknown about aerosol-chemical air-surface reactions, modern industrialism has definitively altered planetary atmospheric chemistry.[98] We are not living in liquid modernity, as Zygmunt Bauman has declared, but in *aerosol modernity*. Because atmospheric climate change leaves no stratigraphic trace, and attempts to model it are extraordinarily difficult, it is ghostly in the most material sense of the word: "giving up the ghost," or breathing one's last breath. Melville leaves us in the eco-eschatological time of Revelations, inhaling haunted sprays of planetary precarity. We are healed only by a pitilessly honest, wind-inspired art, kept from despair by our poetic faculty for making and remaking ourselves into artistic communities of belonging and mourning.

As Melville's spindrift ecologies accumulate clustering minerals, spiraling plants, honeycombing bees, and spraying rosmarine, they produce over a lifetime of writing the non-additive, emergent property of authorial understanding and the strangely embodied intimacy of mouthing another's words out of the pages of a book. Melville makes intimate in the act of reading the most distant and microscopic spindrifts of planetary existence. So, given his dazzling articulations of our planet's mineral-vegetal-animal-atmospheric complexity, it would not have been surprising to Melville that, in 2013, over a century after his death, the Mars Curiosity rover discovered pebbles that indicate the presence of ancient streambeds thirty-five million miles from Earth. In the pebble, he might say, hides the spinning purpleness of the universe.

Conclusion

Books be but part of nature. Oh,
'Tis studying nature, reading books.
—Derwent, *Clarel*

The majority of this book was written in Montana, in terrain so beautiful and vast that it makes you feel, as Clarel puts it, that man cannot "solve the world.... Too wild it is, too wonderful."[1] The sparsely populated remoteness of Montana—and its proclaimed status as the "last best place"—certainly opens it to fantasies of ecological purity and libertarian daydreaming, but the preservation of wildernesses in Yellowstone and Glacier National Parks also make it the front lines for environmental activism. Montana is a place where indigenous peoples celebrate their culture with wider communities and where the protection of bison remains a hot issue; at the same time, it is a place where, in Butte for example, scars of copper mining have left behind one of the largest and most toxic Superfund sites in the world. Montana is a purple state, ecologically and politically. Similar levels of party support among voters creates political moderation, some compromise, and, especially around environmental issues, consensus about conservation (usually centered on fishing and hunting). It offers, in sum, a unique vantage point to consider how a concept like *purpleness* might migrate beyond Melville's extravagant prose and into the discourse of contemporary environmental ethics.

Originally a shade of crimson dye distilled from the hypobranchial glands of Mediterranean mollusks, the color purple was used in antiquity to adorn emperors of Rome. Over the centuries, purple has come to signify richness or abundance—like the "Imperial Purple Majesty" of Mount Greylock to whom *Pierre* is dedicated—as well as deeply felt or extravagantly expressed emotions (in Catholic liturgies, for instance, purple vestments are worn during times of penitence and mourning). But purple is also the color of deoxygenated venous blood visible in moments of suffering and death, as when *Moby-Dick*'s sperm whales, harpooned and dying, spew "gush after gush of clotted red gore, as if it had been the purple lees of red wine."² And, as we saw in chapter 2, "purple" is a catchall term for excessive, bad, or explicit writing. Dorri Beam has argued that Melville's investment in *Pierre*'s "purple prose" was a way to wrestle—as nineteenth-century writers like Margaret Fuller and Ann Stephens did—with "the limits of language, enticed by its potential as a transformative medium" for gender, social, and political issues.³ Melville's "purpleness" congeals all of the etymological dimensions of purple, humbling us in its linguistic and ecological imprecision and aligning literary ambiguity with the unfathomable complexity that creates the gorgeous "purple haze" effect of *Mardi*'s equator-twilights.⁴

In the broader spectrum of Melville's color schemes, purpleness has been obscured by the whiteness of the whale and the greenness of Pacific archipelagos. But as a way of concluding *Magnificent Decay*, I want to suggest that purpleness is a cornerstone of Melville's ecological imagination and, perhaps, a useful new term in the ongoing vocabulary of the environmental humanities. Purpleness captures the familiar but hard-to-articulate feeling of being surrounded, of being enmeshed in systems and processes beyond one's body, as in *Omoo*'s tropical nights where "one purple vault hung round with soft, trembling stars."⁵ Furthermore, purpleness is an index of difference—Queequeg, remember, is a "purple rascal"—and this awkward term color-codes the experience of encountering human and nonhuman others, of dwelling among hues and intensities of all kinds.⁶ Dwelling on purpleness is a way to see beyond the black-and-white rigidity of contemporary discourse, in which nuance and fine distinction are too often chromatic signs of vulnerability and weakness. Purpleness is an embrace of uncertainty that draws together the three other insights that this book has tried to limn in Melville's work: life's shared minerality, the power of mourning to create communities of environmental concern, and the diffusive, spindrift energy ecologies that return all living things to dust or dew but are, simultaneously, the basis for future forms of planetary complexity.

Purpleness has therefore become, for me at least, a byword for the intersection of science, ecological thinking, writing, and teaching. Working through the notion of purpleness with Montana students—especially first-generation students from rural ranching and farming communities on the high plains—has been one of the most challenging and rewarding undertakings of my life. These students, often with deeply conservative values, have a lived understanding of ecological relations that complements and sometimes contests prevailing intellectual models of environmental study. If students miss class because of a sick horse or because wildfires need control lining, their absence reorients the priorities of the classroom and the praxis of my educational philosophy. Such ecological pragmatism comes to bear on discussions of literary texts in the most unexpected ways. Largely oblivious to tired discussions regarding the fraught state of literary study in the twenty-first century, my students are nonetheless familiar with practices of slow labor that are the essence of careful reading and writing. On a wintery morning in a flyover state far from the frenzy of the coasts, they translate onto the page their habits of noticing, of slowing time to monastic origins, of perceiving purpleness. They largely agree with Alice Walker: "I think it pisses God off if you walk by the color purple in a field somewhere and don't notice it."[7]

But as we saw in *The Piazza Tales*, noticing is not enough. Together, my students and I take up the knottiness of thinking beyond noticing, the way that "thoughts knot with thoughts," as Melville put it in *Battle-Pieces*.[8] In this sense, purpleness extends past literary style or ecological phenomena to the very process of knowledge creation itself. The work of research and writing—for English majors as much as environmental science majors—means undoing the knots "that bind a given system of interpretation to a certain order of knowledge," to quote Francesco Vitale, "and tying together again, in a different way, the propositions that constitute that system."[9] I hope that *Magnificent Decay*, by tying Melville into new knots, will open ways forward in nineteenth-century studies so that a new generation of scholars can more fully take up his ecofeminism, eco-formalism, and eco-spirituality in ways that bear on other authors in the period. I also hope that *Magnificent Decay* gives readers of Melville fresh sets of coordinates: new rules for environmental theory in which textual knots are taken seriously for their material implications and their renditions into the narratives that guide our lives. Refashioning the etymological and literary roots of environmental consciousness renovates our rules for life by expanding the power of our noticing. In other words, living in ecological end times can be generative. "As the vine flourishes, and the grape empurples close up to the very walls and muzzles of cannoned Ehrenbreitstein," the narrator of *Pierre* concludes, "so do the sweetest joys of life grow in the very jaws of its perils."[10]

Again, however, my students check this joyful view by reminding me of the ironies of the Anthropocene and the limits of theory. They consistently arrive at the paradox of human exceptionalism, a question of responsibility and of remediation. Vicki Kirby succinctly summarizes the problem: "Can we condemn anthropocentrism and human exceptionalism on the one hand—the human is the ultimate culprit—while embracing and reaffirming these centrisms with the other—the human is the only one who can save the day?"[11] Without resolving this double bind, art is a fleeting slide on a projector or, worse, a masking agent that shields us from the toxicities, literal and figurative, that pervade our environments. In his late poem "After the Pleasure Party," Melville observes that art can "inanimate" its viewers only for so long. Only for so long will it "Inspire."[12] Many of my students have concluded, moreover, that the death of faith, its petrification, has created a vacuum in American culture, one not so easily filled with consumerist nostalgia, nationalistic slogans, Netflix binges, or evangelical belonging. In *Clarel*, Melville gives voice to this felt absence:

> . . . is faith dead *now*,
> A petrifaction? Grant it so,
> Then what's in store
> what shapeless birth?
> Reveal the doom reserved for earth?[13]

Young Americas in the digital age are looking to redraw the contours of culture around various forms of faith, and not predominantly the purely religious or scientific varieties. The fact that science, for example, explains many aspects of ecological phenomena, "Bides no less / The true, innate mysteriousness" of the world.[14] Mysteriousness and ambiguity, dyed purple by Melville, are invitations to curiosity and a summons for ecological devotion to the incredible complexity of our planet. Purpleness is a mandate for planetary preservation and a command to adapt to the material reality, the fleshiness, of interspecies dwelling. If literature gives shape to the shapeless, a process renewed and reordered by each generation of readers, then the stories themselves remain no less mysterious, purple, and inexplicable now as when they were written. They address us and ask for hospitality. We sign ourselves, in the vows and bonds of silent reading, over to their worlds. As Agamben has argued, the truly philosophical dimensions of a literary work are those that have remained unnoticed and unspoken, awaiting readers to witness them in such a way that "it is not possible to distinguish between what is ours and what belongs to the author we are reading."[15] So it is fitting that the final pages of this book should conclude with the greatest and most mysteriously ecological signature of its subject, an 1877 letter from Melville to his brother-in-law John Hoadley:

> Thine
> In these inexplicable fleshy bonds
> H.M.[16]

May we continue to address one another in words not our own, making ourselves hospitable once again to these, our fleshy bonds of magnificent decay.

Acknowledgments

Ecologies of writing incur debts unbounded. Although the influences on this book are impossible to account fully, I would like to thank, first of all, my parents Tom and Elaine and my brother Patrick, whose lived environmental philosophy is an uncompromising challenge and an ethical calling. Thanks to the editors and external reviewers for the University of Virginia Press, and to the many readers of the manuscript in various forms, including Laura Dassow Walls, Cody Marrs, Corey McCall, Abby Goode, and Andy Dumont. Thanks as well to my students and colleagues in the Department of English at Montana State University Billings, particularly Tami Haaland, whose support and mentorship led the way forward. Finally, and most importantly, I dedicate *Magnificent Decay* to my wife Meagan, whose light makes our art and our family possible. Thine, in these inexplicable fleshy bonds, always, T.N.

A version of chapter 1 was originally published as "Mineral Melville" in *J19: The Journal of Nineteenth-Century Americanists* 7.1 (2019), 155–83; © 2019 C19: The Society of Nineteenth-Century Americanists, published by the University of Pennsylvania Press.

Notes

PREFACE

1. See Lynda V. Mapes, "A Mother Orca's Dead Calf and the Grief Felt around the World" *Seattle Times*, August 2, 2018; Hirokazu Ueda et. al., "Plant Communication," *Plant Signaling & Behavior* 7.2 (2012): 222–26; and Robert Hazen et al., "On the Mineralogy of the 'Anthropocene Epoch,'" *American Mineralogist* 102 (2017): 606.

2. See David Quammen, *The Tangled Tree: A Radical New History of Life* (New York: Simon & Shuster, 2018).

3. Herman Melville, *Moby-Dick: or, The Whale*, ed. Harrison Hayford, Hershel Parker, and G. Thomas Tanselle (Evanston, IL: Northwestern University Press, 1988), 320.

4. Lawrence Buell, *Writing for an Endangered World: Literature, Culture, and the Environment in the U.S. and Beyond* (Cambridge, MA: Harvard University Press, 2001), 31.

INTRODUCTION

1. Melville, *Moby-Dick*, 393.

2. Melville, "The Archipelago," in *Timoleon, Etc.*, in Melville, *Published Poems*, ed. Robert C. Ryan, Harrison Hayford, Alma Reising, and G. Thomas Tanselle (Evanston, IL: Northwestern University Press, 2009), 307.

3. See Robert P. McIntosh, *The Background of Ecology: Concept and Theory* (Cambridge: Cambridge University Press, 1985), 16; and David R. Keller and Frank B. Golley, introduction to *The Philosophy of Ecology: From Science to Synthesis* (Athens: University of Georgia Press, 2000), 2–3.

4. The term "protoecologist" is from D. W. Voorhees, *Concise Dictionary of American Science* (New York: Scribner's, 1983).

5. Ralph Waldo Emerson, "Self-Reliance" in *Emerson's Prose & Poetry*, ed. Joel Porte and Saundra Morris (New York: Norton, 2001), 130.

6. Melville, "The Encantadas," in Melville, *The Piazza Tales, and Other Prose Pieces, 1839–1860*, ed. Harrison Hayford, Hershel Parker, and G. Thomas Tanselle (Evanston, IL: Northwestern University Press, 1987), 137.

7. The tree-patting anecdote is from Maunsell B. Field, *Memories of Many Men* (1874), cited in Jay Leyda, *The Melville Log*, vol. 2 (New York: Harcourt, 1951), 506.

8. Charles Darwin, *The Origin of Species* (Oxford: Oxford University Press, 1996), 52, 53; and Melville, *The Confidence-Man: His Masquerade*, ed. Harrison Hayford, Hershel Parker, and G. Thomas Tanselle (Evanston, IL: Northwestern University Press, 1984), 124.

9. Melville, *Moby-Dick*, 456.

10. Jean-Baptiste Fressoz, "Losing the Earth Knowingly: Six Environmental Grammars around 1800," in *The Anthropocene and the Global Environmental Crisis: Rethinking Modernity in a New Epoch*, ed. Clive Hamilton, Christophe Bonneuil, and Francois Gemenne (London: Routledge, 2015), 82.

11. Yves Cochet, "Green Eschatology," in Hamilton, Bonneuil, and Gemenne, *Anthropocene and Global Environmental Crisis*, 119. See also Nathaniel Rich, "Losing Earth," *New York Times Magazine*, August 1, 2018.

12. Melville, "A Canticle," in *Battle-Pieces and Aspects of the War*, in Melville, *Published Poems*, 102.

13. Melville, *Correspondence*, ed. Lynn Horth (Evanston, IL: Northwestern University Press, 1993), 19.

14. Richard Hardack, *"Not Altogether Human": Pantheism and the Dark Nature of the American Renaissance* (Amherst: University of Massachusetts Press, 2012), 8.

15. Scholarship on Melville and science dates to the 1940s. See Elizabeth Foster, "Melville and Geology," *American Literature* 17:1 (1945): 50–65; and three essays by Tyrus Hillway: "Melville's Geological Knowledge," *American Literature* 21:1 (1949): 232–37, "Melville as Critic of Science," *Modern Language Notes* 65 (1950): 411–14, and "Melville's Education in Science," *Texas Studies in Literature and Language* 16:3 (1974): 411–25. But it wasn't until Richard Dean Smith's *Melville's Science: "Devilish Tantalization of the Gods!"* (New York: Garland, 1993), Brett Zimmerman's *Herman Melville: Stargazer* (Montreal: McGill-Queen's University Press, 1998), and Sam Otter's *Melville's Anatomies* (Berkeley: University of California Press, 1999) that scholars explored Melville's engagement with science in detail. In the past decade, the field has seen work on paleontology, electricity, skepticism, evolution, planetary scale, and other materialisms in Melville's writings. See Sam Halliday, *Science and Technology in the Age of Hawthorne, Melville, Twain, and James: Thinking and Writing Electricity* (New York: Palgrave Macmillan, 2007); Maurice Lee, *Uncertain Chances: Science, Skepticism, and Belief in Nineteenth-Century American Literature* (Oxford: Oxford University Press, 2011); Jennifer J. Baker, "Dead Bones and Honest Wonders: The Aesthetics of Natural Science in *Moby-Dick*," in *Melville and Aesthetics*, ed. Samuel Otter and Geoffery Sanborn (New York: Palgrave Macmillan, 2011); Karen and R. D. Madison, "Darwin's Year and Melville's 'New Ancient of Days,'" in *America's Darwin: Darwinian Theory and U.S. Literary Culture*, ed. Tina Gianquitto and Lydia Fisher (Athens: University of Georgia Press, 2014); Geoffrey Sanborn, "Melville and the Nonhuman World," and Tim Marr, "Melville's Planetary Compass," in *The New Cambridge Companion to Herman Melville*, ed. Robert S. Levine (Cambridge: Cambridge University Press, 2014); and Michael Jonik, *Herman Melville and the Politics of the Inhuman* (Cambridge: Cambridge University Press, 2018).

16. Melville, *Typee: A Peep at Polynesian Life*, ed. Harrison Hayford, Hershel Parker, and G. Thomas Tanselle (Evanston, IL: Northwestern University Press, 1968), 205.

17. See Brian Yothers, *Sacred Uncertainty: Religious Difference and the Shape of Melville's Career* (Evanston, IL: Northwestern University Press, 2015).

18. See Smith, *Melville's Science*, 19–89.

19. On Melville's education in science, see Smith, *Melville's Science*, xxxv–vii; and Meredith Farmer, "Herman Melville and Joseph Henry at the Albany Academy; or Melville's Education in Mathematics and Science," *Leviathan* 18:2 (2016): 9, 11, 16. On nineteenth-century transatlantic science and literature, see George Levine, "One Culture," in *One Culture: Essays in Science and Literature* (Madison: University of Wisconsin Press, 1987); Noah Heringman, *Romantic Rocks, Aesthetic Geology* (Ithaca: Cornell University Press, 2004); Adelene Buckland, *Novel Science: Fiction and the Invention of Nineteenth-Century Geology* (Chicago: University of Chicago Press, 2013); and Benjamin Morgan, *The Outward Mind: Materialist Aesthetics in Victorian Science and Literature* (Chicago: University of Chicago Press, 2017).

20. Jacob Bigelow, *Elements of Technology*, 2nd ed. (Boston: Hilliard, Gray, Little, and Wilkins, 1831), 1–2.

21. Ralph Waldo Emerson, "Poetry and Imagination," in Emerson, *The Complete Works*, vol. 8 (Boston: Houghton, Mifflin, 1904), 10.

22. Melville, *Mardi: and A Voyage Thither*, ed. Harrison Hayford, Hershel Parker, and G. Thomas Tanselle (Evanston, IL: Northwestern University Press, 1970), 489.

23. Melville, *Confidence-Man*, 173.

24. Ibid., 70.

25. Ibid., 238.

26. Ibid., 239.

27. Thomas Paine, *Common Sense* (New York: Penguin, 1982), 82; and Emerson, "The Young American," in Emerson, *Complete Works*, vol. 1 (Boston: Houghton, Mifflin, 1904), 379.

28. Washington Irving, *The Sketch-Book of Geoffrey Crayon, Gentleman* (London: John Murray, 1822), 154.

29. Melville, "Benito Cereno," in *The Piazza Tales*, 68.

30. Cornel West, afterword to *Melville among the Philosophers*, ed. Tom Nurmi and Corey McCall (Lanham, MD: Rowman & Littlefield, 2017), 237.

31. Melville, *Confidence-Man*, 81.

32. Ibid., 79, 84.

33. Ibid., 106–9.

34. See Robert V. Bruce, *The Launching of Modern American Science, 1846–1876* (New York: Alfred A. Knopf, 1987), 55–74.

35. Ibid., 68.

36. Melville, "The Piazza," in *The Piazza Tales*, 8.

37. Bruce, *Launching of Modern American Science*, 13.

38. Nathan Reingold, *Science in Nineteenth-Century America: A Documentary History* (Chicago: University of Chicago, 1964), 163.

39. Thomas Allen, *A Republic in Time: Temporality and Social Imagination in Nineteenth-Century America* (Chapel Hill: University of North Carolina Press, 2008), 146, 151.

40. David I. Spanangel, *DeWitt Clinton and Amos Eaton: Geology and Power in Early New York* (Baltimore: Johns Hopkins University Press, 2014), 10.

41. Melville, *Clarel: A Poem and Pilgrimage in the Holy Land,* ed. Harrison Hayford, G. Thomas Tanselle, and Hershel Parker (Evanston, IL: Northwestern University Press, 1991), 2.26.13.

42. Darwin, *Origin of Species,* 389.

43. Stephen Gould, *Time's Arrow, Time's Cycle: Myth and Metaphor in the Discovery of Geological Time* (Cambridge, MA: Harvard University Press, 1987), 3.

44. Melville, *Mardi,* 363.

45. Charles Brockden Brown, "The Difference between History and Romance," *Monthly Magazine and American Review* 2.4 (New York: T. & J. Swords, 1800), 251–53.

46. Melville, *Confidence-Man,* 125, 145.

47. Melville, "Inscription Epistolary to W.C.R.," in *John Marr,* in Melville, *Published Poems,* 192.

48. Unsigned review, *London Leader,* April 11, 1857, 356.

49. Emerson, "Self-Reliance," 125.

50. Ibid., 126.

51. Max Weber, *The Protestant Ethic and the Spirit of Capitalism* (London: Routledge, 2001), 32.

52. Walt Whitman, "A Backward Glance o'er Travel'd Roads," in Whitman, *Leaves of Grass* (New York: Norton, 2002), 475–76.

53. See, for example, Anne Bradstreet's "The Four Elements" (1650) and "Meditations Divine and Moral" (1664), Jonathan Edwards's "A Self-Trained Berkeleian" (1719), and Emily Dickinson's "J.451" (1862).

54. Melville, *Moby-Dick,* 349.

55. See Derek Woods, "Scale Critique for the Anthropocene," *Minnesota Review* 83 (2014): 133–42; and Timothy Clark, "Scale as a Force of Deconstruction" in *Eco-Deconstruction: Derrida and Environmental Philosophy,* ed. Matthias Fritsch, Philippe Lynes, and David Wood (New York: Fordham University Press, 2018), 81–94.

56. Clark, "Scale as a Force," 92.

57. Karl Marx, "Estranged Labor," from *Economic and Philosophic Manuscripts of 1844,* in *The Marx-Engels Reader,* 2nd ed. (New York: Norton, 1972), 75.

58. Melville, *Omoo: A Narrative of Adventures in the South Seas,* ed. Harrison Hayford, Hershel Parker, and G. Thomas Tanselle (Evanston, IL: Northwestern University Press, 1968), 270.

59. Stacy Alaimo, *Bodily Natures: Science, Environment, and the Material Self* (Bloomington: Indiana University Press, 2010), 10–11.

60. Charles Olson, "Equal, That Is, to the Real Itself," *Chicago Review* 12:2 (1958): 100.

61. Ibid.

62. Ibid., 104.

63. In November 1892, a year after Melville died, Ellen Swallow used the term "Oekology" in the *Boston Globe,* marking its first appearance in American print.

64. See Donald Worster, *Nature's Economy: A History of Ecological Ideas* (Cambridge: Cambridge University Press, 1997), x.
65. McIntosh, *Background of Ecology*, 7, 9–11.
66. Ernst Haeckel, *Generelle Morophologie der Organismen*, vol. 1 (Berlin: Georg Reimer, 1866), 8; and Haeckel, *Wonders of Life: A Popular Study of Biological Philosophy* (New York: Harper Brothers, 1905), 80.
67. McIntosh, *Background of Ecology*, 26.
68. See Worster, *Nature's Economy*, x.
69. See Jonathan Bate, *Romantic Ecology: Wordsworth and the Environmental Tradition* (London: Routledge, 1991).
70. Henry David Thoreau, "Letter to Thomas Cholmondeley: October 20, 1856," in Thoreau, *Correspondence*, vol. 2 (Princeton: Princeton University Press, 2018), 472.
71. George Perkins Marsh, *Man and Nature* (Cambridge, MA: Harvard University Press, 1965), 464.
72. See Sharon E. Kingsland, *The Evolution of American Ecology, 1890–2000* (Baltimore: Johns Hopkins University Press, 2005), 15; and Bruce, *American Science*, 124–25.
73. Aaron Sachs, *The Humboldt Current: Nineteenth-Century Exploration and the Roots of American Environmentalism* (New York: Penguin, 2006), 2, 12.
74. Alexander von Humboldt, *Cosmos: A Sketch of a Physical Description of the Universe*, vol. 1 (New York: Harper Bros, 1858; repr., Baltimore: Johns Hopkins University Press, 1997), 23.
75. Sachs, *Humboldt Current*, 4. See Laura Dassow Walls, *Seeing New Worlds: Henry David Thoreau and Nineteenth-Century Natural Science* (Madison: University of Wisconsin Press, 1995); and Walls, *The Passage to Cosmos: Alexander von Humboldt and the Shaping of America* (Chicago: University of Chicago Press, 2011).
76. Humboldt, *Cosmos*, 24, 27.
77. Ibid., 79.
78. Ibid., 25.
79. Ibid., 49.
80. See Sachs, *Humboldt Current*, 12–13; and Walls, *Passage to Cosmos*, 18–20.
81. Many thanks to Laura Dassow Walls for this insight.
82. Charles Darwin, *Journal of Researches* (London: John Murray, 1845), 398.
83. Charles Darwin, *Voyage of the Beagle* (New York: Penguin, 1989), 272.
84. See Mary Bercaw, *Melville's Sources* (Evanston, IL: Northwestern University Press, 1987), 74.
85. Melville, *Typee*, 9; Melville, *Mardi*, 3; and Melville, *Moby-Dick*, 528.
86. Melville, *Moby-Dick*, xxviii; and Baker, "Dead Bones," 94.
87. See Madison and Madison, "Darwin's Year," 92–99; and Smith, *Melville's Science*, 247–55.
88. Gillian Beer, "Darwin's Plots," in *Darwin: A Norton Critical Edition*, 3rd. ed., ed. Philip Appleman (New York: Norton, 2001), 651.

89. George Levine, "Darwin among the Novelists," in *Darwin*, 661, 663.

90. Melanie Mitchell, *Complexity: A Guided Tour* (Oxford: Oxford University Press, 2009), x. See also Frank B. Golley, *A History of the Ecosystem Concept in Ecology: More than the Sum of the Parts* (New Haven: Yale University Press, 1993).

91. Mitchell, *Complexity*, 4.

92. See G. Evelyn Hutchinson, *Introduction to Population Ecology* (New Haven: Yale University Press, 1978), 215.

93. Keller and Golley, *Philosophy of Ecology*, 15.

94. Melville, *Pierre, or The Ambiguities*, ed. Harrison Hayford, Hershel Parker, and G. Thomas Tanselle (Evanston, IL: Northwestern University Press, 1971), 67.

95. Julian Yates, *Of Sheep, Oranges, Yeast: A Multispecies Impression* (Minneapolis: University of Minnesota Press, 2017), 25.

96. Melville, *Omoo*, 240, 257.

97. Martin D. F. Ellwood and William A. Foster, "Doubling the Estimate of Invertebrate Biomass in a Rainforest Canopy," *Nature* 429:3 (2004): 550.

98. John Locke, "Essay Concerning Human Understanding" (1690), in *The Philosophical Works of John Locke*, 12th ed. (London: George Virtue, 1843), 2: 12 (164).

99. Emerson, "Goethe; or, the Writer," in Emerson, *Collected Works*, vol. 1 (Boston: Houghton Mifflin, 1906), 394.

100. Charles Darwin, "To Charles Lyell, 11 October 1859," from *The Darwin Correspondence Project* (www.darwinproject.ac.uk/).

101. John H. Holland, *Complexity: A Very Brief Introduction* (Oxford: Oxford University Press, 2014), 9–10.

102. Hans-Georg Gadamer, *Truth and Method*, 2nd ed., trans. Joel Weinsheimer and Donald G. Marshall (London: Continuum, 2006), 301.

103. Giorgio Agamben, *Creation and Anarchy: The Work of Art and the Religion of Capitalism* (Stanford: Stanford University Press, 2019), 1.

104. Marjorie Levinson, "Of Being Numerous," *Studies in Romanticism* 49:4 (2010): 635.

105. Greta LaFleur, *The Natural History of Sexuality in Early America* (Baltimore: Johns Hopkins University Press, 2018), 15.

106. Melville, *Omoo*, 162.

107. Melville, *Typee*, 49.

108. Ibid., 126.

109. Melville, *Omoo*, 14, 39.

110. Ibid., 39–40.

111. Ibid., 115, 120–21.

112. Ibid., 191.

113. Ibid., 253.

114. Ibid., 74.

115. Melville, *Moby-Dick*, 449–50.

116. Mitchell, *Complexity*, 13.

117. Melville, *Omoo*, 100.

118. Mitchell, *Complexity*, 252.

119. Dorri Beam, *Style, Gender, and Fantasy in Nineteenth-Century Women's Writing* (Cambridge: Cambridge University Press, 2010), 33.

120. Samuel Otter, "Melville's Style" in *The New Melville Studies*, ed. Cody Marrs (Cambridge: Cambridge University Press, 2019), 123, 137.

121. Melville, *Typee*, 24.

122. Melville, "The Encantadas," 128.

123. P. Glansdorff and I. Prigogine, *Thermodynamic Theory of Structure, Stability and Fluctuations* (New York: John Wiley Sons, 1971), 93.

124. Melville, "The Encantadas," 133–34.

125. Ibid., 135.

126. Gaston Bachelard, *The Poetics of Space*, trans. Maria Jolas (Boston: Beacon Press, 1994), 103.

127. Ibid., 104.

128. See Michael L. Cain et. al., *Ecology*, 3rd ed. (Oxford: Oxford University Press, 2014), 406.

129. Melville, "The Encantadas," 136.

130 Graham Thompson, *Herman Melville: Among the Magazines* (Amherst: University of Massachusetts Press, 2017), 32.

131. Thoreau, *Walden, Civil Disobedience and Other Writings* (New York: Norton, 2008), 69.

132. Melville, *Correspondence*, 186.

133. Melville, *Omoo*, 216.

134. Melville, *Moby-Dick*, 260.

135. Melville, *Clarel*, 4.35.18–20.

136. See, for example, Serpil Oppermann and Serenella Iovino, eds., *Material Ecocriticism* (Bloomington: Indiana University Press, 2014); Oppermann and Iovino, eds., *Environmental Humanities: Voices from the Anthropocene* (London: Rowman & Littlefield, 2017); Jussi Parikka, *A Geology of Media* (Minneapolis: University of Minnesota Press, 2015); Jeffrey Jerome Cohen, *Elemental Ecocriticism* (Minneapolis: University Minnesota Press, 2015); David Wills, *Inanimation: Theories of Inorganic Life* (Minneapolis: University of Minnesota Press, 2016); Elizabeth A. Povinelli, *Geontologies: A Requiem to Late Liberalism* (Durham, NC: Duke University Press, 2016); Todd S. Mei, *Land and the Given Economy: The Hermeneutics and Phenomenology of Dwelling* (Evanston, IL: Northwestern University Press, 2017); and Nathan Brown, *The Limits of Fabrication: Materials Science, Materialist Poetics* (New York: Fordham University Press, 2017).

137. Martin Heidegger, *The Fundamental Concepts of Metaphysics: World, Finitude, Solitude*, trans. William McNeill and Nicholas Walker (Bloomington: Indiana University Press, 1995), 185.

138. Giorgio Agamben, *The Open: Man and Animal* (Stanford: Stanford University Press, 2004), 40: and Jeffrey Nealon, *Plant Theory: Biopower and Vegetal Life* (Stanford: Stanford University Press, 2015), 96.

139. N. Brown, *Limits of Fabrication*, 55. See, for example, Cary Wolfe, *Animal Rites: American Culture, the Discourse of Species, and Posthumanist Theory* (Chicago:

University of Chicago Press, 2003); and Wolfe, *Zoontologies: The Question of the Animal* (Minneapolis: University of Minnesota Press, 2003).

140. Maxwell Masters, *Botany for Beginners: An Introduction to the Study of Plants* (London: Bradbury, Agnew & Co. 1872), 73–75.

141. See Melville, *Typee*, 83; Melville, *Mardi*, 168; and Melville, *Moby-Dick*, 142, 262.

142. Melville, "A Way-Side Weed," in *Weeds and Wildings*, in Melville, *Billy Budd, Sailor and Other Uncompleted Writings*, ed. Harrison Hayford, Alma A. MacDougal, Robert A. Sandberg, and G. Thomas Tanselle (Evanston, IL: Northwestern University Press, 2017), 90.

143. Nealon, *Plant Theory*, 115, 121.

144. Buckland, *Novel Science*, 2.

145. Ibid., 19.

146. Nathan Brown, "Ten Theses on Poetics" (centreforexpandedpoetics.com/ten-theses/).

147. Rebekah Sheldon, "Form/Matter/Chora: Object-Oriented Ontology and Feminist New Materialism," in *The Nonhuman Turn*, ed. Richard Grusin (Minneapolis: University of Minnesota Press, 2015), 206.

148. Giorgio Agamben, *The Highest Poverty: Monastic Rules and Form-of-Life*, trans. Adam Kotsko (Stanford: Stanford University Press, 2013), ix.

149. Melville, *Moby-Dick*, 260, 263; and Melville, *Billy Budd*, 68.

150. Melville, *Billy Budd*, 69.

151. Melville, *Moby-Dick*, 414.

152. Melville, *Pierre*, 124.

153. Ibid., 353, 68.

154. Melville, "The Piazza," 8.

155. Melville, "The Encantadas," 134.

156. Wendy Wheeler, *Expecting the Earth: Life, Culture, Biosemiotics* (London: Lawrence and Wishart, 2016), 206.

157. See Sam Mickey, Sean Kelly, and Adam Robbert, *The Variety of Integral Ecologies: Nature, Culture, and Knowledge in the Planetary Era* (Albany: State University of New York Press, 2017), 1–19.

158. Melville, *Clarel*, 2.4.95–97.

159. Melville, *Mardi*, 555.

1. PEARL

1. For more detail on this period of Melville's life, see Hershel Parker, *Herman Melville: A Biography*, vol. 1 (Baltimore: Johns Hopkins University Press, 2005), 496–98.

2. See Paul Johnson, *A History of the American People* (New York: Harper, 1997), 384–87; and Ralph P. Bieber, *Southern Trails to California in 1849* (Glendale, CA: Arthur H. Clark, 1937), 18.

3. See Merrill Davis, *Melville's Mardi* (New Haven: Yale University Press, 1952), 67; and Parker, *Melville: Biography*, 1:576–77.

4. Melville, *Mardi*, 229, 397.

5. On propulsive worlds, see Cohen, *Stone*, 22. On the earth's givenness, see Mei, *Given Economy*, 7–13.

6. Melville, *Pierre*, 122.

7. Christopher F. Jones, *Routes of Power: Energy and Modern America* (Cambridge, MA: Harvard University Press, 2014), 2.

8. Ibid., 185.

9. LaFleur, *Natural History of Sexuality*, 16.

10. Jean-Baptiste Lamarck, *Hydrogeology* (Urbana: University of Illinois Press, 1964), 4.

11. Bruno Latour, "Morality and Technology: The End of the Means," trans. Couze Venn, *Theory, Culture & Society* 19:5/6 (2002): 249.

12. Melville, *Moby-Dick*, 431.

13. Olson, "Real Itself," 101.

14. Melville, *Mardi*, 576.

15. Parker, *Herman Melville*, 1:632.

16. Melville, *Mardi*, 575.

17. Ibid., 283.

18. Melville, *Moby-Dick*, 456.

19. See Bercaw, *Melville's Sources*, 67, 73–74, 99; Smith, *Melville's Science*, 17–19, 46–47; and Foster, "Melville and Geology," 54–58.

20. Melville, *Mardi*, 211.

21. Melville, *Redburn: His First Voyage*, ed. Harrison Hayford, Hershel Parker, and G. Thomas Tanselle (Evanston, IL: Northwestern University Press, 1969), 162.

22. Melville, *Clarel*, 3.1.136.

23. Melville, *Correspondence*, 107. In his reply to Murray on January 1, 1848, Melville erased his description of the novel as "authentic," instead writing: "it shall have the right stuff in it" (*Correspondence*, 100–102).

24. Melville, *Mardi*, xvii.

25. Melville, *Correspondence*, 105, 106.

26. Melville, "Hawthorne and His Mosses," in *The Piazza Tales*, 244.

27. Melville, *Pierre*, 258; and Melville, *Moby-Dick*, 164.

28. Melville, "Encantadas," 132, 126; and Melville, *Clarel*, 2.28.30–31, 2.20.48–50.

29. Hershel Parker, *Herman Melville: A Biography*, vol. 2 (Baltimore: Johns Hopkins University Press, 2005), 805.

30. Melville, "Mosses," 253.

31. Melville, *Pierre*, 285; and Melville, "Mosses," 253.

32. Melville, *Mardi*, 228.

33. Latour, "Morality and Technology," 249.

34. Hazen et al., "Mineralogy," 606.

35. Ibid., 598.

36. Jan Zalasiewicz, "The Extraordinary Strata of the Anthropocene," in Oppermann and Iovino, *Environmental Humanities*, 120.

37. Graham Harman, *Tool-Being: Heidegger and the Metaphysics of Objects* (Chicago: Open Court, 2002), 1.

38. Charles Fletcher, *Physical Geology: The Science of Earth* (New York: Wiley, 2010), 144.

39. See Julie Michelle Klinger, *Rare Earth Frontiers: From Terrestrial Subsoils to Lunar Landscapes* (Ithaca: Cornell University Press, 2017).

40. Emerson, "Experience," in *Emerson's Prose and Poetry*, 205.

41. Andreas Malm, *Fossil Capital: The Rise of Steam Power and the Roots of Global Warming* (New York: Verso, 2016), 8.

42. William Phillips, *An Elementary Treatise on Mineralogy*, 5th ed. (Boston: William B. Ticknor, 1844), xv.

43. Emerson, "The Poet," in *Emerson's Prose & Poetry*, 190.

44. *The Penny Cyclopaedia of the Society for the Diffusion of Useful Knowledge* (London: C. Knight, 1833–43), 5:147–48.

45. Heringman, *Romantic Rocks*, 269. See also Allen, *A Republic in Time*, 146–85; and Buckland, *Novel Science*, 2–18.

46. Parikka, *Geology of Media*, 5.

47. See Vince Beiser, *The World in a Grain: The Story of Sand and How It Transformed Civilization* (New York: Riverhead Books, 2018).

48. Melville, *Moby-Dick*, 136.

49. Phillips, *Treatise on Mineralogy*, xvi.

50. See Smith, *Melville's Science*, xxxvii; and Rebecca Bedell, *Anatomy of Nature: Geology & American Landscape Painting, 1825–1875* (Princeton: Princeton University Press, 2001), 3–4.

51. "Works of Sir William Hamilton," *Putnam's Monthly: A Magazine of American Literature, Science, and Art*, November 1853, 476.

52. Allen, *Republic in Time*, 151.

53. Bedell, *Anatomy of Nature*, xi.

54. Parker, *Herman Melville*, 1:556, 879.

55. Melville, *Moby-Dick*, 22, 508.

56. Michael Marder, *Pyropolitics: When the World Is Ablaze* (London: Rowman & Littlefield, 2015), xiv.

57. Melville, *Pierre*, 220.

58. Ibid.

59. See Parker, *Herman Melville*, 1:187, 2:892.

60. Melville, *Pierre*, 86.

61. Melville, *Moby-Dick*, 42; and Melville, "The Encantadas," 126.

62. Melville, *Moby-Dick*, 507.

63. Ibid., 263, 245.

64. Jacques Derrida, *Archive Fever: A Freudian Impression*, trans. Eric Prenowitz (Chicago: University of Chicago Press, 1995), 4n1.

65. Melville, *Mardi*, 525.

66. Melville, *Redburn*, 149.

67. Melville, *Mardi*, 540.

68. See Davis, *Melville's Mardi*, 92.

69. Bieber, *Southern Trails*, 71.

70. James Knox Polk, "State of the Union Address, December 5, 1848," in the James K. Polk Papers: Series 5: Messages and Speeches, 1833–1849 (Library of Congress, www.loc.gov/item/mss365090065/).

71. Melville, *Mardi*, 620.

72. Ibid., 60, 206, 478–80.

73. Ibid., 547, 552. Oro was the Polynesian god of war, but *oro* also means gold in Spanish and Italian.

74. Melville, *Mardi*, 552.

75. See Wai Chee Dimock, *Empire for Liberty: Melville and the Poetics of Individualism* (Princeton: Princeton University Press, 1989), 46–75.

76. Melville, *Mardi*, 525.

77. Dipesh Chakrabarty, "The Climate of History: Four Theses," *Critical Inquiry* 35 (2009): 201.

78. Ibid., 206.

79. Dipesh Chakrabarty, "Climate and Capital: On Conjoined Histories," *Critical Inquiry* 41 (2014): 3.

80. James Hutton, *Theory of the Earth*, vol. 1, pt. 2 (Edinburgh: Royal Society of Edinburgh, 1788), 304.

81. Melville, *Mardi*, 460.

82. Mark McGurl, "The New Cultural Geology," *Twentieth-Century Literature* 57:3/4 (2011): 384.

83. On the origin of all heavy elements from collisions of neutron stars, see E. Berger et al., "An r-Process Kilonova Associated with the Short-Hard GRB 130603B," *Astrophysical Journal Letters* 774:2 (2013).

84. Tobias Menely, "'The Present Obfuscation': Cowper's *Task* and the Time of Climate Change," *PMLA* 127:3 (2012): 490; and Rob Nixon, *Slow Violence and the Environmentalism of the Poor* (Cambridge, MA: Harvard University Press, 2013), 3.

85. Menely "'Present Obfuscation,'" 482.

86. Virginia Zimmerman, *Excavating Victorians* (Albany: State University of New York Press, 2008), 1.

87. Melville, *Mardi*, 652.

88. Wai Chee Dimock, *Through Other Continents: American Literature across Deep Time* (Princeton: Princeton University Press, 2006), 132–34.

89. On the labor of reading *Mardi*, see Cindy Weinstein, "The Calm before the Storm: Laboring through *Mardi*," *American Literature* 65:2 (1993): 239–53. On the environmental ironies of book production, see Stephanie LeMenager, *Living Oil: Petroleum Culture in the American Century* (Oxford: Oxford University Press, 2014), 11–18, 201–9.

90. Melville, *Moby-Dick*, 331.

91. *OED Online*, s.v. "subtilize" (https://www.oed.com).

92. Melville, *Mardi*, 352.

93. Ibid., 595.

94. Ibid., 597.

95. Golconda is a mining region in southwest India known for its mineral riches, including the Hope Diamond.

96. Melville, *Mardi*, 194, 651.
97. Ibid., 651.
98. Ibid., 654.
99. See Petr Sima and Vaclav Vetvicka, *Evolution of Immune Reactions* (London: Taylor & Francis, 1990).
100. *Penny Cyclopaedia*, 17:351. On Melville's use of the *Cyclopaedia*, see Bercaw, *Melville's Sources*, 18, 26, 108.
101. Aldemaro Romero, "The Case of the Depletion of Pearl Oyster Beds in Sixteenth-Century Venezuela," *Conservation Biology* 17:4 (2003): 1013–23.
102. Melville, *Mardi*, 137–38.
103. Dimock, *Empire for Liberty*, 10, 61.
104. Melville, *Moby-Dick*, 380.
105. Melville, *Mardi*, 137–38.
106. Melville, *Pierre*, 119, 160, 150.
107. Melville, *Moby-Dick*, 263.
108. Melville, *Mardi*, 652, 653.
109. Dimock, *Through Other Continents*, 71.
110. Olson, "Real Itself," 101. For the Olsonian geometry of *Moby-Dick*, see Jonik, *Inhuman*, 49–61.
111. Wills, *Inanimation*, 25.
112. Melville, *Mardi*, 210.
113. Ibid., 575.
114. Ibid., 547.
115. Ibid., 427.
116. Ibid., 414, 415.
117. Ibid., 415, 416. British geologist William Whewell called rocks "geological alphabets" and languages "geological layers" in "Address Delivered at . . . the Geological Society of London" (London: R. and J. E. Taylor, 1838), 14.
118. Melville, *Mardi*, 415.
119. Ibid., 417.
120. Ibid. See Foster, "Melville and Geology," 55.
121. Melville, *Mardi*, 418.
122. See Hillway, "Melville as Critic of Science," 411.
123. Melville, *Mardi*, 507.
124. Ibid., 425.
125. See Lee, *Uncertain Chances*, 55–82.
126. Melville, *Mardi*, 229.
127. Robert Hazen et al., "Mineral Evolution," *American Mineralogist* 93 (2008): 1713.
128. Ibid., 1712.
129. Robert Hazen and J. M. Ferry, "Mineral Evolution: Mineralogy in the Fourth Dimension," *Elements* 6:1 (2010): 9; and Hazen et al., "Mineral Evolution," 6.
130. Hazen et al., "Mineral Evolution," 1706.

131. Melville, *Mardi*, 230.
132. Ibid., 554–55.
133. Zimmerman, *Stargazer*, 29, 19.
134. Bruce, *American Science*, 102–3.
135. On Melville and astronomy, see Davis, *Melville's Mardi*, 67; Zimmerman, *Stargazer*, 11, 14; and Farmer, "Albany Academy," 9, 11, 16.
136. Melville, *Mardi*, 178.
137. Melville, *White-Jacket; or, The World in a Man-of-War*, ed. Harrison Hayford, Hershel Parker, and G. Thomas Tanselle (Evanston, IL: Northwestern University Press, 1970), 398; and Melville, *Moby-Dick*, 478.
138. Melville, *Correspondence*, 100.
139. J. P. Nichol, *Views of Astronomy: Seven Lectures Delivered before the Mercantile Library Association of New York in the Months of January and February, 1848* (New York: Greeley & McElrath, 1848), 6.
140. Melville, *Mardi*, 576.
141. Melville, *Moby-Dick*, 195.
142. Melville, *Mardi*, 236.
143. Ibid., 238.
144. N. Brown, *Limits of Fabrication*, 55.
145. Wills, *Inanimation*, x.
146. Melville, *Mardi*, 613.
147. *Penny Cyclopaedia*, 5:147.
148. Ibid., 5:149–50, 22:75–76.
149. Bachelard, *Poetics of Space*, 113.
150. Melville, *Mardi*, 237.
151. See Franklin Damman, "Bacterial Symbionts and Taphonomic Agents of Humans," 161, and Soren Blau, "The Effects of Weathering on Bone Preservation," 203, in *Taphonomy of Human Remains*, ed. Eline M. Schotsmans, Nicholas Márquez-Grant, and Shari Forbes (New York: John Wiley & Sons, 2017).
152. Cohen, *Stone*, 33.
153. Melville, *Moby-Dick*, 448.
154. Ibid., 349.
155. Ibid., 469.
156. Ibid, 471–72.
157. Ibid., 516.
158. Melville, *Mardi*, 336.
159. Ibid., 352.
160. See Harris Lieberman, Robin B. Kanarek, and Chandan Prasad, *Nutritional Neuroscience* (London: CRC Press, 2005). 78.
161. Melville, *Mardi*, 576.
162. Melville, *The Confidence-Man*, 9, 78.
163. Melville, *Mardi*, 505.
164. Ibid., 649.

165. Ibid., 594.
166. Latour, "Morality and Technology," 256.
167. Melville, *Mardi*, 238.
168. Graham Harman, "The Well-Wrought Broken Hammer: Object-Oriented Literary Criticism," *New Literary History* 43 (2012): 187.
169. Melville, *Mardi*, 597; and Povinelli, *Geontologies*, 21.
170. Povinelli, *Geontologies*, 21.
171. *OED Online*, s.v. "babble."
172. On karst terrain, see Melville, "The Apparition," in *Battle-Pieces* in Melville, *Published Poems*, 116. On rockslides, see Melville, *Clarel*, 1.17.86–97.
173. See *Typee*, 154–55.
174. Melville, *Omoo*, 192.
175. Melville, *Pierre*, 345.
176. Melville, *Clarel*, 2.10.30–34.
177. Chakrabarty, "Climate of History," 220, 222.
178. Kate Marshall, "What Are the Novels of the Anthropocene? American Fiction in Geological Time," *American Literary History* 27:3 (2015): 525.
179. Melville, *Correspondence*, 130.
180. Dimock, *Through Other Continents*, 75; and Melville, *Correspondence*, 130.
181. Melville, *Moby-Dick*, 311.
182. Ibid., 278–79.
183. Melville, *Clarel*, 2.18.105–6.
184. Melville, *Moby-Dick*, 344.
185. Daniel Lord Smail, *On Deep History and the Brain* (Berkeley: University of California Press, 2008), 110.
186. Lorraine Daston, *Against Nature* (Cambridge, MA: MIT Press, 2019), 25.
187. Londa Schiebinger, *Nature's Body: Gender in the Making of Modern Science* (New Brunswick, NJ: Rutgers University Press, 2006), 10.
188. Daston, *Against Nature*, 15.
189. Elizabeth Grosz, *The Incorporeal: Ontology, Ethics, and the Limits of Materialism* (New York: Columbia University Press, 2017), 248.
190. Letter to Lemuel Shaw, April 23, 1849, Melville, *Correspondence*, 130.
191. Letter to Evert Duyckinck, February 2, 1850, Melville, *Correspondence*, 154.
192. Ibid.
193. Branka Arsić, *Bird Relics: Grief and Vitalism in Thoreau* (Cambridge, MA: Harvard University Press, 2016), 188.
194. Melville, "The Piazza," 7; and Hubert Zapf, "Creative Matter and Creative Mind: Cultural Ecology and Literary Creativity," in Oppermann and Iovino, *Material Ecocriticism*, 51.
195. Melville, *Mardi*, 230.
196. Melville, *Moby-Dick*, 42.
197. Ibid.
198. Ibid., 497.
199. Melville, *Confidence-Man*, 206.

2. TENDRIL

1. Melville, *Pierre*, 122.

2. See Sianne Ngai, *Ugly Feelings* (Cambridge, MA: Harvard University Press, 2005), 236–47; Charlene Avallone, "Calculations for Popularity: Melville's *Pierre* and Holden's Dollar Magazine," *Nineteenth-Century Literature* 43:1 (1988): 82–110; Cindy Weinstein, "We Are Family: Melville's *Pierre*," *Leviathan* 7:1 (2005): 19–40; and Weinstein, *Family, Kinship, and Sympathy in Nineteenth-Century American Literature* (Cambridge: Cambridge University Press, 2004), 159–84.

3. Duyckink's phrase is from an 1848 review of Emily Bronte's *Wuthering Heights*. See Parker, *Herman Melville*, 2:55.

4. See Saburo Yayama, "The Stone Image of Melville's 'Pierre,'" *Studies in English Literature* 34 (1957): 31–58; Milton Stern, *The Fine-Hammered Steel of Herman Melville* (Urbana: University of Illinois Press, 1968), 101–3, 151; and Jonik, *Inhuman*, 67–104.

5. Melville, *Pierre*, 353, 68.

6. Ibid., 347.

7. Ibid.

8. Melville, "Rip Van Winkle's Lilac," in Melville, *Uncompleted Writings*, 111.

9. Roberto Esposito, *Immunitas: The Protection and Negation of Life*, trans. Zakiya Hanafi (Malden, MA: Polity Press, 2011), 14–15.

10. Melville, *Pierre*, 9.

11. Ibid.

12. *Southern Quarterly Review*, October 1, 1852, and *The New York Albion*, October 1852 (qtd. in "Historical Note," in Melville, *Pierre*, 383, 381).

13. *New York Herald*, September 18, 1852, and *The Whig Review*, 1852 (qtd. in "Historical Note," in Melville, *Pierre*, 382, 388).

14. Qtd. in "Historical Note" in Melville, *Pierre*, 379–80.

15. Ibid., 402.

16. Melville, *Pierre*, 344.

17. Ibid., 159.

18. Anna Lowenhaupt Tsing, *The Mushroom at the End of the World: On the Possibility of Life in Capitalist Ruins* (Princeton: Princeton University Press, 2015), 169.

19. Ibid., 14.

20. On Melville's botanical reading, see Bercaw, *Melville's Sources*, 36, 78.

21. Melville, *Pierre*, 106–7.

22. Ibid., 298.

23. Ibid., 128. Note the parallels to Hawthorne's "Rappaccini's Daughter" (1846).

24. Ibid., 119.

25. Nealon, *Plant Theory*, 69.

26. Ibid.

27. Fanny Fern, *Fern Leaves from Fanny's Portfolio* (Buffalo: Derby, Orton and Mulligan, 1853), v. See Gillian Osborne, "Herman Melville, Queen of the Flowers," *Leviathan* 18:3 (2016): 133.

28. On "maple-sap" *Moby-Dick*, see "Letter to Richard Henry Dana: May 1, 1850," Melville, *Correspondence*, 162. On "plant-time" as "literary time," see Osborne, "Queen of the Flowers," 143.

29. Melville, *Pierre*, 110.

30. Ibid., 141.

31. Ibid.

32. Ibid.

33. Emerson, *Nature*, in *Emerson's Prose & Poetry*, 29.

34. Ibid.; and C. S. Holling, "Cross-Scale Morphology, Geometry and Dynamics of Ecosystems," *Ecological Monographs* 62:4 (1992): 447–502.

35. Melville, *Pierre*, 346.

36. Tsing, *Mushroom*, 47.

37. Melville, *Pierre*, 343.

38. Benoit Mandelbrot, *The Fractal Geometry of Nature* (New York: W. H. Freeman, 1977), 93.

39. Melville, *Pierre*, 158.

40. Letter to Lemuel Shaw, October 6, 1849, Melville, *Correspondence*, 138–39.

41. Letter to Richard Bentley, June 5, 1849, Melville, *Correspondence*, 132.

42. See Nealon, *Plant Theory*, 31.

43. Letter to Lemuel Shaw, October 6, 1849, Melville, *Correspondence*, 138–39; and Melville, *Journals*, ed. Howard C. Horsford with Lynn Horth (Evanston, IL: Northwestern University Press, 1989), 13.

44. There are exceptions; *White-Jacket*, for instance, opens with a discussion of "capillary action" and closes with atoms and phase changes (4, 502). See Smith, *Melville's Science*, 99–100.

45. Letter to Hawthorne, June 1, 1851, Melville, *Correspondence*, 191.

46. Melville, *Moby-Dick*, 289.

47. Melville, *Typee*, 154; and Melville, *Omoo*, 261–62.

48. Melville, *Moby-Dick*, 537.

49. Ibid., 12. On oak, see Melville, *Moby-Dick*, 333, 357. On oars, see 354.

50. Ibid., 325, 327.

51. Ibid., 499.

52. Ibid., 373, 270.

53. Letter to Hawthorne, June 1, 1851, Melville, *Correspondence*, 193.

54. Melville, *Pierre*, 71.

55. Ibid.

56. Jennifer Greiman, "Feeling Green: Goethe, Melville, and the Color of Democracy," *J19: The Journal of Nineteenth-Century Americanists* 3.2 (2015): 428.

57. Ibid., 422.

58. Heather I. Sullivan, "The Ecology of Colors: Goethe's Materialist Optics and Ecological Posthumanism," in Oppermann and Iovino, *Material Ecocriticism*, 91.

59. Melville, "The Encantadas," 132.

60. Tsing, *Mushroom*, 138.

61. Ibid., 137.

62. Melville, *Moby-Dick*, 180; and Melville, *Pierre*, 10.
63. Melville, *Mardi*, 112, 123.
64. Melville, *Moby-Dick*, 417.
65. Cain et al., *Ecology*, 511, 526.
66. Melville, *Pierre*, 32.
67. Melville, *Moby-Dick*, 237.
68. Nico Israel, *Spirals: The Whirled Image in Twentieth-Century Literature and Art* (New York: Columbia University Press, 2015), 23, 7.
69. Ibid., 32. See G. W. F. Hegel, *Phenomenology of Spirit*, trans. A. V. Miller (Oxford: Oxford University Press, 1977), §79; Marx, *Capital*, 1:727, 780; and Friedrich Wilhelm Nietzsche, *The Gay Science*, trans. Walter Kaufmann (New York: Penguin, 1974), §285, §341.
70. Johann Wolfgang von Goethe, *Goethe: Die Schriften zur Naturwissenschaft*, ed. Dorothea Kuhn (Weimar: Harmann Böhlaus Nachfolger, 1977), 1.4.251.
71. Brian Goodwin, *How the Leopard Changed Its Spots: The Evolution of Complexity* (Princeton: Princeton University Press, 2001), 76, 77.
72. Israel, *Spirals*, 10.
73. Jeffrey Jerome Cohen, "Monster Culture (Seven Theses)," in *Monster Theory: Reading Culture* (Minneapolis: University of Minnesota Press, 1997), 4.
74. Emerson, "Circles," 175, and "Nature," 27, in *Emerson's Prose & Poetry*.
75. Melville, *Moby-Dick*, 572.
76. Otter, *Melville's Anatomies*, 246.
77. Stern, *Fine-Hammered Steel*, 174.
78. Melville, *Pierre*, 289.
79. Emerson, "Experience," in *Emerson's Prose & Poetry*, 198.
80. Otter, *Melville's Anatomies*, 209.
81. Melville, *Pierre*, 189, 62.
82. Ibid., 189, 19.
83. Ibid., 175.
84. Grusin, introduction to *The Nonhuman Turn*, xix–xx.
85. For overviews of spinorial geometry, see Élie Cartan, *The Theory of Spinors* (New York: Dover, 1981).
86. See Bruce, *American Science*, 41.
87. Zachary Turpin, "Melville, Mathematics, and Platonic Idealism," *Leviathan* 17:2 (2015): 19, 28.
88. Melville, *Pierre*, 181.
89. "Historical Note," in Melville, *Pierre*, 385–86.
90. Jacob L. S. Bellmund, Peter Gärdenfors, Edvard I. Moser, and Christian F. Doeller, "Navigating Cognition: Spatial Codes for Human Thinking," *Science* 362 (2018): 2.
91. See Bruce, *American Science*, 185–86.
92. Melville, "Conflict of Convictions," in *Battle-Pieces*, 10.
93. Max Planck, *Where Is Science Going?* (New York: Norton, 1932), 217.
94. Melville, *Pierre*, 342.

95. Smith, *Melville's Science*, 194.

96. Karen Barad, "Quantum Entanglements and Hauntological Relations of Inheritance: Dis/continutities, SpaceTime Enfoldings and Justice-to-Come," *Derrida Today* 3:2 (2010): 251.

97. Melville, *Pierre*, 25.

98. Ibid., 324.

99. Ibid., 189.

100. Melville, *Moby-Dick*, 123.

101. Melville, *Pierre*, 54.

102. Melville, *Mardi*, 508.

103. Ibid.

104. Henri Bortoft, *The Wholeness of Nature: Goethe's Way toward a Science of Conscious Participation in Nature* (New York: Lindisfarne Press, 1996), 19.

105. Ibid., 33.

106. Johann Wolfgang von Goethe, *Goethe's Autobiography: Poetry and Truth from My Own Life*, trans. R. O. Moon (Washington, DC: Public Affairs Press, 1949): 53–54.

107. Goethe, *Zur Morphologie* in *Goethe: Die Schriften zur Naturwissenschaft*, 2.9a: 58. See also Robert J. Richards, *The Romantic Conception of Life: Science and Philosophy in the Age of Goethe* (Chicago: University of Chicago Press, 2002), 382–406.

108. Humboldt, *Cosmos*, 41.

109. Alexander von Humboldt and Aime Bonpland, *Essay on the Geography of Plants*, ed. Stephen T. Jackson, trans. Sylvie Romanowski (Chicago: University of Chicago Press, 2009), 73.

110. Ibid., 64.

111. Goethe, *Goethe's Autobiography*, vol. 2, *Letters from Switzerland and Travels in Italy* (London: Bohn, 1849), 448 (Melville Marginalia: melvillesmarginalia.org/Share.aspx?DocumentID=47&PageID=11255).

112. Gunther Schmid, introduction to R. Magnus, *Goethe as a Scientist*, trans. Heinz Norden (New York: Henry Schumann, 1949), xiii. See also Amanda Jo Goldstein, *Sweet Science: Romantic Materialism and the New Logics of Life* (Chicago: University of Chicago Press, 2017), 23, 72–99.

113. Bortoft, *Wholeness of Nature*, 84.

114. Parker, *Herman Melville*, 2:10.

115. On Melville's reading of Goethe, see Bercaw, *Melville's Sources*, 84–85; and Jonik, *Inhuman*, 79–95.

116. See Melville, *Published Poems*, 899 (Melville Marginalia: melvillesmarginalia.org/Share.aspx?DocumentID=51&PageID=12323).

117. *Penny Cyclopaedia*, 22:354–56.

118. Melville, *Mardi*, 176.

119. Melville, *Correspondence*, 193.

120. Ibid., 194.

121. Emerson, "The Poet," in *Emerson's Prose & Poetry*, 195.

122. Melville, *Pierre*, 302.

123. Ibid., 208.

124. Ibid., 209.
125. Ibid., 3, 9.
126. Ibid. 209.
127. Letter to Hawthorne, June 1, 1851, Melville, *Correspondence*, 194.
128. Melville, "Mosses," 250.
129. Jonik, *Inhuman*, 84.
130. Melville, *Mardi*, 458.
131. See Agamben, *The Open*, 51–68; Derrida, *The Beast & the Sovereign*, vol. 2 (Chicago: University of Chicago Press, 2010), 6–30; Michael Naas, *The End of the World and Other Teachable Moments* (New York: Fordham University Press, 2015), 8–9; and Clayton Crockett, *Derrida after the End of Writing: Political Theology and New Materialism* (New York: Fordham University Press, 2018), 67–70.
132. Goethe, "Preliminary Notes for a Physiology of Plants," in Mueller, *Goethe's Botanical Writings*, 90.
133. Melville, *Mardi*, 458.
134. *OED Online*, s.v. "unit."
135. Ibid.
136. Cain et. al., *Ecology*, 550.
137. Bortoft, *Wholeness of Nature*, 15.
138. Mitchell, *Complexity*, 34, 38.
139. Ibid., 39.
140. Mandelbrot, *Fractal Geometry*, 1.
141. Ibid., 149.
142. Melville, *Mardi*, 4.
143. Hannes Bergthaller, "Limits of Agency: Notes on the Material Turn from a Systems-Theoretical Perspective," in Oppermann and Iovino, *Material Ecocriticism*, 40.
144. Ibid., 43.
145. Ibid., 44.
146. Ibid., 47.
147. Melville, *Pierre*, 258.
148. Jacques Derrida, "Freud and the Scene of Writing," in *Writing and Difference*, trans. Alan Bass (Chicago: University of Chicago Press, 1978), 254.
149. Karen Michelle Barad, *Meeting the Universe Halfway: Quantum Physics and the Entanglement of Matter and Meaning* (Durham, NC: Duke University Press, 2007), 72.
150. Melville, *Moby-Dick*, 492.
151. Ibid., 279–80.
152. "The Spiral Tendency" was published in the last year of Goethe's life, in the 1831 edition of *The Metamorphosis of Plants* (cited in Mueller, *Goethe's Botanical Writings*, 129). Another version—"On the Spiral Tendency in Plants"—was found after Goethe's death and published posthumously in 1833 (cited in Mueller, *Goethe's Botanical Writings*, 132).
153. Derrida, "Force and Signification," in *Writing and Difference*, 15.
154. Goethe, *Italian Journey* (New York: Penguin, 1962), 366.

155. Goethe, "The Spiral Tendency," cited in Mueller, *Goethe's Botanical Writings*, 129.

156. Goethe, "On the Spiral Tendency in Plants," cited in Mueller, *Goethe's Botanical Writings*, 139; and Goethe, "The Spiral Tendency," 129.

157. Charles Darwin, *The Power of Movement in Plants* (New York: D. Appleton, 1897), 1.

158. Richards, *Romantic Conception*, 407.

159. Goethe, "The Spiral Tendency," cited in Mueller, *Goethe's Botanical Writings*, 142.

160. Goethe, *Natural Science in General; Morphology in Particular*, vol. 2 (1823), cited in Mueller, *Goethe's Botanical Writings*, 116.

161. Goethe, "An Attempt to Evolve a General Comparative Theory," cited in Mueller, *Goethe's Botanical Writings*, 83.

162. Smail, *On Deep History*, 80.

163. Wheeler, *Expecting the Earth*, 75.

164. Melville, *Moby-Dick*, 497, 539.

165. Ibid., 376, 455, 304.

166. Ibid., 383, 385, 389.

167. Ibid., xv.

168. Israel, *Spirals*, 21.

169. Erik Kielland-Lund, "Existential Incest: Melville's Use of the Enceladus Myth in Pierre," in *American Studies in Scandinavia* 28 (1996): 54.

170. Jonik, *Inhuman*, 103.

171. Melville, *Pierre*, 342.

172. Ibid., 343.

173. Ibid., 389.

174. Ibid., vii.

175. Ibid., 347.

176. Ibid., 339.

177. Ibid., 9.

178. Ibid.

179. See Jeffory Clymer, "Property and Selfhood in Herman Melville's *Pierre*," in *Nineteenth-Century Literature* 61:2 (2005): 171–72.

180. Marx, *Capital*, 1:727, 747.

181. Ibid., 1:780.

182. Melville, *Pierre*, 342–43.

183. Ibid., 344.

184. Ibid., 345.

185. See F. O. Matthiessen, *American Renaissance: Art and Expression in the Age of Emerson and Whitman* (New York: Oxford University Press, 1968), 484; and Paul Royster, "Melville's Economy of Language," in *Ideology and Classic American Literature*, ed. Sacvan Bercovitch and Myra Jehlen (Cambridge: Cambridge University Press, 1986), 330.

186. Milton, *The Poetical Works of John Milton*, vol. 1 (Boston: Hilliard, Gray, 1836), 3:353 (Melville Marginalia: melvillesmarginalia.org/Share.aspx?DocumentID=107& PageID=36301).

187. These lines are from Book 3 of William Cowper's *The Task* (1785).

188. Royster, "Melville's Economy," 330.

189. Melville, "Conflict of Convictions" in *Battle-Pieces*, 9.

190. Melville, *Pierre*, 198–99.

191. Wheeler, *Expecting the Earth*, 2.

192. See J. Hoffmeyer, "Semiotic Individuation and Ernst Cassirer's Challenge," *Progress in Biophysics and Molecular Biology* 119:3 (2015): 607–15; and David B. Dusenbery, *Sensory Ecology* (New York: W. H. Freeman), 1992.

193. Melville, *Pierre*, 344.

194. Ibid., 342.

195. Thomas Pynchon, *Gravity's Rainbow* (New York: Penguin, 2000), 720.

196. Jonik, *Inhuman*, 76.

197. Melville, *Pierre*, 343.

198. Ibid., 67.

199. James Bridle, *New Dark Age: Technology and the End of the Future* (New York: Verso, 2018), 8, 9.

200. Nealon, *Plant Theory*, 92.

201. Melville, *Mardi*, 505.

202. Beam, *Style*, 44.

203. Ibid., 45, 38.

204. Ibid., 25.

205. *Illustrated London News*, November 1, 1851, qtd. in Parker, *Herman Melville*, 1:134.

206. Melville, *Confidence-Man*, 9.

207. Nealon, *Plant Theory*, 50.

208. Daniel Dennett, *Darwin's Dangerous Idea: Natural Selection as an Algorithmic Process* (New York: Simon & Shuster, 1995), 59.

209. Melville, *Pierre*, 353, 25.

210. Ibid., 181.

211. Humboldt, *Cosmos*, 1:79.

212. Ibid., 1:25.

213. Tsing, *Mushroom*, 4.

214. Sullivan, "Ecology of Colors," 93.

215. Melville, *Confidence-Man*, 194.

216. Melville, *Pierre*, 124.

217. Ibid., 122.

218. See, for example, H. Bruce Franklin, *The Wake of the Gods: Melville's Mythology* (Stanford: Stanford University Press, 1963), 114; and Rogin, *Subversive Genealogy*, 167.

219. Melville, *Pierre*, 122.

220. Mary Shelley, *Frankenstein; or the Modern Prometheus* (Toronto: Broadview Press, 2013), 136, 143.

221. Ibid., 50, 60, 70.

222. See D. L. Macdonald and Kathleen Scherf, introduction to *Frankenstein*, 19–24.

223. See Erasmus Darwin, "The Economy of Vegetation," in *The Botanic Garden* (London: J. Johnson, 1791), I:383–412.

224. Erasmus Darwin, *Temple of Nature, or the Origin of Society* (London: J. Johnson, 1803), 4:398–99.

225. Shelley, *Frankenstein*, 78–79.

226. Ibid., 99.

227. Ibid., 169.

228. Melville, *Moby-Dick*, 79, 123.

229. Melville, *Pierre*, 122.

230. Walter Benjamin, *The Arcades Project*, trans. Howard Eiland and Kevin McLaughlin (Cambridge, MA: Harvard University Press, 1999), 462–63: N3.1

231. Melville, *Pierre*, 152.

232. Ibid.

233. Ibid., 170.

234. Ibid., 139.

235. Ibid., 151.

236. Humboldt, *Cosmos*, 1:49.

237. Halliday, *Writing Electricity*, 98.

238. Ibid., 98.

239. Emerson, "Self-Reliance," in *Emerson's Prose & Poetry*, 132–33; Hawthorne, "The Birth-Mark," in *Hawthorne's Short Stories* (New York: Knopf, 2011), 177; Poe, "Eureka" in *Selected Writings of Edgar Allan Poe* (New York: Norton, 2004), 575; Whitman, "I Sing the Body Electric," in *Leaves of Grass and Other Writings* (New York: Norton, 2002), 81. See also Cristin Ellis, *Antebellum Posthuman: Race and Materiality in the Mid-Nineteenth Century* (New York: Fordham University Press, 2018), 96–134.

240. Melville, *Moby-Dick*, 327, 125.

241. Melville, "Bartleby, the Scrivener: A Story of Wall-Street," in *Piazza Tales*, 34–35.

242. Melville, *Pierre*, 88.

243. Ibid., 88–90.

244. Ibid., 198.

245. Ibid.

246. Ibid., 40–41.

247. Ibid.,

248. Ibid., 7.

249. Ibid.

250. Humboldt, *Cosmos*, 1:37

251. Melville, *Mardi*, 427–28.

252. Melville, "Buddha," in *Timoleon* in *Published Poems*, 281.

253. Ibid.
254. *OED Online*, s.v. "aspire."
255. Sullivan, "Ecology of Colors," 83.
256. Melville, *Pierre*, 274.
257. William Shakespeare, *King Lear* (New York: Norton, 2008), 1.1.90.
258. William Shakespeare, *The Tempest* (New York: Norton, 2003), 4.1.148–51.
259. Melville, *Pierre*, 259, 169.
260. Thomas H. Ford, "Punctuating History circa 1800: The Air of *Jane Eyre*," in *Anthropocene Reading: Literary History in Geologic Times*, ed. Tobias Menely and Jesse Oak Taylor (University Park: Pennsylvania State University Press, 2017), 87, 92.
261. Ibid., 85.
262. Thoreau, *Walden*, 73.
263. Jonik, *Inhuman*, 67, 71.
264. Ibid.
265. Goldstein, *Sweet Science*, 90–91.
266. Melville, *Pierre*, 105.
267. Ibid., 300.
268. Melville, "The Encantadas," 139.
269. Melville, *Confidence-Man*, 149.
270. Melville, *Billy Budd*, 65, 68.
271. Mandelbrot, *Geometry of Nature*, 133.
272. Peter Sloterdijk, *Foams, Plural Spherology*, trans. Wieland Hoban, vol. 3 of *Spheres* (Pasadena, CA: Semiotext(e), 2016), 50, 52.
273. Chambers, *Vestiges*, 204.
274. John Archibald Wheeler, "Geons," *Physical Review* 97:2 (1955): 511–36.
275. Melville, *Pierre*, 14.
276. Sloterdijk, *Foams*, 48.
277. Ibid., 38, 25.
278. Melville, *Moby-Dick*, 39, 412.
279. Hawthorne, *The Celestial Railroad and Other Stories* (New York: Signet, 2006), 213.
280. Melville, *Confidence-Man*, 234.
281. Ibid.
282. Melville, "Benito Cereno," 85; and Melville, "The Encantadas," 127.
283. Melville, *Mardi*, 194.
284. Melville, *Moby-Dick*, 140, 286.
285. See Parker, *Herman Melville*, 2:111.
286. See Thompson, *Magazines*, 36–39; and Bruce, *American Science*, 241.
287. Bruce, *American Science*, 144.
288. Melville, *Pierre*, 147.
289. Franciso Vitale, *Biodeconstruction: Jacques Derrida and the Life Sciences*, trans. Mauro Senatore (Albany: State University of New York Press, 2018), 22.
290. Zapf, "Cultural Ecology," 68.
291. Milton, *Poetical Works*, 4:306–7; and Melville, *Pierre*, 362.

292. Melville, *Pierre*, 5.
293. Ibid., 4.
294. Ibid., 112.
295. Ibid., 189.
296. Ibid., 149.
297. *OED Online*, s.v. "immaculate."
298. Shelley, *Frankenstein*, 84.
299. Melville, *Pierre*, 192.
300. Melville, *Moby-Dick*, 415.
301. "Historical Note," in *Pierre*, 385–86, 380.
302. Melville, *Pierre*, 253.
303. Ibid., 284.
304. Ibid.
305. Ibid., 63.
306. Ibid., 191.
307. Ibid., 69.
308. Elaine Miller, "Vegetable Genius," in *Rethinking Nature: Essays in Environmental Philosophy*, ed. Bruce V. Foltz and Robert Frodeman (Albany: State University of New York Press, 2004), 116.
309. Andreas Malm, *The Progress of This Storm: Nature and Society in a Warming World* (New York: Verso, 2018), 61.
310. Melville, *Clarel*, 4.18.98–101.
311. Derrida, *Beast & Sovereign*, 2:131.
312. Emanuele Coccia, *The Life of Plants: A Metaphysics of Mixture*, trans. Dylan J. Montanari (Cambridge: Polity, 2019), 5.
313. Melville, *Pierre*, 231.
314. Ibid.

3. HONEYCOMB

1. William Hazlitt, *"Lectures on the English Comic Writers" and "Lectures on the English Poets,"* vol. 1 (New York: Derby & Jackson, 1859), 25 (Melville Marginalia: melvillesmarginalia.org/Share.aspx?DocumentID=67&PageID=23506).
2. Ibid.
3. See Naas, *End of the World*, 8.
4. Melville, *Confidence-Man*, 117.
5. See Parker, *Herman Melville*, 2:136–89; and Parker, "*The Isle of the Cross* and *Poems*: Lost Melville Books and the Indefinite Afterlife of Error," *Nineteenth-Century Literature* 62:1 (2007): 29–47.
6. Jennifer Ackerman, *The Genius of Birds* (New York: Penguin, 2016), 18, 40.
7. Ackerman, *Genius of Birds*, 104–5; and Dale Peterson, *The Moral Lives of Animals* (New York: Bloomsbury, 2011), 56–61.
8. Ackerman, *Genius of Birds*, 132–33; and Barbara J. King, *How Animals Grieve* (Chicago: University of Chicago Press, 2013), 1–2, 106–14.

9. See Wolfe, *Animal Rites*, 5–10; and Wolfe, *Zoontologies*, 1–19.
10. Melville, *Mardi*, 53.
11. Jacques Derrida, "The Animal That Therefore I Am (More to Follow)," trans. David Wills, *Critical Inquiry* 28 (2002): 383.
12. Ibid., 380.
13. Melville, *Moby-Dick*, 388.
14. Melville, "The Encantadas," 129; and Melville, *Clarel*, 4.9.85–86.
15. Melville, *Moby-Dick*, 274, 308.
16. Melville, *Typee*, 125.
17. Nealon, *Plant Theory*, 64.
18. Melville, *Moby-Dick*, 163.
19. Melville, "The Encantadas," 164.
20. Stacy Alaimo, "Sexual Matters: Darwinian Feminisms and the Nonhuman Turn," *J19: The Journal of Nineteenth-Century Americanists* 1:2 (2013): 390.
21. See James Mallett, "Darwin and Species," in *The Cambridge Encyclopedia of Darwin and Evolutionary Thought*, ed. Michael Ruse (Cambridge: Cambridge University Press, 2013), 109–15.
22. Mitchell, *Complexity*, 76, 83.
23. Ibid., 86.
24. Ibid., 277, 280–81.
25. Melville, *Confidence-Man*, 226.
26. Melville, *Moby-Dick*, 276.
27. Ibid., 273.
28. Derrida, "The Animal," 416.
29. Ibid., 409.
30. See Kyla Schuller, "Specious Bedfellows: Ethnicity, Animality, and the Intimacy of Slaughter in *Moby-Dick*," *Leviathan: A Journal for Melville Studies* 12 (2010): 3–20; and Jennifer Mason, *Civilized Creatures: Urban Animals, Sentimental Culture, and American Literature, 1850–1900* (Baltimore: Johns Hopkins University Press, 2005).
31. See Bercaw, *Melville's Sources*, 191, 186, 124, 52.
32. Harold J. Morowitz, "Herman Melville, Marine Biologist," *Biological Bulletin* 220:2 (2011): 83–85.
33. Melville, *Omoo*, 35, 63; Melville, *Israel Potter, His Fifty Years of Exile*, ed. Harrison Hayford, Hershel Parker, and G. Thomas Tanselle (Evanston, IL: Northwestern University Press, 1982), 5; and Melville, *John Marr*, 219, 230, 243.
34. Melville, *Pierre*, 267.
35. Melville, "The Encantadas," 133.
36. Ibid., 132.
37. Letter to Harper & Brothers, November 24, 1853, Melville, *Correspondence*, 250.
38. Wolfe, *Animal Rites*, 5.
39. Naas, *End of the World*, 30.
40. Ibid.
41. Melville, "The Encantadas," 165.
42. Ibid., 166–67.

43. Wolfe, *Animal Rites*, 84.
44. Marx, "Estranged Labor," 76.
45. Bachelard, *Poetics of Space*, 7.
46. Charles Baudelaire, *Curiosites Esethetiques* (Paris: Michele Levy Freres, 1868), 221.
47. *New Bedford Daily Mercury*, qtd. in the "Historical Note" to Melville, *The Piazza Tales*, 508.
48. Paul R. Ehrlich, foreword to Robert Dyball and Barry Newell, *Understanding Human Ecology: A Systems Approach to Sustainability* (New York: Routledge, 2015), xv.
49. Malm, *Progress of This Storm*, 162. For a classic Marxist account, see John Bellamy Foster, *Marx's Ecology: Materialism and Nature* (New York: Monthly Review Press, 2000), 1–20.
50. Sophia Psarra, *Architecture and Narrative: The Formation of Space and Cultural Meaning* (New York: Routledge, 2009), 2, 3.
51. Ibid., 5.
52. Melville, *Moby-Dick*, 136.
53. Melville, *Pierre*, 265.
54. Ibid. 266, 269.
55. Melville, "Greek Architecture," in *Timoleon*, 305.
56. Wyn Kelley, "An Introduction to Benito Cereno," in Melville, *Benito Cereno* (Boston: Bedford/St. Martin, 2008), 15.
57. Melville, "The Encantadas," 131, 136, 172.
58. *OED Online*, s.v. "monastery."
59. Agamben, *Highest Poverty*, 4.
60. Ibid., ix.
61. Melville, *Typee*, 264; and Melville, *Clarel*, 2.18. Nehemiah is himself a "hermit" who wears "the habit gray" (1.22.63, 1.9.67).
62. Melville, "Bartleby," 38.
63. Melville, *Pierre*, 6.
64. Melville, "The Encantadas," 136; and Darwin, *Voyage*, 288. Melville also notes the "remarkable tameness" of Galapagos and Marquesan birds in *Typee* (211).
65. Melville, "Benito Cereno," 61.
66. Melville, "The Lighting-Rod Man," 122.
67. Melville, "The Bell-Tower," 184.
68. Ibid.
69. Melville, "The Ravaged Villa," in *Timoleon*, 266.
70. Melville, *Moby-Dick*, 413.
71. Melville, "Bartleby," 29.
72. Melville, "The Encantadas," 142.
73. Ibid., 170, 71, 72.
74. Ibid., 172.
75. Ibid., 127.
76. Darwin, *Voyage*, 377.
77. Goethe, *Goethe on Art* (Berkeley: University of California Press, 1980), 73.

78. See Julia Voss, *Darwin's Pictures: Views of Evolutionary Theory, 1837–1874*, trans. Lori Lantz (New Haven: Yale University Press, 2010), 4–6, 40–50.
79. Melville, *Moby-Dick*, 263.
80. See Thompson, *Melville among the Magazines*, 228n26.
81. *Putnam's* even omitted "Sketch Seventh" in both the original printing and in *Putnam's Compilation*, vol. 3 (January to June 1854).
82. Melville, "The Encantadas," 152.
83. Melville, *Moby-Dick*, 464.
84. Melville, "The Encantadas," 172; and Melville, "An Afternoon in Naples," in Melville, *Uncompleted Writings*, 187.
85. Melville, "The Piazza," 3.
86. Ibid., 1.
87. Ibid., 2.
88. Ibid., 4, 5.
89. Ibid., 6.
90. Ibid., 8.
91. Ibid.
92. Ibid.
93. Ibid., 9.
94. Ibid., 3.
95. Ibid., 11.
96. Ibid., 6.
97. Ibid., 7.
98. Ibid., 2.
99. Agamben, *Highest Poverty*, xiii.
100. Melville, "The Piazza," 10.
101. Ibid., 12.
102. Ibid.
103. Melville, "The Bell-Tower," 174–75.
104. Ibid., 175.
105. Ibid., 176, 61.
106. Ibid., 178.
107. Ibid., 185.
108. Ibid., 183.
109. Ibid., 184.
110. Ibid., 182.
111. Ibid.
112. Melville, "The Tartarus of Maids," 333.
113. Ibid.
114. Emerson, "History," in *Prose & Poetry*, 116.
115. Melville, *Moby-Dick*, 202.
116. Melville, *Mardi*, 229.
117. Gerard M. Sweeney, "Melville's Hawthornian Bell-Tower: A Fairy-Tale Source," *American Literature* 45:2 (1973): 279–80.

118. Hawthorne, *Tanglewood Tales* (London: Knight & Son, 1853), 42.
119. Agamben, *Highest Poverty*, 19.
120. Ibid., 23–24.
121. John T. Hamilton, *Security: Politics, Humanity, and the Philology of Care* (Princeton: Princeton University Press, 2013), 81.
122. Melville, "The Lightning Rod Man," 120, 121.
123. Ibid., 120.
124. Ibid., 123, 124.
125. Ibid., 123.
126. See, for example, Robert Nozick, *Anarchy, State, and Utopia* (New York: Basic Books, 1974); Ursula K. Heise, "Narrative in the World Risk Society," in *Sense of Place and Sense of Planet: The Environmental Imagination of the Global* (Oxford: Oxford University Press, 2008); and Deborah Cowen, *The Deadly Life of Logistics: Mapping Violence in Global Trade* (Minneapolis: University of Minnesota Press, 2014).
127. Arjun Appadurai, *Banking on Words: The Failure of Language in the Age of Derivative Finance* (Chicago: University of Chicago Press, 2016), 3.
128. Melville, "The Lightning Rod Man," 122.
129. Ibid., 124.
130. On indulgences and capitalism, see David Harvey, *A Companion to Capital* (New York: Verso, 2010), 1:72.
131. Melville, "The Lightning Rod Man," 124.
132. Appadurai, *Banking on Words*, 68.
133. Ibid.
134. Gilles Deleuze, "Postscript on Control Society," *Negotiations, 1972–1990*, trans. Martin Joughin (New York: Columbia University Press, 1995), 181.
135. Melville, "Bartleby," 13, 27.
136. Ibid., 45; and Melville, "Benito Cereno," 103. On the source material in "Benito Cereno," see the "Historical Note," in *The Piazza Tales*, 580–82.
137. Melville, "Bartleby," 28.
138. Ibid., 14.
139. Ibid., 25, 36, 27.
140. Ibid., 21.
141. Ibid., 35, 40.
142. Ibid., 41.
143. Ibid., 36.
144. Ralph Waldo Emerson, "Literary Ethics: An Oration Delivered before the Literary Societies of Dartmouth College, July 24, 1838" (New York: T. Y. Crowell, 1890), 16.
145. Melville, "Bartleby," 41.
146. Melville, *Moby-Dick*, 155.
147. Melville, "Bartleby," 44.
148. Ibid., 26.
149. Agamben, *Highest Poverty*, 9.

150. Ibid., 3.
151. Ibid., 13.
152. Ibid., 50.
153. Marx, *Capital*, 1:352.
154. See Agamben, *Highest Poverty*, 38.
155. Ibid., 56.
156. Ibid., 100.
157. Melville, "Bartleby," 21.
158. Ibid., 38.
159. Ibid., 13.
160. Augustine, *Confessions*, trans. R. S. Pine-Coffin (London: Penguin, 1961), 114.
161. Agamben, *Highest Poverty*, 27.
162. Ibid., 35, 39.
163. Ibid., 360.
164. Melville, "Bartleby," 19.
165. Michael Marder, "Ecology as Event," in *Eco-Deconstruction*, 144.
166. Appadurai, *Banking on Words*, 149.
167. Melville, "Bartleby," 44.
168. Darwin, *Origin*, 53.
169. Melville, "Benito Cereno," 67.
170. Ibid., 46, 78.
171. Ibid., 49.
172. Ibid., 54.
173. Ibid., 64–65.
174. Ibid., 75.
175. Ibid., 97.
176. Ibid., 77.
177. Ibid., 77, 84.
178. Ibid., 51.
179. See Colin Dayan, *The Law Is a White Dog: How Legal Rituals Make and Unmake Persons* (Princeton: Princeton University Press, 2011), 115–16.
180. Melville, "Benito Cereno," 102, 53, 60, 100.
181. Ibid., 73.
182. Ibid., 72.
183. Ibid., 75, 76.
184. Ibid., 56.
185. Ibid., 97.
186. Ibid., 88.
187. Ibid., 53.
188. Ibid., 47, 96.
189. Ibid., 98.
190. Ibid., 99, 49.
191. Ibid., 99.

192. Ibid., 107.
193. See Greg Grandin, *The Empire of Necessity: Slavery, Freedom, and Deception in the New World* (New York: Metropolitan Books, 2014).
194. Melville, "Benito Cereno," 50.
195. Ibid., 74.
196. Ibid., 82, 83.
197. Ibid., 94.
198. Ibid., 69.
199. Ibid., 68.
200. Ibid., 116.
201. Ibid.
202. Ibid., 111.
203. Melville, *Clarel*, 2.11.67, 2.12.63–64.
204. Melville, "Supplement" in *Battle-Pieces*, 185.
205. Bachelard, *Poetics of Space*, 79.
206. Melville, "Benito Cereno," 48.
207. Ibid., 75.
208. Ibid., 48.
209. Ibid., 82.
210. Ibid., 52, 57, 103, 114.
211. Ibid., 57.
212. See John Paul II, "*Bula Inter Sanctos* Proclaiming Saint Francis of Assisi as Patron of Ecology" (1979).
213. Agamben, *Highest Poverty*, 111.
214. Melville, "The Encantadas, 135.
215. Henry Louis Gates, "The Literature of the Slave," in *Figures in Black: Words, Signs, and the 'Racial' Self* (Oxford: Oxford University Press, 1989), 101.
216. Melville, "Benito Cereno," 93, 62.
217. Agamben, *Highest Poverty*, 109, 110.
218. Melville, "Benito Cereno," 116.
219. Jenny Franchot, "Melville's Traveling God," in *The Cambridge Companion to Herman Melville*, ed. Robert Levine (Cambridge: Cambridge University Press, 1998), 162, 179.
220. Melville, "Benito Cereno," 116.
221. Agamben, *Highest Poverty*, 143.
222. See Ted Toadvine, "Thinking after the World: Deconstruction and Last Things," in Fritsch, Lynes, and Wood, *Eco-Deconstruction*, 56.
223. Melville, "The Encantadas," 126.
224. Ibid., 128, 127.
225. Edward Wilson, *The Creation: An Appeal to Save Life on Earth* (New York: Norton, 2007), 91.
226. Melville, "The Encantadas," 127.
227. See Darwin, *Voyage,* 271; and Melville, "The Encantadas," 129.
228. Derrida, "Animal," 389.

229. Melville, "The Encantadas," 144.
230. Ibid., 144–45.
231. Ibid., 146.
232. See Gary Shapiro, "Beasts, Sovereigns, Pirates: Melville's 'Enchanted Isles' beyond the Picturesque," in Nurmi and McCall, *Melville among the Philosophers*, 89.
233. Melville, "The Encantadas," 147, 149.
234. Ibid., 125.
235. Ibid., 128–29.
236. Ibid., 129.
237. Ibid., 131.
238. Ibid.
239. Ibid., 132.
240. Melville, *Clarel*, 4.3.1–98.
241. *OED Online*, s.v. "cope."
242. Melville, "The Encantadas," 152.
243. Ibid., 154.
244. Sigmund Freud, "Mourning and Melancholia," in *Complete Psychological Works of Sigmund Freud*, vol. 14, *1914–1916* (London: Hogarth Press, 1957), 244.
245. Ibid., 245.
246. William Shakespeare, *Hamlet* (New York: Norton, 2010), 1.2.94–108.
247. Judith Butler, *Precarious Life: The Powers of Mourning and Violence* (New York: Verso, 2006), 30.
248. Melville, "The Encantadas," 155.
249. Melville, *Moby-Dick*, 34.
250. Melville, "The Encantadas," 155.
251. On Darwin and mourning, see Darwin, *Autobiography*, 90; and George Levine, "Darwin and Pain," in *Darwin: A Norton Critical Edition*, 3rd ed., ed. Philip Appleman (New York: Norton, 2001), 643–44.
252. Elizabeth Kolbert, *The Sixth Extinction: An Unnatural History* (New York: Holt, 2014), 250. On Melville's knowledge of Neanderthals, see Madison and Madison, "Darwin's Year," 88–89.
253. Wolfe, *Animal Rites*, 76–77.
254. Hamilton, *Security*, 78.
255. Melville, *Clarel*, 1.19.2–4.
256. Melville, "The Encantadas," 151.
257. Ibid., 157.
258. Ibid., 162.
259. Ibid., 172.
260. Melville, *Mardi*, 192.
261. Melville, *Clarel*, 3.22.16.
262. Agamben, *Highest Poverty*, 33.
263. Tim Morton, *Hyperobjects: Philosophy and Ecology after the End of the World* (Minneapolis: University of Minnesota Press, 2013), 196.
264. Melville, *Clarel*, 3.24.40

265. Ibid., 1.17.181–82.
266. Derrida, *Beast & Sovereign*, 2:30–31.
267. Fletcher, *Physical Geology*, 144.
268. Melville, "The Encantadas," 173.
269. See Derrida, *Cinders* (Minneapolis: University of Minnesota Press, 2014), 23.
270. Melville, "The Encantadas," 157–58.
271. Melville, "Benito Cereno," 112.
272. Melville, *Battle-Pieces*, 72.

4. PEBBLE

1. Letter to Daniel Shepherd (Allan Melville's law partner), July 6, 1859, Melville, *Correspondence*, 338.
2. Letter to Richard Dana, May 1, 1850, Melville, *Correspondence*, 162.
3. Hazlitt, *Lectures*, 2:3 (Melville Marginalia: http://melvillesmarginalia.org/Share.aspx?DocumentID=67&PageID=23712).
4. Melville, *Clarel*, 4.7.75.
5. Audre Lorde, "Poetry Is Not a Luxury," in *Sister Outsider: Essays and Speeches* (New York: Crossing Press, 1984), 39.
6. For the history of Melville's life as a poet, see the "Historical Note" in *Published Poems*, 331–527; Parker, *Herman Melville*, 2:421–53; and Hershel Parker, *Melville: The Making of the Poet* (Evanston, IL: Northwestern University Press, 2008).
7. Melville, *Clarel*, 2.25.149–50, 2.25.144–45.
8. Ibid., 2.21.39–40.
9. Ibid., 3.5.64.
10. Melville, "The Return of the Sire de Nesle," in Melville, *Uncompleted Writings*, 317.
11. Parker, *Herman Melville*, 2:895.
12. Melville, "The Haglets," in *John Marr*, in *Published Poems*, 220.
13. See Bruce, *American Science*, 100.
14. Muriel Rukeyser, *Willard Gibbs* (Boston: Dutton, 1942), 353.
15. Melville, *Clarel*, 3.2.67–71.
16. Melville, "Misgivings," in *Battle-Pieces*, in *Published Poems*, 7.
17. Melville, "Aurora-borealis," in *Battle-Pieces*, in *Published Poems*, 111.
18. Leon Howard, *Herman Melville: A Biography* (Berkeley: University of California Press, 1958), 320. Exceptions include Edgar A. Dryden, *Monumental Melville: The Formation of a Literary Career* (Stanford: Stanford University Press, 2004), 148–66; and Jonik, *Inhuman*, 203–7.
19. Malm, *Progress of This Storm*, 11.
20. Ibid, 5.
21. Melville, *Moby-Dick*, 5. See Beiser, *World in a Grain*, 201–56.
22. See Parker, *Herman Melville*, 2:418–53.
23. See Sean Ford, "Authors, Speakers, Readers in a Trio of Sea-Pieces in Herman Melville's *John Marr and Other Sailors*," *Nineteenth-Century Literature* 67:2 (2012): 234–58.

24. See Cohen, *Stone*, 11.
25. See Parker, *Herman Melville*, 2:431.
26. Melville, *Journals*, 135.
27. Melville, "An Uninscribed Monument," in *Published Poems*, 130.
28. Melville, "The Armies of the Wilderness," in *Published Poems*, 72.
29. Melville, "Donelson" and "The Fortitude of the North," in *Published Poems*, 28, 124.
30. Melville, "The Portent" and "Swamp Angel," in *Published Poems*, 5, 78.
31. Melville, "The Armies of the Wilderness," in *Published Poems*, 76.
32. Melville, *Clarel*, 1.34.78.
33. Melville, *Moby-Dick*, 227.
34. Melville, *John Marr*, 195.
35. Melville, *Israel Potter*, 156.
36. Melville, *John Marr*, 197.
37. Ibid., 197.
38. Ibid.
39. Melville, *Mardi*, 554–55.
40. Melville, *Clarel*, 2.31.14–16.
41. Ibid., 2.31.101–2.
42. Ibid., 2.11.37–40, 1.24.81–84.
43. Michael Marder, *Dust* (New York: Bloomsbury, 2016), 55.
44. Melville, "Rosary Beads," in *Weeds and Wildings*, in Melville, *Uncompleted Writings*, 123.
45. Melville, *Clarel*, 1.24.73–76.
46. Melville, *John Marr*, 235.
47. W. H. Smyth and E. Belcher, *Sailor's Word-Book: An Alphabetical Digest of Nautical Terms* (London: Blackie and Son, 1867), 103.
48. See Jorge Assis, Miguel B. Araujo, and Ester A. Serrano, "Projected Climate Changes Threaten Ancient Refugia of Kelp Forests in the North Atlantic," *Global Change Biology* 24 (2018): 55–66.
49. Melville, "The Ground-Vine," in *Weeds and Wildings*, in Melville, in *Uncompleted Writings*, 104.
50. Melville, *John Marr*, 236.
51. Ibid., 197. See also *Clarel*, 2.15.72–73.
52. Melville, *John Marr*, 195–96.
53. Ibid., 198.
54. Ibid., 218.
55. Ibid., 198.
56. Ibid., 199–200.
57. See Paul Royster, "John Marr and Other Sailors: An Online Electronic 'Facsimile' Text of the First Edition (1888)," Faculty Publications of the University of Nebraska Lincoln Libraries 18 (2005), 101–3.
58. Jacques Derrida, *Negotiations: Interventions and Interviews, 1971–2002* (Stanford: Stanford University Press, 2002), 244.

59. Melville, *Mardi*, 49.
60. *OED Online*, s.v. "strain."
61. Melville, *Moby-Dick*, 194.
62. Milton, *Poetical Works*, 4:110, 196.
63. Melville, *Moby-Dick*, 566.
64. Melville, "Fragments from a Lost Gnostic Poem," in *Published Poems*, 284.
65. See Dryden, *Monumental Melville*, 163.
66. See the "Historical Note," in Melville, *Uncompleted Writings*, 358–59.
67. Melville, "Story of Daniel Orme," in Melville, *Uncompleted Writings*, 232.
68. Melville, *John Marr*, 195; and Melville, "Daniel Orme," 234.
69. Melville, *Clarel*, 2.10.63.
70. Latour, "Morality and Technology," 252.
71. Ibid., 251.
72. Bernard Stiegler, *Technics and Time 1: The Fault of Epimetheus* (Stanford: Stanford University Press, 1998), 142. See also N. Brown, *Limits of Fabrication*, 52–53.
73. Melville, *Mardi*, 437.
74. Melville, *Clarel*, 4.18.148–52.
75. Melville, *Moby-Dick*, 384.
76. Melville, *John Marr*, 227.
77. *OED Online*, s.v. "wreck"; and Melville, "Bartleby," 32.
78. *OED Online*, s.v. "wrack."
79. Melville, *Clarel*, 1.10.3–7.
80. Melville, "Rip Van Winkle's Lilac," in *Weeds and Wildings*, in Melville, *Uncompleted Writings*, 110.
81. Ibid.
82. Melville, *Mardi*, 126.
83. *OED Online*, s.v. "wrack."
84. *King James Version of the Holy Bible (KJV)*.
85. Melville, *Moby-Dick*, 563–64.
86. Melville, "Daniel Orme," 234–35.
87. *KJV*.
88. Dryden, *Monumental Melville*, 166.
89. Ben Jonson, *Masque of Queens* in *The Works of Ben Jonson*, vol. 1 (London: Herringman, 1692), 902.
90. Emily Dickinson, "This Was a Poet," J448, Emily Dickinson Archive (edickinson.org/editions/2/image_sets/75099).
91. Shakespeare, *Hamlet*, 4.5.150.
92. See Colin D. O'Dowd et. al., "Biogenically Driven Organic Contribution to Marine Aerosol," *Nature* 431 (2004): 677.
93. John I. Hedges, "Global Biogeochemical Cycles: Progress and Problems," *Marine Chemistry* 39 (1992): 81–84.
94. Melville, *Moby-Dick*, 497.
95. Ibid., 107.
96. Melville, "Buddha" in *Timoleon*, in *Published Poems*, 281.

97. Melville, *Moby-Dick*, 232; and Melville, *Clarel*, 2.11.37–40.

98. See Marianne Glasius and Allen H. Goldstein, "Recent Discoveries and Future Challenges in Atmospheric Organic Chemistry," *Environmental Science & Technology* 50:6 (2016): 2754–64.

CONCLUSION

1. Melville, *Clarel*, 4.3.111–12.
2. Melville, *Moby-Dick*, 286.
3. Beam, *Style*, 22.
4. Melville, *Mardi*, 26.
5. Melville, *Omoo*, 199.
6. Melville, *Moby-Dick*, 21.
7. Alice Walker, *The Color Purple* (New York: Harcourt, 1982), 197.
8. Melville, "Lee in the Capitol," in *Battle-Pieces*, in *Published Poems*, 166.
9. Vitale, *Biodeconstruction*, 5.
10. Melville, *Pierre*, 69.
11. Vicki Kirby, "Un/limited Ecologies," in Fritsch, Lynes, and Wood, *Eco-Deconstruction*, 134–35.
12. Melville, "After the Pleasure Party," in *Timoleon*, in *Published Poems*, 263.
13. Melville, *Clarel*, 3.5.79–82.
14. Ibid., 1.28.109.
15. Agamben, *Highest Poverty*, 15.
16. Letter to John Hoadley, March 31, 1877, Melville, *Correspondence*, 454.

Index

Aesop, 145
Agamben, Giorgio: *Creation and Anarchy*, 28; *The Highest Poverty*, 39, 155, 164, 168, 173–75, 184–86, 196, 228–29; *The Open*, 37
Agassiz, Louis, 6, 12, 51, 104
Alaimo, Stacy, 18, 149
Allen, Thomas, 14, 58
Andrews, James, 87
animals, xi, 8–9, 30, 34, 43, 93, 142–43, 145–59, 166–67, 178–90, 198, 215; bats, 183; bears, 148, 179; birds, 4, 9, 30, 34–35, 43, 78, 115, 147–48, 151, 162, 167, 177, 178–79, 183, 189, 215, 221; bison, 108–11, 148, 210, 225; camels, 43, 151, 206; cats, 91, 119, 125, 148, 151, 178; coral, 18, 29, 73, 79, 151, 210; crustaceans, 29, 35, 150; deer, 178–79; dogs, 43, 148, 151, 163, 178, 187; fish, 33, 35, 143, 148, 150, 156, 178, 210; foxes, 145, 181, 183; horses, 30, 135, 141, 148, 150, 169, 178, 227; insects, 30, 80, 105, 120, 162, 166, 181–82, 186, 201, 206; lizards, 151, 159, 186; mollusks, 29, 35, 50, 67, 95, 164, 209, 220, 225; and mourning, xi, 194, 198; sharks, xii, 148, 210, 215, 218; sheep, 30, 162, 169, 178–79, 184; snakes, 84, 91, 127, 151, 186; squid, 93, 150; and technology, 60, 145, 147–48, 165–67; tortoises, 3, 43, 47, 149, 151, 155, 159, 186–90; whales, xi, 2, 3,17, 24, 32–33, 36, 39–40, 43, 50, 76, 91, 93, 110, 113–14, 136, 148–50, 202, 223, 226; wolves, 178, 184; worms, 30, 79, 127, 130, 163, 184; zebras, 198. *See also* biology; zoology
animal studies, 37, 43, 96, 147–59
Anthropocene, the, 4, 203, 218, 228; challenges of, xiii, 19–20; and geology, xi, 53–54; mourning in, 186–87, 196, 198; politics of, 176; responsibility for, 156–58, 171, 179–80, 186; witnessing, 37–39, 48, 64, 79–81, 164
Appadurai, Arjun, 170, 176
architecture, 8, 43, 60, 143, 152–55, 166–67, 175, 196. *See also* dwelling
archives, 60, 70, 160, 161
Aristotle, 105
Arnold, Matthew, 106
Arsić, Branka, 81–82
astronomy, 72–73, 205–6; Mars, 224; Saturn, 17, 72, 106; Venus, 106
Augustine of Hippo, 175
automaton, 158, 166–67. *See also* technology

Bachelard, Gaston, 34, 74, 153, 182
Baker, Jennifer, 24
Barad, Karen, 100, 103, 111–12
Basho, 204
Bataille, Georges, 175
Baudelaire, Charles, 153
Bauman, Zygmunt, 223
Beale, Thomas, 150
Beam, Dorri, 34, 122, 226
Bedell, Rebecca, 58

Beer, Gillian, 24
Bell, Alexander Graham, 7
Belousov-Zhabotinsky reactions, 98. *See also* chemistry; spirals
Benjamin, Walter, 128
Bentley, Richard, 92
Bergthaller, Hannes, 110
Biblical references, 132, 219, 221, 222. *See also* religion
Bigelow, Jacob, 6
biology, 5, 7, 8, 85, 120, 134; history of, 14, 20–24, 37–38, 149; philosophy of, 89–90, 111–14; relation to complexity, 26–27. *See also* biosemiotics; chemistry
biopolitics, 37, 39, 96, 193–94
biosemiotics, xi, 82, 105, 119–20, 137, 152
Blake, William P., 208
Bond, William, and George, 72
bones, 73–77
Bortoft, Henri, 104–5
botany, 6, 20, 23, 38, 87, 95, 122. *See also* plants
Bradstreet, Anne, 16, 236n53
Bridle, James, 121
Brown, Charles Brockden, 15–16, 99
Brown, John, 206
Brown, Nathan, 37, 39, 74
Bruce, Robert, 13, 72, 137
Bryant, William Cullen, 6
Buckland, Adelene, 39
Buddhism, 132, 218, 223. *See also* eco-spirituality; religion
Buell, Lawrence, xiii
Butler, Judith, 193

capitalism, 3, 17, 21, 48, 62, 96, 117, 157–58, 167, 169, 173–74. *See also* finance
Chakrabarty, Dipesh, 64, 65, 79
Chambers, Robert, 134, 150
chemistry: biochemistry, 48–49, 83, 134; history of, 6, 13, 20, 137, 209; marine chemistry, 18, 223; physical chemistry, 56, 81, 202; and writing, 35. *See also* biology

Church, Frederic Edwin, 57–58. *See also* landscape paining
Cicero, 174
Civil War, American, 4, 7, 13, 147, 198, 201, 205–6
Clark, Timothy, 17
coal, 48–49. *See also* fossil fuels
Coccia, Emanuele, 143
Cochet, Yves, 4
Cohen, Jeffrey Jerome, 98
Cole, Thomas, 47, 58, 61, 78, 160. *See also* landscape painting
Colon, Christopher, 180–81
complexity, 26–27, 33, 109–10, 121–24. *See also* scale
Comstock, J. L., 58
Cooper, James Fenimore, 118
Crockett, Clayton, 132
Cuvier, Georges, 6, 38, 51, 70, 150

Dalton, John, 6
Darwin, Charles, 8, 9, 17, 23–24, 38, 51, 65, 70–71, 80, 112–13, 143, 146, 149–50, 160, 197, 234n15; and complexity, 26–27, 121; correspondence, 13, 26; *Descent of Man*, 24, 149; and grief, 130, 147, 195, 205, 263n251; *Journal of Researches* (*Voyage of the Beagle*), 6, 23–24, 150, 156, 186; *Origin of Species*, 3, 14, 24, 177; *Power of Movement in Plants*, 112. *See also* biology; evolution
Darwin, Erasmus, 22, 126–27
Daston, Lorraine, 80
Davy, Humphry, 126
Dayan, Colin, 178
decay, 34, 45, 60–61, 85, 88–89, 94–95, 113–14, 126–27, 210. *See also* energy ecology; taphonomy
Deleuze, Gilles, 122, 170; and Félix Guattari, 124
Dennett, Daniel, 123–24
Derrida, Jacques: "The Animal That Therefore I Am," 148, 150, 187; *Archive Fever*, 60; *Beast & Sovereign*, 143, 152, 196; *Negotiations*, 213; *Of*

Grammatology, 137; *Writing and Difference*, 111, 112
Descartes, Rene, 97, 166
Dickens, Charles, 160
Dickinson, Emily, 16, 222–23, 236n53
Dimock, Wai Chee, 65, 68, 69, 79
Drake, Daniel, 23
Draper, John, 72
Durand, Asher B., 58
Dutrochet, Henri, 106, 112
Duyckinck, Evert, 81, 84
dwelling, 7, 11, 20, 35, 40, 43–44, 55, 104, 108–10, 119, 142–43, 146–47, 152–64, 172–77, 181–89, 195, 197, 210, 217, 226, 228. *See also* architecture; philosophy of ecology

eco-fascism, 196
eco-formalism, 40, 69–70, 79–80, 90–91, 93, 96, 204–6, 227. *See* poetics; style
eco-futurism, 165
ecology, 2, 19–26, 32, 90–91, 94–96, 176–77, 187; atmospheric ecology, 41, 72, 83, 127–29, 133–34, 201–2, 205–6, 208–10, 221–24; disease ecology, 11–12, 23, 30, 49; energy ecology, 18, 25, 43, 87, 128–29, 202–4, 218; human ecology, 6, 43, 91, 137, 143–44, 153–54, 158, 167, 171, 173, 179–80; marine ecology, 2, 18, 29, 82–83, 209, 220, 223; philosophy of, 108–15, 117–25; sensory ecology, 120
eco-spirituality, 43, 130–33, 188–89, 227. *See* religion
Edwards, Jonathan, 16, 236n53
Ehrlich, Paul, 153
electricity, 128–29. *See* lightning; technology
Ellms, Charles, 190
Emerson, Ralph Waldo, 16–17, 22, 57, 70, 90, 116, 125, 204; "Circles," 99; "Experience," 54, 99; "Goethe; or the Writer," 26; "History," 167; *Journals*, 1, 12–13; "Literary Ethics," 173; *Nature*, 90, 99; "The Poet," 55, 106; "Poetry and Imagination," 6–7; "Self-Reliance," 2, 16, 129; "The Young American," 9
Enceladus, 79, 90, 114, 115–17, 118–19, 132, 162, 188
energy, xii, 18, 48–50, 53, 62, 65, 116; solar, 94, 167. *See also* energy ecology; thermodynamics
Esposito, Roberto, 85
Espy, James P., 201
Euclid, 79
evolution, xiii, 3, 8–9, 13–14, 20, 23–24, 29, 42, 44, 67, 70–72, 74, 112–13, 142, 149, 161, 195–96, 198, 220; and literature, 24, 137–38; mineral evolution, 71–72. *See also* Darwin, Charles; reproduction

Falconer, William, 49–50
Faraday, Michael, 6, 13
Farrar, John, 101
Fern, Fanny, 88
Ferrel, William, 102
Fibonacci sequence, 98. *See also* mathematics; spiral
finance, 170, 176–77. *See also* capitalism; risk
fire, 58–59, 129–30, 161, 167
foam, 134–36. *See also* biology; chemistry
Ford, Thomas, 133
fossil fuels, 19, 49. *See also* coal; oil
fossils, 9, 31, 51, 55, 70, 74, 78, 134. *See also* geology
Foster, Elizabeth, 70
Foucault, Michel, 96, 149, 169, 175
fractals, 44, 69, 91, 110, 135, 202. *See also* geometry
Francis (pope), 184
Fressoz, Jean-Baptiste, 4
Freud, Sigmund, 14, 112, 193
Fuller, Margaret, 226
fungi, 85, 94–95, 188–89, 210

Gadamer, Hans-Georg, 27
Gates, Henry Louis, 184

272 INDEX

geology, 13–14, 47–48, 56–72, 197, 203–5, 207–8, 213–16. *See also* minerals
geometry, 69, 79–80, 100–101, 110, 114, 123, 125. *See also* fractals; mathematics
Gibbs, Josiah Willard, 202
Goethe, Johann Wolfgang von, 5, 22, 26, 90–91, 104–8, 112–13, 126, 160; *Autobiography*, 104, 105; correspondence, 97; "Dissipation, Evaporation, Exudation," 133; *Italian Journey*, 104; *Metamorphosis of Plants*, 104, 106; "Preliminary Notes for a Physiology of Plants," 108; "The Spiral Tendency," 112; *Theory of Colors*, 94
gold, 47, 52, 61–63, 76. *See also* minerals
Gold Rush, California, 61–62
Goldsmith, Oliver, 38
Goldstein, Amanda Jo, 133
Goodwin, Brian, 98
gothic literature, 98–99, 126, 131
Gould, Stephen Jay, 14
granite, 47, 52–53, 72. *See also* minerals
Gray, Asa, 13, 87, 90, 104
Greiman, Jennifer, 94
grief, xii, 43, 103, 129–32, 147–48, 161, 186–87, 192–97. *See also* mourning
Grosz, Elizabeth, 81
Grusin, Richard, 100

Haeckel, Ernst, 20
Halliday, Sam, 129
Hamilton, John, 169
Hardack, Richard, 5
Harman, Graham, 54, 77, 217
Harper's New Monthly Magazine, 146
Haseltine, William Stanley, 58
Hawthorne, Nathaniel, 36, 106–7, 129, 135, 168, 199
Hayden, Ferdinand, 208
Hayes, Rutherford B., 7
Hazen, Robert, 71
Hazlitt, William, 145
Hedges, John I., 223
Hegel, Georg Wilhelm Friedrich, 97
Heidegger, Martin, 37, 108, 217
Henry, Joseph, 13

Heringman, Noah, 55
Herrera, Juan Felipe, 204
Herschel, William, 15, 72
Hillway, Tyrus, 70
Hitchcock, Edward, 58
Hoadley, John, 168, 229
Homer, 219
Hoppe-Seyler, Felix, 49
Howard, Leon, 203
Hubble, Edwin, 114
Humboldt, Alexander von, 22, 104–5, 124, 129, 132
Hutton, James, 6, 51, 64
Huxley, Thomas, 24

indigenous peoples, 134, 156, 190, 207, 210, 225
Irving, Washington, 9, 160, 220
Israel, Nico, 97–98

Jefferson, Thomas, 58
John Paul II (pope), 184
Jones, Christopher F., 48
Jonik, Michael, 107, 114, 120–21, 133
Jonson, Ben, 222

Kant, Immanuel, 129
Keats, John, 115
Kelly, Wyn, 155
Kelvin, Lord, 202
Kensett, John Frederick, 58
King, Clarence, 208
Kirby, Vicki, 228
Kolbert, Elizabeth, 195

LaFleur, Greta, 28, 50
Lamarck, Jean-Baptiste, 22, 50
landscape painting, 58. *See also* Church, Frederic Edwin; Cole, Thomas
Latour, Bruno, 50, 77, 217
Levine, George, 24
Levinson, Marjorie, 28
lightning, 2, 36, 78, 85, 91, 125–30, 169–70. *See also* electricity; weather
Lincoln, Abraham, 176
Linneaus, Carl, 6, 51

Locke, John, 5, 26, 129, 154, 169
Loomis, Elias, 201
Lorde, Audre, 199
Luther, Martin, 170
Lyell, Charles, 6, 23, 24, 26, 51, 65, 70, 149. *See also* geology

Malm, Andreas, 54, 142, 154, 203
Malthus, Thomas, 149
Mandelbrot, Benoit, 91, 110, 134. *See also* fractals
Marder, Michael, 59, 176
Marsh, George Perkins, 21
Marshall, Kate, 79
Marx, Karl, 97, 154; *Capital,* 117, 174; "Estranged Labor," 17, 152
Masters, Maxwell, 38, 87
mathematics, 80, 98, 99, 101–3, 123–24, 202, 204–5. *See also* geometry; physics
Maury, Matthew, 102
Mayo, Sarah Carter Edgarton, 87
McGurl, Mark, 64
McIntosh, Robert, 19, 20
Meek, Fielding, 208
Melville, Herman: "The Apple-Tree Table," 151; *Battle-Pieces,* 4, 78, 102, 119, 147, 151, 182, 198, 200, 202, 204, 205–6, 221, 227; *Billy Budd,* 40, 134, 204, 217; *Clarel,* vii, 14, 37, 45, 52, 78, 79, 143, 147, 148, 151, 156, 182, 189, 195, 196, 199, 200, 202, 204, 206, 208–9, 217, 218, 223, 225, 228; "Cock-A-Doodle-Doo!," 151; *The Confidence-Man,* 3, 7, 9, 11–12, 77, 83, 123, 125, 134, 135–36, 145, 147, 149; *Correspondence,* 36, 52, 72, 79, 81, 92, 93, 106–7, 151, 199, 229; "The Fiddler," 161; "The Happy Failure," 161; "Hawthorne and His Mosses," 52, 107; *Isle of the Cross,* 147; *Israel Potter,* 147, 151, 154, 207; *John Marr,* 43–44, 151, 200–222; *Journals,* 92, 205; *Mardi,* 15, 41–42, 45, 47–56, 60–81, 95, 104, 108–11, 132, 136, 154, 167, 196, 199, 207–8, 214, 218, 226; *Moby-Dick,* xii, 1, 3, 17, 32–33, 39–40, 52, 56, 58–59, 65, 72, 76, 80, 82–83, 92–93, 95, 99, 103, 112–14, 129, 148–51, 154, 156, 158, 161, 167, 173, 194, 201, 204, 206, 215, 219, 221, 223, 226; *Omoo,* 18, 26, 29–32, 79, 92, 154, 226; *Pierre,* 25, 42, 52, 59, 68, 78, 79, 84–103, 115–44, 151, 154, 156, 221, 225; *Poems,* 200, 205; "Poor Man's Pudding and Rich Man's Crumbs," 157; *Redburn,* 51, 61, 92, 154, 190; "Rip Van Winkle's Lilac," 220–21; and science, 6–7, 71, 128–29, 234n15, 235n19; "Story of Daniel Orme," 217, 222; "The Tartarus of Maids," 35, 136–37, 157, 167; *Timoleon, Etc.,* 1, 132, 154, 158, 200, 204, 216, 223, 228; "The Tortoise-Hunters," 151; "The Two Temples," 154; *Typee,* 5, 34, 78, 92, 149, 154, 156; *Weeds and Wildings,* 38, 200, 208, 210; *White-Jacket,* 72, 92, 156. See also *Piazza Tales, The*
Mendel, Gregor, 149, 155
Menely, Tobias, 64–65
metaphor, 94, 100–101, 107, 122, 123. *See also* poetics
meteorology, 102, 121, 133–34, 201–2, 221–21. *See also* weather
Mexican-American War, 7, 58
Miller, Elaine, 142
Milne-Edwards, Henri, 166
Milton, John, 118, 138, 199, 215
minerals, 29, 48–58, 70, 74, 76–77, 95, 110, 182; biominerals, 29, 67, 72, 74, 77; mineral criticism, 78–81; mineral unconscious, 68–69. *See also* geology
Mitchell, Melanie, 25, 33
monasteries, 43, 146, 155–56, 159, 161, 164, 168–69, 173–75, 183–86, 189, 196, 198, 258n61; Augustinian, 216; Benedictine, 155; Dominican, 170, 183–84, 200; Franciscan, 175, 184–85. *See also* eco-spirituality; religion
Montana (state), 225–27
Moran, Thomas, 58
morphology (biology), 20, 69, 97, 105, 113
morphology (linguistics), 120–23
Morrill Land Grant College Act, 201

Morton, Tim, 196
mourning, xi, 7, 129–31, 136, 145, 148, 161, 186–87, 190–98, 205, 218. *See also* grief
Murray III, John, 6, 52–53, 72
Musk, Elon, 157

Nass, Michael, 152
Nealon, Jeffrey, 37–38, 88, 96, 122, 123
neuroscience: cognitive, 101; nutritional, 77. *See also* biology
Newberry, John S., 208
Newton, Isaac, 15
Nichol, John P., 47, 73
Nietzsche, Friedrich, 97, 159
Nixon, Rob, 64–65

Oersted, Hans, 129
oil, 48–49. *See also* fossil fuels
Olson, Charles, 18–19, 50
Osgood, Frances Sargent Locke, 87
Otter, Samuel, 34, 99

Paine, Thomas, 9
Pammel, L. H., 23
Parikka, Jussi, 55
Parker, Hershel, 106, 201
pearls, 66–68. *See also* minerals
Penny Cyclopaedia of the Society for the Diffusion of Useful Knowledge, 67, 74, 106
Phelps, Almira, 87
Phillips, William, 38, 55, 56
photography, 56, 72, 187, 192. *See also* technology
physics, 101–3, 141, 202; astrophysics, 64; quantum physics, 101, 103, 111, 121, 134, 141. *See also* geometry; mathematics
Piazza Tales, The (Melville): "Bartleby, the Scrivener," 35, 57, 59–60, 96, 129, 141, 147, 155, 158–59, 165, 168, 171–77, 220; "The Bell-Tower," 155, 157–58, 165–69; "Benito Cereno," 96, 136, 147, 151, 155–56, 158–59, 168, 171, 177–86, 197–98; "The Encantadas," 2, 34–35, 52, 59, 95, 134, 136, 149, 151–56, 159–61, 168, 184, 186–98; "The Lightning-Rod Man," 155, 157–58, 169–71; "The Piazza," 13, 43, 155, 157, 161–65, 168
Planck, Max, 102
plants, 86–90, 92–94, 104, 136–37, 182; algae, 82–83, 112, 209–10; aloe, 81, 210; amaranth, 117–19; aster, 210; catnip, 118; ferns, vii, 3, 26, 32 69, 85, 162; lilacs, 220–21; mosses, 3, 29, 69, 90, 95, 115, 164, 188, 210, 220; roses, 210; trees, 2, 3, 9, 12, 26, 30, 32, 79, 82, 84, 86–87, 89, 91–93, 95, 108, 113, 122–23, 126–27, 130–31, 199, 220–21; violets, 220. *See also* botany
Plateau, Joseph, 134
Plato, 80, 97
Poe, Edgar Allan, 99, 129
poetics, 19, 26, 33, 35, 40, 55, 69, 100–101, 121, 154, 204–6. *See also* ecoformalism; style
Polk, James K., 62
Pope, Alexander, 190
posthumanism, 149
Povinelli, Elizabeth, 78
Powell, John Wesley, 208
Priestly, Joseph, 71
Prigogine, Ilya, 34
Prometheus, 60, 115, 119, 127, 157, 166–68, 171, 218
Psarra, Sophia, 154
purpleness, 10–11, 115, 120–21, 124, 128, 140, 142–43, 225–27. *See also* ecoformalism; style
Putnam's Monthly Magazine, 57, 59, 146, 159, 161, 165, 202
Pynchon, Thomas, 120

Redfield, William, 201
Reingold, Nathan, 13
religion, 71, 131–32, 185, 200, 215–17, 226. *See also* Biblical references; monasteries
reproduction, 8, 42, 82, 85, 89, 110, 114, 127, 136–46, 172. *See also* evolution; sexuality

Richards, Robert, 113
risk, 12, 153, 157–58, 165, 169–71, 180, 193. *See also* security
Royster, Paul, 118
Rukeyser, Muriel, 202

sand, 199, 203–4, 208–9. *See also* geology; minerals
scale, 16–18, 64–66, 79–81, 109–10, 134–35, 214–15. *See also* complexity
Schiebinger, Londa, 80
Schopenhauer, Arthur, 5
security, 12, 68, 84, 119, 153, 157–58, 165, 169–71, 179, 181, 193. *See also* risk
sexuality, 122, 138–40. *See also* reproduction
Shakespeare, William: *Hamlet,* 193, 223; *King Lear,* 132; *The Tempest,* 133; *The Winter's Tale,* 190
Shaler, Nathaniel Southgate, 21
Sheldon, Rebekah, 39
Shelley, Mary, *Frankenstein,* 91, 125–27, 138, 140, 166
Silliman, Benjamin, 13
slavery, 158–59, 178–86
Sloterdijk, Peter, 134, 135
Smail, David Lord, 80
Smith, Adam, 154
Smith, Titus, 23
Sophocles, *Antigone,* 193–94
Spahr, Juliana, 204
Spanangel, David, 14
Spenser, Edmund, 187, 199
Spinoza, Baruch, 5, 126
spiral, 42, 89–91, 96–100, 111–13, 121; spiral phyllotaxis, 98. *See also* ecoformalism; geometry
Stephens, Ann, 226
Stiegler, Bernard, 218
style, 33–34, 84–86, 120–24. *See also* ecoformalism; poetics
Sullivan, Heather I., 94, 125, 132
Sweeney, Gerard M., 168
systems theory, 110–11, 153–54, 202. *See also* complexity

taphonomy, 75–76, 87. *See also* biology; energy ecology
technology: history of, xii–xiii, 6–8, 60, 129, 202; and human ecology, 153–55, 157–58, 165–71, 206; and knowledge, 114, 121, 146–47, 209, 217–19; and mining, 48–49, 53–56, 62, 64. *See also* electricity
Tetzel, Johann, 170
Thackery, William Makepeace, 160
thermodynamics, 197, 202–3, 220. *See also* energy; physics
Thomas, Harry, 201
Thompson, Graham, 35, 160
Thoreau, Henry David, 21, 36, 133
time: and capitalism, 174; and evolution, 23–24, 113, 121, 195; geologic time, xi, 13–17, 34, 40–41, 45, 49, 53, 54–55, 58, 60, 63–65, 68, 71–72, 76, 106, 135, 197, 207–9, 214; human time, 4, 27, 56, 74, 132, 168–71; and literature, 11, 16, 65, 80–81, 160, 190, 227; and mourning, 161, 168, 186–87, 192–95; philosophy of, 19, 50, 91, 146; plant time, 81–82, 93, 132; and slavery, 184; spacetime, 134. *See also* mathematics; scale
Tsing, Anna Lowenhaupt, 86–87, 91, 95, 124
Turing, Alan, 98
Turpin, Zachary, 101

Vitale, Francesco, 96, 137, 227
Volta, Alessandro, 129

Waddington, Conrad, 113
Walker, Alice, 227
Walls, Laura Dassow, 22
Ward, Lester Frank, 21
Watson, James, and Francis Crick, 114. *See also* biology; spiral
weather, 113, 121, 126–27, 169–70, 201–2, 205, 208–9, 221–22. *See also* atmospheric ecology; meteorology
Weber, Max, 16
Webster, Daniel, 193
West, Cornel, 9

Wheeler, George, 208
Wheeler, John, 134
Wheeler, Wendy, 44, 113, 119
Whewell, William, 244n117
Whitman, Walt, 17, 22, 39, 57, 202; *Leaves of Grass;* 16, 129, 254n239; "When Lilacs Last in Dooryard Bloom'd," 193
Whitney, Josiah, 62
Wills, David, 69, 74, 217
Wilson, Edward O., 186

Wöhler, Friedrich, 49
Wolfe, Cary, 37, 96, 151–52, 195
Woods, Derek, 17

Yates, Julian, 25–26

Zalasiewicz, Jan, 53
Zapf, Hubert, 82, 138
Zimmerman, Virginia, 65
zoology, 6, 9, 20, 27, 38, 139, 150–51, 166, 214. *See also* animals

Recent Books in the Series
UNDER THE SIGN OF NATURE: EXPLORATIONS IN ECOCRITICISM

Tom Nurmi • *Magnificent Decay: Melville and Ecology*

Elizabeth Callaway • *Eden's Endemics: Narratives of Biodiversity on Earth and Beyond*

Alicia Carroll • *New Woman Ecologies: From Arts and Crafts to the Great War and Beyond*

Emily McGiffin • *Of Land, Bones, and Money: Toward a South African Ecopoetics*

Elizabeth Hope Chang • *Novel Cultivations: Plants in British Literature of the Global Nineteenth Century*

Christopher Abram • *Evergreen Ash: Ecology and Catastrophe in Old Norse Myth and Literature*

Serenella Iovino, Enrico Cesaretti, and Elena Past, editors • *Italy and the Environmental Humanities: Landscapes, Natures, Ecologies*

Julia E. Daniel • *Building Natures: Modern American Poetry, Landscape Architecture, and City Planning*

Lynn Keller • *Recomposing Ecopoetics: North American Poetry of the Self-Conscious Anthropocene*

Michael P. Branch and Clinton Mohs, editors • *"The Best Read Naturalist": Nature Writings of Ralph Waldo Emerson*

Jesse Oak Taylor • *The Sky of Our Manufacture: The London Fog in British Fiction from Dickens to Woolf*

Eric Gidal • *Ossianic Unconformities: Bardic Poetry in the Industrial Age*

Adam Trexler • *Anthropocene Fictions: The Novel in a Time of Climate Change*

Kate Rigby • *Dancing with Disaster: Environmental Histories, Narratives, and Ethics for Perilous Times*

www.ingramcontent.com/pod-product-compliance
Lightning Source LLC
Chambersburg PA
CBHW021654230426
43668CB00008B/625